Polyamory

PRAISE FOR *POLYAMORY*

"*Polyamory* is a book that should be on every sex and relationship therapist's shelf. It is an indispensable and comprehensive guide to not only understanding polyamorous relationships but also providing affirmative therapy for clients with diverse relationship structures. Casual readers looking to enhance their relationship skillset can also benefit from the book's straightforward approach and practical exercises."—**Justin J. Lehmiller, research fellow at the Kinsey Institute and author of *Tell Me What You Want: The Science of Sexual Desire and How It Can Help You Improve Your Sex Life***

"Martha Kauppi has written a book on much more than polyamory. To be poly informed, she skillfully teaches how one needs to understand other populations such as LGBTQIA, kink and fetish communities, and other erotic orientations. Her work is based on current research and recognizes clinicians' need to be versed in understanding relationships focusing on differentiation. It is exhaustive and includes the nuances, complexities, and diversities that exist within the poly community. This book is destined to become a classic."—**Joe Kort, author of *Is My Husband Gay, Straight, or Bi?***

"In the tremendous new book *Polyamory: A Clinical Toolkit for Therapists (and Their Clients)* Martha Kauppi examines the clinical side of serving polyamorous clients in a mental healthcare setting. Using data from her own and others' research, Kauppi provides a solid grounding in theory, explains the intersections between consensual nonmonogamy and kink/BDSM and LGBTQ+ populations, and takes on therapeutic bias and ways for therapists to look beyond CNM to other issues in the relationship. Kauppi offers clinicians tools to approach clients' common issues such as forming agreements, managing jealousy, cheating, healing from past relationship trauma, and a mismatch in desire for CNM. *Polyamory* concludes with ethical and professional considerations and a wealth of useful worksheets and handouts. The most comprehensive toolkit for therapists serving clients in consensually nonmonogamous relationships to date, *Polyamory* is required reading for culturally competent CNM mental health care provision."—**Elisabeth Sheff, author of *The Polyamorists Next Door, Stories from the Polycule, When Someone You Love Is Polyamorous*, and *Children in Polyamorous Families***

Polyamory

A Clinical Toolkit for Therapists (and Their Clients)

Martha Kauppi

ROWMAN & LITTLEFIELD
Lanham • Boulder • New York • London

Published by Rowman & Littlefield
An imprint of The Rowman & Littlefield Publishing Group, Inc.
4501 Forbes Boulevard, Suite 200, Lanham, Maryland 20706
www.rowman.com

6 Tinworth Street, London, SE11 5AL, United Kingdom

British Library Cataloguing in Publication Information Available

Library of Congress Cataloging-in-Publication Data

Names: Kauppi, Martha, 1961–author.
Title: Polyamory : a clinical toolkit for therapists (and their clients) /
  Martha Kauppi.
Description: Lanham : Rowman & Littlefield, [2020] | Includes
  bibliographical references and index. | Summary: "This is the first
  practical, how-to guide to non-monogamy for therapists. It contains
  everything a therapist needs to know to start working confidently and
  competently with polyamorous clients. It covers both the most common
  challenges and the most complex and difficult situations likely to
  present in the therapy room"—Provided by publisher.
Identifiers: LCCN 2020009585 (print) | LCCN 2020009586 (ebook) | ISBN
  9781538129883 (cloth ; alk. paper) | ISBN 9781538129890 (paperback ;
  alk. paper) | ISBN 9781538129906 (epub)
Subjects: LCSH: Non-monogamous relationships. | Open marriage. | Couples
  therapy.
Classification: LCC HQ980 .K38 2020 (print) | LCC HQ980 (ebook) |
  DDC
  306.84/23—dc23
LC record available at https://lccn.loc.gov/2020009585
LC ebook record available at https://lccn.loc.gov/2020009586

Contents

Foreword

I have been waiting for decades for someone to write this book. *Poly-amory: A Clinical Toolkit for Therapists* should be required reading for every therapist, coach, counselor, or helping professional. The number of people engaged in some form of consensually nonmonogamous (CNM) relationship (including polyamory) is increasing each year, as evidenced by the number of rigorous research studies during the past decade. Therapists are bound to encounter such relationships in the therapy room unless they actively *avoid* them. And when they do encounter them, they will need at least some of the treasure trove of information that is packed into this volume.

I have been a nurse, counselor, and hypnotherapist in private practice in Berkeley, California, for almost 30 years. Most of my clients are in some type of CNM relationship, and most of them tried working with other therapists before coming to me out of sheer desperation. These clients need smart, skilled, well-informed therapists to help them successfully navigate this challenging and complex relationship style. But because so many therapists have had incorrect information—or none at all—about nonmonogamies and made false assumptions, there is often much trauma and damage to be undone for these clients.

Likewise, every week I receive phone calls and e-mails from therapists, psychologists, and even psychiatrists who find themselves sitting across from clients who are in CNM relationships and realizing they lack professional knowledge and skills for working with this population. There is in the clinical community an egregious gap between the traditional view that healthy relationships depend on monogamy and the modern reality that a full spectrum of healthy sexual and relationship orientations exist. Perhaps in another decade, most therapists will be clinically and culturally competent in this area. It will certainly have been this book that helped them get there.

Therapists reading this book will be both thrilled and relieved to discover that when working with polyamorous clients, there is both an art and a science to creating an effective treatment plan. In this way, clients in CNM relationships are no different from other clients: They come with presenting problems that are causing distress, and there are specific strategies they can develop to resolve their current problems and restore or achieve satisfying and connected relationships. Any skilled therapist who can work with monogamous clients to facilitate solutions to relationship problems can also learn to work effectively with clients in CNM relationships. Such work requires strength in four areas.

First, a therapist needs a basic understanding of what motivates people to engage in consensually nonmonogamous relationships. Second, the therapist needs to have working knowledge of the different types of CNM relationships that exist, how each one works, and the "pros and cons" of each model. Third, any therapist working with clients in CNM relationships must be willing and able to set aside any biases or negative past relationship experiences of their own that may prejudice them against nonmonogamy. Fourth, they need to understand the most common pitfalls and problems that are likely to occur in these relationships and be able to offer strategies and support for solving them.

Polyamory: A Clinical Toolkit for Therapists offers an accessible way for therapists to develop competence in each of these four areas and feel confident and comfortable working with a rapidly growing demographic of clients who are eagerly seeking their help. I am so grateful to Martha Kauppi for providing this fantastic resource for filling in the gaps that exist in professional training.

Kathy Labriola
Counselor/Nurse
Author of *The Polyamory Breakup Book*,
The Jealousy Workbook, and *Love in Abundance*

Acknowledgments

In the past couple of years, I've given considerable thought to what it takes to write a book, particularly one about a topic many people—even many therapists—find controversial. It turns out it isn't as much about personal gifts and talent as I used to think; instead, it's about the team. Rather than create long lists of names in an attempt to include everyone who has contributed to this endeavor, I will take a more narrative approach here. I hope you can find yourself in the following descriptions and know I am grateful for your part in my life and work.

I am deeply grateful to my mentors and teachers, past and present. Without thought leaders, renegades, rebels, and gifted thinkers encouraging, questioning, challenging, heckling, uplifting, and pushing me, I wouldn't have developed my thinking to the point where I have a book to share. There have been many such influencers in my life, including my parents, who were brilliant thinkers and saw little need to conform to society's rules about pretty much anything. Also heading up this category are Ellyn Bader and Peter Pearson, creators of the Developmental Model of Couples Therapy. Ellyn and Pete's work transformed my thinking about relational systems, enabling me to consolidate a lot of previous learning and experience, and take it to the next level, and the next level after that, and then they encouraged me to take it public. Much of the clinical grounding in this book can be attributed to them, either directly or indirectly, and I cannot say enough about how important they and their work have been to me. If you need more training in couples therapy, take a deep dive into the Developmental Model. You won't be sorry.

Much of my thinking about polyamory, and indeed relationships in general, has developed as a result of observing thousands of relationships at close range. It may have been my fingers writing this book, but if you have ever shared your complex and beautiful relationship with me up close or from a distance, or consulted with me about your or your clients' relationships, or written to me with a question or challenged something I wrote about on my blog or taught in a course, you are very much a coauthor. You have my deepest gratitude, and it is my sincere hope that my work lifts you up.

If, as you read this book, you become entranced by an especially well-crafted phrase, you are almost certainly noticing the elegant work of Amelia Soth, who brings significant creative gifts to the co-creation of the written materials that issue from my desk, as well as many other tasks associated with my business. Without her, my book would not see the light of day for several more years. Vanessa Harvell and Jim Fleckenstein assisted significantly with research, making it possible for me to spend time actually writing. Thank you.

You can look forward to some beautiful personal accounts of polyamory sprinkled throughout this book. These were generously contributed by real people, all of whom have this in common: They care enough about polyamory to offer their own experiences to help therapists see how their relationships actually work. Thank you from the bottom of my heart; your willingness to share your personal challenges and breakthroughs is an amazing gift to me and my readers.

And then there is love. This book is the direct result of my family and larger community of friends and colleagues lifting me, encouraging me, and supporting me, every day. My work exposes controversy, and I certainly would not have had the courage to put myself out there as I have without being grounded by the steadfast values, incisive skills, and moral compass of my community of support. Standing by me is no easy task. JoAnne, Kaya, Tracy, the Badass Sisterhood, Erik, Laura, Jacob, Ellyn, Pete, and my mentor group respond to texts, e-mails, and calls with just the right balance of support and challenge, unconditional regard, and tough love. Thank you.

The community of AASECT professionals is a vast network of unparalleled experts who offer resources anytime I'm stuck. If you ever need anything, go find a sex educator, counselor, or therapist, because they are amazing. If you regularly have questions about sex therapy, join AASECT and get on their listserv. As free resources go, this one can't be beat. I'm especially grateful for Russell Stambaugh's expert feedback on my chapter covering BDSM.

The friends and community members who are willing to connect with me now and then as time allows deserve special appreciation. As many before me have noted, writing a book takes time, and I haven't yet worked out the balance of things to my satisfaction. I know it, and you know it. Let's have tea soon.

Finally, a book requires an audience. Thank you so much for being curious enough about some aspect of polyamory to pick up this book and read it. I hope it benefits you and those you care about. I am continually humbled by the international community of therapists who read, share, digest, interact with, respond to, and support my work. Please keep telling me how I can best help and support you in your work, and in your relationships, because the world needs you to express your gifts.

Introduction

CAN POLYAMORY REALLY WORK?

The most common question therapists and clients ask me about poly-amory is, "Have you ever actually seen a polyamorous relationship that works for more than just a few months?" I hope you get a lot from this book. But if you could only take away one thing, I'd want it to be this: Polyamory absolutely can work. There are lots of healthy, happy polyamorous relationships that are functioning well, both with and without therapy. These are healthy relationships in every sense of the term: They are fulfilling and joyful, enriched by deep intimacy, and supported by a strong sense of teamwork. In my experience, it's just not true that monogamy is necessary for true intimacy or long-term relationship success. Just like monogamous relationships, some poly-amorous relationships last for a short time and some for a long time, and many polyamorous relationships succeed for the long haul.

In addition to my clinical experience, I also have many friends and some family members who are in consensually open relationships, most of which are functioning very well. A developing body of re-search bears out my experience, demonstrating that polyamory is a valid relationship structure, with happy and satisfied participants, lon-gevity, deep intimacy, and secure attachment.

There are also polyamorous relationships that are struggling. Just like many struggling monogamous relationships, many of these just need a skillful therapist to flourish. If you are a therapist, counselor, or relationship coach, that can be you. All you need is a little background information, a willingness to work with people who craft unique relationships to suit their individual needs, and a set of go-to strategies for conceptualizing cases and tackling the problems that commonly come up in therapy with polyamorous clients and relationships. That's where this book comes in.

I divide my time between training and consulting for therapists and seeing clients in my own practice. Most of my clients don't hear me describing how I do therapy, and most of the therapists I train don't hear me working with clients; this book crosses the line in both directions.

It may seem like this book is primarily directed toward therapists, but it describes strategies and concepts I use regularly with my clients. I love being a therapist because I love helping people identify their goals, dreams, and aspirations, and then support the change process as they move toward creating the life they desire, including grappling with challenges and personal blocks when they arise. Helping people create happiness and joyful relational connections is extremely satisfying. When I teach therapists, I am doing the same job, but on a different level. The material is the same; the audience and goals are a little different.

There are a lot of little moments in therapy that can seem like magic when done well. The biggest risk to reading this book from a client perspective is that peeking behind the curtain might make the process seem a little less magical. That said, I see no reason why you shouldn't be able to work the magic without having a therapist present, and if you choose to do so, I think that is fabulous, and it is the reason I wrote this book for both audiences.

If you are a therapist, coach, or helping professional, are you intimidated by the prospect of working with polyamorous clients? Do you worry you don't know enough or won't be able to help? Do you have questions about the variety of consensual nonmonogamies and how to approach related issues? Is it hard for you to wrap your head and heart around this alternative relationship style because of your personal history or belief system? Do you lack a strong therapeutic plan for working with common polyamorous relationship challenges? Have you had some clients in consensually open relationships and felt a little uncertain where to start or how to structure therapy, or encountered challenges you didn't know how to handle? Have you had some polyamorous clients and been overwhelmed by the complexity of the relationship systems? Do you lack the resources, worksheets, and exercises that might help you and your clients? If you answered yes to any of these questions, this book is written especially for you.

If you have a lot of experience working with polyamorous and other ethically nonmonogamous relationships, you may find you don't have enough support for your work, and could use a deep dive into how another therapist conceptualizes cases and works with expectable challenges with nontraditional relationships and marginalized populations. If this describes you, I wrote this book for you, too.

If you are reading this book as a support for your own personal relationship(s), you might have questions and information needs that are not so different from the therapists. Few people have many great role models of well-functioning polyamorous relationships, not because they don't exist, but because many are closeted. When you can't see or imagine something, it can be difficult to achieve it.

This book is intended to be a practical guide. It's designed to serve as a full toolkit for tackling both the most common and the most complicated situations that are likely to arise with open-relationship structures. I hope to address your concerns about polyamory by giving you the in-depth information and solid strategies you need to move forward with confidence. By the time you turn the last page, I hope that you'll feel capable and confident, and supported, whatever your own personal connection to polyamory might be.

WHY POLYAMOROUS CLIENTS MAY BE YOUR BEST CLIENTS EVER

Before I start sharing techniques for how to work with polyamorous clients, I want to explain why I think you might want to develop the skills to work with this population. The long and short of it is that I love working with polyamorous clients, and I think you will too.

People in polyamorous relationships are breaking out of the monogamy mold and creating unique, carefully crafted, intentional relationships based on the needs and desires of those involved and no one else. There is no template to follow, relatively little research or guidance, and plenty of cultural stigma to contend with, and there are few visible role models. Despite this, many polyamorous people still manage to craft strong relationships. That takes an impressive and unusual set of qualities: strength, courage, vision, caring, and substantial relationship skills.

I'm a great believer in individuality, authenticity, and transparency. I have never fit comfortably into any mold. I've rebelled against most labels and boxes my entire life. I strongly believe outside-of-the-box thinkers and relationship pioneers deserve every chance to thrive. They deserve a place in our society, they deserve to live and love in the absence of stigma, and they *certainly* deserve excellent therapy and relationship support when they seek it.

Polyamory culture strongly values communication, transparency, consent, and personal growth. As a result, even if your polyamorous clients aren't yet great at communicating or being transparent (after all, there's a reason they're in your office), they are likely to believe that building those skills is worthwhile and be willing to challenge themselves and invest the time and effort to grow in those areas. This is a population that generally acknowledges that therapy can be a big help in navigating relationship complexities. Imagine what your practice would look like if all of your clients started out with this perspective.

Here's something else I love about working with polyamorous clients: It's never boring. In fact, it can sometimes be quite complicated, because there are multiple people, needs, desires, and feelings involved. I love working with self-aware, motivated clients, and I relish the challenge of sorting through complex relationships and interesting dilemmas. I also love generating individually crafted solutions that are somewhat outside of the cultural mold.

But the most important reason I love working with polyamorous clients is that I believe in the viability of polyamory. I have seen polyamory work so well, so many times, that I think it should be part of our cultural narrative about relational possibilities. While that may take some time to accomplish, I see no reason whatsoever that therapists shouldn't include polyamory in our narrative about relational possibilities. This is not to say I think *every* polyamorous relationship is a healthy one or that monogamy is bad. It's just that I've seen it work so well that I can't discount it as an option. Consider: Would you rather have complicated cases and highly motivated clients or clients with low motivation who don't believe in transparency and instead come to you for infidelity? I'm clear on which I prefer.

There's another important reason why you might want to work with polyamorous clients: They need you. There are far too few therapists who are qualified to work with polyamory. In fact, many polyamorous people complain that it's prohibitively difficult to find a polyamory-friendly therapist. In part, that's because of a persistent belief that polyamory is an unworkable relationship structure. Several leaders in the field of psychotherapy have taken open stands against polyamory, stating that it isn't healthy and can't function well or asserting that polyamorists are essentially sex addicts. Although some of these leaders have since recanted, the sentiment lingers. Add to that the huge amount of misinformation and bias this marginalized group experiences, and you can begin to see why polyamorous people might be a little cautious when choosing a relationship therapist.

Most of my clients come to me via word of mouth. My experience has shown me that, once you demonstrate that you are open to working with polyamory and back up that willingness with cultural competence, the clients will come. This means that you will be not only working with delightful clients who value relationship skills, transparency, and therapy, but also setting yourself apart from other therapists in your area at the same time.

WHAT YOU'LL NEED TO BECOME A POLYAMORY-COMPETENT THERAPIST

When it comes down to it, if you are a practicing coach, counselor, or therapist working with individuals, you likely already have most of the basic skills you need to work with polyamorous clients. Polyamorous clients are just people, and polyamorous relationships are a lot like any other relationships. It will also serve you well if you have some skill and additional training in working with couples and relationships, as relational therapy is very different from individual therapy.

So, what sets working with polyamorous clients apart? Even though you probably have most of the essential skills for working with polyamorous relationships, there are still a few missing pieces of the puzzle for most therapists. This book is designed to provide you with those missing pieces and fill in some gaps with relational therapy skills as well.

The first piece is cultural competence working with consensually nonmonogamous people. Most therapy and coaching training programs don't provide specific information on this topic. Even if you have the perspective that polyamory is a workable relationship structure, it can be difficult to get a good education about polyamory and consensual nonmonogamy, and even more difficult to find therapy-specific information. In addition, consensually nonmonogamous people are a marginalized population, which means that misconceptions, negative stereotypes, and misinformation are all too common.

On top of that, not all training programs take into account the complex relational dynamics and multiple systems that surround *all* relationships. Much therapy training focuses on linear processes rather than systemic dynamics, and I find a systemic perspective to be crucial when working with any relational system. Also, relational therapy training often focuses on attachment concerns, sometimes to the near-exclusion of differentiation. In my work, I've found that lack of differentiation is a common underlying source of many serious relationship problems. Developing skill in helping clients create a secure bond is very important, but having a solid understanding of how to help clients build differentiation of self as well adds a foundational piece for working effectively with all relationships. This will serve you well when working with clients whose relational connection and happiness depends on congruent communication, self-awareness, and the ability to craft good agreements—and whose relationship doesn't depend on those things? In this book, I've provided a section that describes how to conceptualize cases using the perspective of the Developmental Model of Couples Therapy, based on the combined concepts of attachment, differentiation, and neuroscience. I take a deep dive into differentiation of self and how to support growth in this important area. I think it will offer you additional skills and confidence that will serve you well with all your clients, polyamorous and monogamous.

BIAS, MARGINALIZATION, AND CULTURAL NORMS

As a marginalized population, polyamorous people face persistent cultural bias. Therapists aren't immune to our culture's messages about marriage, fidelity, and intimacy. In fact, many couples therapists and counselors have been specifically trained to believe that upholding and reinforcing these cultural norms is the most effective way to help clients have securely functioning relationships. But perpetuating this bias, particularly when it is unexamined and unconscious, excludes and further marginalizes the many thoughtful, insightful, intelligent, and unique individuals who don't fit into that cultural box. I go more deeply into how to assess and work with your personal bias in chapter 6.

While we're talking about bias, it's important to mention that there is a lot of overlap between several marginalized communities. Particularly relevant to the topic of polyamory in therapy is the overlap between the polyamorous community, the BDSM/kink community, and the LGBTQ+ community. Because therapists who work with one of these populations will probably find themselves working with all of them, I discuss the overlapping marginalized populations and make treatment recommendations in chapter 3.

It is easy to see how working cross-culturally with this group may be a significant challenge for many therapists, as it requires looking closely at personal belief systems and getting clear on how to help people who may be very different from you. Happily, doing therapy with other people's polyamorous relationships does not require that you have personal experience with polyamorous relationships. The primary requirement is simply that you believe a healthy polyamorous relationship is possible and are willing to learn a little more about it. If, after reading this book, you still have doubts, I discuss ethical considerations and scope of practice in chapter 20.

Throughout this book, I've included anonymous stories from polyamorous people about their relationships, told in their own voices. Some provide illustrations of how warm, loving, and flexible polyamorous relationships can be, and others offer examples of how real people have transcended some of the thornier relationship challenges associated with polyamory. If you've never seen a polyamorous relationship in the wild, if you've only seen dysfunctional ones, or if you tend to feel overwhelmed when things don't go ideally, I hope these stories will provide you with some examples of how real-life polyamorous relationships function, in their amazing diversity.

On the other hand, if you are polyamorous yourself or know lots of people who are, working with polyamorous clients will require that you are able to see the unique relationship in front of you with its own challenges and strengths, and recognize that it isn't the same as any other relationship or situation. The more you have in common with your clients, the more challenging it can be to avoid the pitfall of assuming that what has worked for you will work for others. In that case, I hope this book will provide you with ways to assess, conceptualize, and treat unique situations uniquely, and with confidence.

WHO IS THIS BOOK FOR?

In this book I provide a therapist's-eye view of polyamory, including a deep dive into case conceptualization, treatment strategies for multiple clinical challenges that crop up frequently in the therapy room, a discussion of ethics and practice considerations, extensive background information about every aspect of polyamorous relationships, and a selection of handy worksheets and exercises for use with your clients.

I wrote this book primarily for therapists, coaches, counselors, and other helping professionals. It is my hope that I can help you feel comfortable, competent, and confident working with this population. I truly believe working with clients who have consensually nonmonogamous relationships will benefit you, your practice, and your larger community. The polyamorous people in your area deserve excellent therapy. With the help of this book, I believe that you can provide it.

But I also wrote this book for the polyamorous community and the relationship pioneers within and around it, who (like everyone else) could use a little help once in a while, particularly when it comes to making relationships work. There is enough information here for an insightful, highly motivated person or polycule to do a self-help deep dive. If you don't have access to therapy or there are no polyamory-knowledgeable therapists in your area, or you want some worksheets and foundational concepts to support the therapy you are already in, this book is for you.

HOW THIS BOOK IS ORGANIZED

Part I, "Polyamory from a Therapist's Perspective," is a primer on polyamory aimed at building cultural competence for therapists and consolidating information for those who need it for any reason. Here you'll find a glossary of important terms, as well as an explanation of the difference between polyamory and other consensual nonmonogamies, for example, swinging. You'll learn about the overlap between the polyamory community, BDSM/kink, and LGBTQIA+, and discover the foundational theories and belief systems that underlie polyamorous relationships. Plus, I'll describe what current research says about polyamory, including the results of my own study.

Part II, "Creating a Strong Foundation for Therapy with Polyamory," lays the groundwork for therapy, which is also the groundwork for effectively creating personal change. I discuss my theoretical perspective regarding relational therapy, which is grounded in the Developmental Model of Couples Therapy (created by Ellyn Bader and Peter Pearson of the Couples Institute). The concepts I discuss here will come in handy throughout the rest of the book, and I show you how to apply them to common problems that arise in polyamorous relationships. You'll also find worksheets to help guide your thinking as you consider your own past experiences and belief systems with regard to polyamory, alternative lifestyles, fidelity, and your therapeutic position.

Part III, "Polyamory in the Therapy Room: Common Presenting Problems," is a practical primer on working with polyamory in therapy. In this section, I share strategies for working with a variety of common issues related to polyamory that often arise in the course of therapy. For each clinical challenge, I discuss how I conceptualize the issues and offer treatment strategies that I have found to be effective, illustrating relational dynamics and intervention opportunities and strategies with the help of hypothetical composite case examples drawn from my own practice and those of the many therapists for whom I have consulted. You'll also find practical worksheets and exercises for clients to support the therapy. If you are doing a self-help deep dive, this section is quite deep and wide. Don't take it too fast; when considering applying a book about therapy to your own relationships, remember that you are learning about challenges you might not be facing, and for those that are immediately relevant, the growth and change process might take weeks, months, or years. Some goals can be tackled simultaneously, and some follow more sequentially as necessary skills develop and evolve. As you read this book, you are engaging with years of goals, challenges, and exercises in mere hours of actual reading. Pick the book up, lay it down, skip around, use the worksheets, and don't hurry. If you find yourself needing or wanting additional support, locate a coach or therapist. If you have a therapist you love but he or she doesn't yet know much about polyamory, hand them a copy of the book.

Part IV, "Professional Considerations," focuses on professional and ethical issues related to working with polyamorous clients. I discuss how to assess and decide if you want to and are qualified to work with this population. I also explore strategies for marketing yourself as a polyamory-friendly therapist and ethical pitfalls you may face when working with this population.

The appendixes provide a selection of worksheets and exercises for both clients and therapists. Each one describes an exercise or piece of work I frequently use in my practice. They are intended to support your work, and that of your clients, as you move forward.

FINAL THOUGHTS

I wrote this book for the many polyamorous people I've met who have had painful experiences in therapy, whether because they felt judged by their therapist, because their therapist did not yet have the tools to work effectively with their relationships, or because they simply couldn't find a therapist who was prepared to work with them. I firmly believe that every person deserves access to helping professionals who are equipped to treat their relationships' unique challenges with warmth, empathy, and respect. I hope that, in the very near future, high-quality relationship support for polyamorous clients will no longer be hard to come by.

I wrote this book for the many therapists who have reached out to me to say that they wish they had the skills to work with polyamorous people but that continuing education was sparse or prohibitively expensive. I wrote it in the knowledge that, with just a little background and a set of tools, these therapists can make a huge difference in their polyamorous clients' lives. I wrote it with deep gratitude and admiration for those who take the leap of setting aside culturally normative assumptions about fidelity, intimacy, and sexuality to open their minds to some potentially new and challenging ideas. I wrote it for you, the person holding this book. Thank you for taking this leap with me.

Part I

POLYAMORY FROM A THERAPIST'S PERSPECTIVE

CHAPTER 1

Consensual Nonmonogamies
What Are the Options?

Polyfidelity, relationship anarchy, monogamish: The world of consensual nonmonogamy comes with a language all its own. In this chapter, I'll be defining some helpful terms and providing a road map to the wide world of consensual nonmonogamies, in all their many varieties, shapes, and structures.

This guide is necessarily incomplete, and it's inevitable that many people will disagree with me on the definitions I offer. This is because, as our culture evolves, the language for polyamory, queerness, and all matters that diverge from the cultural hetero-cis-normative script is evolving with it. Plus, the terms people use may vary from region to region, since polyamorous communities tend to be tight-knit and very local. The more consensual nonmonogamy is openly discussed, the more language will evolve. Eventually, there may be a coherent vocabulary to describe relational styles. Until then, we have a mishmash of overlapping, ever-evolving terms and concepts; therefore, I offer these definitions with a caution: Please keep in mind that they should be regarded as broad strokes at best.

I never assume I know what someone means when they offer me a label to describe themselves or their relationship. Rather, I assume the label just gets me in the ballpark. From there, I will need to listen carefully and ask good questions to truly understand how someone sees themselves and their relationships. As always, the best way to understand what someone means when they use specific terms is to ask them.

For these reasons, my goal here is not to give you an encyclopedia, but to provide you with enough information about polyamorous relationship shapes and options that you will be able to ask your clients intelligent questions. Hopefully, that will lead to deeper conversations and a shared understanding of what the terminology they use means to them.

If you're a polyamorous or polyamory-curious person considering how you want to structure your relationships, this chapter may provide some fertile ground for discussion and exploration. I hope you'll treat the definitions that follow as a starting point and not a prescription; there are infinite ways to structure a relationship, with your imagination and preferences being the only limits.

This chapter addresses types of nonmonogamies and explains common language that is used to describe aspects of polyamorous relationships.

GLOSSARY OF USEFUL RELATIONSHIP-RELATED TERMS

Consensual nonmonogamy (CNM): An umbrella term for relationship structures that include agreements that permit outside sexual and/or romantic connections. This includes polyamory, as well as other forms of nonmonogamy, like swinging, but it doesn't include infidelity, which is nonmonogamous but not consensually so.

Ethical nonmonogamy (ENM): This term refers to the aspect of consensual nonmonogamy whereby all partners are fully aware of and in agreement about the open relationship structure, in contrast to infidelity. Some use this term interchangeably with CNM.

Metamour: Derived from "paramour," this term describes one's relationship to one's partner's partner. For example, if Sandy is dating Jack and Jack is married to Daniel, then Sandy and Daniel are metamours.

Monogamish: Coined by Dan Savage, this term refers to being in a committed couple relationship with some agreement that, in certain circumstances, sex or specific types of intimacy with others is permissible. For instance, some might agree to one-night stands, or sex when out of town traveling, or just for kinky play, or flirtation/romance only but no sex, and so forth. There isn't a rule book for what it means to be "monogamish," so if you want to understand the contours of the agreement, you will need to ask.

Monogamy: Refers to a dyadic relationship with an expectation that there will be no extradyadic sexual or romantic relationships. This can be either by explicit or implicit agreement. By "implicit," I mean that one or both partners are making an assumption that their relationship is monogamous, rather than having a discussion specifically about it. When this is the case, partners can have vastly different ideas of what is and is not allowable or what "fidelity" means, which can lead to some interesting therapy down the line. For example, is watching porn okay? What about flirting with other people? What about fantasizing about other people—while having sex with your partner? Many relationships suffer from strong disagreements about what counts as crossing the line, especially when both partners assume that what crosses the line should be obvious. For this reason, I encourage partners in any intimate relationship to have an explicit discussion about what fidelity means to each of them. The complexity of that discussion can feel like a big deal, but it can save a lot of heartache.

Mono-polyamorous: This is my term for a relationship in which one partner has, seeks, or remains open to extradyadic sexual and romantic connections, while the other partner remains monogamous. Many people, including some experts on polyamory, consider this form of relationship to be unworkable, but I personally have seen it work well many times. I discuss this relationship style in much more detail in chapter 15, "Working with Mono-Polyams and Reluctant Polyams."

Nesting partners: Refers to cohabitating partners. This term provides nonhierarchical language for describing the increased level of day-to-day complexity and interconnectedness that comes with sharing a home and related responsibilities.

Network: A group of people, usually in community, in which it is agreed that anyone can choose to be sexual or intimate with any others as long as they are consenting.

Nonhierarchical polyamory: In brief, this is a style of polyamory for which there is no expectation of a power differential between partners, in contrast to a primary/secondary structure in which one partnership is primary and any others are secondary. There is a huge amount of variation in how this actually looks.

Nonmonogamy: Most often used as an umbrella term referring to all forms of nonmonogamy. Sometimes used interchangeably with "open," referring to an open relationship with an expectation that there will be outside sexual connections but no "love" or romantic connections.

Open relationship: An umbrella term for many forms of open relationships. Often used to describe a form of consensual nonmonogamy in which extradyadic romance or love are not expected or allowed.

Pod: A group of people who are connected to one another by interconnecting intimate relationships. Used interchangeably with the word *polycule*, or occasionally *family*.

Polyamory: A form of consensual nonmonogamy (sometimes abbreviated to *polyam*, or less correctly, *poly*) in which one, some, or all partners engage openly in more than one romantic and (often) sexual relationship. There are many forms and styles, but polyamory implies love and romance will be involved, and that the arrangement is consensual for all participants.

Polycule: Used interchangeably with "pod," this refers to a group of people who are connected to one another by interconnecting intimate relationships. It does not assume all involved are sexual or romantic with one another, but usually the inference is that the connections are intimate. Also sometimes refers to a diagram of a group of people connected by polyamorous relationships, similar to a diagram of a molecule depicting interconnected atoms.

Polyfidelity or polyfi: A form of polyamory in which a group of people in an interconnected polyamorous configuration of any type agrees to close their relationship for a particular period of time or permanently. In this agreement, all participants agree not to become involved with anyone new without further renegotiation. This, like all other forms of fidelity, works a lot better when agreements are explicitly discussed and agreements are crystal clear.

Primary/secondary: In brief, this refers to an agreement that one partnership, the primary one, will take precedence over all others, which are considered secondary. There is a huge amount of variation in how this actually looks. This form of polyamory has its detractors; nonetheless, it is common.

Relationship anarchy (RA): Describes an ever-evolving relationship philosophy. Proponents of RA believe that relationships should be nonhierarchical, that sexual and romantic relationships should not be prioritized over platonic ones, and that relationships should be structured according to the preferences of the participants rather than based on a preexisting set of rules. Believers in RA tend to value not imposing rules or "needs" on others and may prefer to go separate ways rather than hold one another back in pursuing happiness and connection.

Serial monogamy: A common expression of monogamy in our current world. The mindset of monogamy, meaning just one intimate partner at a time, requires that, when new attractions develop, choices are made between old and new relationships. This can result in a sequential string of monogamous relationships, or serial monogamy. This is relevant because polyamory provides an alternative solution to the problem of multiple attractions and (some would say) saves many a perfectly good marriage by not making a new crush into an emergency that requires a big decision-making moment.

Solo polyamory: A way of being polyamorous whereby a person identifies primarily as single, either for now as a result of circumstance or as an aspect of identity. A person may consider themselves to be practicing solo polyamory even if they have one or more relationships and even if those relationships involve meaningful commitments. It's more a matter of how they think about and prioritize relationships, rather than whether they have any. There is some overlap between the definition of solo polyamory and relationship anarchy, but there is considerable difference in usage. If your client uses either of these terms, you will probably want to ask for more information about what the term means to them.

Swinging (often referred to as "the lifestyle"): A form of couple sexual exploration or play, usually involving other couples. The assumption is generally that the sexual connections will be for the enrichment of the couple and that romance won't be part of the picture.

Swingers find one another at special events, key parties, and hotel takeovers. Couples may connect with other couples and continue their relationships outside of the swinger events or they may not.

Unicorn: A unicorn isn't a relationship type, but the term is relevant to polyamory discussions and relational challenges, so I include it here. The term *unicorn* is frequently used (somewhat derogatorily) to describe a heterosexual dyad seeking a "hot bi babe" (or HBB) to join their relationship but only on their terms. In this scenario, the dyad would be described as "unicorn hunters." I have a few problems with this usage. First of all, I have known many emotionally healthy bi- or pansexual people of various genders who are interested in dating a couple, so in my experience there is no reason to think that is either particularly hard to find or unhealthy, and it's certainly not impossible to have a functioning triad that starts with a heterosexual dyad who wants to date a bisexual woman. I wouldn't denigrate that desire by using derogatory language to describe its origins; however, I don't think relationships reach their greatest potential when any of the participants determine the terms without consideration of the others, and most would agree with me about that, which is why "unicorn" and "unicorn hunters" are derogatory terms in the first place; they imply lack of consideration. If there *is* a troubling power dynamic at play, then the power dynamic needs to be addressed, in my opinion—which isn't the same thing as writing off an entire potential kind of relationship as inherently impossible or inherently problematic. For these reasons, when I have a client who uses "unicorn" or "unicorn hunter" to describe themselves or someone they seek for a relationship, I'm very interested to better understand what they actually mean. This often leads to me providing some information that helps clear up misunderstandings about what makes a strong relationship or what is possible and realistic.

POLYAMOROUS RELATIONSHIP STRUCTURES— HIERARCHY OR NO HIERARCHY?

No matter how a relationship is structured, situations will arise in which the people involved will need to make important decisions concerning all participants in the relationship. *Can so-and-so move in with us? Should we share our finances? Is it okay if we add a new partner to our polycule?*

In any relationship structure, there is a person, pair, or group of people responsible for making major decisions that determine how the relationship is structured and the shape and nature of the relationship. I refer to that person or group of people as the *decision-making body.*

Each of the relationship structures I describe here represents a specific way of allocating power and therefore a specific kind of decision-making body. Many polyamorous relationships have a hierarchy to some degree, but many others have expressly nonhierarchical structures. RA, or relationship anarchy, for example, is a relationship philosophy that embraces nonhierarchical structure.

It is important that the participants are clear about how their relationships are structured in terms of power, priority, and decision-making, so much so that this can be an important focus of therapy if participants aren't clear about it. It's also important that you fully understand how this aspect of your clients' relationships works. Among other things, this consideration has everything to do with how I decide who should attend therapy in the initial stages of treatment.

Primary/Secondary Structure

The way you can identify a primary/secondary structure is that, according to the agreements of the relationship, there is one relationship—the "primary" one—that will be prioritized over all other romantic or sexual relationships, which are considered "secondary." Primary/secondary structures usually look like a pair of people who consider themselves particularly committed to one another and the relationship between them, although one or both may have outside romantic and/or sexual connections. Sometimes this is a married couple, sometimes not. It can be two people who are just dating but who are interested in creating a primary relationship. Primary/secondary structures are currently the most common kind of polyamorous relationship structure, although in my experience the culture is starting to shift toward more nonhierarchical relationships (more on those later in this chapter).

When previously monogamous couples consider opening their relationships, this is the relationship structure that most often springs to mind, because it can serve as a way of holding on to some of the sense of security that being an exclusive couple implies while also engaging in new relationships. Of course, no relationship structure ensures that nothing will go wrong and everyone will always feel chosen, but primary/secondary can feel comforting to some. There may be rules in place to preserve the hierarchy: for instance, that either partner can veto the other partner's dates or connections, that meetings with other partners must be limited in some agreed-upon manner, that the needs of the family come first when it comes to scheduling, and so forth; any agreement you can imagine has certainly existed for someone, somewhere. Alternatively, there may be very few rules in place; rather, participants will trust one another's judgment when it comes to making choices that are respectful of everyone involved. Some people choose a primary/secondary structure because it implies security, some to ease the anxiety of exploring polyamory, and others because they don't know there is such a thing as nonhierarchical polyamory or have difficulty navigating it.

The success of any polyamorous relationship of any structure depends on the relational skills, beliefs, values, and capacity of everyone involved. Having a primary/secondary structure does not prevent broken agreements or keep difficult emotions from arising, but this relationship structure is popular for a reason. It can work beautifully, particularly when a couple has a lot of shared responsibilities, like a mortgage and children, or when one or both partners want a little extra sense of emotional security while they check out how polyamory works for them.

One of the potential pitfalls of a primary/secondary structure is that the other people involved—the "secondaries"—may not have much power at all. When that is the case, it can be a tough position to be in. How much decision-making power a secondary partner has varies tremendously from relationship to relationship. Some secondary partners are very content, some less so. Some don't need a high degree of predictability, and some truly appreciate their metamour's position and preferences, and have no desire to compete for decision-making power. Similarly, some primary partners have a lot of compassion and empathy for the position of the secondary metamour, others much less so.

Relationships between metamours vary a lot as well. In some cases, the metamours may know and like one another, which can result in more flexibility when they have competing preferences. In other cases, metamours may not know one another or prefer to have no communication at all. Sometimes there may be a tense relationship. In other cases, even if metamours don't know or don't like one another, there can be a peaceable and respectful coexistence, as they have empathy and appreciation for the challenges the other faces, and do what they can to make the entire system work well for everyone involved. I elaborate on the complexities of primary and secondary relationship roles, as well as the challenges hinges experience, in chapter 17, "Role-Related Challenges and Benefits: Primaries, Secondaries, Hinges, Etc."

Nonhierarchical Structures

Some polyamorous relationships do not have any hierarchy at all between partners. In this case, one, some, or all participants reject the concept that one partner's needs and desires should "rank" higher than another's. Nonhierarchical polyamory serves people who find designations of "primary" and "secondary" to be somewhat arbitrary or even downright unethical or offensive. In a nonhierarchical polyamorous structure, there is no primary partner whose needs automatically take precedence. Instead, conflicts between different partners' desires are worked out on a case-by-case basis.

Nonhierarchical relationships are increasingly common. While this is not something that has been researched yet to my knowledge, it is my perception that nonhierarchical polyamory is more common with younger and queer people. It may also be more common when people choose a polyamorous relationship right from the start, rather than transitioning from monogamy to polyamory. It also often evolves throughout time out of primary/secondary structures, as people become more trusting of the ability of their partner(s) to take into account differences and handle them well.

In addition to relationships, or groups of people with nonhierarchical structures, there are also *individuals* who identify as having a nonhierarchical way of understanding and expressing themselves relationally. Solo polyamory and RA or relationship anarchy are examples.

UNDERSTANDING DECISION-MAKING POWER

It can be hard to understand how polyamorous people negotiate between the desires of multiple different partners unless you've seen the process in action. Most people think that the slate of decision-making options is limited to three possibilities: one partner makes the decision, the other partner makes the decision, or the decision is made together. But this way of thinking about decision-making is overly simplistic. It's neither entirely accurate nor particularly helpful.

There are many ways a couple (or any group) might make a decision. There may be times when there is an actual 50/50 decision, but I think that is quite unusual. Much more often, the people involved in the decision are not equally enthusiastic about the options or the outcome. Yet, the decision still gets made peaceably and effectively. I think this happens because the partners agree to agree. They're happy to come to a "good-enough" agreement. Some would call this choosing your battles, and it is an aspect of a well-functioning relationship that isn't discussed enough. Often, it is understood that one partner will get a little more decision-making power in some circumstances, and the other will have the edge in other domains. In the Developmental Model of Couples Therapy, this is referred to as 49/51% decision-making.

There may also be times when one person clearly makes the decision, but that doesn't necessarily make the decision unilateral. It's likely that the decision-maker is actually taking the other partner's preferences into account. After all, making a unilateral decision to cook a certain food for dinner won't feel that good if everyone else hates the meal you serve them. Taking other people's preferences into account when making a decision is a relational way of being. Most of us do it automatically and probably would still say we made the decision ourselves. Even decisions that may seem unilateral or that not everyone is happy about probably have some amount of give-and-take or consideration of others behind them.

It's neither necessary nor realistic to come to complete agreement in decision-making. It is completely adaptive and healthy for each partner to have a little more authority in one area or another. Ideally, they discuss the issue and come to understand one another's perspective, including why things feel important to the other, and then one ultimately makes the final decision, taking everyone's opinions into account.

When it comes to helping people make decisions, whether individually or in groups, the skills of differentiation are foundational; see chapter 8 for a deep dive into differentiation. People who have difficulty feeling secure emotionally will need some help gaining the necessary skills for balancing their preferences with those of other people and holding steady when others make decisions that affect them. In your therapy room, you can help by normalizing the many shades of decision-making power.

The initiator/inquirer process from the Developmental Model of Couples Therapy is a tool that I often use to help clients build the parts of differentiation. You can read more about that in chapter 9. For more on the kinds of decisions people in polyamorous relationships are likely to encounter, see chapter 12.

BLURRING THE LINES OF POWER

No book of rules or relational guidelines is fail-safe or foolproof. Stuff happens, all the time. The following is an example of the kind of nuanced situation that often arises and generally goes better if relational decision-making is discussed ahead of time.

Liz and Joe have a primary/secondary relationship, with an agreement that Joe will prioritize Liz's preferences over Michelle's. All goes well until Michelle experiences a health crisis, and Joe has a hard decision to make and a few different options for how to handle it.

- Does he cancel a dinner date with Liz to go support Michelle at the emergency room?
- Does he tell Michelle, "Sorry, I have a dinner date?"
- Does he discuss the situation with Liz and ask her permission to let him go to the ER with Michelle?
- Does he ask one of the partners what their advice is about how to handle the situation?

I've seen this type of situation unfold in every imaginable way, with outcomes ranging from spectacularly positive to spectacularly negative, and everything in between.

Here is another example of a different but equally common situation: Mark and Susan have a primary/secondary relationship, with an understanding that Susan will prioritize Mark's preferences over her other partner, Julie's. This goes well until Susan develops strong romantic feelings toward Julie, during a week when she and Mark happen to be disagreeing about a number of large issues in their lives. Mark and Julie both ask to spend a quiet evening with Susan on the same night, and while Susan knows she "is supposed to" pick Mark, she thinks she and Mark would fight all evening, while she and Julie would enjoy themselves. She very much prefers to spend the evening with Julie. How does she decide to handle this? Again, I've seen this unfold in a vast array of ways.

I present these examples to get you thinking about some nuances of hierarchy. Here are some further questions, to help you dig into the complexities of these situations:

How did you feel as you read the examples? Were some parts uncomfortable to read or think about?

Did you find yourself having an opinion about what they should do? If so, are there assumptions you are making about the circumstances or participants in each situation that your opinion is based on?

Put yourself in their shoes. Imagine you are, in turn, each of the three participants in each scenario. Notice what your preferences would be from each separate perspective. Are they different?

Consider if the relationships were nonhierarchical. How would that change the perspective from each participants' viewpoint? Would it be harder or easier for you?

Consider how outside stresses and/or the general happiness level and resilience of each participant might affect the system in each case.

Notice all the opportunities for either speaking up about a preference or deciding not to speak up. Note how tempting it might be to choose to stay quiet or do what you want to do and not mention it to the other parties involved. Consider what specific skills and capacities it would take on the part of each participant to steer both of these scenarios toward happy, positive outcomes.

Lastly, consider how it would change things if each participant in both scenarios felt at least 75% safe and secure in their relationship. That is, they aren't worrying about being left nor are they thinking about leaving. They may be having a good week or a bad week, but they feel loved and chosen, and know how to connect on purpose, even in a brief encounter. They are not worried that anyone is trying to take something away from them, get away with something nefarious, or fool them.

Can you start to see how the capacity of the participants is more important than the "rules" of the power dynamics in the relationships? Consider the example of Liz, Joe, and Michelle. In similar situations, I have many times seen something akin to Joe having a conversation with Liz in which Liz asks Joe to hurry up and go to the ER, and take good care of Michelle, and sends along her best wishes and maybe some flowers. I've seen that happen even if Liz and Michelle are not close or don't even like one another. Taking the example of Mark, Susan, and Julie, I've often seen something akin to either Susan, Julie, or both expressing concern for the connection between Mark and Susan, and choosing to prioritize strengthening that bond over any particular date or momentary preference they might have. These responses are made possible when all people involved are aware of the ways they can stabilize their relational system and inoculate it against stress by offering respect and consideration, particularly in stressful situations.

The lines of power and hierarchy get blurry because it benefits all concerned for everyone to be happy and for their relationships to be stable. When participants in polyamorous relationships begin to experience positive effects from their relationship structure, everyone starts to relax. As anxiety comes down and appreciation goes up, safety increases, most relationships become more flexible, and any existing hierarchy, while probably still there, becomes much less obvious.

The aforementioned examples look at how primary/secondary hierarchies can blur and shift. Sometimes, depending on circumstances, they end up looking very nonhierarchical. Circumstances also can make nonhierarchical polyamory look somewhat hierarchical. For instance, if two partners share a mortgage, household responsibilities, and children, they will necessarily sometimes prioritize one another's or the household's needs over those of other partners with whom they have less complicated commitments. The term *nesting partner* was developed to address this. Without implying hierarchy (as in "primary partner"), the term acknowledges a level of shared responsibility that will occasionally (or frequently, as in the case of sharing children) result in choices that may seem hierarchical when viewed from the outside.

POLYAMOROUS RELATIONSHIP SHAPES, OR "POLYCULES"

Let's look at some of the shapes polyamorous relationships take. Start by imagining a map of a relationship. In this map, each participant is charted as a point, and the connections between them are dashes connecting the dots; therefore, a relationship between two people would look like two dots connected by a line, a triad would look like three dots connected by three lines in a triangle shape, and so forth. Consider this an intimate relationship genogram, diagramming connections between people, some of whom have multiple partners, some of whom also have other partners.

People often become confused when I discuss relationship shapes. Rest assured, it's not terribly important. I only include it here because many polyamorous people describe their relationships in these terms, and I'd like you to have some idea of what they are talking about.

There are infinite potential configurations of individuals in polycules, pods, or polyamorous groups/families; however, there are some frequently occurring relationship shapes you will surely encounter in your work. This glossary will take you through the most common terms, as a truly exhaustive list is impossible. Note that people often describe their relationship in terms of the people most actively connected with them, but there may be other connections as well.

V or Vee: This refers to a relationship structure in which one person has two partners who are not romantically or sexually involved with one another (if they were, it would be a triad). This term is in common use, and you certainly might hear someone say "I'm in a V." V relationships often have primary/secondary structures. In that case, the person depicted by the center point of the V (the hinge person or, sometimes, pivot person) would have one primary partner and one secondary partner. A V can also have a nonhierarchical structure, in which the hinge person does not prioritize either of their partners over the other. For role-related challenges, for instance, those faced by hinges, primaries, and secondaries, see chapter 17.

N: This is a common variant of the V, in which two people, each part of another couple, are together sexually and/or romantically: Picture two Vs connected. Imagine Marina and Joe are a couple, and Chris and Roberto are a couple. If Marina and Chris are having a relationship, this would be an N. Throughout time, in my neck of the woods at least, I have noticed fewer people describe their relationships this way. Instead, Marina and Chris would both just say they each are in a V. It is good to know that someone who describes themselves as being in a V might very well be describing a portion of a polycule that has more than three people. I have most often seen an N described as a V when the fourth partner isn't really part of the day-to-day life of the person doing the describing. They are metamours but may not have much contact. It is also possible that the metamours have never met.

Asterisk: An asterisk describes a person who has several or many other partners. They are the center of the asterisk, and the other partners are the points radiating off the center. In my region, this is now most often described as solo polyamory. A person who practices this style of polyamory might also describe themselves as a free agent, a solo, or as practicing RA (relationship anarchy).

Triangle, triad, or throuple: A triad of three people who are usually all romantically and/or sexually involved with one another and function as a polyamorous family. Any of the connections in a triad may be romantic and sexual, or just romantic and not sexual, or just sexual and not romantic, but the main thing is that all are intimately connected. Any polyamorous family may be a closed group, meaning they have agreed not to engage in intimate relationships outside of the current group (polyfidelity), or they may have an agreement they are open to other connections. The family unit may be primary or there may be a nonhierarchical structure if some of the participants have other relationships.

Usually a triad has a family decision-making body but not always. Occasionally, there might be an originally existing dyad who retain the vestiges of a primary/secondary structure, particularly if the triad is still forming and full commitments are not yet cemented. While they may make decisions together as a family, there will always be some decisions that mainly affect two participants, and there may be areas in which two participants make decisions together more than the other partner—for instance, issues of child-rearing. Remember the 49/51 decision-making idea. In any group of two or more, there will rarely be total and complete accord; 49/51 is healthy and adaptive.

Square, quad: A quad is a group of four people who are all in some way intimately connected. It is in every way similar to a triad but with four people. Usually, a quad will have a family decision-making process; however, the more people involved in any given family, the more interpersonal complexity there will be, especially when it comes to decision-making. Often a quad will have originated with two couples who may have lots of shared family commitments and responsibilities, and who may be raising children together. Sometimes a quad may have one or more solo polyamorous people in it. A quad may be closed or open, meaning they may have an agreement that the participants may have other partners, or they may have a polyfidelity agreement to not engage in other relationships for a time.

Network: A community within which people have the option to have any sexual or romantic connections they wish. There may or may not be rules about who can and can't sleep with whom or have what kind of intimacy with whom. The diagram of this relationship configuration resembles a web and may be constantly changing as people come and go. Decisions may be made in any manner: sometimes by a dyad, sometimes by the community, and sometimes solo or nonhierarchically.

SUMMING UP DECISION-MAKING BODIES

As you can see, it can be a bit complicated to discern the decision-making body in a polyamorous relationship. Some relationships have one or more individual decision-makers, as in nonhierarchical polyamory, solo polyamory, or relationship anarchy. There might be a dyad making decisions, as in primary/secondary polyamory. There might be multiple dyads making decisions, as in a polycule in which two secondary partners each have a primary or spouse. There might be a family making decisions, which could be three people in a triad, four in a quad, or more. Additionally, in any particular group or situation, there may be some decisions that will be made by one or more people that are the primary stakeholders in that particular situation, in which case it varies by content of the decision. There might be nesting partners or coparents, even in a nonhierarchical situation. Moreover, most decisions are actually made 49/51, with someone having slightly more of a say in any given domain.

Many people have explicit agreements about who has decision-making power. For instance, there may be clear agreements about primary/secondary status. In other cases, however, there may not have been a clear discussion about it. In any particular situation, it can be important to understand who the decision-makers are, particularly if there are disagreements among partners about how things are going or how decisions are being made. If some participants are not entirely respectful of how their decisions affect others in the polycule or pod, tensions will certainly arise.

WHO SHOULD COME TO THERAPY?
DECISION-MAKING BODIES

Now that you know some language your polyamorous client might use and have a ballpark idea of what sort of thing they might be talking about when they identify themselves as being RA, polyfidelitous, or in a V, you might be wondering what the significance of all this is, beyond simply vocabulary.

I think it is important to understand how the power dynamics are structured in any given relationship. When there are multiple people involved, things can get confusing. The most confusing decision a therapist might need to make comes right away with the first contact you make with your first polyamorous client: Who should you invite to come to the first therapy session? My short answer: the decision-making body. I'll expand on this in chapter 10, "Getting Polyamory Therapy Off to a Strong Start: Understanding the Change Process."

CHAPTER 2

Polyamory
What the Research Tells Us

This chapter provides an overview of what the current body of research has to offer regarding polyamory. But before I dive into the details, I want to put these research findings into perspective. This book draws on information obtained from research conducted by others and myself, but it relies much more heavily on experience. This includes my clinical experience working with this population, experience with supervision and consultation for many other therapists who work with open relationships, and, of course, the experiences of my clients. I also draw heavily on my own personal connections with people in my life (including family members, friends, colleagues, and acquaintances) who are in consensually nonmonogamous (CNM) and polyamorous relationships. That's an extremely important dimension of my experience, because those relationships provide a unique and hard-to-find viewpoint: that of polyamorous people who are not self-selected for being in active therapy.

The body of knowledge is evolving and expanding constantly as researchers continue to contribute new findings. Right now, in fact, the research is exploding as the cultural visibility of polyamory increases. I'm certain that much more research-based knowledge about polyamory will emerge in the next few years. The research as it stands definitely bears out what I observe in my practice: Polyamorous relationships work, and polyamorous people are happy, healthy, and satisfied in their relationships.

But research has its limitations. No study is perfect. Research requires time, money, expertise, and other resources; this limits who can do research and therefore limits the scope of research to those topics that interest the people who have the resources and ability to conduct it.

Studies are limited by their design and methods of data collection. By definition, they can look only at a small sliver of the world and attempt to generalize from that to the population as a whole. Since there are regional differences in polyamorous populations and since study size tends to be small, the picture we glean is limited. That said, some things are fairly well-established by multiple studies with similar findings. In this chapter, I discuss a number of these well-established findings. My goal is not to provide an exhaustive literature review, but to focus on the findings that I think are particularly important for cultural competence and conceptualizing therapeutic treatment.

CLINICAL APPROACHES: THE RESEARCH

It is difficult to get approval to conduct comparative research on clinical practices. As a result, the research about clinical strategies and interventions for working with people in consensually open or polyamorous relationships is currently very limited. In fact, I would argue that the research on clinical strategies and interventions for relationship therapy *in general* is limited as well.

The existing body of literature about clinical guidelines for working with polyamory sheds light on a few different topics. One is the importance of acknowledging the possibility of clinician bias and finding effective ways to work with bias, including supervision, consultation, further study, and active strategies for building self-awareness, for example, self-reflection and journaling. This literature frequently emphasizes the need for accurate information about the population to build cultural competence, as well as the importance of recognizing the client as the expert in their own lives and acknowledging that polyamory may or may not be the focus of treatment.

One study by Berry and Barker (2014) recommends existential sex therapy as a treatment modality. It defines this style of therapy as

> grounded in a nonpathologizing model of sexuality, which views human sexual behaviors as existing within a broad and diverse spectrum . . . reject[ing] a binary view of "healthy" and "pathological," or "normal"

and "abnormal." Instead, the existential sex therapist sees sexuality and sexual behavior as subjectively situated within the context . . . of one's individual life. (p. 22)

Another, Zimmerman (2012), highlights the need for self-awareness, honesty, authenticity, and boundaries in nonmonogamous relationships, and discusses a multisystemic approach to therapy. The study recommends that therapists bring up nonmonogamies as viable relationship options that offer specific benefits. The overall focus in multiple research studies is on the importance of a nonpathologizing, systemic perspective, along with the need for honesty and agreements about disclosure and the ability to set boundaries. This is quite compatible with my clinical approach, which is informed by the Developmental Model of Couples Therapy, based on concepts of attachment, differentiation, and neuroscience.

There are many studies that offer insights into useful therapeutic approaches for LGBTQIA+ people. They shed light on general approaches that are effective when working with other marginalized populations, for example, participants in consensual nonmonogamies or kink. In addition, the heavy overlap between LGBTQIA+ populations and consensually nonmonogamous populations points to a direct link: If you are working with polyamorous clients, you will almost certainly also be working with some LGBTQIA+ clients, as well as some kinky clients.

In a nutshell, what I have gleaned from this body of work is that multisystemic, nonpathologizing, feminist, narrative, or other postmodern therapy approaches are useful, because they focus on individual definitions, narratives, strengths, power structures around marginalization, and meaning-making rather than adhering or adapting to culturally normative relational constructs. Many studies have recommended talking about the clients' experience of discrimination when working with marginalized populations and cultivating awareness of the issues LGBTQIA+ people face, including coming-out issues, identity concerns, and marginalization, with the goal of helping clients deal with these stressors. It is not necessary to identify as LGBTQIA+ to provide therapy for these populations, nor do therapists need to have a lot of prior experience working with the population; however, clients do appreciate cultural competence in their therapist with regard to their identity, and they generally do not want to be their therapist's only source of information about the populations they are in.

My colleagues, Atala Mitchell and Madeline Barger, did an unpublished study looking at what polyamorous clients want from a therapist. You can see the entire study on my website, https://instituteforrelational intimacy.com/wp-content/uploads/2020/05/MitchellBargerPolyamory .pdf. Mitchell and Barger identified several key characteristics polyamorous clients seek in therapists, including "listens attentively," "respects client's communication style," and "addresses the client's issues whether or not they relate to polyamory." Participants specifically reported they did not feel it was important that their therapist actually be polyamorous themselves; however, participants who had not yet had a therapist reported it was very important that their therapist identify their practice as polyamorous-friendly. These findings are congruent with those I have seen relating to working with other marginalized populations.

FASCINATING DEMOGRAPHICS: WHO, WHAT, WHY, HOW?

Haupert, Gesselman, Moors, Fisher, and Garcia (2017) used two separate U.S. Census–based quota samples of single adults in the United States. They found that more than one in five participants reported engaging in consensual nonmonogamy at some point in their lifetime and write,

> This proportion remained roughly constant across age, education level, income status, religion, region, political affiliation, and race. The prevalence of open relationships did vary significantly by gender and sexual orientation across both studies, with men [compared to women] and those identifying as gay, lesbian, or bisexual [compared to those who identify as heterosexual] being more likely to report previous engagement in CNM relationships. (p. 436)

Levine, Herbenick, Martinez, Fu, and Dodge (2018), and Rubin, Moors, Matsik, Ziegler, and Conley (2014) found that approximately 4 to 5% of Americans are currently involved in a consensually nonmonogamous relationship.

Page (2004), in evaluating the demographics of her bisexual sample, found that 33% were involved in a polyamorous relationship at the time of the study. Richards (2010) found that trans people are more likely than cis people to embrace nonmonogamy, and Sherrer (2010) found the same of asexual people.

The overlap between the polyamorous community and the kinky community is also well-established (Sheff, 2005, 2006; Wosick-Correa, 2010; Bauer, 2010). Sheff and Hammers (2011) found that polyamorous and kinky communities shared a heavy overlap. Richters, De Visser, Rissel, Grulich, and Smith (2008) found that people involved in BDSM were more likely to have been nonexclusive in a regular relationship than people who weren't involved in BDSM. Carlström and Andersson (2019) further explored the relationship between BDSM and nonmonogamy, and found that the transgression of one norm makes it easier to transgress other norms as well. Sheff and Hammers (2011) found that people who engage in consensual nonmonogamy are largely white, college-educated, middle- and upper-class professionals between their late 30s and early 50s, with race being especially homogenous. Jenks (1985) and Levitt (1988) found similar demographics in the swinging community. That's not to say there are not people of color or low-income people in the polyamory community—there certainly are, and sampling methods in marginalized communities can easily lead to demographically skewed samples. Although the demographics appear to be skewed toward whites and the middle class, African American polyamorous people are becoming increasingly visible; a quick search online will get you more information on recent developments, organizations, and community supports.

There are other interesting cultural overlaps between the polyamory community and various other subcultures that are perhaps worthy of further study. Wilkins (2004) and Aviram (2010), for instance, investigated the connections between polyamory culture and pagan, goth, and geek communities.

By the time you read this, there will probably be many new developments in subcultures of polyamory and CNM. If there is a community or resource you think would benefit your clients, even if I haven't mentioned it, definitely look for it. Chances are you will find what you are seeking.

One question therapists often ask me is whether choosing polyamory is an indication of attachment wounds or psychopathology. Nowhere in the research is there any indication of a higher incidence or different type of psychopathology in the polyamorous community than in the population at large. My clinical experience is definitely congruent with this finding. You can read more about attachment as it relates to relational therapy with polyamorous clients in chapter 8, "Conceptualizing the Case: If Polyamory Isn't the Problem, What Is?" Jessica Fern also covered this ground exceptionally thoroughly in her book *Polysecure: Attachment, Trauma, and Consensual Nonmonogamy*.

Many of my clients tell me they and their community members agree that ongoing support for personal growth through therapy and self-help is important to them and their relationships. Studies bear this out: The research indicates that polyamorous people tend to be very much like the population at large regarding levels of trust, satisfaction, commitment, and mental health (Conley et al., 2017; Rubel & Bogaert, 2015).

There is also plenty of research that shows that polyamorous people are concerned about their health and, in particular, are knowledgeable about sexually transmitted infections and careful about safer sex (Fleckenstein & Cox, 2015; Conley, Moors, Ziegler, & Karathanasis, 2012; Lehmiller, 2015; Levine et al., 2018). Again, this fits with my experience. Many people in the polyamorous community get regular health care; those who are quite sexually active generally get regular STI testing. This is another aspect of this population I admire: It is lovely to work with clients who are proactive and knowledgeable about their health, and concerned about and protective of the health of their partners.

MY STUDY

In 2011, I did a study on polyamory with my colleague, Nicholas Wittwer. Common mainstream thought at that time held that monogamy is necessary for true intimacy and that polyamorous relationships don't stand the test of time. There was, and still is, an overarching assumption that polyamory equals promiscuity. None of that reflected what I had observed in my life or practice, so we decided to do a study and see what we could discover.

You can see the entire study on my website (https://institutefor relationalintimacy.com/wp-content/uploads/2020/05/Longevity-and -Intimacy-in-Polyamorous-Relationships.pdf), but I want to highlight some particularly interesting findings. Everyone who participated self-identified as being in a consensually polyamorous relationship. When we asked them how many relationships they were currently in, the average was a little more than two. That definitely doesn't imply promiscuity. The range was huge, with many people being in only one relationship currently; the outlier for the number of current relationships was 23. We spent some time speculating about how a person might be in 23 current relationships, and our hypothesis was that this might be someone who lives in a community with many others, with an open-relationship network agreement; however, we will never know.

Juicy as the outlier number is, the real lesson is that many polyamorous people are in only one relationship currently, and most are in two or three. Some of those in one relationship are probably monogamous-polyamorous people, and others currently may not be seeing more than one person for any number of reasons.

Nick and I asked our study participants to distinguish between their primary and other relationships. For those who did not identify a primary, we asked them to distinguish between their first and subsequent relationships. The largest category of relationship length for primary or first relationships in our study was 12-plus, and the mean was 8.3 years. For me, that demonstrates clearly that polyamorous relationships can stand the test of time.

The largest category of duration of all relationships, meaning a combination of primary/longest relationships and all other relationships, was less than one year, reflecting that many subsequent or secondary relationships were of fairly brief duration; however, the second, third, and fourth-largest groups for duration of all relationships were almost the same size. They were 1 to 2 years, 4 to 6 years, and more than 12 years' duration. It seems clear from this finding that secondary/ subsequent relationships can also have substantial longevity, which coincides with my clinical observation. I know of secondary relationships that function very well and have lasted more than a decade, and are still going strong; the same goes for many nonhierarchical polyamorous relationships.

We looked at relationship structures as well. The majority of our respondents were in primary/secondary relationships; however, the second largest group was people in family structures, in which all participants participate equally in decision-making. The remainder were in some variety of nonhierarchical relationships. My sense from what I observe clinically is that this is shifting throughout time. I still see more primary/secondary relationships than any other form, but I notice increasing numbers of nonhierarchical relationships in my practice.

Nick and I also asked people why they were polyamorous, offering a list of possible reasons and asking them to choose all that applied. The following are the reasons people selected for being polyamorous, ranked from most to least popular:

It's just the way I am
Desire for more intimacy/closeness
Freedom/independence
Desire for more variety in partners
Philosophical reasons
Desire for other kinds of sex/sex practices
Desire for sex with another gender
Desire for more sex
It just happened and I went with it
My partner wanted to explore polyamory
Other
Protection from being alone
Religious reasons

By far, the winning response was, "It is just the way I am," which implies that, for many polyamorous people, polyamory is a congruent expression of an aspect of their identity. Few respondents selected protection from being alone or religious reasons.

Finally, we looked at intimacy. In my experience, when people are considering opening their relationship, they worry (or their friends, family, or therapists worry) that if their partner has another partner, it might reduce the intimacy they experience in the original relationship. That doesn't appear to be true. Unfortunately, I didn't ask respondents to compare their intimacy before opening up and after opening up, but the intimacy levels were high enough (especially in primary/original relationships) to make it unlikely that opening up diminished intimacy.

My observations of polyamorous relationships certainly bears out the idea that opening up doesn't destroy intimacy or even diminish it. In fact, often the opposite occurs. Some studies have confirmed that some respondents report intimacy increasing after opening up, perhaps as a result of the unique benefits of the relationship structure and perhaps as a result of experiencing a congruent expression of self. I also want to note that, although intimacy levels in my study were a little lower in secondary/subsequent relationships, they were still pretty high. Secondary relationships face particular challenges, but it doesn't appear that low intimacy is typically one of them.

WRAPPING UP

For my purposes, there are a few findings discussed here that I consider to be particularly useful to therapists. The first is the extensive overlap between polyamorous people, LGBTQIA+ people, and kinky people, which I believe suggests an important dimension of cultural competence for therapists; I discuss this in more depth in chapter 3, "Overlapping Marginalized Populations and Intersectionality." The second is the lack of any indication that polyamorous people have any higher rates of psychopathology and attachment wounds than the general population; this finding is important because it addresses a common question therapists ask me and supports what I've seen in my practice: Polyamory is not a reflection of pathology, but a healthy and adaptive relationship style. The third is the finding, from my own study, indicating that many polyamorous relationships were long-lasting and had high levels of intimacy.

Research can provide us with a valuable (if limited) snapshot of what tends to exist in nature. In my therapy room, however, I'm not concerned with the statistical proportion of people who flourish or struggle in any specific relationship structure; I'm concerned about the people sitting across from me, what they want for themselves, and what's possible for them. I'm interested in helping them craft a relationship that is tailored to their desires, beliefs, inner compass, and sense of self. From that perspective, it doesn't matter so much if the relationship structure they're interested in creating is statistically common or even if it's ever existed before. It matters whether they're excited to explore the territory; flexible enough to experiment and negotiate; and committed to warm, empathetic, honest communication about their desires, beliefs, and preferences. If that's the case, I'm happy to help them create any kind of relationship they can imagine. Where some of those qualities are lacking, rather than tell them they cannot create the type of relationship they desire, I focus on helping them develop the skills they need to create the life they aspire to.

CHAPTER 3

Overlapping Marginalized Populations and Intersectionality

Polyamorous people comprise a marginalized population that intersects with many other marginalized populations. It is worth noting that while there is overlap, these communities are far from identical. Plenty of your clients will fall into one community and not others; however, if you work with clients in polyamorous relationships, you are certainly going to find yourself working with some people who also identify as gay, lesbian, bisexual, pansexual, asexual, gender nonconforming, and/or kinky, or who want to explore some of those areas or practice related behaviors. Similarly, if you work with the LGBTQIA+ and/or kink community, you will have clients who identify as polyam or want to explore polyamory. Knowing something about these populations will be helpful, in part to give you a jumping-off place for further learning and in part to help you avoid some common misunderstandings due to lack of information.

If you're reading this book for support in your own relationship journey and you are curious about exploring diverse erotic orientations, attractions, gender identity, kink, or a fetish, this chapter covers the basics and can serve as a starting point. There are also numerous references on the topic to support your exploration, as well as supportive and informative communities.

When working with marginalized communities, it is important to remember that intersectionality is in play. Intersectionality refers to how different categories of oppression (based on race, class, gender, sexuality, ability, etc.) combine and overlap. People who are in more than one oppressed group have particular experiences of oppression greater than the sum of the parts. For instance, the discrimination experienced by black women is not just "racism plus sexism," but a *distinct* form of marginalization with its own particular characteristics. That means that, to understand the marginalization your clients experience, you need to be aware of not only homophobia, transphobia, sexism, and so forth, but also how those categories overlap.

I think the most important stance for a therapist to take when working with marginalized groups is to acknowledge the marginalization and invite feedback and frank discussion in the course of the therapeutic relationship. Invite your client to talk about ways in which they feel marginalized as a result of being polyamorous, as well as being in any other marginalized group. Honor their experience and invite feedback about their experience of having a therapeutic relationship with you. Openly explore any feedback they may have for you or any experience of marginalization between you. Initiate discussion of racial differences, power dynamics, and other aspects of marginalization. As with other thorny topics, it is the therapist's responsibility to bring it up. Most clients won't go there, unless you make it clear you are able to have those conversations by opening the door to the topic yourself. Even if you don't feel confident, remember that being yourself, and letting your authenticity and caring show is the ticket to a strong therapeutic relationship.

If you are the client in a therapeutic relationship, please give your therapist honest feedback about this and any other matter that is important to you. I'm sure they genuinely want to help you and know the real you. Moreover, if they can't handle receiving feedback from a client on a topic that is this important to the therapeutic process, you definitely need a new therapist. If you are fuzzy on why, take a look at chapter 8, with special attention to the topic of differentiation. It is commonly accepted that a therapist can't help a client achieve a level of differentiation they themselves have not yet achieved; it is possible that you might outgrow your therapist in the differentiation department. Hopefully this does not become the case, but if they don't accept feedback well, that is a red flag. Meeting your relationship goals will probably include leveling up in the differentiation department; find a therapist who can help you achieve that.

The join between therapist and client is more important than any other factor. In fact, there's research about this as it relates specifically to polyamory. My colleagues, Atala Mitchell and Madeline Barger, conducted a study that demonstrated that most polyamorous clients don't feel they need a polyamorous therapist. Research participants also reported being willing to be a therapist's first polyamorous client. Their primary desire was to have a therapist who is open to and accepting of their relationship choices, and willing to educate themselves about polyamory, rather than expecting their clients to provide their education.

That's good news, because there certainly aren't enough polyamorous therapists to work with all the polyamorous people who would like to have therapy. This is broadly true of marginalized populations: There generally aren't enough in-group therapists to serve everyone in any given marginalized population, so referring to an in-group therapist isn't usually an option. In my opinion, it isn't necessarily the best solution even when it is possible; the understanding that comes with personal experience of being in a marginalized group is counterbalanced by the risk in-group therapists run of thinking they and their clients are more alike than they actually are. There is no therapeutic situation that doesn't require acknowledging differences and striving for empathy; sharing a demographic doesn't guarantee an effective shortcut for any of that.

This doesn't mean that you should ignore differences and issues related to being different, including experiences particular to marginalization, cultural knowledge deficits on the part of the therapist, and power imbalances that affect the therapy. Developing ways to talk openly with clients, supervisors, supervisees, and colleagues about these issues is key. Much healing can come from an attuned, connected relationship that features genuine caring and curiosity, open acknowledgment of differences, and a collaborative approach. Invite and honor the experiences, perceptions, and feedback your clients offer, and you will be off to an excellent start.

In this chapter, I provide some information about working with each of the subgroups that commonly overlap with the polyamory community. My goal is to debunk a few common myths and help you avoid making potentially damaging assumptions. I want you to feel like you can get started with your intersectional polyamorous clients *without* already being an expert in all these areas. The world needs more polyamory-competent therapists, and right away, so please don't wait until you're an expert in working with all of these groups. Instead, read on, stay open and curious, model curiosity about differences and acceptance of diversity, invite feedback, accept it with grace, and go ahead and get started.

Each of these populations offer enough nuance and fascinating material to fill entire books, which is obviously beyond the scope of this chapter. I invite you to get curious and explore beyond the overview I provide here. It's also important to note that language and knowledge about some of these populations are evolving quickly, so remember to stay open to learning more and rethinking your assumptions continually as you work with these groups. Things change fast and vary regionally for these populations; as with polyamory, I always ask my clients to describe what they mean by the labels they use rather than assume I understand. Please consider this chapter to be merely a brief introduction to overlapping marginalized populations, not a complete manual.

BDSM/KINK

If you work with polyamorous clients, you will almost certainly also be working with kinky clients, even if you don't know it. I say "even if you don't know it" because your clients might not come out to you as kinky. Of course, not all kinky clients are polyamorous, and not everyone who is polyamorous is kinky, but the overlap is significant enough that if you're planning to work with polyamory, you should be prepared to work with kink, too. Because it can be difficult to find information about this population, I provide quite a bit of information about BDSM/kink, as it relates to therapy, here. For much more information including recent research about BDSM, refer to Brad Sagarin and others' work at www.scienceofbdsm.com.

What Is BDSM/Kink?

"Kinky" describes a way of being that includes engaging in one, some, or all of multiple erotic and/or sexual practices, including, but not limited to, bondage (B), discipline (D), dominance (D), submission (S), sadism (S), masochism (M), sensation play, power play, role play, and fetishism. Kinky play encompasses a huge range of activities, from quite common and mild to quite extreme and unusual. Kinky play, like polyamory, can be experienced as an aspect of identity or simply a behavior that is enjoyable and may be practiced occasionally, situationally, often, or always. The following are just a few examples of what kink can mean to give you an idea of the range:

Restraint: Playing with handcuffs, bondage, being held down, holding someone else down, etc.

Role play: Pretending to be strangers who meet in a bar, dressing up in costume for private play at home or going out (think nurse or school girl outfit), pretending to be a different age or species, etc.

Sensation play (which can range from mild to intense): On the mild side, touching or being touched with feathers or fur and light spanking with a fuzzy paddle; on the intense side, flogging, caning, wax, needles, blood, fire, piercing, branding, etc.

Eroticizing objects, body parts, or fictional characters, for example, shoes, underwear, balloons, diapers, feet, fur, My Little Pony, etc.

Imposing relational dynamics involving power exchange, including a range of such roles as master/slave or mistress/slave relationships, and ranging from occasional play to 24/7.

Kink 101 for Therapists

There are several important things to understand about kinky play and kinky relationships.

Kink Is Not the Problem

Adults are free to engage in whatever erotic or sexual activities they want to, as long as their play is consensual and legal. Being able to help clients navigate any challenges related to kink requires that you truly understand that their erotic preferences and expressions are normal, healthy, and not an indicator of a problem. Of course, occasionally there will be a situation that is not actually healthy. Being able to discern between adaptive and maladaptive behavior is part of being an effective therapist with any population. Consider couples therapy; while we can spend a lot of time and energy strengthening the connection in couple relationships, it is also true that sometimes we see a relational dynamic that is maladaptive, and we need to be able to tell the difference and also intervene effectively. Kink is no different; you'll need to be able to distinguish between a maladaptive, unhealthy dynamic and a perfectly normal, perfectly healthy expression of sexuality. When it comes to kink, the line between adaptive and maladaptive often boils down to consent. This chapter provides a lot of information about the nuances of consent and how to help in complicated situations.

If you are still in doubt about the normalcy of the kinky play your clients are engaging in, get supervision or talk to a consultant who specializes in BDSM/kink. Being able to normalize kink is a requirement of working with this population, but being able to intervene, if needed, is part of being an effective therapist for any population. Get the support you need to feel comfortable, confident, and competent as you enter new areas of specialty.

Kink Isn't a Sign of Pathology

There is no evidence that kinky people have more or less psychopathology than other sectors of the population. Read that again, because this is the biggest misconception I encounter. Wanting to engage in even intense forms of sensation play, dominance, submission, fetishism, or any other kink isn't an indication of past trauma, attachment wounds, or other psychopathology.

Assuming that there is a connection or there must be psychopathology underlying or resulting from a person's kinky behavior or identity is a form of marginalization. Therapists communicating this belief to their clients is the primary way I have gotten my kinky clients; they have left the therapist with whom they felt marginalized and sought out one who is accepting of diverse sexual practices and can help them think through the things that are important to them, like consent, negotiation, and creating strong relationships, without getting distracted by a passing mention of dramatic erotic practices.

That said, of course there are kinky people who have depression, anxiety, attachment wounds, trauma histories, and every other issue you would encounter in the general population, That's simply because kinky people are a part of the general population and are dealing with the same problems everyone else is.

Consent Is an Important Part of Kink

Kinky clients who are experienced with kinky play generally know a lot about consent and take it very seriously. Any problem that can occasionally come up in kinky play is at least as likely to come up with people who are not kinky—i.e., triggers arising during a sexual interaction, someone getting hurt physically or emotionally, or consent violations, both subtle and overt. The reason these things are at least as likely to occur in "vanilla" (nonkinky) relationships is because the kink community is founded on precepts of consent. Keep this in mind, because while it can be tempting to blame the kinky play for the problem, it's much more therapeutic to discuss *how* consent broke down. Otherwise, you're focusing on the window dressing at the expense of the real issue. If you have a client who is relatively new to kink and/ or who is not involved in the kink community, they are more likely to be fuzzy on some of these ideas, and your help understanding consent may be very important.

Kink Can Provide a Path to Healing

Kinky play can be a way of healing past hurts, whether large or small. It can be extremely therapeutic to act out a past trauma and create a felt experience of a new and empowered outcome. Examples of empowered outcomes range from vanquishing the abuser to eroticizing the traumatic events and everything in between; topics range from childhood abuse to rape to race play. Not everyone who is kinky is taking control of or reworking past trauma, but some are, and helping your client set up this type of play for success is not an uncommon therapeutic agenda. This can be extremely effective and result in deep healing. It is also true that there are some potential pitfalls that bear discussion ahead of time; I discuss this in detail later in this chapter.

Kink Is an Erotic Template

An erotic template is a core type of turn-on. Your erotic template is the specific scenario or narrative that turns you on most and tends to run as a central theme in your most prominent fantasies. Everyone has one, and although no one really knows how erotic templates develop, we do know they are outside of our conscious control and that no erotic template is "abnormal." We also know erotic templates can be added to, but they usually don't go away.

For example, let's say you have a core erotic desire to be powerless in a violent sexual situation (which is a common fantasy, by the way). You will probably always have that turn-on. If that is your only red-hot turn-on and you would like to diversify, it is possible to add more and expand your potential for having fulfilling vanilla (nonkinky) sexual interactions. But it is not likely that the rape fantasy will go away. It is possible to have an erotic template/preference/interest that is illegal, in which case you must make the decision to preserve health and safety by choosing not to act on it, and reserve it for fantasy life. If you have a client in this type of situation, you might want to engage a consultant to make sure you are dotting your Is and crossing your Ts, just in case your client ends up acting on their illegal turn-on. Never skimp on obtaining professional education and support, particularly when you are stretching into new areas of specialty. Trust your gut, and get help if you feel uncomfortable.

Kink can be a powerful way to explore a broad range of erotic interests in the framework of role play with consenting adults. In some cases, it provides the only safe or semisafe way to experience certain expressions of eroticism.

Kink Comes with a Huge Community

Kinky play and relationships don't need to exist in a vacuum. There is a huge international kink community. Many people who engage in kinky play are not connected to a larger community, but there are many benefits of being connected. Clients who are connected to the kink community in their region are likely to be keenly aware of in-group expectations about communication before play; negotiations about what is both desirable and off-limits during play; strategies to communicate "more please," "slow down," or "stop"; discussion of potential risks, aftercare, or ways to help one another get grounded and recover after play; and so on. They also are likely to have direct and normalizing experiences regarding kinky practices, because they are part of a community of people with similar interests and likely more experience.

If your clients are newly exploring kink and aren't yet aware of the community that can both support and entertain them, you can and should help them connect. The kink community offers a lot in the way of resources, support, education, events, and even mentoring for newcomers. A good place to start is an internet search for "BDSM in (your town and state)." I also encourage clients to do some reading to learn more about managing safety, getting consent, maintaining flexibility, addressing triggers that may arise, and other more nuanced aspects of kinky play.

The kink community broadly embraces a variety of guidelines to encourage nonharmful play. You may hear terms like SSC (safe, sane, and consensual), RACK (risk-aware consensual kink), and PRICK (personal responsibility, informed consensual kink). SSC was coined to help the public distinguish between kink and abuse; however, throughout time, kinky people realized that the slogan was inherently flawed, because safety cannot be guaranteed. For that reason, the acronym RACK was created, to acknowledge that, while you can't completely remove risk from kinky play, you can be aware of it and do your best to reduce it through processes involving informed consent. This is similar to the dilemma that occurred years ago in the earlier days of the AIDS epidemic, when health care providers coined the term *safe sex* to distinguish between lower- and higher-risk behaviors. Now we use the term *safer sex* instead, which acknowledges that no sexual activity can be guaranteed "safe"; there is always a risk of contracting an infection and no fail-safe strategy for prevention other than total abstinence. PRICK is an even more recent term, developed to acknowledge that personal responsibility for one's choices and actions is paramount to ethical erotic expression.

It is not important that you remember these terms, but it is crucial that you are aware that the kink community is actively working to understand, work with, and accurately describe nuanced distinctions involving risk, choice, responsibility, and, of course, the all-important cornerstone, consent. These concepts can also help you distinguish between abuse and ethical kink when you are uncertain.

Kinky Play Is (Usually) Normal

While your clients may talk with you about engaging in some fairly intense forms of kinky play, and those conversations can be jarring, don't immediately jump to the conclusion that "this is not normal." In fact, it probably is very normal, common, and accepted within the kink community, and just new or surprising to you. I have gotten quite an education from my kinky clients. I understand what it feels like to be surprised or shocked and to have to take a second to get grounded. When someone tells me about a kinky activity that brings up uncomfortable feelings in me, I am interested to know how the client feels about it. If the answer is "fine," I see no signs of lack of consent, and my client doesn't have unfinished business or unresolved feelings about it, I see it as my responsibility to move on, rather than allow my own feelings to hijack the session. If I still feel unresolved about it after the session, I get supervision or consult with an expert to get a "gut check" and/or debrief my own reaction. I don't discount my own "gut," but I am also aware that occasionally a story about perfectly adaptive, consensual kinky play can cause me some discomfort.

The most intense forms of kinky play to come up in my therapy room have involved people who were well-connected to the local kink community, knew their play partners well and/or were able to check references, had lots of experience with consent, took responsibility for their own decisions regarding their choices, and had a supportive community with which to debrief if things went amiss or got surprisingly intense.

Kink Isn't Always about Sex

Kinky play is often not overtly sexual. Sexy, sexual, and erotic, yes. But explicitly sexual touch is optional. Spanking, bondage, dominance/submission, role play, and fetishism do not by definition require genital contact, fluid exchange, or any other specific sexual contact. These specifics are open for negotiation between partners.

This creates an opportunity for someone to explore kinky play while crafting relationship agreements that don't necessitate totally sexually opening up their relationship(s). This is a handy thing to understand, because this potentially semisexual aspect of BDSM/kink has enabled lots of couples to create monogamish relationships that honor differing sexual interests, without having to go full-on polyamorous.

Fetishes

A fetish is an erotic interest in an object, activity, or situation. Think high-heeled shoes, furries (dressing in a fursuit), or diapers (role playing an infant or child). The fetishized object or situation may be a sexy adjunct to an erotic encounter or a necessary part. Fetishes are expressions of eroticism (see the earlier information regarding erotic templates).

Understanding Consent

The single most important thing to understand about BDSM/kink is that it describes *consensual interactions between adults*. Consent seems like a simple thing, but it actually requires a sophisticated skill set to do it well, which is why sometimes things go amiss. Additionally, it is actually quite nuanced and cannot be reduced to "just say no." I'm going to go into it pretty deeply here because it is so important. Stay with me; this section is kind of detailed and dense but hopefully also thought-provoking. If you understand consent well, including its nuances and underlying skills, and have a repertoire of ways to help clients build those skills (see chapter 8, "Conceptualizing the Case: If Polyamory Isn't the Problem, What Is?"), you are in a great position to work effectively with a huge range of sex issues, not just kink and polyamory.

Consent, as I describe it, is an ongoing and ever-shifting process that requires self-awareness, self-assessment, other-awareness, and attunement, in an atmosphere of sincere mutual respect, achieved through verbal and nonverbal communication, with the clear intention of collaboration between partners for the mutual pleasure of everyone involved. Much of our world is spectacularly bad at consent, due, in part, to a lack of understanding of what consent actually entails and, in part, to underdeveloped skill at reading and responding to self and others in adaptive ways.

I think it is important to note that the kink community is far above average in the ability to understand and practice consent well. In my practice, I work with a broad range of clients, and I see far more consent-related problems with my "vanilla" (nonkinky) clients than I do with the kinky ones, probably because practicing kink, by definition, involves practicing consent, explicitly. It is refreshing to work with a population that values consent, openly discusses it, and forms explicit agreements about erotic play. That's not to say that consent issues don't crop up with kinky clients, but even when there are consent violations in kinky play, this tends to be a group of clients with a base understanding of consent and an interest in upholding it. This is not always true with the vanilla population, many of whom haven't really thought through the nuances of consent.

This raises an interesting question: Why is it that kinky clients tend to have a better grasp of consent than vanilla ones? I believe it's because most people never got sufficient sex education, and what they did get probably didn't include much nuance about consent. Without a reason to have to learn it, most people won't be exposed to these ideas. But if someone gets involved in the kink community or does any reading about BDSM, they will immediately start learning about consent. It's nothing to do with the nature of being kinky or the nature of being vanilla; it's about the fact that being part of BDSM culture is more likely to expose you to nuanced discussion of consent, which, unfortunately, you're not likely to get in mainstream culture.

Nuances of Consent   Consent describes an ongoing state of self-assessment and communication about desires and preferences. The ability to take an accurate internal read of one's desires and communicate them, even if someone else might be disappointed, is actually a sophisticated skill set and one that is underdeveloped in many people (see chapter 8, "Conceptualizing the Case: If Polyamory Isn't the Problem, What Is?" specifically the section on differentiation of self).

Consent isn't just "yes" or "no." The ability to consent involves a nuanced vocabulary that includes "maybe," "in certain circumstances," "until I indicate otherwise," "go slow and I'll let you know how I feel," "maybe we could work up to it by doing something else first," etc. Typical "safe words" in kinky play are "red," "yellow," and "green," as in traffic signals indicating "stop," "slow down" or "take care," and "go." It is also worth noting that individuals make their own safe words that might be unique to them alone, as in "broccoli," "lasagna," "peanut butter," or anything you can imagine. The important concept is that there are safe words involved in kinky play as an important part of practicing nuanced consent.

It isn't really consent unless it is freely given. There must be no overt or covert coercion, internal pressure, external pressure, cultural pressure, peer pressure, or any other kind of pressure. Anyone involved in any consensual activity should feel absolutely certain that they and anyone involved can and will say "no" if they want to, for any reason, and participants must actively make sure anyone can say "no" without negative consequences.

Once given, consent can also be withdrawn, any time, for any reason or for no reason at all. Many people suffer from a flawed construct, which is the idea that when a person agrees to participate in any given activity it can be assumed that they will always consent to that activity. Not necessarily so. A similarly flawed idea is that it might be assumed that a person consents to participate in some other, possibly related, activity once they consent to any particular activity. This belief does a huge amount of relational damage. It is equally flawed to assume the person wants to continue any given activity for any particular amount of time. It is better not to assume; it is much better to check assumptions by asking or, if engaging in activities that involve stretching into unknown or uncomfortable realms, employing safe words.

On the other hand, this philosophy can lead to cumbersome, obsessive, antierotic checking: "Is this okay? Is this still okay? Is *this* okay? How about this?" I would argue that this is still better than rushing ahead and violating a boundary, but anxiety and eroticism don't go together well. It is definitely possible to walk a line between checking in for purposes of ongoing consent and maintaining eroticism. For instance, partners might have a conversation before a sexual situation to discuss everyone's preferred style with this type of checking. Some people don't want to be asked if everything is okay, in which case it would be ideal to arrive at some other way for consent to be understood to have been given, and withdrawn. Moreover, some people have a difficult time saying no or giving any direction at all in an intimate context; in that situation, partners will need to build attunement through debriefing before and/or after the fact to see how things are going, what they liked and didn't like, and how their partner should interpret their cues. Once in a while I will have a client who doesn't want to have these uncomfortable conversations about consent; for more on this see chapter 8, "Conceptualizing the Case: If Polyamory Isn't the Problem, What Is?"

Because consent is a skill set that depends on judgment and awareness, a person's ability to give or withdraw consent can be changed by the use of substances or altered states of being. If you are working with a client who has run into problems involving consent violations, assess substance use, because substance use and impaired judgment go hand in hand.

One of the goals of kinky play for some people is to *achieve altered states of being*, for instance, those that can be brought about naturally, in kinky play, by the release of endorphins that help the body and mind cope with pain. For some, achieving a sense of release of control, heightened awareness, or some other altered state of being is one of the main goals of engaging in kinky play. Of course, these, or any, altered states of being can change a participant's judgment and thereby affect their ability to consent or withdraw consent. This is one of the complexities of kinky play; one of the primary goals of play can also potentially result in unintended consequences of play through altering judgment. Ideally, only one partner in any given scene is in an altered state of consciousness at a time, so there is at least one other person close by who has access to executive function and good decision-making and judgment. Tuning in to one's partner and taking some responsibility for helping them discern where they are, what they want, and what they do not want is part of responsible erotic play. Kinky play may include exploring the erotic quality some people experience when they are not able to say no. This commonly involves having a "safe word" other than "no," so a person can experience saying "no" and being ignored (but when they say "red light" or "broccoli" or whatever the safe word is, the action stops). But it might also involve more physical ways of not being able to say "no," for instance, being gagged and bound or even having one's lips sewn shut. The point is, if the erotic play is about not being able to say "no" and their ability to speak is removed, how does a person withdraw consent? Communication in intimate situations may be verbal or nonverbal. The ability to read one's partner reasonably well is helpful in managing consent well. In situations where a partner is unable to speak, it is crucial that they have nonverbal ways of signaling their consent or withdrawal thereof. Obviously, the more experience partners have together, the better they will be able to "read" one another and the more likely they will be able to manage complicated situations like this without negative consequences. I wouldn't recommend that a couple who has never played together before start out with a scene requiring skill reading subtle cues. The people I know who have engaged in this type of play do so with partners with whom they have a strong connection, a fair amount of experience, and/ or a lot of trust, and of course that minimizes the risks associated with this type of play.

To put this in perspective, there are vanilla expressions of granting overarching consent ahead of time as well; this isn't just reserved for kinky play. For instance, if I hear a client describe their partner initiating sex with them while they slept, I would ask a question about consent. It is not uncommon to have a relationship with sufficient trust to make it perfectly fine to grant a blanket consent for certain types of interactions, for instance, allowing a partner to initiate sex when one is asleep, without fear that it will result in trauma of any kind. There are also plenty of people or situations in which this might very well be traumatic. Being a therapist who can help clients think through this type of nuance without blaming, shaming, or overreacting is my goal. Having a differentiated sexual relationship involves learning about self and other, figuring out what is (and is not) acceptable, and communicating it. Running experiments is creative and sexy, and learning from mistakes is the other side of that coin; if someone has a theory that sleep sex will be fine and then wakes up afraid, it would be important to revise the theory, and ideally partners would collaborate on facilitating repair and healing. The same goes for bondage, gagging, or any other practice.

Identity

Like polyamory, kink can be either a behavior or an identity. To one person, kink may be something they enjoy now and then or only with certain partners, while to another person, kink may be a way of being that makes up an important aspect of their sense of self, either erotically or relationally, or both.

Identity is important for many reasons. When a client tells you something about their identity, they are revealing deep and potentially vulnerable aspects of how they see themselves, including relationally. Someone who connects their identity with a marginalized community or population is more likely to have been profoundly affected by cultural assumptions and oppression compared to someone who merely dabbles now and then. Additionally, there can be dissonance between childhood values and belief systems and emerging identity later on. For instance, if a person were raised believing aspects of kink are deeply sinful or disgusting, they will probably have some challenges in coming to understand and accept their emerging eroticism as an adult.

Sometimes a therapist will ask me if I think it is advisable for them to question or challenge a client's perception of an emerging identity, particularly if it is creating tension in their relationship(s). While there is a lot of potential for nuance here depending on the specific situation, I think identity is an internal perception of an aspect of self, and the first part of differentiation is being able to look inside, get grounded in oneself, and identify one's own thoughts, feelings, perceptions, beliefs, and desires. When someone is able to do that and then express it, I think it is a very good thing and likely something of a developmental leap.

Sometimes a client will specifically ask me to help them sort out some internal questioning or confusion regarding their identity, in which case I ask questions intended to help them sort through thoughts and feelings rather than offer my own opinion. Learning to access and interpret internal guidance is an important therapeutic goal.

Treatment Considerations

Easily half of my clients either identify as kinky or engage in kinky behaviors. Yet, kink is rarely the focus of therapy. Usually kink just exists in the background, as a way a client expresses themselves erotically or sexually, not causing any problems or creating any dissonance for them. That said, now and then kink comes up as part of an intrapsychic issue, personal dilemma, or interpersonal interaction, in a problematic or distressing way, in which case it becomes part of therapy.

Here are some ways kink might come up as an issue in therapy and some treatment strategies I have used. There is enough detail earlier in this chapter to get you off to a good start with these treatment strategies. If you need more, of course engage a consultant and do some research to expand your knowledge base. This list is not intended to be exhaustive.

- Your client wants to explore kink and doesn't know where to start.
  - Supporting, normalizing, empowering, and helping your clients connect with the kink community and other like-minded people is the way to go here. Do an internet search for BDSM plus your city/state to find out what kink events and get-togethers there are locally. A "munch" is a common first Q/A type activity that is nonsexual and informational. While most people who engage in kinky play are not connected with the kink community, I would certainly advise anyone to access the many benefits of the community connection. There are also good books to guide this journey; you will find some of them in the bibliography of this book, in the "BDSM/Kink" section.
- One partner is interested in exploring kink or a fetish and their partner is less interested.

- ∘ Normalize the kink. Most people have misconceptions about kink, so providing accurate information about sexual templates, normalcy of all forms of erotic expression, importance of consent, lack of psychopathology, etc., can go a long way toward providing relief.
- ∘ It's often helpful in this situation to guide clients toward additional written and internet resources, and the kink community in their area. You might want to do a little research and familiarize yourself with available written resources.
- ∘ When there is a difference in desire to explore kink, I treat it more or less like any other desire discrepancy or difference between partners. Check out chapter 8, "Conceptualizing the Case: If Polyamory Isn't the Problem, What Is?" and chapter 11, "Negotiating Polyamory: Forming Good Agreements." Because kinky play is not always sexual, it is sometimes possible for a client to explore their kinky desires in nonsexual or semisexual ways that are individually negotiated and can fit within a relational agreement that is "monogamish." Providing the freedom for a person to explore their kinky sexual template is one situation in which polyamory or some form of consensual nonmonogamy can be a huge benefit to both partners. The partner who wants to explore can do so with other partners who truly enjoy it and/or have extensive experience in that area, which has the potential to provide the other partner with a lot of security. This type of situation can also spare the less interested partner from feeling pressure to try things they don't want to explore or allow them to participate only occasionally. For more on this theme, refer to chapter 5, "Who Can Benefit from Consensual Nonmonogamy?"
- Your client is engaged in kinky play that seems potentially nonconsensual or you are concerned they may not have the skill to give and withdraw consent.
  - ∘ Refer to the "Nuances of Consent" section earlier in this chapter. What pieces of consent seem to be missing in your client's situation? Is your client aware of what is involved in giving and withdrawing consent? Psychoeducation is often needed in this situation, as there are many people who never learned what

consent means or weren't given permission to both grant and withdraw consent.

- ○ Differentiation of self is the core skill set needed to negotiate well, make and keep agreements, and give and withdraw consent. It is also the skill set for holding steady when a partner has a preference other than yours. There is no magic bullet for this type of issue. I understand that helping your client build the skills of differentiation is a huge and often long-term project, but there isn't a shortcut when consent issues are the problem. If you're feeling stuck, really study chapter 8, "Conceptualizing the Case: If Polyamory Isn't the Problem, What Is?" and consider getting further training in working with sex issues from a differentiation perspective.
- Your client is interested in setting up a kinky experience (called a "scene") to reenact trauma of some sort, with the goal of creating a healing experience.
  - ○ To the best of my knowledge there is no data about healing resulting from kink, but there are plenty of kinky people, including some of my clients, who report experiencing deep healing via kinky play. Of course, the ways it can go wrong are many and varied. Planning, support, a detailed aftercare plan, and deep trust between everyone involved are key to creating a positive experience. The plan should have built-in flexibility, in case things don't go as planned.
  - ○ Oftentimes, clients who plan something like this have a lot of experience with kink, great self-awareness and insight, a community of play partners they are very connected to and between whom there is a lot of trust, and every reason to think they will be able to be flexible and adequately supported during and after the scene even if things don't go as planned. In that case, you might have a session in which you discuss the plan, contingency plans if things don't go as planned, and the aftercare plan, and then have another session to check in after the scene and debrief any unfinished business or maximize gains and cement new awarenesses.
  - ○ If your client does *not* have a fair amount of experience with kink, good self-awareness, a supportive community of play

partners, and every reason to expect flexibility during the scene and think aftercare will go well, you have a different project. In that case, I recommend slowing things down and encouraging your client to take their time creating a situation that is likely to succeed. The last thing a person with a trauma history needs is a potentially healing scene to go badly, resulting in being retraumatized, and then having their team of play partners let them down with aftercare. Heaven forbid.

○ That said, not everyone slows down just because their therapist recommends they do so. One aspect in which there might be some midrange possibilities is the subject of experience with play partners. There might be a local kink event where your client can set up a scene with partners they don't yet have a lot of experience with but who come with excellent references. Or there may be folks in the local scene that have a lot of experience with the type of scene your client is interested in. They can explore and connect with the local community at an event or may be able to get some traction on Fetlife, which is a social media platform for the kink community; however, while it might be possible to find reliable play partners without personal experience with them, there is absolutely no substitute for self-awareness or the ability to identify and communicate a desire to pivot mid-scene if needed. Refer again to chapter 8, "Conceptualizing the Case: If Polyamory Isn't the Problem, What Is?" I would strongly discourage any client from entering into a potentially traumatizing scene without adequate preparation. By that I mean I would try to communicate inspiration and empowerment via a strong pep talk selling the amazing potential gains of taking more time in preparation. I sincerely mean this; I would never try to discourage someone from doing something they think will heal them, but I will always strongly encourage them to do it in a way that is likely to result in the benefits they desire. Doing some strength-based trauma work in therapy might give them some relief while they build the connections or internal safeguards they need to take the risk of entering into a scene that might, or might not, go as planned.

- Your client has experienced unintended consequences of kinky play and gotten hurt either physically or emotionally.
  - Do they need medical care, and have they gotten it? Do they need support for or collaboration with that? Not all medical professionals are kink-aware, and this can be a difficult situation if the medical professionals are concerned about the client's safety. You may need to help explain the difference between domestic violence and unintended consequences of play. Plan to make yourself available for collaboration with health care professionals. In fact, it is a good idea to scope out kink-aware health care professionals in your area if you work with this population. Your kinky clients may also be able to scope this out for themselves through word of mouth in the local community.
  - You may need to parse out whether this is indeed domestic violence, rather than unintended consequences of play. The primary difference is consent, and there are circumstances in which it is not so easy to tell. If your client doesn't feel safe, you will need to proceed as you would with any other domestic violence. Use the concepts from RACK and PRICK to assess if your client is in an adaptive or maladaptive situation.
  - Ask: Was the situation at all times completely consensual? Was there ever a point in the unfolding of the action when your client had a hint of internal knowing that they wanted to stop or alter the plan? If so, what prevented them from speaking up or what happened when they did speak up? This gets at some nuances of consent. Oftentimes a client will make a choice to "just go ahead" when they have an internal sense that they should stop, and this is good fodder for therapy. Sometimes they regret their choice, and sometimes they don't, but it always leads to an interesting conversation. On the other hand, maybe they didn't feel safe speaking up because they feared for their safety or they did speak up and their partner ignored or deliberately went against their wishes, in which case this is definitely problematic and goes directly against the tenets of consent, as well as the expectations of the kink community.

- Was your client aware of the risks and informed about the activities they were engaging in? Did they have an explicit discussion with their play partner(s) ahead of time about potential risks? If not, why not, and if so, how did things diverge from the plan? Not everyone always has a detailed discussion of all scenes ahead of time, but when engaging in something particularly risky, it is best practice, obviously a good idea, and well worth exploring if it didn't happen. Is there anything about the way the scene was discussed (or not discussed) ahead of time that your client would like to do differently next time?

- Is everyone involved taking personal responsibility for their part(s) in the planning, play, and outcome? In particular, I would be curious about how the participants are communicating and caring for one another after the fact. Does everyone involved know about the unintended consequences of play? If not, why not? Was there an aftercare expectation? It's common practice to have an aftercare plan in place. If there was one and it isn't being followed, that is of concern and sheds some light on the character of whoever is not following through on their aftercare agreements. If there was not an aftercare discussion in the planning stages, that would be unusual, particularly if the participants are connected with the kink community, and, in any case, definitely something to discuss and add to the skill set of the participants.

- Is there unfinished business with the play partner or community? Is there any action your client wants to take? It is to be expected that they may feel protective of the community and not want to make a big thing of it, even if it is a clear-cut consent violation or there is a lot of unfinished business. When that is the case, it can be challenging for therapists, including myself, who want there to be some personal consequences or learning for people who engage in irresponsible play; however, this is a marginalized community that has gotten a lot of well-meaning but ill-informed interference from law enforcement, concerned friends and neighbors, physicians, nurses, therapists, and physical therapists. Not everyone, by far, understands the difference between kink and abuse or domestic violence. It is understandable that your client may not want to take the risk of their community, which is important to them, drawing unhelpful or negative attention. Helping your client parse all of this out is great therapy, and very important.

LGBTQIA+

I frequently get questions about nuances of working with the diversity of queer communities. There is plenty of overlap with polyamory and other forms of consensual nonmonogamy and the LGBTQIA+ community, so I'm including some basic information about these populations here. As with the information about kink, this should be considered the merest introduction. Hopefully, I'll clear up a few misconceptions and set you up to go out and learn more.

Happily, at this point in history I think most therapists have had at least some training in cultural sensitivity for LGBTQ populations; however, things change constantly in this realm. In my lifetime, there have been huge shifts, including many that are fairly recent. Part of cultural competence is simply keeping up with cultural shifts and trends as they continue to unfold.

As a start, I'll clarify the acronym: L is for lesbian, G is for gay, B is for bisexual, T is for trans, Q is for queer or sometimes questioning, A is for asexual, and I is for intersex. Plus (+) is for everything that isn't covered by those terms. That includes nonbinary and gender-fluid, which refer to people who identify as neither male nor female, both male and female, or nongendered, or fluid, meaning gender identity shifts regularly.

"Plus" also includes pansexual, which refers to someone who is attracted to all genders or any gender. There's a little bit of controversy about the difference between bisexuality and pansexuality; some people use pansexual to include attraction to nonbinary genders, while others feel that the bisexual label includes attraction to nonbinary people. As always, it depends on the person and how they understand that language.

The + can also refer to related but newer terms, including, I'm sure, some I'm not even aware of yet. Language is developing quickly to reflect broadly diverse experience. Newer terms like *polysexual* and *agender* immediately spring to mind. Also, "questioning" can encompass bicurious, gender questioning, or any other type of exploration.

Queer is a term that people define individually. I think it is fair to say that most people who identify as queer have found some way in which their own beliefs, attractions, behaviors, thoughts, choices, or family structures do not reflect our cultural heteronormative construct of "one man, one woman, marriage, then babies." This language, and the acronym itself, has evolved throughout time and is still evolving as we gain understanding of diversity of sexual identity and expression.

I am a therapist who often works with queer populations, and I also identify as queer and lesbian. My perspective in this section is shaped by both the therapist lens and the personal lens, so I'll weave in information from both. Hopefully my personal perspective and identity, which informs much of my thinking, will provide a helpful and concrete example to illustrate some important aspects of what I think you should know about the LGBTQIA+ community.

I have identified as lesbian since I was 23 years old. That's a long time now. I fall somewhere on the spectrum of bisexuality. I was definitely straight as a youth and teen, and married a man quite young. I didn't really know there was such a thing as a lesbian when I was a child, but even if I had, I suspect I still would have identified as straight. My early fantasies, crushes, and relationships were with men. I discovered my attraction to women in college and came out as lesbian at age 23. Currently, and for the last 25 years and counting, I'm in a relationship with my now-finally-legal spouse, JoAnne. At the time I came out, in the mid-1980s, identifying as bisexual was unusual, because bi identity was marginalized by not only straight people, but also gays and lesbians. This is still true to a lesser but still significant extent. According to the Kinsey Scale, however, I'm clearly bisexual, probably somewhere close to the middle—or pansexual, because I'm attracted to all genders, not just binary ones. Remember that thoughts, feelings, *and* behaviors all count as part of what defines attraction, not just behaviors.

The Kinsey Scale

You have probably heard of the Kinsey Scale, which was developed out of thousands of extensive interviews conducted by Alfred Kinsey's research team and first published in 1948, in *Sexual Behavior in the Human Male*. *Sexual Behavior of the Human Female* followed in 1953. Together, these are referred to as the Kinsey Reports. The Kinsey Scale is an important part of sex history, because it looked at what people actually do, think, feel, and desire sexually, separate from whatever labels they might use to self-identify. Kinsey definitively established that the vast majority of people don't fit into strict categories of hetero- or homosexual. Rather, when taking into account thoughts, feelings, and behaviors, almost no one is exclusively attracted to either the same sex or the opposite sex. Basically, everyone is somewhere in the middle, on the bi-spectrum.

It is also important to acknowledge that Kinsey didn't address all sexual orientations or identities. Hundreds of later studies have provided more nuance, as well as additional measures. For instance, the Klein Sexual Orientation Grid (Fritz Klein) looks at seven variables and three times: past, present, and ideal. The Storms Scale (Michael Storms) places eroticism on an x and y axis, providing for a lot of variability. These and many other measures clearly establish that there is tremendous variation and normalize that variation as being, actually, normative.

Additionally, gender identity and gender expression are a separate topic from sexual attraction, identity, and behavior. We now know thinking of gender in a binary way (in terms of two genders) is overly limiting, as there are plenty of people who experience themselves as not having any gender at all, or having both genders, or shifting around through an infinite spectrum of all gender possibility. Unfortunately, despite a lot of progress throughout the years, our culture still hasn't quite gotten the memo that heteronormativity isn't actually all that normative, and as a result of this lack of awareness in the larger culture, LGBTQIA+ populations are still marginalized.

When you consider Kinsey's findings, it really puts identity issues, not to mention sexual shame, into perspective. If essentially everyone who has erotic experiences and thoughts has them about multiple genders, then anyone who was raised to believe only heterosexuality is normal (which is still a lot of people) is likely to have some confusion, internal conflict, and distress about the thoughts, feelings, or behaviors they experience. That means there is probably just about no one in your practice who doesn't have some issues, however buried and hidden, about queerness and their own sexuality. I find this to be sobering, and also fascinating. I wonder how different the world would be if every therapist knew this and asked about, taught about, and normalized same-sex or nonbinary attractions and identities, as well as kinky thoughts, diverse sexual templates, and polyamory or interest in having multiple consensual partners. Think of the sexual shame that would begin to lift. Think of the energy that could be liberated to use for the forces of good in the world.

Overlap between LGBTQIA+ and Polyamory

Why is there so much overlap between LGBTQ populations and polyamory? There are many reasons.

- Various forms of open relationships, including "open" and "monogamish," have been part of gay male culture forever, and this is still true today. Of course, not all gay men have open relationships or even "monogamish" ones; diversity is the one rule that wins the day in every category.
- It's not uncommon for a person to explore polyamory because of an emerging awareness of sexual attraction to a gender other than that of an existing partner, which is sometimes followed by a desire to explore this part of themselves. This can be challenging for both the person who is experiencing an emergence of a new aspect of themselves and a preexisting partner who didn't see this coming, especially if they are not particularly interested in or familiar with either that form of sexual attraction or polyamory. Working with this emergence is a therapy based in supporting differentiation of self, so refer to chapter 8, "Conceptualizing the Case: If Polyamory Isn't the Problem, What Is?" It can be a challenge to help the client find ways to stay emotionally connected with and intimate with the preexisting relationship (if they want

that relationship to remain in their lives) when a lot of psychic energy and curiosity is focused in the new direction, even if there isn't another intimate relationship in the picture. Some people don't feel it is important to explore the emerging aspect of their sexuality through intimate relationships, whereas others decide they do want to explore that aspect of their sexuality and may end up breaking up with their preexisting partner to do so. Still others want to explore their emerging identity and don't want to end the first relationship. In that case, for some, polyamory can be a workable solution.

Queer culture includes a sizeable population of people who operate from an assumption of nonmonogamy for a variety of ideological reasons, in addition to individual preference. Some don't believe in imposing "rules" on partners but would rather have their partners freely choose what their lives and relationships look like, even if that sometimes turns out to be quite inconvenient for them. This is a group that highly values personal growth, individuality, and differentiation. Some might describe themselves as polyamorous because they don't believe in controlling or placing claims on others. Many people in this category have nonhierarchical polyamorous relationships. Of course, the egalitarian belief system doesn't guarantee a bump-free road. Nor do all people who identify as queer have this perspective about relationships; remember the supreme overarching concept: diversity.

Attraction, Behavior, Identity, and Labels

The most important thing to know about queer identity is that *behavior* is what a person does. This is not the same as *identity*, which refers to how a person conceptualizes themselves inwardly. Behavior and identity do not have to match, although for some people they do or come close. *Attraction* also does not have to match either behavior or identity. A person can identify as gay and sometimes be attracted to or even have sex with members of other genders. A person might identify as straight and engage in fantasy or sex involving members of the same gender. A person can identify as one gender on some days or times and another gender at other times. Everything can shift throughout time—

whether that's a short time or a lifetime. For some people, these things don't shift at all. Throw the rule book out the window: If you can imagine an evolution or a configuration, there are plenty of people who are living it. For that matter, things I can't yet imagine are certainly also being lived out by someone somewhere, and that is a beautiful thing. I love the exciting diversity, new terminology, and evolving understanding of people, possibility, and relationships.

Labels are yet another thing. I think of labels as being a shorthand we offer to other people so they can make assumptions about us. Given that there are no labels that accurately encapsulate the fullness of who any of us really are, I believe everyone should pick and choose the labels that lead to assumptions they are most comfortable with. It is not anyone's responsibility to provide others with accurate and nuanced information about their most interior or intimate life and preferences. Moreover, even if it were possible to choose a list of labels that would be technically accurate, and even if the general population understood what those labels meant, that level of disclosure doesn't fit well with a surface or casual acquaintance, or a desire for personal privacy, let alone the risks incurred by coming out as being in a marginalized group.

Labels can feel restrictive and reductive, but they aren't all bad. They help us avoid having inappropriately detailed conversations about private matters, while still experiencing some degree of feeling seen. For instance, if I don't provide a label (lesbian, in my case), most people will assume I'm straight, which renders my 25-year-long relationship, and an enormous aspect of my day-to-day reality, invisible. So I choose to use the label "lesbian." I think it conveys a picture of a woman facing me at the dinner table and sharing life and intimacy with me. That is a comfortable reflection of my life, given that I'm in a decades-long same-sex relationship.

If, instead, I used the label "pansexual," which is more technically accurate, I would have to explain what it means, because most people aren't familiar with the term. I would also be opening the door to plenty of conjecture, unless I wanted to sit down and explain how it is that I experience attraction to all genders when I'm in a long-term relationship with a woman. That's too esoteric (and personal) a discussion for me to have with acquaintances.

That's just one example of how a person, in this case, myself, might come to terms with the inevitable simplification that comes with assigning a label to the infinite range of human experience and sexual expression. Everyone approaches this issue in their own way. Someone in the same boat as I am might end up choosing a totally different way of defining themselves. That's okay. These are very individual perceptions and choices.

Fluidity is also an important aspect of this discussion. Many years ago, I was married to a man. If you would have asked me about my identity then, I would have provided the label "straight" and the identity "questioning." Now I provide the label "lesbian" but the identity "pan." That is an example of fluidity throughout time.

Someone might also have fluid gender identity if, for instance, they used to identify as one gender and now identify as another. Or someone might always have identified internally as a different gender from what was assigned to them at birth, but the way they present to the world may have shifted throughout time from their assigned-at-birth gender to their current gender identity. Or someone might identify as different genders during the span of a very short time, like a day or a week; that person might identify as gender-fluid or gender-queer.

Why would a person choose any label at all, you might be wondering, when this is personal, private, and no one's business? I imagine if you asked 20 queer-identified people that question, you might get 20 different answers. For me, the answer lies in our heterosexist culture. What I mean by that is, in the absence of any other cues or direction, the assumption most people in the United States make about people is that they are straight. Since my partner is a hugely important aspect of my life, I don't feel like someone knows me until they understand that I have a long-term partner. If I just say I've been married for 25 years, the image people in our current culture get is one of me having a husband. If this is a conversation with an acquaintance or it isn't important to me to feel known, that might be okay with me, although it still feels uncomfortable. It can feel sort of like I lied, which is truly weird because it all started with assumptions made about me, and it's hardly my fault if they mis-assumed. The point is, it is often important to me to feel like someone actually knows me. At that point, I will have to have a coming-out discussion of some sort.

Consider how much more complicated, and pressing, this might feel to someone who feels dissonance between their internal sense of knowing themselves and their gender expression as others perceive it. Many people in this situation experience people using incorrect pronouns to refer to them, which can feel extremely traumatic and dehumanizing. Many cisgender people find the issue of pronouns confusing; here, again, language is ever-evolving. But referring to someone in the way they would like to be referred shows respect for the person and respect for human diversity. In my case, I identify as cis-female, meaning I'm comfortable with the gender I was assigned at birth (that is what *cis-* refers to), which, in my case, is female. Personal pronouns have something to do with how I, and others, communicate about gender identity to others. In my case, I am comfortable with the pronouns she and they, but the pronoun "he" doesn't feel like a good fit for me.

It is worth taking some time to learn about diversity of gender expression and pronouns, and become comfortable with having conversations about it. While you're at it, get comfortable making a repair when you accidentally misgender someone. Perfection doesn't come overnight, if at all; let your heart and your authenticity lead, and you'll be okay.

Marginalization

Anyone who is in any way outside of the cis and heterosexual norm will, unfortunately, have already had to put up with a lot of mistaken assumptions, inconvenient and intrusive conversations, reductionist labels, and assumptions derived from the heterosexist cultural norm, and will continue to do so, in some cases on a more than daily basis. Consider, for a moment, the potential that kind of marginalization has to make someone feel bad about themselves and also angry at others and the culture that puts them through this. Imagine, most importantly, the feeling of not being known or understood that someone might have concerning these issues.

What about someone whose internal sense of their gender doesn't match how they appear to others from the outside, who gets constantly misgendered? Or someone who is extremely principled and doesn't want people to make inaccurate assumptions about them, perhaps sometimes at the cost of their ease, comfort, privacy, and safety? Or someone who is closeted about one or many aspects of their gender, behavior, relationship structure, or identity and never gets to feel truly known because the danger of losing friends, family, or a job is too high? The internal and social consequences of invisibility run deep.

It is also easy to assume that in this day and age, people aren't really discriminated against for being gay, lesbian, trans, bi, queer, nonbinary, asexual, or intersex anymore. Let me assure you, that is far from true. Ask any LGBTQIA+ person about the ways they have experienced marginalization and discrimination, and listen to what they have to tell you. It is heartbreaking. I've been out for many years, and I have kind of come to terms with all of this for myself. But even so, I've experienced plenty of discrimination and marginalization, some of which still feels raw on occasion. I can tell you from personal experience, you will be doing your clients a beautiful service by allowing them to unpack what is almost certainly a big bag of trauma related to being abused, bullied, ignored, blamed, shamed, avoided, attacked, misunderstood, and more—not to mention the associated losses, like holding anxiety about multiple aspects of self and relationship, struggling with mixed feelings about self-disclosure, lost jobs, relationships, feeling afraid of holding hands with a partner in public, and never quite feeling safe. I could go on and on.

Add to this the concept of intersectionality. Being a member of multiple different marginalized groups leads to unique and specific experiences of marginalization, amounting to an experience that is far larger than the apparent sum of the parts. In addition to being members of some or many of the LGBTQIA+ groups, people experience marginalization and discrimination as a result of race, culture, language, accent, class, physical ability, cognitive ability, mental health, body shape and size, clothing choices, and many other aspects of self and self-expression (e.g., sexual practices like kink and such family structures as polyamory).

LGBTQIA+ in Therapy

When I work with LGBTQIA+ clients, usually their LGBTQ-ness is not the focus of the therapy. Rather, it is generally an aspect—or aspects—of themselves that is working fine. As with other populations

I discuss in this book, you don't need to be an expert to get started working with these populations. That's a good thing, because there aren't nearly enough queer-identified therapists to work with the many people who share that identity. But you do need to have some basic understanding and a willingness to embrace a broad diversity of sexual and gender expression to honor those aspects of your clients' selves. You will also have to have ways of demonstrating your openness. Ideally, you should be willing to have a frank discussion of marginalized experience, as well as receive feedback from your client if they feel misunderstood or slighted.

It's important to get good at inviting and responding in an attuned way to feedback, because it can provide an extremely therapeutic reparative experience. Imagine having multiple past experiences of marginalization and then going to a therapist and having some feelings of marginalization come up. Imagine being brave enough to speak up to your therapist about it or, better yet, having your therapist inquire about your experience of them in therapy. Imagine how healing it could be for your therapist to acknowledge and validate your perceptions and experience. Furthermore, imagine how amazing it would feel for your therapist to make a thoughtful repair for any error or misunderstanding on their part, validating your experience and perception.

When you work with populations and clients who have an experience of marginalization, they often choose therapists based on cultural competence, usually as established by word of mouth. Don't be surprised if a new or potential client asks what your level of experience with their marginalized group might be. Figuring out how you want to handle this, including whether you want to self-disclose as being ingroup (or not in-group) is something every therapist who works with marginalized populations faces.

The primary issues that have arisen thus far in my therapy room with LGBTQIA+ clients involve various aspects of exploring identity, behavior, and labels. It has been helpful to discuss and do some education about the differences between and fluid nature of attraction, behavior, identity, and labels (see the section entitled "Attraction, Behavior, Identity, and Labels"). If nothing else, that deep discussion helps identify nuances of what someone is experiencing, thinking, and feeling about themselves and normalize a full range of possible experience, as well as fluidity. It can be very freeing to release a client from a sense of having to pick a label, adhere to an identity, or limit behaviors for reasons imposed by a label, cultural expectations, or fears of having to explain.

Marginalization is also a common theme in therapy. Our culture has come a long way in my lifetime in terms of accepting and understanding LGBTQ people, but there's still a long way to go, and bias against nonheterosexual and gender-nonconforming people is present even in the most liberal communities. Pretending this is not so will almost certainly feel marginalizing to your clients. In particular, gender nonconforming people experience pervasive marginalization, often in very damaging, hurtful ways, including bullying and violence. The lack of understanding of nonbinary gender and lack of acceptance of nonbinary pronouns in our culture is an example of one insidious and pervasive form of aggression against gender nonconforming people. This population is at high risk for self-harm, suicide, and violent death at the hands of others. You're not going to help your clients if you turn a blind eye to the very real trauma, pain, and danger they face. On the other hand, you can make a real difference for your clients by educating yourself about their experience, normalizing their identity and feelings, and demonstrating consistent caring, warmth, and respect.

Another common therapy agenda is discussion and support of a trans person with their internal, public, medical, and sometimes surgical transition. This is an area of specialty that goes beyond the scope of this book, but suffice it to say, it is important work. There are lots of opportunities to get specialized training in this area, and I recommend if you want to work with this population that you do get some extra training. In addition to the importance of giving therapeutic support to people who experience gender dysphoria or other issues concerning their gender identity and/or transition, many physicians who provide hormone therapy or gender alignment surgeries require that their clients obtain a letter from a therapist attesting to their mental health status, sometimes confirming that they experience gender dysphoria, and attesting to the ability of the trans person to make good decisions about their health care.

Needless to say, this has the potential to create an unfortunate gate-keeping role that complicates the therapy. I know if I were the client in this situation, I would be seriously pissed off that I needed to pay someone to say I could think for myself. I also find it to be a bit of a dilemma when I have a client who needs me to confirm a gender dysphoria diagnosis when not all trans people experience dysphoria per se and in my opinion should certainly be able to make decisions about surgical alterations to their body even if they don't have deeply negative or distressful feelings about their body in the form it was assigned at birth. I think it is important for therapists to know that sometimes a trans person will need to build a relationship with a therapist, not primarily because they want or need therapy, but instead primarily because they need an official relationship with a therapist who can write a letter for them. Hopefully one day soon this practice will be obsolete, but until then, we all have to deal with it. I have found that having a frank discussion about the needs, desires, and goals of the client is helpful, and bringing the topic of the power imbalance between client and therapist/gatekeeper right into the open is an important part of that process.

That said, of course medical, transition-related and mental health issues can be complicated depending on the age of the client, emotional developmental stage, mental health status, level of distress, and any number of other factors. This is one reason I think extra training is needed. The trans population is at high risk for self-harm, suicide, and violence against them. As with any population, you certainly want enough training and supervision to not cause harm. That will include gaining some strategies for helping effectively in nuanced situations involving medical and psychosocial issues, as well as, potentially, extreme marginalization and cooccurring conditions.

A Note on Asexuality

It's important that therapists know that asexuality is a perfectly healthy and perfectly normal way of being. It's not an aversion; it's just an orientation, like homosexual, heterosexual, or bisexual. It's also perfectly possible to have a strong, loving intimate relationship as an asexual person. Some asexual people abstain from sex, whereas others may engage in partnered sex and/or self-pleasure; as with any orientation, there is infinite diversity, even under the heading of a single label.

It's most likely that you'll see asexual clients for reasons that have nothing to do with asexuality itself, just as most polyamorous clients come to therapy for issues like depression or anxiety, not polyamory. Still, you may end up discussing asexuality in therapy. For instance, your asexual clients may need you to help them navigate finding a relationship in a world that assumes all romantic partnerships are also sexual, cope with a desire discrepancy in a relationship, or deal with challenges associated with cultural invisibility. You may also work with clients who are just discovering or exploring an asexual identity. In any case, they will need you to normalize asexuality so they can explore their thoughts, feelings, desires, and deepest self, and come to a place of internal affirmation of their identity.

Asexuality and polyamory can go hand in hand. One way this might look is that one partner is simply not interested in having sex and the other wants a sexual partnership, in which case exploring some form of consensual nonmonogamy can be a quite an elegant solution, one that preserves the relationship while meeting the needs of both partners. Another way this might look is that an asexual partner may love flirtatious and romantic connections, and enjoy having more than one romantic partner, whether or not they choose to express themselves sexually. Again, diversity is infinite; if your clients can imagine it, they can move toward creating it. Don't assume an asexual person would not be interested in engaging in multiple relationships.

Making Your Practice LGBTQIA+ Friendly

You can show your openness to LGBTQIA+ clients by making some simple changes in your intake forms. Here are a few choices I've made to make my LGBTQIA+ clients feel more comfortable and welcome. Best practice regarding these decisions is constantly shifting and evolving as the needs and preferences of the community evolve, so be aware that a little internet research will probably be in order to make sure you are up-to-date. The following are categories you should consider, with an eye to being inclusive:

Use a write-in line for gender, rather than checkboxes. Because people have unique and individual ways of identifying their gender, checkboxes, like other forms of labels, are not likely to offer sufficient choices, and I don't like to make people choose from a list of inadequate descriptors. I want to use the descriptor my client chooses for themselves.

Have a write-in line for pronouns. Some people are comfortable with a range of pronouns, and new pronoun options arise every now and then. Also, occasionally someone will coin their own unique pronouns; checkboxes offer overly limited choices, in my opinion.

When speaking about anyone in the third person, use "they," unless you particularly know and want to reference a client's gender through pronouns. This lets people know you're not wedded to the binary. Oftentimes, it is not at all necessary to reference gender. I find this to be good practice in general.

Never make assumptions about behavior as a result of partial knowledge of someone. This stance saves me from having to manage my facial expressions when my clients' behavior doesn't match assumptions based on identity or labels, and I hope it also prevents my clients from feeling judged by me. Believe me, behavior and labels match far less frequently than most people think, so I'm accommodating the vast majority by not making assumptions or acting surprised when this comes up.

Don't refer to someone who is in a same-sex relationship as gay/lesbian automatically. Plenty of people who are in even very long-term same-sex relationships don't identify as gay or lesbian. Before you refer to them that way, ask how they like their relationship or identity to be referenced. Plenty of people who appear to be gay or lesbian actually identify as bisexual, pansexual, or any number of other signifiers.

Don't assume someone's gender identity from the way they present, or look, to you. It is safer and most respectful not to extrapolate based on assumptions.

Consider whether you actually need to know all the details before you ask for more information, and if you do decide to ask, make sure it is out of a desire to respect your client's individuality rather than to know details that aren't really anyone's business and are irrelevant to the therapy.

Get comfortable with the singular "they." It goes without saying that you should refer to your clients using the pronouns they prefer. This can be a challenge for a lot of people who were raised with a binary construct of gender. The singular "they" is a relatively new addition to the lexicon, and it takes some practice to get used to using it. It has helped me to deliberately decouple the way a person looks from their gender. In other words, I was raised to think that things about the way someone looks indicate something about their gender, but that is a belief system that can be changed. Start getting comfortable with the idea that no outside indicator or, for that matter, body part is relevant to gender identity, and refer to everyone as "they" until you know otherwise. The more you practice questioning your assumptions about gender, the more naturally it will come to you.

A Note on Nonbinary Gender

Nonbinary people identify as neither male nor female. Instead, they may identify as agender, third gender, two-spirit, gender-fluid, demigender, or many other ways. Many nonbinary people use the neutral pronouns "they/them/theirs"; some alternate masculine and feminine pronouns; others use neopronouns like "ze/zir/zirs" or "per/per/pers"; and others prefer to use no pronouns at all. Some use "she/her/hers" or "he/him/his" but still identify as nonbinary. The lexicon of neopronouns is large and will probably continue to evolve. Additionally, some people invent uniquely individual pronouns. There is immense diversity, in terms of how people experience and understand their own gender, what pronouns they use, and how they choose to express themselves in dress, posture, speech, and behavior.

Our culture comes with many built-in assumptions about gender. Gender assumptions pervade pretty much every aspect of self-expression. If you're cisgender (meaning you identify internally in congruence with the gender you were assigned at birth) and haven't yet had friends, family members, and clients who are nonbinary, relating respectfully to nonbinary people will involve shedding some of those assumptions—deprogramming yourself. This takes some practice, both interpersonally and internally. Practice using a variety of pronouns in your head; the more you practice, the more easily it will come to you. If you accidentally misgender someone, quickly apologize, repeat the sentence with the right pronouns, and move on.

You can also practice using gender-neutral descriptors for people you see out in public: thinking or saying "the person with the blue glasses," rather than "the man with the blue glasses," for instance. This is an easy way to get in the practice of not assuming gender and may serve you well when working with nonbinary clients.

ETHICAL CONSIDERATIONS

Getting to know other therapists in your area who work with LGBTQIA+ populations, kink, and polyamory is crucial. One feature of working with polyamory is that dual relationships are everywhere. Polyamorous families (polycules) can be large or small and often overlap with other polycules. You can't do all of the therapy for polyamorous people in your region on your own without running into ethical issues concerning dual relationships. For that reason, it's key to make connections with other therapists to whom you feel comfortable referring a polyamorous and/or LGBTQIA+ and/or kinky client. Chapter 20, "Ethical Considerations," provides more guidance on navigating this issue.

CHAPTER 4

Polyamory Theory, or Why
Polyamory Makes Sense to Some

I'd like to start with a disclaimer: I can't see a way to help you understand polyamory for yourself or your clients without explaining how and why some people believe polyamory is a good idea for them and a healthy way for them to relate and form relationships; however, I also can't figure out a way to explain these cultural concepts without sounding like I'm trying to sell you on polyamory.

So before you start formulating objections, remember that empathy is not the same as agreement. Ultimately, you can, and will, decide whatever you want to about your own relationships, and so will your clients.

This chapter is about gaining some understanding of how polyamory makes sense to the people who choose to practice it. My goal is not to convert or convince, but rather to give you some information that may help you understand where some polyamorous people are coming from. My hope is that what I have to share may inspire you to empathize with the theoretical cultural stance of polyamory, so you can relate to your polyamorous clients, family members, friends, and colleagues a little better.

If you are considering opening your own relationship, giving careful consideration to these concepts will be important. For many, successfully opening an intimate relationship requires shifting entire belief systems about fidelity, security, exclusivity, marriage, and commitment. If you find it challenging to imagine shifting those beliefs, you are not alone. The most important predictor of success when changing a belief system is whether *you* actually want to (as distinguished from your partner wanting you to) and how motivated you are to do so, not how close or far you were from your goal to begin with.

"EXPANDING LOVE" VISUALIZATION

Let's start with a brief visualization. The purpose of this exercise is to help you get an intuitive, emotional grasp of one of the most important underlying concepts of polyamory.

Take a moment to get into your own space. Take a few deep breaths. Read this exercise slowly, and put yourself into the scene I'm going to describe. Let yourself experience the thoughts and feelings that come up.

Imagine that you have just been handed your first-born child. (If you can't relate at all to this idea, feel free to substitute something that makes your heart swell. Maybe imagine being handed a new puppy or kitten, or your sibling's new baby.)

You're looking into that new being's face and experiencing the newness and preciousness of their life. Imagine getting to know and experience this little person for the first time. Embrace that sense of falling in love with an amazing, precious being. Feel how your heart overflows with love for this tiny person.

Your partner is right there with you, and they're falling in love too. Linger in this space for a second. Think of the sense you have of the love for your baby, and then tune in to your sense of your love for your partner. What happens to the love you have for your partner when you fall in love with your baby?

Let yourself feel everything that comes along with that. Take note: What are you feeling? Take a moment to hold both your love for your partner and your love for your new baby.

Now, fast-forward two and a half years, to the birth of your second child. In this moment, your second child is being handed to you for the very first time, and you're looking into the face of a brand-new, unique, miraculous baby.

Imagine, as you're looking into the face of your second child, that your first child—now a toddler—is standing next to you. They're acting just like any normal toddler: half-adorable, half-annoying. Yet, you love that little person more than you could have imagined and more than you can easily express. What happens to your love for your precious (yet sometimes annoying) toddler when you hold your second baby, brand new and perfect, for the first time?

Now, imagine that your partner puts their hand on your shoulder and your eyes meet in a tender moment of connection. Observe what happens to your love for your partner, now that you have these two beautiful, miraculous little children with you as well.

Can you feel all the feelings that are blooming within you for these two children? What happens to your love for each one of them, because there are now two of them? Does it change? If so, in what way? How do you respond to your own feelings? How do you express them to your newborn? To your toddler? To your partner?

How do you aspire to be, in your little imaginary family with two children and a partner? What do you do, internally, to support yourself in feeling and expressing your love for all three of your most important people? Is it challenging, or does it seem to come automatically? Either way is fine; just observe how it is for you.

What the "Expanding Love" Visualization Can Show Us

When our family expands in size due to the births of children, it's *culturally normative* for us to expect our love to multiply rather than divide. In fact, if it doesn't happen like that, we worry. Having a new baby can even cause us to love our partner *more* than we did before the baby came. Not only is it culturally normative for love to expand, but also normative for it to *exponentially multiply*.

Of course, familial love doesn't necessarily come easily. Most parents tell me they love their children uniquely but not one more than another. Some tell me they are challenged by one particular child and have difficulty loving them. In that situation, they have to do something internal to continue to show up in that relationship in accordance with their values or what it means to them to be a good parent. Many tell me they feel resentful of their children or one child. Again, they have to challenge themselves to do something internally to manage those feelings and figure out how to parent well, or well enough, while still figuring out how to take good care of themselves and attend to their own dreams and desires.

But, even when it is challenging to love our children or balance their needs with our own, our cultural expectation is *not* that we look for ways to get rid of some of the children. Instead, we are encouraged to find ways to manage feelings, attend to our own interests and self-care, and get support from family and community.

Obviously, the way we love our children is not the same as the way we love our romantic partners. But I do think that this exercise can teach us something meaningful about love and exclusivity. In the family setting, we expect that our love will expand as each new child enters the family. What this shows us is that love is not *necessarily* a limited commodity. In the right circumstances, love can expand, or multiply, rather than be limited or divided. When it is challenging, much depends on what we believe about family, love, and expansion, and how we want to show up in our lives.

What polyamorous people do is apply these same ideas to romantic love. They argue that, just as it's possible to love more than one child deeply and wholeheartedly, it's possible to love more than one partner deeply and wholeheartedly. Additionally, they invite their feelings of love for their partners to expand further *as a direct result* of the unique relationships they are in. The polyamorous community coined the term *compersion*, which describes a feeling of well-being, joy, or pleasure that is derived from having a partner experience pleasure with someone else. This is a new term to express some of the experience of the expansion of love that becomes possible when more than two people are involved; it is the opposite of jealousy.

In our current culture, monogamy is the relational ideal and standard. In that context, it is a common fear that romantic love is, indeed, a limited commodity. Many people fear that if their partner had another lover, it would detract from their intimacy or connection in some very real and frightening ways, potentially leading to comparison—being found lacking and then being left. But does it really have to be that way? If love can expand for multiple children, why must it divide for multiple romantic partners?

Imagine what it would be like if we lived in a culture in which polyamory was the norm and monogamy the exception. In that culture, people would assume that, when you fall in love with someone new, you don't love your current partner any less. You wouldn't ever be expected to choose between the two, and both relationships would be considered valid, important, and meaningful. More partners would mean more love, not love subdivided.

Imagining that may feel like a stretch. Nonetheless, I'd like to ask you to consider this question: Would there be a *benefit* to living in a culture in which it's totally normative for love to multiply, rather than having to compare and ultimately choose? For example, might it save some perfectly viable relationships that fall prey to serial monogamy or the pressure to choose just one?

I posed this question to a group of fellow therapists and got some interesting, thoughtful responses. One pointed out that a "love expands" attitude might make separations and divorces easier, because it would be easier to acknowledge that even when you decide to separate from someone, you don't automatically stop loving them. Acceptance of this fact might make it easier to maintain a loving relationship with a former partner, rather than having to put up a wall to prevent your new partner from feeling jealous.

Another therapist noted that it could reduce jealousy in general if we understood and accepted that a single person isn't going to meet all your needs. It would open up the idea that having multiple needs met by multiple people is normal and not worth the energy expenditure of jealousy, which feels akin to crisis.

In the same vein, it could make it easier to handle the completely normal and expectable differences that all partners experience, because it would take the pressure off our partners to meet all our needs. It could make us feel more fulfilled and less resentful or disillusioned when one partner inevitably isn't everything we could ever hope for in every circumstance.

Finally, another therapist said that it would feel nice to live in a culture with the attitude that love is abundant, rather than scarce; if we believed that there was enough love for everyone, maybe there would be less loneliness and isolation.

This is the most basic premise of polyamory: Love is not a limited commodity that you have to compete for. It's something that human beings have the ability to create from scratch. It can expand to embrace all the people in our lives, and loving more people means we have more love to give. Moreover, we have the ability to create our own emotional state; by feeling love, and dwelling on the feeling, it is possible to make it expand, feel it more, and spread it to areas where the feeling might not previously have been as strong as you would like. This is a mindfulness practice you can learn, repeat, and get better at.

This doesn't mean that everything in polyamorous relationships is always sunshine and roses. Even when it's possible to love more than one, it can sometimes be complicated and uncomfortable. Even when a person believes in the expansion of love, they might experience difficult emotions like envy and jealousy. This is true even in the culturally normative situation of love expanding within a family: Adding more children to the mix can be a little fraught, and finding a new balance doesn't always come easily.

Also, time and money are somewhat more limited commodities, even if love isn't; deciding how to apportion limited resources between multiple partners is a common source of challenge and growth in polyamorous relationships.

Monogamy, as a belief system and relational construct, seeks to solve the potential issues of emotional discomfort and time constraint by limiting our romantic relationships to a single person. For many, that's a perfectly good solution, but it's not the only possible solution. It also creates other issues of its own: infidelity and serial monogamy, for example.

ONE PERSON FOR EVERYTHING?

No one person can be everything to anyone. This basic idea is fairly well accepted in our culture, and many communities and subcultures espouse the importance of multiple supports and connections. Consider the benefits a couple might experience from having other friends: Neither partner has to give up a major interest or hobby just because their partner doesn't share their interest, and neither of them have to participate in something they don't particularly enjoy.

In the culture of monogamy, however, sex and romance aren't handled that way. People may be completely comfortable with accepting that no one can share all their partner's hobbies or opinions but feel completely differently about the idea that no one can fulfill all their partner's sexual desires or match all of their kinks. In fact, many people feel uncomfortable when their current partner has a close friendship with someone else, particularly if their gender suggests romance is possible. Similarly, connections with exes may be discouraged, even though they already proved to their own satisfaction that the relationship with the ex wasn't workable. Monogamy, as most people currently practice it, asks us to find one person who fulfills all our sexual and romantic needs, and stick with them exclusively, for decades. We might find other people to connect with around other interests, but for romance, we're expected to choose just one. And if another comes along, we are expected to choose.

In the world of polyamory, on the other hand, sex and romance are regarded much like other areas of interest. Partners connect around common interests and romance alike, and experience increased flexibility, independence, and connection as a result. This can feel a little alienating or abstract to imagine, so I'd like to guide you in another brief thought exercise.

Imagine that you're in a relationship with a wonderful person. You're compatible in a million ways, and you support and respect one another through thick and thin. But there's just one little thing: You're not particularly sexually compatible.

If you're monogamous, sexual incompatibility might become a big problem. You can't seek out another sexual partner without violating your relationship commitments. You have a few options, none of them particularly appealing: You could end the relationship, you could commit infidelity, or you could choose to suck it up and live without that sexual fulfillment.

For a nonmonogamous person, however, this doesn't necessarily create a problem. That's because they can outsource the sex part, just like how, in a monogamous relationship, you can outsource the person who will get completely involved in that weird or boring hobby that you adore and your partner has no interest in. It's perfectly possible for a polyamorous person to preserve the relationship without committing infidelity *or* relinquishing the possibility of sexual fulfillment.

This, to me, is one of the biggest reasons that polyamory makes sense. It presents a viable alternative to both serial monogamy and infidelity, both of which create significant distress in people's lives and make regular appearances in the therapy room. In fact, I've found that polyamory, when done well, can lead to more stable relationships than monogamy, in that it doesn't depend on deception or making choices out of step with the natural evolution of relationships. It acknowledges that no one relationship will fulfill every aspect of a person's sexual and romantic selves, and allows an outlet for exploration without destabilizing long-term partnerships. In that vein, I'd like to share this story, which illustrates the beauty of a relationship founded on a recognition of the truth that no one person can be everything to anyone:

> I grew up in a very conservative religious family and culture, and came out as lesbian relatively late—in my mid-30s—and through much struggle concerning what that meant for my faith and my relationships with family.
>
> I was taken aback when the second woman I ever dated started right off—the first time we even had coffee together, after meeting on the dance floor at a club—saying, "I assume you're monogamous and want to get married; most lesbians do. Well, I'm not and I don't, so I don't see this working out as a relationship, but I think we could be friends." I found it insulting that she would make assumptions about me. I'm not sure what I said, but it was probably something like, "I don't know whether I'm monogamous or not!"
>
> When I started to come out as a lesbian, in the 1990s, my entire worldview changed in big ways; I didn't have an established set of assumptions about how things would go. I mean, I was already doing something radical and inconceivable to my parents and my childhood church, so why should anyone assume I'd be conventional in other ways?
>
> Currently, I think of myself not as monogamous or polyamorous, but simply as committed to my partner/spouse for life. Beyond that, if I wanted a label, I'd choose autonomous or independent. My sense of being a separate self is very important to me, no matter how close I am to my partner. I've always needed a significant amount of time and space to myself, and I avidly pursue creative work, emotionally intimate friendships, and involvement in social justice activism and a faith community. I just don't happen to be interested in pursuing another sexual relationship. I've always found it disturbing to hear about relationships in which

each person is expected to be everything to the other and meet all of that person's needs. I think those are likely to be unhealthy relationships, actually. I'm glad that my spouse (who, by the way, is polyamorous) has always been supportive of my—you could even call them "other"—relationships with writing, church, and close friends, and I'd feel trapped if that were not the case.

POLYAMORY IN A WORLD OF DIVORCE, SERIAL MONOGAMY, AND INFIDELITY

Here's another foundational idea in the cultural construct of poly-amory: Maybe human beings are not actually built for monogamy. As you can imagine, this is quite a controversial topic. There are more and less extreme versions of this argument. Some believe that monogamy runs counter to the essential nature of human beings, while others argue that *some* people may not be naturally compatible with monogamy.

Here is one way to look at it: Human beings have two aspects or urges to balance. On one hand, we want a deep, close, connected, lasting pair-bond, as well as emotional security and no fear of a breakup or any big surprises. On the other hand, we want the shiny, heart-fluttering experience of a new love, which feels exciting in part *because* it is a little uncertain.

In the culture of monogamous relationships, people are supposed to choose between these two options. The cultural ideal is that (after some early experimentation, perhaps) we ultimately embrace the pair-bond and forego the excitement of new love. But there is an alternative that might come about intentionally or totally accidentally. We could find ourselves having feelings for someone new. In the culture of monogamy, according to which we can only have one relationship at a time, embracing the new love would mean sacrificing the long-term pair-bond.

As therapists, we know that divorce, serial monogamy, and infidelity are rampant in our culture. Is it possible that this is because many people struggle to balance their desire for a deep, lasting pair-bond with their desire for the thrills that come with a new, exciting, fresh relationship?

Imagine that you're in this situation. You can't bring yourself to give up the close, long-term pair bond, but you also want to have that shiny new experience of a fresh love. What options do you have? You don't want to break up, so you can't go the serial monogamy route. You have no culturally approved option.

In this scenario, a lot of people end up going the route of infidelity, as an attempt to hold on to their long-term relationship while also getting that new-love experience. As therapists, we have a unique front-row seat to the harm caused by romantic and sexual deception. It's certainly not a good option if you want to proceed ethically, avoid harming the people you care about, save money on therapy, or preserve your original relationship.

Imagine now that you are a person who thinks you are not really prepared to give up the possibility of having, at some point in the future, a brand-new, sparkling, full-on experience of new love. But imagine you are also clear that you are a person who wants to make a commitment, settle down, and be a good and reliable partner and spouse. You don't want to cheat, lie, and deceive. You want to live up to your promises. What do you do then?

INFIDELITY: THE BEST ARGUMENT FOR POLYAMORY

Infidelity has two components: (1) developing and acting in some manner on romantic or sexual feelings outside of your dyadic relationship agreements, and (2) keeping it secret, and/or actively lying about it. When I'm working with couples in the aftermath of infidelity, it often seems to me that the lies and deception cut even deeper than the extradyadic romance and sex. In fact, many clients tell me so. I'll bet you have had the same experience.

My clients often tell me something like this: "It stings that my partner developed feelings for someone else, but I think I could get over that. It's the betrayal that cuts deepest. I keep going over it in my mind, trying to figure out when they were together, and wondering how I missed it. What was I doing while they were together? Cooking dinner? Picking up the kids? How could my partner look right into my face and lie? I feel so stupid. How can I ever trust them again? I knew something was up, and I asked and asked, and eventually actually confronted my partner, and they denied it, over and over again. How could they choose that other person over me, so blatantly, and in such a hurtful and destructive way? This was my one safest person in the world. How have we come to this?"

In the aftermath of infidelity, partners feel betrayed, taken advantage of, stupid, ashamed, angry, furious, and disillusioned. The partner may have confessed the infidelity, revealed the infidelity when directly asked, or lied repeatedly and then been caught in some manner. The lies may have been direct or indirect. They may have called their partner crazy for even thinking they would cheat. There is a lot of variation, and some scenarios are more difficult to recover from. Yet, many couples recover from the betrayal and successfully rebuild their relationships. I find it fascinating that many people can recover from infidelity but not tolerate the idea of polyamory.

Imagine what it would be like for you or your partner to bring the conversation about romantic and sexual feelings for someone else out into the open. What would that sound like? "Honey, I met someone at the office, and I have to admit, I have a little crush." Could you do it? How about if your partner brought it up? Could you hear it? Could you get curious? Could you remember that the alternative could very easily be deception?

If a person is in a situation in which they are really having strong feelings for someone other than their spouse, they have a choice to make. They could get a grip, make a decision not to act on it, and follow through with integrity by remaining monogamous. Or they could push the boundaries of agreements, incrementally or all at once, and either edge toward infidelity or dive right into the deep end with full-blown deception.

Polyamory offers a third path: Why not have a real conversation about it?

TRANSPARENCY AND FIDELITY

Let's return to that hypothetical conversation about a crush at work. Without a doubt, that is likely to be a difficult conversation for many people to have. Here's the thing: I know a lot of polyamorous people for whom this conversation doesn't even reach a 2 on a scale of 1 to 10 for stressfulness. Amazing, huh?

> Partner 1: "Honey, I met someone at work and I have a little crush; I'm thinking of asking them out on a date."
>
> Partner 2: "Great; be safe and have fun."

No kidding.

In case you are wondering about my bias, here it is: I'm not a fan of deception, either as a human being or a therapist. I deeply honor people who value transparency and personal growth enough to choose polyamory, rather than choosing to go underground with infidelity. I think it is a braver, more forthright, and more differentiated path. I also deeply honor those who choose monogamy, are in touch with their values, and have the integrity to live up to their values and be the person they aspire to be, making good agreements and following through on them. Finally, I deeply honor relationships in which partners tune in to what they want and how they are doing as things evolve throughout the years, and update or renegotiate their relationship agreements to reflect changing circumstances, growth, and interests.

IDENTITY: BEYOND ARGUMENT

Aside from any theory or concept about larger ideas of monogamy and polyamory, the fact of the matter is that for a lot of people, polyamory is an important aspect of how they see themselves and understand themselves relationally. When someone has a perception of who they are at their core, derived from an internal sense of knowing, no amount of theory can, or should, shift it. This account gives a good sense of what it means to identify polyamory as a deep aspect of one's identity:

> Since my preteens I've always known I was, or wanted to be, not monogamous. It's part of my need to be independent and not controlled by someone else. At the same time, my dreams and visions of the future always have a partner in them. My ideal of partnership is that we help one another be the best we can and fulfill our dreams. Not restrict or con-

fine one another. I have no desire to control what another person does, and I do not like it when others try to control me. I do not see this as at all opposed to my desire for a close partnership. It's just how I define partnership or the kind of partnership I want.

I do not always have multiple lovers. I just need to know that I am free to do so. Much of my life I have had multiple lovers or partners, generally in the primary/secondary model. A few times I have promised to be monogamous for a limited time and have held to that agreement, but it's not comfortable for me and not something I would agree to other than for a limited time. It's about independence for me—I do not think asking or allowing this level of control is healthy in a relationship. At least not in a relationship I would care to be part of.

CHAPTER 5

Who Can Benefit from Consensual Nonmonogamy?

There are many situations in which exploring a consensually nonmonogamous relationship makes a lot of sense. Since I've seen polyamory and other consensual nonmonogamies provide elegant solutions to some pretty daunting relationship problems, I think it is worth taking the time to discuss some of those situations.

Please keep in mind that there is no one-size-fits-all relationship solution. What has worked for some may not work for others. There is no substitute for self-awareness and communication, and every fabulously functional relationship situation I've ever seen, monogamous and otherwise, has been individually tailored by the participants to fit their unique personalities, preferences, and values.

OPENING THE TOPIC OF CONSENSUAL NONMONOGAMY WITH CLIENTS

Therapists often ask me if I ever suggest consensual nonmonogamies to my clients, if I think it has the potential to solve some of their relationship problems. The short answer is, yes—fairly frequently, in fact. In part, I do this because many people have never heard of consensual nonmonogamy. If they haven't heard of it, they don't have the chance to decide if it could work for them. Even for those who have heard of it, there are so many misconceptions and so much misinformation out there that it's likely most people have a skewed idea of what polyamory or other forms of consensual nonmonogamy look like in the real world. It is *extremely* likely that they are not aware that many polyamorous relationships work well for the long haul. How could they know that, given how much bias there is against polyamory and how little information is available? Polyamory and other consensual nonmonogamies are showing up in the media more now, so more people are exposed to the concept, but some of those depictions are overly sensationalist and involve extremely quirky characters or unusual relationship styles; this is not always helpful when it comes to understanding what is actually possible in real life. As with sex, media depictions should not serve as substitutes for, or replace, educational offerings.

I'm not in the business of promoting polyamory to anyone; I'm in the business of helping people have happy relationships. But if someone doesn't know open relationship structures exist in happy, healthy forms, or what skills and beliefs create them, their options for how they might structure their own relationships are limited by what they don't know. I also like for people to know that, while monogamy has its unique challenges, it works truly elegantly for some. Whether choosing monogamy or polyamory or another form of open relationship, it is helpful to know something about the difference between fabulously functional relationships and tense, unhappy ones. Knowledge is power. I trust that my clients can figure out what they want, and I don't believe anyone can be hurt by knowing what options exist.

Ultimately, I believe it's important to present consensual nonmonogamy as an option because I believe in informed consent. When I have a medical problem, I want to know all the options, even the long shots and the new stuff that hasn't yet been well-researched. I'm smart enough to do my research and think things through before I take action. If I think it is in my best interest, I might ultimately choose to do something that is against conventional medical advice. I'll always be deeply grateful to the people who were courageous enough to tell me about all the options, without editing out the half they don't think I'm going to consider. I want to provide the same service to my clients, in my area of expertise.

I respect the intelligence of my clients and operate from the position that they are perfectly capable of making decisions that are good for them. I don't need to protect them from knowledge. I also don't make assumptions about who would consider polyamory and who would not. All kinds of people practice consensual nonmonogamy: liberal people and conservative people; people of many ethnicities, genders, and orientations; people with a lot of money and people with hardly any money; people who are deeply religious and people who are definitely not. I have known hippies, Gen Xers, old folks, and lots and lots of midlife folks in long-term marriages who successfully opened their relationships.

Here is an example of someone who identifies as Christian, and polyamorous, discussing how they make sense of these two aspects of their identity coexisting:

> I fit into what is likely a small sliver on the Venn diagram of polyamory and Christianity. I take my Christianity seriously, so it was important for me that if I was going to embrace polyamory, I needed to reconcile it with my Christian belief. My thought process behind how these two seemingly opposing worldviews fit together is quite complex, but one aspect of it is that I see God as being in a relationship with us as humans, and throughout the Bible, the way that relationship was structured profoundly changes from the beginning to the end. But despite those profound changes, the relationship God has with people is valid throughout, and the structure changed to adapt as the relationship evolved. So I believe that as long as the people in the relationship are making it thrive through vulnerability and connection—that's the important part. From there, the structure itself can vary. While some might say that extending that to polyamory is a stretch, I don't agree. There seem to be plenty of examples in the Old Testament of God approving of someone having multiple wives, David for instance. I think the Bible, throughout, teaches that having our heart in the right place is the most important aspect for creating relationships that are God-centered.

One way that I support differentiation of self is by encouraging my clients to think for themselves; I invite them to push back if I say something they don't agree with. In my therapy room, this is not a passive intervention. I tell my clients straight out that I offer options, suggestions, feedback, and observations to support them in their growth, including their own decision-making. Whether they have a new idea, or their partner offers a suggestion, or I do, I encourage my clients to pause, look inside themselves, and take the time they need to identify their own opinion. Then I encourage them to share it, even if it is in opposition to the opinions of others in the room.

Polyamory is merely one of many things I might talk about in therapy that could potentially feel challenging to my clients. Here's how that might sound: "Can I run an idea past you? Feel free to reject it. But you know, I've worked with lots of clients in open relationships, and some people have found it to be a useful way to deal with some of the issues you are struggling with. I've seen it work really well. Have you ever thought about opening your relationship? Would you like to know more about how that works for some people?" Believe me, people don't hesitate to tell me if this isn't something they want to consider. But often one or both partners want a little more information. At some point, they either become clear that consensual nonmonogamy isn't for them, or they decide to further discuss their array of options and how a nonmonogamous relationship might work for them.

With this discussion, as all others, I encourage partners to keep a creative, collaborative conversation about options, thoughts, feelings, and desires going for quite some time before any move toward decision-making. Using the therapeutic environment to build relational skills is a well-established technique, and this is just one example of how to use it to build differentiation around challenging topics. I think it is therapeutic in itself to model careful and creative consideration of a variety of topics far in advance of making a decision. When you actively invite differences of opinion, it expands the field of what options and possibilities are open for discussion. Help your clients keep their exploration lighthearted and generative, while grounding that process in the secure knowledge they will be making their own decisions, and each will make a decision that feels right to them.

If you are the one in the stressful conversation within your own relationship, you're putting theory into practice. It might help to remind yourself that you are just thinking and talking, which is quite different from making a decision. Focus on curiosity, and resist the impulse to debate; if your partner senses you are trying to convince them or bring them over to your opinion, they are likely to dig in their feet.

Let's circle back to a situation in which a client says right away they are not interested in considering opening their relationship. I admit, in a conversation like that I sometimes go one step further. If my clients tell me that they aren't interested in consensual nonmonogamy but they haven't already said *why* they think it's not for them, I might ask them why, just in case they are basing their conclusion on completely inaccurate information. I would do the same for any other possibility a client is considering—for instance, going back to school for an expensive graduate degree or having the aging in-laws move in. If they are factoring in obvious misinformation, I clear it up or suggest further research so they can make choices more effectively. I'm also interested in encouraging self-definition, meaning I want my clients to express their own unique perspective more fully. Asking someone how they came to a conclusion is an expression of curiosity and a desire to know them better, not a challenge to how they think or an attempt to change their minds.

WHO CAN BENEFIT?

Here, for your consideration, is an (incomplete) list of circumstances that could be mitigated or resolved with some form of open relationship, whether that's polyamory, swinging, monogamish, or other nonromantic open structures. Refer to chapter 1, "Consensual Nonmonogamies: What Are the Options?" for a sample of the many flavors of nonmonogamy. I've framed most of these in terms of a couple who might come to you for therapy about particular types of challenges, but the client might just as easily be an individual facing relational challenges or identifying individual preferences.

There is no guarantee, of course, that consensual nonmonogamy *will* solve any particular problem; it's just another set of options to consider. As you read through this list, remember it is not exhaustive; there are many circumstances that might benefit from trying a consensually open relationship. If you, or your clients, think opening the relationship might have some significant benefits, I think it is worth a conversation. For each of the following examples, ask yourself how consensual nonmonogamy, practiced with care, thoughtfulness, and consideration, might serve. If this feels like a stretch, notice what thoughts and feelings are coming up. Uncomfortable feelings you experience when reading these situational examples might relate to a belief system, and in the next chapter, I'll be discussing some ways to think about belief systems.

A couple is struggling with an extreme desire discrepancy. One partner wants frequent sex, and the other wants sex rarely or never. They love one another and want to stay together for multiple reasons, but the higher-desire partner is deeply frustrated and feels trapped: "I don't want to leave my partner, but I don't want to be stuck in a sexless relationship for the rest of my life." The lower-desire partner feels pressured, pestered, sad, guilty, and deeply conflicted: "I want my partner to be happy, and I can see the trap they are in; we signed on for a sexual marriage, and now I actually prefer a sexless one. I see their pain; my lack of desire is hard on them. I want us both to be happy, and I don't want to have sex when it isn't what I want because neither of us enjoys that, but I also don't want to end this otherwise awesome relationship."

One partner has recently realized that they are asexual—that is, they have no desire for or interest in sex. Possibly they are willing to have sex to please their partner, or possibly they are not. In either case, their partner says, "I love my partner and want to stay with them, but I'd also like to have a sexual relationship with someone who enjoys sex and really wants to have sex with me." Both agree this would benefit each of them, because it would take the pressure off of both and make more room for them to appreciate the strengths of their relationship.

A couple has been together for many years, since they were both very young. They have a strong, stable, mature relationship, but they both sometimes feel melancholy about how long it's been since they experienced the rush of falling in love and the headiness of an early crush. "I'm so happy with our relationship and proud of what we've built," one of them says, "but I wish I could experience the amazing feeling of falling in love again at some point before the end of my life."

One partner is bisexual. Maybe they have been for a long time, or maybe this aspect of their identity recently emerged. In any case, they want to explore that aspect of themselves, but neither they nor their partner want to end their current relationship, which has many strengths.

One partner is kinky or has a sexual interest that they want to explore, and their partner is not particularly interested in participating, yet they want to honor their partner's exploration of this aspect of themselves. (As it happens, kink is one situation in which "monogamish" can work really well, because kinky play often doesn't include sexual contact. For more on this, see chapter 3, "Overlapping Marginalized Populations and Intersectionality").

One partner has developed a strong sexual and/or romantic attraction to someone outside the relationship. They don't want to lead a secret life involving secrecy and deception, and they have strong values that don't permit them to have an affair. They see the strengths of their longer-term relationship and don't want to end it, but they also don't want to shut off their feelings or turn away from what the other relationship has awakened in them, although they remain realistic about the new relationship and its limitations.

The partners, because of work or family, or some other reason, spend a lot of time in different locations, and they both get lonely and wish for companionship. They don't want totally casual connections, but they don't want to disrupt their current relationship connection. (This situation also lends itself well to "monogamish" relationship structures; for more on this see chapter 1, "Consensual Nonmonogamies: What Are the Options?").

One or both partners are philosophically interested in nonmonogamy or polyamory and believe in the idea of expanding love. They want to explore it because it makes sense to them and fits with their values.

One or both partners identifies as polyamorous. They have a lot of personal experience that suggests that monogamy is not a good fit for them or simply a strong inner sense that it doesn't fit their beliefs or personality. They think of themselves as polyamorous and envision a stable relationship or family situation with more than one partner.

One partner likes a lot of physical closeness and snuggling, while the other prefers a big bubble of personal space much of the time. The partner who desires touch tends to feel lonely or overly needy, and the other often feels pressured or guilty. They don't want to end their relationship because of this difference, but they don't see a solution as things currently stand.

One partner has an extremely time-consuming job, hobby, set of family obligations, etc., that leaves the other frequently feeling lonely and at loose ends.

One or both partners value the idea of experiencing love, sex, and intimacy with many different people in their lives, as a way of expanding their world. They don't see themselves settling into one relationship.

One partner has a pattern of serial monogamy and/or infidelity. They aspire to be able to commit to a long-term relationship without being dishonest, for the depth of intimacy, connection, and personal growth it will offer, but they also realistically acknowledge they are likely to be drawn to other people at some point and will be tempted to act on those attractions. They want to feel free to explore those attractions but in an ethical and consensual manner.

One partner is not strongly attracted to the other, although they love one another deeply. The first partner would like to experience being with someone they find extremely attractive, and the second partner would like to experience being with someone who is completely into them sexually.

One partner has experienced severe chronic or catastrophic illness that drastically limits their capacity for physical, intellectual, and/or romantic intimacy for the long haul. Their partner loves them and wants to stay by their side, but they are not ready to set aside their own sex life.

One or both partners enjoy having a lot of emotional support at an intimate level or maybe someone has a preference for high levels of reliability and presence, beyond what is reasonable to expect from just one person. They find that having more than one partner spreads the emotional support around, making it more likely that at any given moment, there will be someone available to talk, snuggle, or spend the night.

Do any of these scenarios sound familiar to you from your own therapy room? Sometimes having consensual nonmonogamy as an option can be the difference between saving a marriage and ending it. Naturally, it doesn't work for everyone, but I have seen wonders happen in scenarios much like the ones I describe here. Can you see how, given the right circumstances, a polyamorous or otherwise nonmonogamous arrangement has the potential to provide an elegant solution to a serious impasse?

Desire discrepancy is a common and often painful impasse. From my own clinical experience, and from my work as an educator for other therapists, I know that desire discrepancy can be one of the most challenging issues for relational therapists to work with. That's why I'd like to share this account of a couple who discovered that polyamory served as a creative and elegant solution to their desire discrepancy:

> My husband says that polyamory has helped him to relax. He feels much less stressed and anxious than he used to. Part of the reason we opened our marriage was because of what I guess you would call a desire discrepancy: He wanted my sexual attention, and I was completely wrapped up in work. I felt very little interest in sex. Instead of giving up on me, however, he got creative, inventing all sorts of kinky ways to get me interested in sex. He sexualized his own anxiety. He ended up creating elaborate cuckold fantasies as a way to empower me and intrigue him, and long story short, it worked fantastically well. His invitation to me to explore sexually reignited my libido and gave me self-confidence that had been holding me back for years. I simply had not seen myself as attractive or desirable, and I couldn't remember or understand why sex was such a big deal.
>
> As a result of opening up, my husband says he feels far, far more satisfied with our sexual relationship (because now I show up, for starters). In addition, polyamory allows him to perceive himself in a variety of ways that improve his own self-image. While he loves to feel "under my thumb" as a cuckolded husband, he enjoys dominating his once-a-month girlfriend. He revels in the complexity of this situation.
>
> Clearly, becoming polyamorous gave me back my mojo. But it has done more than that. Precisely because it is emotionally difficult, because it touches so close to the bone, it gives me unparalleled chances to grow. At this point, I have three partners I love. One of them is both 12 years younger than me and much more of a free spirit—precisely the sort of "scary" person I would never have considered marrying. I really don't know what I can count on from him in terms of stability or monogamy. He loves me, and he is honest with me. But there are no guarantees. To think that I am able to handle this—I, who have struggled mightily with jealousy—is an accomplishment. I feel proud. I can't say that I handle all

challenges with ease. Yet, I am growing. I am learning to trust the beauty of my life and the possibilities of relationships in ways that I never, in my wildest imaginings, could have foreseen for myself as a middle-aged woman. My life is interesting, challenging, and deeply rewarding. I am blessed to know three men in a deeply intimate, loving way. What's more, I no longer have time to be such a workaholic. I have far more interesting things on my plate.

As you can see, polyamory helped this couple to revitalize their relationship in a number of ways, both resolving a persistent desire discrepancy and offering them fertile new ground for personal exploration.

In some cases, when situations like these arise, the client comes to therapy already wanting to explore polyamory. Their partner may or may not be on the same page. As an exercise in understanding how nonmonogamies might serve in a variety of situations, I invite you to imagine what a variety of options might look like. Consider polyamory, other forms of open relationships, monogamish, monogamy, and anything else you can imagine. What circumstances would need to be in place for each option to work?

In other cases, when situations like those listed here arise in therapy, the partners may not have considered polyamory. Moreover, they may not know anything about the range of options they could craft for themselves and may have never considered that they might create their own definitions of fidelity and commitment. Imagine yourself suggesting a variety of forms of consensually open relationships as potentially viable options. Consider what types of solutions might serve them and in what circumstances. Imagine how you might feel in these conversations.

Of course, each of the aforementioned scenarios could also lead to participants choosing monogamy. Think through how complex that could potentially be in some of these scenarios. I think you will find that exploring the option of monogamy is not always the easiest road, and exploring the range of nonmonogamies is not always the most complicated.

THE MAGIC OF FEELING FREE TO CHOOSE

Let's consider again the possible scenario of someone in a monogamous relationship who has just realized they are bisexual and wants to act on their same-sex attraction. If there is no discussion of opening the relationship, they may feel a huge amount of pressure to set aside those desires. They may feel trapped or coerced. Sometimes when people feel trapped, they dig in. Using this example, the desire to act on bisexual attraction could expand beyond what it otherwise might. They might think, "I didn't know before that I had these feelings. I decided to be in this relationship before I knew this about myself. It's not fair that I'll never be able to explore this part of myself. I'm angry with my partner for holding me back from exploring this." This train of thought could easily lead to infidelity or push them to end the relationship.

If, on the other hand, the partners have a rich, nuanced, pressure-free discussion of the pros and cons of opening up, they are more likely to feel heard and like their partner is treating this important aspect of themselves with the respect it deserves. They may choose to act on their attractions, or they may not, but because their decision was made freely and their perspective fully considered, they are less likely to feel cornered or resentful, and their relationship will benefit as a result.

For some people, it can be a new and tremendously liberating realization that they have total freedom to decide what they want their relationship to be like. This is just as true in a long-standing relationship as in a new one: As people evolve throughout time, so do their needs and desires. Their relationships should be able to flex and evolve with them. They get to decide what that looks like, based on what's important to them. What does commitment mean to them? What does fidelity mean? What are each partner's dreams, desires, preferences, limits, values, and boundaries? How do they feel about sexual exclusivity? How about romantic exclusivity?

There isn't just one recipe for romance, love, companionship, support, marriage, fidelity, or intimacy. There are infinite possibilities and plenty of evidence that flexibility throughout a lifetime is the most important ingredient for successful long-term relationships. This suggests to me that, even for monogamous couples, periodically revisiting the question of, "What kind of relationship do we want to create?" will help them craft and maintain a relationship that meets everyone's needs for a long time to come.

Part II

CREATING A STRONG FOUNDATION FOR THERAPY WITH POLYAMORY

CHAPTER 6

The Therapist
Bias, Strengths, and Challenges

This chapter is about honestly assessing belief systems that, if they remain unexamined, can make it hard to remain grounded and open-minded when considering someone else's point of view. This is relevant to helping professionals because we often find ourselves challenged by our own biases, belief systems, or past experiences when working with clients. But it is also relevant to anyone who finds themselves having a significant difference of opinion or belief from their partner or partners. In fact, differences of opinion surface in every long-term relationship, and learning how to look more deeply at what thoughts, feelings, and beliefs are under the surface is an important relationship skill. As you read this chapter, which on the surface may seem to be directed at therapists, consider the viewpoints of not only the therapist, but also a potential client seeking a therapist, a friend who might be grappling with something that is hard for you to hear, or yourself when considering a partner's viewpoint that shakes you to the core.

The first step in cultural competence for therapists is separating your choices and belief systems from those of your clients. For people in relationships, the first step is separating your opinions, choices, and beliefs from those of other people. Both require developing curiosity about how things look from the perspectives of others, while remaining grounded in your ability to make independent choices for yourself. This is foundational to good therapy of any kind, with any population.

Unfortunately, it can be especially difficult to separate our own beliefs and preferences from those of our clients when it comes to polyamory and other forms of consensual nonmonogamy, because the very concept of having multiple concurrent intimate relationships goes directly against our cultural indoctrination toward monogamy. Therapists can have an even more complex challenge, because training in couples therapy often holds that it is not possible to be effective with relational therapy when one partner has romantic feelings for a third party. This leads to therapists requiring their clients to end any extradyadic relationships to engage in dyadic relational therapy. On the face of it, that makes sense, and it can be useful guidance in some cases. But the problem with applying this approach automatically and in every case is that polyamory by definition involves having significant romantic feelings for more than one person. A client might have a goal of becoming successful in engaging in multiple concurrent relationships, rather than a goal of being monogamous. In that case, it might not make sense for them to have no contact with their other partner during the therapeutic process. In some cases, they also might not be willing to do so or interested in doing so. In such a case, therapy goals have to go far beyond ending an extradyadic romantic connection.

Sometimes the entry point for polyamory is infidelity, by which I mean someone might see themselves as having more than one relationship, and live that out, without having any language for, or understanding of, how to do it consensually. I know that this is a hot-button issue. As relationship therapists, we know how damaging infidelity can be, and it can be hard to imagine how it's possible to start with an infidelity case and end up with happy, healthy polyamory. But, in the story I want to share with you, that's exactly what happened. This is a personal account from a person who has a successful marriage of more than 20 years and has now been in a wonderful polyamorous relationship for more than 10 years, despite the fact that it started with a messy affair:

> I always thought of myself as someone who would have a wife and a mistress; I didn't have language for polyamory until I was in my 40s, but when I heard the word and the concept, I knew it described me. I had absolutely zero communication skills; I couldn't have stood up for myself or said a feeling to save myself or my relationship. I just had no idea; that was not how we operated in my family. We did not talk, negotiate, discuss, or anything like it; rules came down from on high. So I sneaked and lied my way through my childhood and then my marriage as well.

When my wife caught me in an affair with a close friend, there was a big blow up, and we separated temporarily.

We saw a couples therapist, and after a few meetings she said we were done with therapy if I didn't end the affair. I had been learning about polyamory from a close friend, pretty much nonstop thinking about it and trying to figure out what to do and what I wanted. I saw an individual therapist for a while too, which helped. When our couples therapist gave me the ultimatum, I realized this is the moment I can speak up and start being me, or I can say nothing once again and go back to lying, deceit, heartbreak, rinse, and repeat, as it has always been my entire life. So I told my wife, and the therapist, I wasn't going to stop seeing my lover. I explained, if it wasn't her, it would be someone else, this is just the way I am and how I want to live my life. We never went back to therapy, and we probably never will. I don't know how my wife decided not to leave me, but we're still together, years later. It's just insane when I realize that I could have cleanly made a situation like this work if I had been equipped with better communication skills and knew that polyamory existed. It wasn't until I started talking about my feelings and what I wanted that my life started to work out.

This story illustrates why, despite the conventional wisdom, it's not always the most helpful course of action to require that clients either commit to monogamy or give up on relationship therapy entirely. In this case, the therapist's choice to require that the client end his affair precipitated a healing crisis that the couple in question resolved on their own by opening their relationship and terminating therapy. Neither partner feels that the therapy was particularly helpful—not even the monogamous partner, even though she was not in favor of opening their relationship. This story has a happy enough ending, but I can't help but wonder if some support for the transition to polyamory could have given them a stronger foundation. I also wonder what would have happened if the partners in question had not had the will, information, or emotional skills that ultimately allowed them to rebuild their relationship on their own, once relational therapy was no longer an option. What if the therapist's insistence that the affair be ended had pushed our storyteller back underground, leading to further lies and deeper betrayal? Things could have turned out very differently.

I want to share another story with you now, one that I think illustrates the powerful impact a polyamory-competent therapist can make. This story comes from someone who has a lifetime of experience with polyamory and is now in a happy primary relationship of seven years, and also has other partners regularly. This person's relational therapy experience lasted more than two years.

When we started couples therapy, both of us were not at all sure our relationship of six years could continue. We were causing each other so much pain almost every day, we knew we could not go on like this. It was either take radical steps to fix it or give up with a whimper. We were a mess—not hearing one another well, easily triggered, assuming the worst, making up crazy stories in our heads, middle-of-the-night meltdowns— we were both miserable. Jealousy and control stuff were the presenting symptom, the crisis. So we had to start with that. But really I think the issues in our relationship, and the solutions, were mostly in the way we related to one another, not mainly in our affairs with others.

Much of what we worked on was just like any other couples therapy— communication skills, not getting triggered, coping and getting-over-it skills, learning to understand our differences, etc. Not really issues specific to polyamory. We did carefully select a polyamory-experienced therapist, and I'm glad we did. He could support our lifestyle, and he had good specific examples and tools. But a good, skilled therapist with some familiarity with polyamory, or just one who could hold their tongue about doubts about nonmonogamy, might have done 90% as well.

We came into therapy talking about our differences. I've been polyamorous my entire life, and my partner has been mono-ish. And, of course, we are different in many other ways. I was trying to minimize our differences: "See, we're nearly the same, we want the same thing." And she was maximizing them: "We're so far apart, how can we ever satisfy one another." Now with the therapist's help we have a different understanding of our differences. We went from anxiety, through tolerance, through understanding, to now supporting and appreciating one another and our differences.

In this example, an experienced, polyamory-knowledgeable therapist made a big difference in the clients' ability to connect effectively and build a secure bond while still actively participating in an open relationship.

THINKING ABOUT BIAS

Many therapists, and indeed many people, have belief systems or values that don't condone multiple simultaneous relationships. Many have past personal histories that make it particularly challenging to consider consensual nonmonogamy. Negative experiences with infidelity, broken agreements, trust issues, abandonment, jealousy, or even of polyamory gone wrong in your own life can affect how you react to your partner, friend, or client when the topic of polyamory arises. Every human being has bias, and therapists are no exception. It's not possible or even desirable to avoid being shaped by our experiences. The trick is learning how to hold your own beliefs and those of another person as well, and still think clearly about how you want to show up, what your role is, and how to move forward in ways that foster connection and healing.

If you struggle with the idea of consensual nonmonogamy or polyamory, that's understandable. It doesn't mean anything bad about you, and you're certainly not alone. If you're reading this book, I assume you are curious to find out if you want to work with this population, or perhaps if you want to stretch in your understanding of what your own relationships could become. That's all you need right now. If you can continue to cultivate that spirit of curiosity, you are already well on your way to figuring it out. The act of careful consideration and respect for diversity is the key. Any choice you make with due consideration of your bias and deep respect for others will be an honorable path.

While in this chapter I have focused on ways unexplored differences can challenge our ability to connect authentically, I think it is also important to consider ways our similarities can do the same. My working assumption is that every relationship is a cross-cultural relationship. In fact, while having personal in-group experience can be a real asset to understanding another person's culture, I think it can also be a bit of a liability. I always feel cautious when working with a client who appears to be much like me, because I think I am at high risk of making assumptions about them based on my own experience. When I do that, I know I am not making enough of an effort to see things through their eyes. When I'm working with clients who have relatively little in common with me, on the other hand, I find it easier to get curious about their experiences and perspectives, because it is obvious to me that I have no other way to understand them deeply. This is also true with friendships and partnerships; it is easy to say "if I can do it, you can too," when it might be more honest, and respectful, to ask the other person what they think sounds easy or difficult about it, or other questions that acknowledge more than one answer, choice, or challenge.

WHAT DOES IT TAKE TO BE A THERAPIST FOR POLYAMOROUS CLIENTS?

Here's your "must-have" list:

  The ability to separate your choices and values from your client's and tailor therapy to address their goals for the relationship(s) they want to create
  A basic level of cultural competence about polyamory and other forms of consensual nonmonogamy
  A therapeutic approach to some common presenting problems
  A working understanding of available resources

This book can provide you with the last three, but the first requires that you to make a decision about how you want to approach any differences in values between you and your clients. It will be important to develop strategies for recognizing when your own biases and assumptions may be starting to intrude on either your equanimity or their therapy. This is always a challenge, but it becomes particularly pressing when you're working with anyone whose relationships are not culturally condoned, as is the case with polyamorous people.

ASSESSING BIAS

We all have bias. Our culture, upbringing, family, lifetime of experiences, and other influences shape who we are, what we value, and what we believe. That, in turn, shapes our actions. The goal isn't to free ourselves from bias, but rather to make sure we're aware of what our bias is and where it comes from. That way, we have the option to correct for it—whereas if our bias remains unexamined, it's likely to sneak in and cause trouble without our realizing it.

To avoid that, we have to intentionally examine our bias. We have to consider what we believe, what assumptions we make about people and relationships, and what our own values are. In my opinion, this should be regular practice for therapists, and all humans in relationships with other humans, regardless of who they work with or relate to. Each individual is unique, a universe unto themselves, and therefore every relationship calls on us to continually reassess our perspectives. But taking a close look at your own bias can be quite uncomfortable, and I have nothing but respect for you as you undertake this important process of self-reflection.

To give you a sense of how to start analyzing your own bias, I'm going to share some of my own experiences. I want you to get a sense of what my bias is and where it comes from. I'm hoping that you can come along with me and really open yourself to considering the nature and sources of your own bias, whatever it may be. To that end, I've included a worksheet to guide you in a reflection on your own experiences and influences at the end of this chapter.

MY STORY

My mother and stepfather were married in 1968. They had a consensually nonmonogamous relationship. (Did you know that consensually nonmonogamous relationships even existed in 1968?) He traveled the world for his work, and their agreement was that he could have relationships when he traveled. Although I don't have many details, I believe that they had a don't ask, don't tell arrangement. I was about nine or 10 when my mom told me about this agreement. I recall that it was really no big deal to her. Her attitude was, "As long as it's not in my state, it's not an issue."

This was a foundational family influence for me. At a young age, I learned that my mother and stepfather had created a relationship agreement that was unique and individual, based on the needs of the people involved. That's what I was raised to believe in, not nonmonogamy per se, but individually crafted relationships.

My brother is another huge influence in my life. He and his wife were together for 18 years before she passed away. My brother has always considered himself to be a polyamorous person, and their relationship was polyamorous from the beginning. During the almost two decades they were together, he had another partner, and sometimes more than one. My sister-in-law was monogamous and did not have any other partners. (I call this kind of relationship structure mono-polyam; it's discussed in more depth in chapter 15). They also had a primary/secondary relationship structure, which means their relationship was primary and any other relationship came second. They had an ongoing conversation about what was feasible for them. To me, it seems clear that their relationship evolved through a process of differentiation. If it hadn't been a well-differentiated conversation and their relationship agreements a living document that flexed and changed throughout time, it seems very likely that something would have gone amiss and the relationship would never have lasted for 18 years.

Incidentally, many people, including many people who study polyamory, believe that mono-polyam is not a workable relationship structure. But I witnessed my brother's relationship with his wife, and it was a beautiful, long-lasting relationship. It worked, and that's what matters to me. I've seen many other mono-polyam relationships since that time, and I have no reason to think it isn't a potentially workable relationship style.

Another major influence on how I view polyamory is that I have been in a same-sex relationship for more than two decades, and I identify as lesbian. There's a huge overlap between the LGBTQIA+ community and the polyamorous and consensually open community. Because of that, I know many polyamorous people just from interacting with my own community. That means that I see a lot of the polyam people that never come in to couples therapy because their relationships are working already. Additionally, my partner and I crafted our relationship agreements and discussed balance of roles and responsibilities according to our gifts, strengths, and challenges. This is because in our household of two women, there is no rule book for who fixes the dryer, shovels the snow, cooks, cleans, or performs any other tasks of daily life that might otherwise be aligned with or proscribed by gender roles. I have always considered this aspect of my life to be a tremendous gift; far from being held back by gender stereotypes, we have had to transcend them.

Can you see how these influences combine to give me the perspective that polyamory can work? I've seen it work with my mother and stepfather. I've seen it work with my brother and his wife. I've seen it work, time and time again, with people in my community. On top of that, I believe in crafting unique relationship agreements because my parents modeled it, and my partner and I did it. These are the experiences that prepared me to work with polyamorous clients, because these experiences provided me a front-row seat in real-life demonstrations of beautiful, strong, loving, lasting unique relationships, some of which had nonmonogamous agreements in place.

In graduate school, I had an interesting experience that threw my own perception and understanding of relationships into stark relief. I was taking a class on couples therapy with a brilliant professor. One day, I asked him, "What are your thoughts about working with polyamory?"

He replied, "I've worked with a few, and what I've noticed is that the mother of at least one of the partners always seems to have a personality disorder."

I can certainly say, from my therapy room and my community, that's far from a universal truth. Yet, my professor was working from a small sample and a sample that only included people who needed relationship therapy. That's inherently going to offer a skewed perspective. It's important to remember that, as relationship therapists, we work almost exclusively with people whose relationships aren't doing so well. If you don't encounter polyamorous people in happy relationships in your everyday life and the only image of polyamory you have comes from the people you see in therapy, you might draw the conclusion that polyamory leads to, or arises from, dysfunction and conflict. One of the things I love about my own cultural influences is that I get to see the polyamorous relationships that work. That means that when a couple comes to me looking to move toward a nonmonogamous relationship, I already have plenty of examples for how that can work really beautifully. Most importantly, having access to well-functioning mono-polyam and don't ask, don't tell relationships, which are generally thought of as being not ideal, shows me just how wrong the conventional wisdom can be about nonmonogamy. Questioning the limitations people tend to place on what kind of relationship structures are workable comes to me naturally.

That said, these experiences and influences have their own inherent limitations. When I work with a monogamous person who identifies strongly as monogamous and isn't interested in exploring polyamory, I can easily feel an internal pull toward convincing them of the possibility that polyamory might work. I have to remind myself that me going to bat for the underdog (polyamory as a marginalized population) is not relevant to this individual's therapy goals. I have to consider carefully what will be therapeutic for them and what I can do to help them meet *their* goals. That can take a fair amount of careful consideration, since polyamory's marginalized status means that people rarely have accurate information and therefore psychoeducation is often necessary. I have gathered a number of interventions that keep me out of the middle, which I share in this book. I love these interventions because whenever I feel my personal bias might be coming into the room, I like to have strategies to make sure the clients are making their own decisions and having their own conversations, with one another and also with aspects of themselves. (For example, I make ample use of initiator/inquirer and resolving a dilemma using two-chair work.)

Additionally, I am quite aware of my own bias when I work with long-term same-sex white female couples, especially those in my age range. It is easy for me to identify with their cohort, challenges, culture, and situation; I'm in danger of projecting my own values and beliefs on them. I can easily make assumptions about them that are untrue and obscure their individuality. Ideally, I want to connect with and come to understand the real person in front of me rather than an aspect of myself, projected on them. It takes a deliberate effort to not take shortcuts based on what would probably end up to be false assumptions.

WHAT ARE YOUR INFLUENCES?

When I talk to therapists about working with polyamorous clients, I often hear about internal conflicts and blocks. Here are a few things I hear a lot:

"I've just seen things go wrong so often and so badly with nonmonogamy, and I feel uncomfortable letting my clients put themselves in a situation that could turn disastrous."

"Some of the things this client is telling their partner sound manipulative or narcissistic; I'm not sure I can tell the difference between a healthy situation and an unhealthy one, so we should veer away from a discussion of polyamory to avoid an entire category of pitfalls that can be damaging."

"I've tried nonmonogamy at one point in my life, and it turned out terribly."

"I don't understand how nonmonogamy can be compatible with a secure attachment style."

We all have ideas about what goes into a good relationship. These ideas are shaped by any number of factors: our own personal experience, our perceptions of the people around us, our religious belief systems, our consumption of the media, and so on.

If you haven't had a lot of experience talking and thinking about polyamory, it might make you uncomfortable at times. It may even bring up some internal conflict that you haven't been aware of before. You might have some ideas about when it can and cannot work or how. Sorting through that discomfort can be a really interesting project, if you're open to it. Think of this as an invitation to learn more about yourself and an opportunity to stretch and challenge yourself.

GUIDED REFLECTION: MY RELATIONSHIP IDEAS

I'd like to invite you to take a little time to consider your personal history. How have your experiences shaped your perspective on relationships? Beliefs and biases are close cousins; a belief is a thought we think a lot; it becomes a bias when we can't see past it sufficiently to engage with the reality of a situation or understand a different viewpoint. By examining your beliefs, you can stay aware of your internal processes and identify where your beliefs stop and a client's beliefs and choices begin. When you lose track of your own beliefs and the line between you and your life versus your client and their life, you are in the territory of acting from bias.

To guide you in reflecting on this subject, I've created a worksheet with a series of questions intended to lead you through a process of self-assessment, starting with looking at what beliefs and values you hold about relationships, fidelity, commitment, and so on, based on past experiences. The goal is to identify your influences, notice which beliefs may be lingering vestiges of a mindset you no longer consciously hold, and explore what you hope for in a long-term relationship or relationships.

"My Relationship Ideas: Reflection Worksheet" is the first in the Relationship Concepts worksheet set (see appendix A), a series that invites people to consider the assumptions that shape, and potentially limit, the possibilities for what a relationship can look like (the other two worksheets in appendix A are discussed in chapter 7, "What Makes a Good Relationship?"). These worksheets are simply tools, intended to be used as jumping-off places for deeper reflection and, ultimately, guides for how to go about changing a belief system, habit, or ineffective behavior you would prefer to leave behind. The change process involves multiple steps and makes an exciting and challenging course of therapy or a very interesting self-help project.

The first step involves identifying goals that you have the power to achieve (see the "Getting Clear on Your Goals" worksheet). The second step is to clearly see where you are and get your sights set on where you want to go in terms of thoughts, feelings, and actions that are related to your goal (see the "Creating Personal Change" worksheet). The third step is an action plan for implementing your change process (see the "Creating Change Action Plan" worksheet). The worksheets for these three steps are part of the Creating Change worksheet set in appendix E.

You can read through the worksheets and reflect on any thoughts and memories the questions evoke for you. If you want to go more in-depth, however, I recommend writing down some thoughts about each of the questions or discussing them with a partner, friend, coach, or therapist. You can do a full-on journal project or just jot down a few notes to remind yourself of what came to mind.

If you have clients who are considering opening their relationship or might benefit from some deep self-reflection about what kind of relationships they want to create, feel free to use any of these worksheets with them. In that case, first you might want to do a deep dive and go through the worksheets yourself so you can understand what it will be like for your client to engage in this process (see appendix A, "My Relationship Ideas: Reflection Worksheet"). Modify or adapt the worksheets as needed.

STANDING AT THE CROSSROADS

I wonder how you're feeling now, at the end of this chapter. If you did the exercise, you will have just finished a pretty deep reflection on your history with relationships. Maybe you picked up on a pattern you hadn't noticed before. Maybe you remembered an interesting experience you had forgotten. Maybe it sparked some curiosity about what experiences have shaped your loved ones' beliefs about relationships. There's always more ground to cover and deeper work to do.

When you meet someone who challenges your beliefs about relationships in some way, that will serve as another opportunity to reflect on your perspective and challenge your assumptions. Try to get curious and understand why they think what they do. I believe that it's when we are confronted with different perspectives that we learn the most about our own beliefs, and especially our values and our capacity for connecting with others. Engaging deeply with another person's viewpoint forces us to reflect on our own; as a result, we may shift our ideas, allow for new exceptions, or even deepen our commitment to what we believe by thinking through it more fully.

CHANGING A BELIEF SYSTEM

Changing a belief system is one of the most liberating things a person can do. Remember that a belief system isn't a global truth or mystical entity; it is a thought you have repeated so many times it becomes automatic and assumed (by you); however, you are in control of your thoughts. If you uncover a belief system you hold (an often-repeated thought) that you would prefer not to hold anymore, you can change it. And in so doing, you will also change something about your emotional experience because thoughts and emotions are closely connected. In fact, one way to identify a belief you might want to change is to notice if it makes you feel good, or bad. If you hold a belief that makes you feel bad about yourself or disconnected from people you love, it makes a lot of sense to change that belief into one that makes you feel good about yourself and more connected, loved, and loving.

Exercise: Creating Personal Change

Given the subject matter of this book, one belief a reader (or their client) might want to change is that monogamy is the only healthy and workable relationship structure, or that polyamory cannot ever work. I'm providing a lot of information to combat those beliefs, but if you really want to change your belief about this, it will help to look at how your actions, thoughts, and emotions are connected and work together to support the belief you currently hold. Additionally, it is important to figure out what you would prefer to believe and how thoughts, emotions, and actions would intertwine to support that desirable belief as well. To dig into the process of creating this or any other change, check out the worksheet "Creating Personal Change" in appendix E. I often use the format of this worksheet on a whiteboard in therapy and coaching sessions with clients, and it works equally well when done as a self-help project. It is very powerful to identify where you are; where you want to go; and what thoughts, feelings, and actions create and also result from each position. The process guided by the worksheet leads to choosing action steps. This might be taking one or some of the actions identified as desirable. Or it might be engaging in blocking or countering thoughts that support the old belief and cultivating thoughts that support the new one. Another way to work with the change process is to develop a mindfulness practice of feeling the feelings you want to experience. It all fits together, wherever you begin, but change involves shifting thoughts, actions, and emotions, and repeating often enough to create and then strengthen a new neural network.

To work further with changing a belief system, refer to the "Creating Change Worksheet Set" in appendix E, which includes "Getting Clear on Your Goals," "Creating Personal Change," "Accessing Motivation," "Creating Change Action Plan," and "Resolving a Dilemma Using Two Chairs."

CHAPTER 7

What Makes a Good Relationship?

Good relationships between adults have some things in common. Consider strong relationships between adult children and their parents, best friends, siblings, and extended family members, as well as romantic partners. Every healthy adult relationship has some key qualities: respect, empathy, curiosity about the perspectives of others, warm but firm boundaries, flexibility, the ability to understand and communicate one's desires and thoughts clearly, the ability to make and keep agreements, and the trust that comes from that. I could go on and on, and I'm sure you can think of some I have forgotten. In addition to the aforementioned attributes, intimate relationships also have some unique romantic, sexual, or otherwise intimate bond.

Think of a healthy relationship between two people. Imagine, for example, an intimate couple, a pair of adult siblings, two friends, or an adult child and their parent. It would be ridiculous to think that these dyadic relationships can't be successful unless the participants had already achieved a high level of secure attachment and differentiation, even under stress. We are all works in progress, and that doesn't stop us from having relationships. Moving toward increased congruence between thoughts, feelings, and actions; becoming more reliable; building the skills needed to discuss difficult topics; increasing our emotional endurance for ongoing hard conversations; sharing joys and sorrows well; collaborating as a team; and creating a life that is values-led and personally meaningful are important aspects of becoming increasingly strong individuals—the type of strong individuals who create strong relationships.

The more skilled the participants in any given relationship, the better the relationship functions, particularly during times of stress.

Now consider relationships among three or more people. Imagine a sibling group, a family unit, a church community, the people on a small committee, a group of close friends. Are there differences in the skills needed to make this type of situation function well as compared to the skills needed for a dyad?

I would say the same skills apply, but the potential for complexity is geometrically more, because there are more people, more variables, more unique circumstances and preferences, more moving parts shifting all the time, and more unique connections between people. That added complexity will show up especially starkly in stressful situations, particularly when a lot of emotions are involved and tempers may run high, which is often the case in romantic or intimate relationships.

Additionally, when there are more people involved, there are more opportunities for triangulation, indirect communication, going behind someone's back to discuss something that concerns them, making assumptions, and so forth. The partners may need more systems in place that provide guidelines for emotional boundaries in complex situations. They certainly may need help understanding the basic concepts of emotional boundaries, which may be new to them. As a therapist, I think this calls for a bit of a special skill set. You'll need to be good at spotting emotional contagion, triangulation, and other types of indirect communication, and helping clients practice good emotional hygiene and direct, appropriately boundaried communication. Developing this skill set will serve well and be worth cultivating for anyone in any relationship, but certainly anyone in a polyamorous relationship. Throughout this book, I offer steps for developing these skills, and for helping others develop them too. In the next chapter, "Conceptualizing the Case," I discuss in depth how I analyze relational challenges and support skill-building in polyamorous (and other) relationships using a framework combining concepts of differentiation, neuroscience, and attachment.

EXERCISE: EXAMINING ASSUMPTIONS
ABOUT RELATIONSHIP STRUCTURES

Oftentimes it is helpful for a person, whether therapist, coach, or client, to consider potential benefits and pitfalls of a broad range of relationship styles. Why might someone choose a monogamous relationship? Why might someone choose to have multiple concurrent sex partners without a romantic attachment? Why might someone choose to have multiple concurrent romantic partners? Coming, as most of us do, from a culture of monogamy, it may be a new idea that there are many potential benefits, and many potential drawbacks, to any given type of relationship. Looking deeply into this material might require imagination beyond one's own experience.

Once having identified some benefits and drawbacks to various types of relationships, it is useful to wonder if those benefits and pitfalls are actually related to the relationship type. For instance, if we imagine a person might choose monogamy because they want to feel emotionally secure, we can ask whether monogamy actually creates emotional security. From there, I wonder how a monogamous relationship might be structured to create emotional security and, then, if any form of open relationship could be structured to create emotional security. As you can see, the answers will vary according to the thoughts, beliefs, and preferences of the person who is asking themselves these questions.

I operate from the assumption that most, if not all, relationship benefits and pitfalls could hypothetically occur in any structure of relationship. Remember, I'm not interested in promoting polyamory, I'm interested in helping people imagine success for anything they might undertake and then use their ability to freely choose (or say no) when it comes down to decision-making time. I'd hate to see a relationship dream fail due to a simple failure of imagination. To this end, I developed an exercise called "Examining Assumptions About Relationship Structures" to guide you, or your clients, through this process (see appendix A, "Examining Assumptions About Relationship Structures" worksheet).

EXERCISE: DREAMS AND DESIRES

Another exercise that is important to the formation of a healthy, juicy, alive relationship that brings joy to everyone concerned is that of identifying what is desirable and important in life. Again, this will be a very individual exploration of dreams, desires, and possibilities, and might be done alone, in therapy, or with a partner, depending on personal preference and individual circumstances. Desire is often overlooked in relationships, and here I am talking about much more than sexual desire. The very word *desire* suggests some positive generative energy, as opposed to resignation, boredom, or defeat. It is too easy to settle for what seems possible rather than asking ourselves or our partner(s) about dreams and desires.

Remember that a discussion of what each of you desires, or what your client desires in their relationship or life, is not the same as a decision-making discussion about problem-solving or change. Furthermore, many people expect their partners or friends to ignite desire for them, rather than figuring out how to ignite their own desire and then choosing with whom to share it. For a worksheet about exploring dreams and desires, and taking a look at how to create as much fabulous juiciness as possible in your life, see appendix A, "Dreams and Desires" worksheet.

To close this chapter, I want to share a story that stands as a beautiful example of polyamorous partnership that displays all the qualities of a truly exceptional relationship—mutual respect, warmth, open communication, and lasting regard—even after the relationship comes to an end:

> I discovered polyamory when I was single, dating, and going to graduate school. I learned about polyamory in a graduate school class. About a year later, I met a man while online dating who told me up front that he was married and polyamorous.
>
> Intrigued and curious to learn more about polyamory, I agreed to a first date. We got along really well, and we could tell there was mutual attraction. Then, he introduced me to his wife over coffee at our next meeting. I didn't realize at the time, but I suppose she had "veto power" over me, which turned out to be just fine with me. If his wife hadn't ap-

proved of me, I would personally want nothing to do with that dynamic. But she and I got along swimmingly from the first meeting.

The three of us started getting to know one another and liked one another a lot. I admired their communication patterns, which I observed more and more regularly as we spent time together. Within a month or so, we found ourselves pretty naturally stepping into a triad situation, and I was finding being their girlfriend to be easy, fun, relaxing, hot, and rewarding.

The sex was phenomenal and so different from any sex I'd had before. I loved the ability to "tap out" during partnered sex when I needed a break and have the attention not be on me for a while. Then I'd rejoin, turned on so much by the hot sex between just the two of them. Voyeurism was one of my favorite parts of being a secondary.

Being their secondary opened me up to learn about healthy communication between two married, emotionally mature adults. My parents' marriage was such a disastrously abusive, alcoholic relationship that I never knew that conflict could be healthy until my lovers showed me firsthand. They would have a normal discussion or disagreement and then get over it with resolution or empathy. Mind-blowing! I don't honestly know a better way I could have learned healthy marital communication aside from being immersed in it, in their private home. It was almost like a foreign exchange program to me, being immersed in an entirely new culture and language, that worked.

The other huge thing that being their secondary did for me was open me up to my pansexuality. Getting to know the wife, both sexually and emotionally, and being vulnerable and passionate with her, showed me a lot about how gay I was. I'm not sure I would have been able to meet my (now) wife and open up to her if this woman hadn't taught me so much about my own sexual fluidity.

We all three mostly got on harmoniously for about two years. The relationship as we knew it ended when they decided they needed to move to a different part of the state for work and life, and I knew I wanted to move back to my hometown. We are close friends to this day. They just danced the night away with my wife and me at our wedding.

Conceptualizing the Case
If Polyamory Isn't the Problem, What Is?

Let's say a couple comes to you with a difference of opinion about opening up their relationship. There you are, in your therapy room, on the first visit, and one partner is distressed because they don't want to open the relationship, while the other partner is distressed because they do. Both have good points, both are upset, and both are hoping you will solve the problem for them, probably by taking sides in their favor and helping them change their partner's mind. If we start from a working assumption that polyamory itself is not the problem, then there has to be some way of thinking about the case, and each person's unique feelings and thoughts, that acknowledges that polyamory is a valid relationship option.

This chapter is about how I conceptualize cases: how I think about the problem at hand without pathologizing my clients or any particular belief system or relationship structure, while still identifying areas in which growth is needed to create a secure, happy, collaborative relationship of any kind. Forming an opinion myself about whether someone else should open their relationship is not part of my strategy; I don't have a stake in that game, and it is none of my business. I see my job as helping people become more relational with one another and helping them develop themselves in ways that open the door for co-creating something that works for everyone involved.

While this chapter is heavy on therapy-related concepts, I think it is also relevant to self-help, because these are concepts I find utterly essential in not only my work, but also my own life. If you're reading this to find support for your own personal and relational growth, please don't be intimidated. I discuss these concepts with my own clients in the same language I use in this chapter, and they tell me they find it useful to understand how I think about relationships. The concepts in this chapter have made huge differences in many lives, including the lives of many therapists who have studied them. High-quality personal growth experiences and concepts should be available to everyone.

Much of my thinking about case conceptualization is informed by the Developmental Model of Couples Therapy and the work of Ellyn Bader and Peter Pearson. If you want to read more, I recommend their books, website (couplesinstitute.com), and other materials for further study, in addition to my own blog (instituteforrelationalintimacy.com).

CONCEPTUALIZING THE CASE: WHERE IS DIFFERENTIATION BREAKING DOWN?

Where is differentiation breaking down in the relationship? This is the primary question I ask myself to figure out where things are going wrong and how I might be of help, whether I'm working as a therapist with an individual or relationship client, or having a hard conversation with my partner at our own kitchen table. Almost every relevant relationship skill requires differentiation: the ability to create strong agreements and follow through on them, the skills involved in recovering from broken agreements, the distress tolerance required to have a good discussion about what is meant by fidelity, and so on. There are a million reasons why someone might have difficulty differentiating and a correspondingly wide range of approaches to helping them gain those skills. But, ultimately, if the goal is a relationship in which everyone involved has a voice and a vote, differentiation is the key ingredient.

To find out where differentiation is breaking down, I must assess the presence, or absence, of multiple aspects of differentiation of self. As I talk with my clients, I focus on assessing which parts of differentiation they are strong in and which need some bolstering. Figuring out what is missing enables me to help clients build skills exactly where they need them.

I think of differentiation of self as having three parts:

1. The ability to look inside yourself and identify what you feel, think, believe, and prefer, separate from what anyone else might think, prefer, or want from you.
2. The ability to hold steady while you communicate your unique thoughts, feelings, perceptions, and desires to another person, regardless of what you imagine their response might be.
3. The ability to hold steady and access genuine curiosity and empathy when someone tells you something about their thoughts, beliefs, and perceptions that you find difficult to hear.

It helps me in my work to separate these distinct aspects of differentiation of self, because I've noticed that usually people are stronger in one aspect of differentiation than another. For instance, you might find it relatively easy to hold steady while your partner tells you something challenging but struggle to express your own difficult truths to them or vice versa. Or you (or a friend or partner) might have difficulty identifying what you prefer, especially when there is someone you care about voicing a strong opinion or having a big emotional reaction. Using the parts of differentiation to identify growth areas allows me to focus my efforts for the greatest gain. It also gives me language and a construct to help my clients understand what skills will make the biggest difference for them and why, which helps increase motivation, and therefore success.

CULTURAL CONSIDERATIONS, DIFFERENTIATION, AND MARGINALIZATION

Differentiation of self is all about individuality. In the Western world, it is pretty common to value individuality more than family or cultural assimilation. But that's not necessarily a universal value, and it's important to let your client make the choice about whether they actually *want* to differentiate.

If a person aspires to a relationship in which they feel seen, known, and accepted as their unique and individual self, they will need to develop all three aspects of differentiation of self. Most of my clients get very excited when I talk about the three aspects of differentiation, and most are completely on board with building that skill set. They clearly see where they are challenged and also where their strengths lie. Maybe they have absolutely no idea how to get there, but they can easily see how their life and relationship would improve if they increased those skills. They're on board.

But what if you, or your client, don't actually want to differentiate, don't believe in differentiation, or are very conflicted about it?

Not everyone aspires to being seen and accepted as a unique individual. Some people, and some cultures, value upholding the family connection or carrying forward cultural norms over individuality and unique expression. They may or may not want to shift to a set of cultural values that includes individuation. There are also cultures and subcultures with values systems that include upholding and supporting the decisions of a leader: perhaps a religious leader or a head of family or household. Expressing unique individual opinions that differ from those of the leader is not always encouraged. Most importantly, not everyone wants to change that.

I have often had clients who are wrestling with an internal dilemma: Differentiate from family belief systems or let go of some individual dreams and desires, and uphold the family belief system. When this happens, the first order of business is to resolve that impasse. There is no rule book for life. Rebellion is not for everyone, nor is it a higher form of being. Shifting cultures is a big deal. If someone I care about gets clear that they don't want to differentiate, that is a valid resolution to a complicated dilemma.

Consider the complicated feelings that will arise when a person discovers an aspect of their personal expression or identity that is in direct conflict with family or cultural belief systems. Weighing dilemmas like this often means making some very hard choices. If they choose to differentiate, there will probably be significant losses associated with that choice, or that may be their fear but not actually come to pass, in a best-case scenario. But some people do stand to lose family, friends, or an entire cultural identity. If they choose to uphold the family or cultural belief systems, they will have to let go of some dreams and desires, and possibly even some important parts of themselves. It's not an easy choice, but both options are valid. Your job as a therapist, or good friend, is not to push anyone down one path or another. As a therapist, it is particularly important to hold a space for them to fully explore the tension they are experiencing, so that they have the opportunity to make their own choice.

I don't want to work at cross-purposes with anyone's values or belief system, or set them up for family or cultural disaster they don't see coming and freely choose. For someone who is choosing between their family or culture and their personal identity, it doesn't always have to be all or nothing. There are many valid cases of quiet cultural or family rebellion through the use of secrecy (often referred to as being "in the closet"). This is differentiation plus a twist of privacy. Some would consider that to be a form of cutoff that limits the depth of relationships. I consider it to be a valid choice that sometimes preserves relationships that would otherwise be lost. (If you're looking for more guidance on how to help your clients work through an impasse, refer to the worksheet "Resolving a Dilemma Using Two Chairs" in appendix E.)

The discussion of privacy, being closeted, and cultural identity is relevant to our discussion of polyamory, because relatively few people in polyamorous relationships are "out" to all of the important people in their lives. For many people, whether they will be able to safely come out as polyamorous weighs heavily in their considerations about whether polyamory will be a workable relationship form for them.

DIFFERENTIATION VERSUS INDIVIDUATION

Differentiation and individuation are related but distinct: One is relational, while the other is individually focused. Both refer to identifying one's desires and preferences, but differentiation invites other opinions and takes into account how actions affect everyone involved, whereas individuation involves attaching to one's desires with limited concern for others and, in some cases, regardless of how they might affect others.

Here's an example of an individuated stance: "I've realized I need to return to school. I am not going to be able to get the kind of job I need without an advanced degree. I'd like you to support my decision." A differentiated stance, by contrast, might sound like this: "I have been thinking a lot about going back to school for an advanced degree. I am aware that this is a big decision that will affect us all. I'd like to tell you more about why it feels important to me, and I'd like to hear your thoughts about it as well. In my ideal world, you support this decision, but I recognize it is a big step and one I would like to discuss until we are both clear about what will be best for our family."

Individuation has a "my way or the highway" flavor. Depending on the people involved, it might be subtle or quite abrasive. It is your job as a therapist to be able to identify whether a person's self-definition is relational and whether they *want* it to be relational. Sometimes, particularly when polyamory is part of a person's identity, it might feel to them like opening the relationship is indeed a do-or-die situation, and this can result in a relationship ultimatum.

The question I ask my client is, "Are you sure your happiness actually does depend on exploring or expressing this aspect of yourself?" Sometimes it does. If you have a client who is grappling with identity issues, for instance, with regard to discovering bisexuality, gender identity, or a kinky or polyamorous identity, they are in fact individuating, and the therapy can be difficult simply because they are in a less relational psychic and emotional space. They are engaging in a cost–benefit analysis regarding choosing emerging aspects of themselves versus maintaining the status quo or trying to find a way to merge the two.

If you have clients in this boat and you are finding it to be challenging, that is because doing relational therapy with an individuating client is, indeed, challenging. Having them explore some of their intrapsychic impasses using chair work (see "Resolving a Dilemma Using Two Chairs") in the relationship therapy or coaching session will help their partner understand their perspective more deeply and vice versa, if they can tolerate the discomfort and manage their emotions sufficiently to make progress. Otherwise, collaborating with a good individual therapist might be in order. If you or a friend or partner are individuating, this can also be a very challenging situation, and I strongly recommend therapy to support both the individuation and the relationships that are important to everyone involved. The "Resolving a Dilemma Using Two Chairs" exercise may also be helpful and can be used alone, as well as with a therapist or coach.

DIFFERENTIATION AND POLYAMORY

Polyamory requires people to depart from the rulebook of monogamous relationships and embark on the challenging project of envisioning a new kind of relationship, in collaboration with their partner(s). Succeeding in that project inherently requires that they figure out what they think and want, communicate it to someone else, and hear someone else's opinion and concerns. In other words, it requires a substantial amount of differentiation.

I often say that polyamory is a pressure cooker for differentiation of self. If you don't have the skills going in, you're going to start building them fast. Polyamory can challenge even people who are generally quite differentiated. In part, that's because polyamorous relationships have a way of challenging participants in precisely the areas they find most challenging; in part, it's because differentiation is a lifelong project for everyone, and new relationships are always an opportunity to grow.

The level of differentiation required to do polyamory well is a huge part of why polyamory can be so challenging and why so many people who explore it quickly run into the pitfalls of "polyamory gone wrong." Polyamory puts the hard work of differentiation in front of its participants every day. They may rise spectacularly to meet the challenge— particularly if they have the help of a skilled therapist or had strong relational skills to begin with—or stumble over all kinds of obstacles. In the early phase of transitioning to a polyamorous relationship, most partners end up doing a bit of both.

Discussing opening a relationship can be such a challenging project that people often try to take shortcuts or avoid the hard parts. When that happens, it can easily result in people opening up their relationship before building the skills required to identify, speak up about, and invite others to express feelings, preferences, and desires. (What could go wrong? I'm sure you can guess the answer: pretty much everything.)

Polyamory is a form of consensual nonmonogamy, the operative word here being "consent." Consent requires some skill with every aspect of differentiation of self. To truly consent, you must be able to do a thorough internal self-assessment of what you want, feel, think, and prefer without being unduly influenced by the preferences of others. You also need to be able to share your thoughts, feelings, and preferences with someone else, and manage your own tendency to wobble, waffle, or change your stance completely if you get a lot of pushback. You may need to continue to show up for that conversation over and over again, if it turns out to be a hard conversation. Endurance in tough conversations is foundational to long-term relational health.

Fortunately, it is possible to pinpoint the most pressing growth edge for differentiation pretty quickly. Here are some diagnostic questions I ask to help figure out which parts of differentiation need some strengthening. You can ask yourself these questions too to find out where to focus your personal growth efforts. Knowing where your partner(s) are struggling can help too, because then you know when and how to give them more space and encouragement to express themselves in areas in which they struggle:

> Did you know what you wanted and just couldn't say it, or were you unable to figure out what you wanted?
>
> What prevented you from speaking up about what you preferred?
>
> How did you decide to agree to try it?
>
> Do you have a way of checking in with yourself to figure out what's going on for you?
>
> Do you have a way of bringing up a conversation about your feelings and desires with your partner?
>
> When your partner comes to you with something important, are you able to welcome a discussion of their viewpoint?
>
> When your partner has an opinion that differs from yours, how do you handle that internally?
>
> What do you tell yourself to keep yourself calm enough to say something hard?
>
> What do you tell yourself to keep yourself calm enough to hear something hard?
>
> Can you feel your love for your partner even when you disagree?
>
> Can you feel your partner's love for you, even when you disagree?

IS DIFFERENTIATION A PREREQUISITE FOR POLYAMORY?

Many therapists have offered the opinion that a certain level of differentiation is a necessary prerequisite to opening a relationship. I don't disagree, in theory, but whenever I hear a blanket statement of this kind about any given relationship structure, I like to check it for bias. To check my bias, I ask myself if I also believe this about monogamy. If not, I ask myself whether the differences I perceive are actually valid. So let's apply that strategy here. The twin questions would then be: Is differentiation a prerequisite for monogamy? Is differentiation a prerequisite for polyamory?

I definitely believe that a certain level of differentiation is needed to have a strong, happy, monogamous relationship that honors the preferences, feelings, and dreams of both partners, and demonstrates flexibility and resilience to life's challenges throughout time. I believe the same for polyamory. I would go further and assert that building every aspect of differentiation of self is the primary objective of most of the relational support I do in my practice, whether for monogamous or polyamorous people. So, is differentiation important? Very.

However, what about that word *prerequisite*? I have noticed that some people engage in relationships, whether monogamous or polyamorous, before they have attained a high level of differentiation of self. This makes sense, because building differentiation is a relational project. We learn it by practicing it and discovering what happens when we fail to practice it.

Also, the differentiation that is needed to consent (or object) to trying a polyamorous relationship is the same differentiation that is necessary for engaging in *any* sexually intimate relationship. People generally do not postpone their first sexual relationship until they have a level of differentiation sufficient to give and withdraw consent reliably. Instead they jump in; hope for the best; struggle; and, hopefully, build skills along the way.

The same is true for engaging in a monogamous relationship. People tend to go for it and hope for the best, even though differentiation is indeed helpful for long-term success.

The problems that arise from deficits in differentiation skills are often what bring people to therapy. I find that I am often able to help clients build the skills of differentiation while they struggle in their relationship(s), and I've heard the same from other therapists. In any type of relationship, growth and struggle can, and often do, happen side by side, rather than sequentially. Oftentimes, their relationships grow along with their relationship skills. I've found this to be true for both polyamory and monogamy, even though opening a relationship can be a significant relationship challenge. Often the relationships (whether polyamorous or monogamous) grow and ultimately blossom as the result of the challenge. Of course, sometimes the relationships end, which, although painful, is not necessarily a bad outcome for relational therapy; my objective as a therapist is to support relational connection and growth, including honoring the unique gifts and challenges of everyone concerned, not preserve every relationship.

HOLDING STEADY: THE FOUNDATION OF DIFFERENTIATION

Of course, sometimes the hot-button issues in the relationship are just too upsetting for the partners to handle, and they can't find a way to talk about them that leads to progress and fosters connection between them. Any topic can potentially fall into that category, but I have seen it quite often with infidelity and polyamory.

When one or both partners cannot hold steady, the relational dynamics can become too messy for me to consider the process to be therapeutic. This dysregulation comes in many forms: anger, attacks directed toward the partner, internal collapses like hysterical crying or despair, and even suicidality. It can also be turned outward toward the therapist. Dysregulation can also show up in the opposite way, by shutting down, disassociating, or stonewalling.

Going from experiencing dysregulated (or extremely distressed) emotional responses to holding steady (or feeling grounded and balanced) is an important personal and therapeutic objective. Holding steady underlies the other aspects of differentiation, and developing the skill to hold steady is a matter of addressing underlying attachment wounds and building emotional security, as well as finding new ways of responding in times of stress. I have had clients who made significant progress on emotional regulation and building relational security, both in monogamous relationships and polyamorous ones, simultaneously with discussing hot-button topics. I have also worked with people who were too distressed to participate in the conversation at first and have needed to mend trauma, attachment wounds, past betrayals, and so on, before feeling secure enough to discuss polyamory.

There are a number of strategies for working with this type of challenge if you are a therapist. Sometimes I have seen partners separately, in between relational therapy sessions, to support skill-building in the less fraught environment individual sessions can offer. Alternatively, I might recommend they have individual therapy with another therapist concurrent with the relational therapy. Occasionally, I recommend they postpone the relational therapy entirely for a time and put their energy into their individual therapy goals first. That has been most effective when I've been able to clearly communicate to them or their individual therapists what skills are needed for me to feel comfortable proceeding with the relational therapy.

Strengthening "holding steady" almost always includes work on mending attachment wounds and creating a stronger internal self. That strong internal sense of safety and self-reliance provides the basis for being able to listen and respond with a modicum of balance in difficult conversations and disagreements, and feeling connected and attached even when there is disagreement. This is a project a therapist can be very helpful with, and while challenging in any circumstances, it is also possible as a self-help project. For more on building skill with holding steady, see the section on attachment and regulation later in this chapter.

THE THREE ASPECTS OF DIFFERENTIATION: DEEP DIVE

The First Aspect of Differentiation: Do You Know Who You Are?

The first part of differentiation is the ability to look inside yourself and identify what you feel, think, believe, and prefer, separate from what anyone else might think, prefer, or want from you. This aspect of differentiation is foundational. Without the first aspect of differentiation, the second simply isn't possible: You can't share your beliefs, feelings, and preferences with someone else if you don't know what you think in the first place.

Several major skills that are necessary for a successful polyamorous relationship (and really, any relationship) are built on this foundation. Knowing your preferences and desires enables effective discussion; negotiation; and, eventually, decision-making. It also makes it possible to form an agreement that is in accordance with what you actually want. Given that people tend to break agreements that they don't believe in, that's pretty foundational to negotiating a relationship successfully and building emotional security.

Challenges with the first aspect of differentiation can show up in many ways. The following are a few examples:

Difficulty identifying individual unique thoughts separate from the thoughts, opinions, and belief systems of others who are important to you or stakeholders in the decisions at hand.

Difficulty identifying individual feelings separate from the feelings of others and/or difficulty resisting "catching" or adopting the emotions or thoughts of others.

Difficulty identifying preferences or desires. (If someone wants you to voice an opinion, are you able to generate one?)

Difficulty separating thoughts from feelings, making it hard to figure out what's going on internally.

Believing you have no thoughts, feelings, or desires.

Preferring to be a chameleon, shifting thoughts and desires to match those of others around you.

Struggling with the concept of disagreeing with certain people, organizations, or belief systems.

Judging oneself for having thoughts, feelings, or preferences.

If you have a client with little practice recognizing their own feelings, beliefs, and preferences, it will take some work to develop those skills. The good news is that the payoff is huge, and it gets much easier with practice.

Exercise: Identifying Thoughts and Feelings

If you have little practice identifying your thoughts, feelings, beliefs, and preferences, you are in for a treat. When you get good at knowing what you think and want, it's good for not only you, but also everyone around you, and your relationships. Anyone who cares enough about you to want to know you actually wants to know what you think and how you feel, even if it is sometimes a little hard to talk about or involves disagreement.

I think it's useful to draw a distinction between thoughts and feelings. People often confuse the two, in their actions if not in their language.

Some people feel their emotional reactions in physical ways. For instance, some people feel a knot in their stomach when they feel anxious or afraid. Some people feel an expansion in their chest when they experience joy. If you have a body sensation that seems to be linked to an emotion, the body sensation is a cue that it might be a good time to ask yourself what emotion you are experiencing.

Thoughts are different. Thoughts lead to feelings, but thoughts on their own aren't usually felt in the body. Thoughts emerge from the brain. They express something about ideas and beliefs or how concepts are connected to one another, but they aren't, on their own, sensations.

However, oftentimes thoughts and emotions happen at the same time or close to one another. This is because thoughts create emotions, and sometimes emotions lead to thinking. We often have trouble disentangling the cause from the effect. For instance, if I tell myself, "I'm never going to be able to do this," I'm *creating* an emotion of hopelessness or anxiety. I could change that thought and get a different emotional response. For instance, I could tell myself, "I've got this! I can do it! One step at a time!" Then I would probably experience a more uplifted feeling of hope, determination, or increased focus.

Sometimes emotions just happen, seemingly arising from nowhere. Then we often come up with a thought to make some sense of the emotion. For instance, I might wake up feeling a little blue and then tell myself, "I'm not going to be able to do what I need to do today," which is a thought that matches the emotion. I might also ask myself, "Why me?" or "Why do I feel this way?" and get into a thought loop about why I feel blue. In both cases, I could choose to think a different thought and deliberately create a new emotion. I could also hold space for the emotion and just be with it but not allow myself to pile on with a bunch of negative thoughts or a negative story to go with the feeling.

Can you see how, in each case, you (and your clients) have an option for creating a different emotional experience by choosing a different thought? Feelings are strong and often overpowering, but they are shaped by our patterns of thinking, which we have the power to change.

I created a worksheet to support exploration and developing awareness of thoughts, feelings, and preferences, and beginning to learn to have some control of them; you can use it to develop skill with your own emotion-generating process or help your clients (see the "Daily Practice Identifying Thoughts and Feelings" worksheet in appendix B).

This kind of daily practice will help develop the ability to identify what you're feeling, separate feelings from thoughts, understand how your thoughts and feelings influence one another, and gain some control of how your thoughts end up shaping your feelings. Those are the skills that underpin the first and most foundational aspect of differentiation of self.

Additionally, throughout part III, "Polyamory in the Therapy Room," you will find specific suggestions for how to work with every aspect of differentiation in various situations.

The Second Aspect of Differentiation: Can You Hold Steady while You Share Your Truth?

The second part of differentiation is holding steady while expressing unique and individual thoughts, beliefs, feelings, and preferences to someone else. The goal is to communicate about one's own perspective as clearly, deeply, and fully as possible, regardless of the reaction from the listener. It's important to know that even if the listener is doing a terrible job, it is still possible to hold steady and continue to express yourself clearly and fully.

The person speaking has a great deal of power over how the communication goes. One perspective is that it is important to spit it out, no matter how messy it is, and cleaning it up can come later. In a sense, that's true; for a person who struggles mightily just to speak up at all it is probably a necessary starting point. But it's not the only option.

There are ways of expressing ourselves that are more likely to result in defensiveness on the part of the listener, and there are ways to communicate that make it a lot easier for the listener to stay steady and really understand what is being said. With practice, it serves us better to become more skilled at *how* we speak up.

Ultimately, the goal is for each partner to get so good at maintaining emotional boundaries and cultivating curiosity that they can stay steady and be a leader in the conversation even if the other person is really struggling. But none of us starts there. Managing ourselves in difficult communications is a sophisticated skill set and involves a lot of personal development and practice.

If the communicator is mean, blames or shames their partner, insists on ultimatums, or avoids taking responsibility for their own perceptions, thoughts, and actions, it is not reasonable to still expect that their partner be warm, curious, engaged, and have a lot of stamina for the interaction and warm feelings for the communicator. The second part of differentiation of self has to do with communicating about ourselves, and the success of the communication to some extent depends on *how* we do it. Empowering the communicator to be clear about their ideas, thoughts, feelings, perceptions, preferences, desires, and beliefs is important and exciting work.

Difficulties with the second aspect of differentiation of self can show up in a number of ways. Some examples include the following:

Losing your temper easily, dissolving into tears, being overly dramatic, or shutting down when you meet any resistance while expressing yourself.

Lying, distorting, or omitting the truth when you know (or assume) it's not what your partner wants to hear.

Avoiding difficult conversations.

Not being clear about what you think, feel, believe, desire, and perceive before you engage in the conversation, so your communication is convoluted, confused, confusing, or otherwise difficult to engage with.

Holding in your emotions until you reach a boiling point and explode—as if you have to reach the level of being "angry enough to speak the truth."

Framing desires as needs to communicate emphasis or degree of importance (e.g., "I need you to agree with me about this"), rather than communicating a desire and then adding emphasis in the form of a feeling ("This is what I think, and it feels very important to me because of x, y, z.").

Being passive when it comes to expressing an opinion and then expressing dissatisfaction with how someone else took action.

Making promises you know you can't keep.

Being unclear about your part in a situation or avoiding taking responsibility for your own thoughts, feelings, preferences, actions, and perceptions.

No doubt you've seen plenty of clients who exhibit these patterns in one way or another. It's easy to see how these habits can wreak havoc on a relationship, and yet people are usually just doing their best with the limited tools they have. They may never have been told that it's okay for them to have preferences. They may have been trained from an early age to smooth things over and never rock the boat with an unpopular opinion. They may not have gotten the message that every healthy relationship involves a certain degree of tension and conflict, and that it is not a sign of emergency when partners disagree. As a therapist and, for that matter, as a participant in your own relationships, you have the opportunity to demonstrate that handling tough topics doesn't require passive aggression, deception, blaming others for one's own experience, or stifling our true self.

One way you can help your clients and others around you develop the second aspect of differentiation of self is by modeling it yourself. Your presence can become a place where others experience both speaking and hearing difficult truths in safety. With an individual client, you can provide a safe environment for them to practice getting in touch with and sharing their honest thoughts, feelings, and so on, as well as practice hearing you express some challenging perceptions you have about areas in which your client might be blocked or struggling.

With a relationship or couple client, you can help create a space for the truths and perceptions of each partner to be both spoken and heard, and support all clients in holding steady as they either voice or receive information about others. In any kind of therapy, if your client is courageous enough to provide you with pushback or feedback, you can model differentiation by holding steady, getting curious, and thanking them for trusting you enough to share their thoughts and feelings.

You don't have to be a therapist to model differentiation. In fact, how you show up in your relationships is extremely important. Becoming reliable and steady with your ability to express genuine curiosity, as well as taking responsibility for your own thoughts, feelings, and preferences rather than blaming them on others, will elevate the tone of all of your interactions and show others what is possible.

The initiator/inquirer (I/I) process (see chapter 9 and the worksheets in the appendixes) is a great exercise for helping people practice sharing and receiving challenging information in active, compassionate ways that move the conversation forward. I use it in session and in my own relationships of all kinds. My clients use it at home, too. It provides a foundational structure for any communication, particularly when the discussion is difficult for one or some participants. One of the great strengths of the I/I process is that it encourages depth when exploring a subject. Oftentimes, people, left to their own devices, make the mistake of staying on the surface of the topic, rather than going deep. It might seem like depth would be more difficult for the listener to receive gracefully, but the opposite is more often true. Providing enough depth helps the listener access empathy for the speaker. A full communication should cover not only what was perceived to have happened, but also the feelings that occurred for the person who is speaking and the stories or meaning made by them about the events and feelings. The I/I process strengthens the second aspect of differentiation by inviting the speaker to share in depth.

Exercise: Needs Versus Desires

One strategy to help partners hold steady with difficult conversations is to recognize the difference between needs and desires. Confusion about needs versus desires is common. And it can cause huge problems in communication. This matters because when we talk about what we need, we bring a real urgency into the discussion. "I need . . ." or "I need you to . . ." can sound close to an ultimatum, and that puts a lot of strain on the conversation—strain that tends to be counterproductive when we are trying to nurture the kind of deep, thoughtful conversation that helps partners understand one another more fully. Using the word *need* in a conversation with a partner is rarely a good strategy. Let me explain.

Consider these statements:

"I need you to support my decision."
"I need to cut back my work hours."
"I need to have a more active sex life."
"I need to be in a polyamorous relationship."
"I need you to be monogamous."

Notice how you felt when you read these statements. Now compare to the following:

"This decision is important to me, and I would really like you to understand where I'm coming from."
"I've been thinking about cutting back my work hours and would like to discuss it with you."
"Having an active sex life is very important to me."
"Being in a polyamorous relationship feels very important to me. I would like to discuss it further with you, because I would like you to understand where I'm coming from, even if you don't agree."
"I feel very uncomfortable when you talk about opening the relationship. I've always thought of myself as a monogamous person and imagined myself being in a monogamous relationship."

Posing desires and preferences as needs is not a good strategy for fostering an honest exchange of ideas, as it invites the other person to be defensive. "I need . . ." puts a lot of pressure on the partner to agree, as compared to "I would really prefer . . ." One closes the door, and the other opens the door to a discussion involving multiple perspectives.

Inviting others to express themselves fully is an art form, and the language you use can make a huge difference in the emotional tenor of difficult conversations. I like to use the words "I want" or "I prefer," rather than "I need." If added emphasis is required, I suggest, "This feels very important to me because . . ." If I'm not discussing food, water, safety, or shelter, I remind myself that I'm describing a desire, not a need. I don't want to minimize the importance of the topic or the depth of feeling behind it, I'm just trying to avoid becoming overly dramatic and resist using language that tends to invite reactivity and escalation.

Sometimes someone expresses a desire that they really believe is a need for them. When that happens, it does have the feeling of an ultimatum. That makes it harder for the listener to stay calm and nonreactive, and access curiosity. Although it's not ideal when this happens, I nonetheless encourage the listening/inquiring partner to stay steady and challenge themselves to ask questions that keep their partner expressing themselves more deeply.

In every conversation, the goal is for the discussion to go somewhere it hasn't gone before; ideally somewhere deeper. *Why does it feel so urgent? What does it mean to them? How does it hit the panic button to think about not getting their way?* These questions are more useful than something akin to, "I will leave if you don't give me what I want."

This brings up an interesting distinction. If polyamory is an identity for some and monogamy an identity for others, doesn't that suggest that opening the relationship (or not opening it) is actually a need, more than a desire? It may turn out that there truly is an impasse and partners decide they want very different things. Still, we won't know that until there is some discussion. The more flow, flexibility, and curiosity those conversations can have, the more likely it is that the partners will understand one another and actually have realizations that shift their perspectives.

If a person wants to give the relationship they are currently in a chance of survival and they are really hoping their partner will experience a perspective shift (about, for instance, opening the relationship or not), I truly believe their most effective strategy is to challenge themselves to stay open to all possibilities. It is not realistic to expect our partners to stretch if we aren't willing to stretch. Nobody *has* to change their mind about anything, but allowing your mind to explore many possibilities in a deep and real way can lead to unexpected outcomes.

If you, or your client, would benefit from exploring the differences between needs and desires further, see the "Needs Versus Desires" worksheet in appendix B. For more specific clinical strategies for working with this and the other aspects of differentiation, check out the I/I process in chapter 9.

Exercise: Preparing to Communicate

Another useful practice for communicating effectively is acknowledging the role of your own perspective in what you have to say: "I feel this way, because I believe that . . ." It is important that communication be explicitly framed as being about the speaker's perceptions, feelings, opinions, preferences, thoughts, beliefs, and meaning-making. It's much easier for your listener to avoid getting defensive when you explicitly frame what you're saying in terms of your perspective, rather than asserting it as a universal truth.

You may have heard of "using I statements," which gets at this concept. The idea is that, when I talk to my partner, if I start with "I think . . ." or "I feel . . ." it is a stronger, more empowered, and more boundaried, beginning than, "You . . ." The latter approach invites defensiveness and is likely to be perceived as an attack. My position in the conversation would be much stronger if I could identify my perceptions as perceptions and clearly acknowledge that my partner likely experiences something quite different from me. Strong communication includes open acknowledgment that the participants are different human beings and likely have different ideas, preferences, and opinions.

When it comes to perceptions of events, particularly events that occurred a while ago, two or more people will almost always have different and possibly conflicting memories. This is because we tend to filter everything through our own narratives and perceptions, which are individual and unique. It's particularly true when it comes to arguments: Stressful conversations are hard to remember accurately because the brain focuses on perceived threat, not objective fact. The person who is expressing their thoughts can help their partner not get distracted by trying to square up history by being explicit that they are describing their perceptions, not *the truth of how it happened*.

When I am preparing to communicate something difficult to someone I care about or helping a client do the same, I like to be intentional about the process. Just jumping in and hoping for the best is not as good a strategy as thinking carefully about what you want to say and how you want to say it. I often hear people say they are "waiting for the right time" before bringing something up with their partner, which often results in the conversation never happening or coming up in an angry burst when things really come to a head. I think the timing of difficult conversations can be important but less so if the person who is bringing up the topic becomes skilled at preparation. I consider a conversation to be successful if the person who is bringing up the topic is able to actually say what they intended to say and hold steady while doing so. (Notice that I do not think the success of the conversation to be based on avoiding disagreement or uncomfortable feelings.) To accomplish that, it is important not to communicate from an emotionally activated state or without thought about how you can take full ownership of your own perceptions and avoid blaming, shaming, defending, judging, and other sure-fire reactivity-inviting behaviors. I think preparation helps a lot with this, so I developed a worksheet to guide a fairly involved sequential process (see the "Preparing to Communicate" worksheet in appendix C).

Exercise: Rehearsing Tough Conversations

I oftentimes rehearse my own hard conversations ahead of time, and I recommend you and your clients do the same. Whether you are bringing up a difficult topic with a friend, partner, or family member, or presenting a new exercise or intervention in a therapy session and are uncertain about how it will go, rehearsal can help you sort out what you want to say, actually spit it out, and then work through how you want to respond if things go sideways.

I do this using two chairs, and it is a fun and frequently used strategy in my therapy room. Accessible for self-help, I also use it myself at home. It gives me the opportunity to explore how I might want to respond if the other person becomes upset and results in considerably lowering my anxiety about the conversation because I have explored all of my worst-case scenarios ahead of time (see the "Rehearsing Tough Conversations" worksheet in appendix C).

The Third Aspect of Differentiation: Can You Hold Steady and Engage Actively when Someone Shares Their Truth with You?

The third part of differentiation is holding steady and accessing curiosity and empathy while someone else expresses their thoughts, beliefs, and preferences to you, even if it is hard for you to hear or you don't agree. It requires cultivating curiosity but also the ability to hold two different perspectives simultaneously, which is just about as hard as it sounds.

When someone is struggling with the third aspect of differentiation, it might show up in some of the following ways:

Getting angry and defensive or going on the attack.

Withdrawing emotionally or giving the cold shoulder: "Well, I don't want to hear about this anymore, I'm just going to bed."

Losing focus and engaging elsewhere, like checking e-mail, leaving the room, etc.

Catastrophizing, for instance, creating a story about what a disastrous situation they're in or making dire claims about themselves, their partner, or their future: "You don't love me anymore, I'm a terrible person, this relationship is doomed . . ."

Becoming defensive and trying to explain why their partner's perspective is incorrect, whereas they are blameless and/or misunderstood: "Well, that wouldn't have happened if you had just remembered to . . ." or "You totally missed that I had already done that! You're blaming me for something that isn't even true!"

Minimizing or explaining away their partner's feelings: "You're just grouchy because you didn't have your coffee this morning."

Scrambling to "fix" the situation too quickly, conceding everything and making ill-advised promises: "Of course, you're completely right, whatever you say, I promise never to do anything you don't like ever again."

Agreeing to something they know they can't follow through on, don't believe in, or don't want.

When people don't know how to sit quietly with an uncomfortable emotion, they often do the first thing they think will dispel their discomfort, often unconsciously. That might mean creating a smoke-screen or distraction to change the subject or take attention away from the topic at hand. It might mean shutting down or becoming more activated and going on the attack. However this looks in the moment (and there are an unlimited number of variations), these are ineffective coping strategies that protect from vulnerability. These strategies also prevent the conversation from moving forward in any useful way. Few of us have had great role models for actively engaging with differing viewpoints, and it can take quite a bit of practice to grasp that there are options available and that those options really work well.

To be able to actually hear what a partner is saying and listen long enough to get the full, nuanced picture, you will need to be able to tolerate your own discomfort and possibly also your partner's discomfort. You'll also need to be able to deeply engage with your partner's perspective without abandoning your own (and without even engaging about your own for the time being). That's a project that involves a few different pieces:

Identifying the benefits *to you* of deeply understanding your part-ner's perception, preferences, and situation.

Recognizing your own emotional reactions and patterns, in particu-lar, their earliest signs, so that you notice your defensiveness kick-ing in and manage it *before* you react in a damaging way.

Learning how to self-soothe, so that you can successfully modulate your reaction and control your response, thereby staying with the conversation more productively and for longer.

Disrupting the cycle of negative meaning-making, so that you hear what your partner is telling you without it being distorted by your fears and assumptions.

Cultivating curiosity, so that you can encourage your partner to share the most nuanced version of their perspective.

Setting aside your perspective and engaging with theirs in a deep and open manner, including both being open to seeing it their way and not fearing that seeing it their way will obligate you to abandon a position that feels important to you.

Managing difficult discussions in a thoughtful way by taking breaks when necessary and intentionally building pleasant, connecting time together into your schedule.

Postponing a need to reach resolution, building understanding from every angle, and cultivating empathy and appreciation for your partner's experience and opinion rather than moving prematurely to decision-making.

To tune into what your partner is really saying, you need to be able to set aside your own reactivity, imagined stories, past slights, defensiveness, or desire to argue about "what really happened." This requires holding multiple realities at the same time: your perception of what happened and their perception of what happened. It is also helpful to be aware that you can love someone and express that love while still disagreeing about something or even feeling angry, scared, or disappointed.

This is a challenging project, and it requires going against the brain's automatic defensive responses. During periods of stress, the self-protective part of your brain wants to fight, flee, or freeze; these reactions are helpful in a life-threatening situation but unhelpful when you're just trying to have a tough conversation with a loved one. If a person aspires to respond from their heart with compassion and love, and from their rational brain, which is able to think and experience empathy, they will need to cultivate multiple strategies for managing these automatic responses.

Understanding Automatic Responses and the Self-Protective Brain

I've found a little psychoeducation about neuroscience to be one of the most effective interventions for increasing emotional regulation, regardless of the cause. Learning the basics of neuroscience as it relates to automatic self-protective responses, emotional regulation, and creating change has also made a huge difference in my life; I can personally recommend the project. If you are interested in becoming a happier person, responding in ways that connect rather than distance, and developing new habits or ways of being, you are in luck. With amazing developments in the field of neuroscience in the past 20 or so years, there is a lot of information now available about how to actually accomplish these things.

It is so depathologizing to realize that when you have an out-of-proportion freak-out response, it's just the brain's way of trying to protect you from having something bad you experienced in the past happen again. Our brain, in its effort to keep us safe, remembers every negative thing, so that it can scan for look-alike disasters. But it skips over a lot of positive things, which can leave us with a perception of overarching negativity. When that is applied to our perception of our spouse or our relationship, it can really undermine or prevent a feeling of security, safety, or connection.

It is also helpful to realize that the degree of danger we perceive is generally far out of proportion to most of what we actually encounter these days. We are talking here about the part of the brain that is responsible for the survival of the species. Every single one of us is the most recent descendant of a long line of survivors. The part of our brain that causes us to spot and escape from a predator has been extremely successful in each of our genetic lines—that's why we survived. Eons ago, when the self-protective mechanisms of the brain evolved, there were life-and-death dangers everywhere. Now, we still have the saber-toothed tiger level of freak-out, even when we're in much less danger.

That means, in my opinion, we are all wound *way too tight* when it comes to perceiving threat. The part of our brain that saves us when we are in danger evolved in times when there were saber-toothed tigers, but evolution is a slow process, occurring gradually in a span of millions of years. We still respond in essentially the same way, with a burst of stress hormones that increase our heart rate, sharpen our reflexes, and give us a lot of strength and intensity with which to save our lives. That works out well if someone is coming into your house with a machine gun or you need to single-handedly lift an automobile off of a child, but it's a little bit out of proportion when the threat is actually just your partner pointing a finger at you and saying, "I can't believe you did that!" or your boss getting annoyed with you when you arrive at work 15 minutes late; therefore, most of us experience a lot of disproportionate worry, anxiety, and reactivity until we learn how to control our automatic responses and counteract our natural negativity bias.

I am deliberately painting a vivid image of how this aspect of survival works. I want to acknowledge that when I suggest we might take the more relational stance of managing our automatic responses to get curious in the face of perceived threat, what I'm suggesting feels impossible. It feels impossible because our very survival up to this point has depended on us doing just the opposite. Nonetheless, this is the project that must be undertaken to feel connected, create a secure connection with your closest loved ones, and build a strong teamwork-driven relationship.

The Importance of Motivation

So how does someone go against their most potent survival mechanisms to get genuinely curious about what their partner experienced in yesterday's fight? Well, it takes a lot of self-control and determination. No one ever does this without a very good reason.

Imagine this: Your partner is angry. They are pointing a finger at you and yelling. You feel wronged, like they don't understand you. What they are saying doesn't agree with your perception of what is true. You feel flushed, and you feel the urge to point your finger back at them and defend yourself. Instead, you remember the kind of relationship you want to create. You remember that you want to feel heard when you are upset and that to experience that, you will need to provide that for your partner as well. Besides, it is the kind of person you want to be. You want to be someone your partner can talk to about anything. So you make a decision to go against your strongest instincts in this moment. This is when the rubber meets the road. You bring to mind an image or word that reminds you of your strongest motivation, you take a deep breath, and you say, "I can see you are very upset. Can you tell me more about what has happened to upset you? What did I do that got under your skin?" As you listen, you nod. You can actually relate to what they are telling you. You say, "I can see how that would be very upsetting. I can see how that thing I did really didn't work for you, and now that I understand how that looked from your perspective, I get it."

This is a little like looking right at a saber-toothed tiger and saying, "Here kitty kitty, let me help you get that thorn out of your paw. Where exactly does it hurt?" You would have to believe it was possible or at least worth taking the risk of things going badly. You would need some really gritty personal motivation. You would probably need enough calm, grounded energy to both manage yourself well and share some with the distressed tiger.

Exercise: Accessing Motivation If you, or your client, aren't able to get in touch with internal motivation (that is, any really good reasons of their own) to manage automatic emotionally reactive responses, this will create big problems in relationships and enormous blocks in relational therapy. In my practice, this type of motivation is one of the things I assess early on, because I'm not likely to have much luck helping with difficult partner interactions and tough discussions if one or both partners are not really interested in tackling their emotional reactivity.

If you are interested in learning to manage your own automatic reactions more effectively, the first step is to take a good look at why a part of you is interested in doing so. "Because my partner wants me to" is usually not a good enough reason when the rubber actually meets the road.

Personally, I had to do a lot of work to learn how to manage my automatic reactions. I really understand how hard it can be, and also how worthwhile and rewarding. Here I offer a few ways I can think of that I benefit from managing my automatic emotional responses, in the hopes my reasons might help you get in touch with your own unique motivation.

I really want to know the truth. When I am skilled at hearing the truth from my partner and can get to the point of encouraging difficult disclosures, I have much more confidence that my partner will not hide, distort, or omit the truth. Plus, then I feel like I know my partner better, not just the easy parts, but all the parts. And that helps me feel love for my partner, including their struggles.

When I have more control of my reactions and act in the way that *I* choose, not the way determined by my stressed-out, freaked-out lizard brain, I feel like I'm acting more in accordance with who I truly am. I have less to apologize for the next day and feel better about myself as a person. I experience much less misery; there is nothing more miserable than feeling totally freaked out and triggered. It is fabulous to have some real strategies for getting there less often and out of it more easily when it happens.

Acting on assumptions wastes a lot of time and emotional energy. I would rather spend my energy understanding all of the perspectives that both of us have (frequently there are more than two; one person can hold more than one perspective). It actually feels creative and kind of intellectually stimulating to consider a lot of possibilities, once I remove myself from worrying about the eventual outcome.

When I fully understand what is going on for my partner and more deeply understand what is going on for me, too, we are able to make more thoughtful decisions. We always make great decisions together as a result of having a deeper understanding, so this definitely benefits me. We function well as a team, and we both have one another's interests at heart. Together, we can solve any problem. But to solve a problem well, we both need to understand every facet of the issue.

For a worksheet that walks you through finding your own motivation for change, see the "Accessing Motivation" worksheet in appendix E.

HOLDING STEADY: DIFFERENTIATION GLUE

Let's start the discussion of holding steady by assuming that we are describing smart, insightful people who truly care about one another. I believe that if people can manage their automatic responses, access genuine curiosity, ask excellent questions, draw one another out, and work together for a fuller understanding of a topic, without rushing to any conclusion or decision-making outcome, they *will* be able to figure out solutions that work for both of them. But first, each will need to understand not only what *they* think and feel about the topic, but also what their partner thinks and feels. This requires considerable skill with holding steady.

When I use the term *holding steady*, I mean getting grounded, managing emotions, controlling automatic reactions, and remaining calm enough to express yourself effectively *and* put yourself in someone else's shoes. This is necessary in every aspect of effective communication. There is no part of differentiation that doesn't require holding steady. If you believe in individuality and the strengths associated with diversity of thought, opinion, and experience, there is no relationship structure that isn't strengthened by differentiation.

Dan Siegel developed the concept of a "window of tolerance." It's a construct that can help therapists and clients understand and manage their emotions, particularly the emotions that accompany difficult experiences and interactions. The window of tolerance is the level of emotional arousal in which we are still able to think, get curious, and respond congruently. A person can be outside their window of tolerance either in the direction of hypoarousal (checked out, shut down, disassociated) or hyperarousal (angry, acting out, yelling). When a person is outside of their window of tolerance, they will have difficulty interacting or expressing themselves in effective ways. First, they need to get back within their window of tolerance. Clients with a history of trauma or attachment wounds often have a much smaller window of tolerance than other people, meaning they have more difficulty regulating their emotions and are more likely to feel unsettled to the point of having difficulty thinking, processing, and responding.

This is an example of how attachment, neuroscience, and differentiation cannot be separated. Your relational therapy client will need to be able to figure out what they want and feel, express that to their partner, and stay steady when their partner shares something with them that they may find hard to hear. But if they cannot tolerate some aspect of this differentiation skill set without dysregulation (whether in the form of hyperarousal or hypoarousal), they'll need to learn how to self-regulate sufficiently to participate in the discussion first. If they have attachment wounds or trauma in their past, they may have a reduced window of tolerance, making it particularly difficult to self-regulate.

The aforementioned terms and techniques can be easily researched on the internet, and there is a lot of information out there about emotional regulation. My purpose here isn't to provide a primer on neuroscience, but rather to let you know there are many ways to approach the issue, and it is inevitable that you will have to work with automatic emotional self-protective responses and managing the window of tolerance if you are going to work with relationship issues or other types of distressful content in therapy.

The good news is that a person absolutely can heal their trauma and expand their window of tolerance as a result. A good therapist, counselor, or coach can help. Sometimes this deep personal work can be done in conjunction with relational therapy. Other times it is accomplished more effectively with individual therapy, perhaps with a trauma specialist.

Regulation

There are a number of techniques that can help a client (or yourself or your partner) come back into their window of tolerance, and it's good to have a repertoire on hand. There is little point in continuing a conversation once any participant becomes significantly dysregulated, flooded, or unsettled, so when this happens, whether in therapy or life, I take it as an opportunity to do some in situ practice with regulation. When there are two or more people involved, you can experiment with self-regulation and co-regulation techniques. With practice, everyone can get better at bringing themselves back into the window of tolerance, whether that means getting more present and active (less checked-out) or more present and calmer (less activated). The following are some strategies you might explore:

Using EFT tapping or other forms of energy work, including tapping the karate-chop point on the side of the palm or crossing arms over the chest and tapping alternate sides near the collar bones in a calm, steady rhythm.

Tossing a ball back and forth until things calm down and conversation is possible again; you might continue tossing the ball while continuing to talk.

Taking long, slow, pressurized exhales; imagine holding a candle flame at arm's length and blowing just enough to make the flame wobble but not hard enough to extinguish it.

Taking a time-out; this may be needed when the level of dysregulation is high, because it takes quite a bit of time for the stress hormones associated with distress to be metabolized. You might take a break and walk around the block or get a glass of water if just a brief break will suffice. Sometimes that is not sufficient; if at home, definitely take a full time-out. If in a therapy session, rather than end the session, I would take the opportunity to help clients regulate by shifting the focus of the session to a mindfulness practice about being embodied, calm, and in the moment rather than wrapped up in thinking and reacting.

Spreading your arms to hold an enormous imaginary ball in front of your body; lift it and lower it, breathing into your expanded rib cage.

Holding hands with your partner or sitting back-to-back with backs touching to calm the body and lead to relaxation. Some people like to take a break every five or 10 minutes with a difficult conversation and just hug, hold hands, or otherwise co-regulate until calm before resuming the conversation.

Getting in motion by doing jumping jacks or dancing to uplifting or inspiring music for a few minutes as a state-changer.

Whatever technique you use the goal is to break the chain of thinking and meaning-making; become embodied and aware of the present moment; create a feeling of safety in the moment; and get the breath expanding the chest and belly, and fully exhaling, rather than being locked up tight in the upper chest. The most effective strategy will depend on the client's preferences and whether they need to increase or decrease their level of arousal to get back to the window of tolerance.

Self-Regulation and Co-regulation

Self-regulation, co-regulation, and differentiation are important parts of any relationship, including an open one. Most therapists already have a strong repertoire for helping clients increase self-regulation and co-regulation. That said, some relationship therapy modalities focus heavily on co-regulation and don't attach as much weight to self-regulation and differentiation. Personally, I think that they are just as important, and a relationship can't truly flourish without all three firmly in place. Without the ability to figure out what you desire, feel, and prefer, and share that information with your partner, you would be left praying for your partner to be an accurate mind reader. That's an *extremely* shaky construct for pursuing an open relationship (or, for that matter, happiness in general). Focusing on co-regulation to the exclusion of differentiation and self-regulation can also set up an environment where it is hard for people to strongly disagree. The potential pitfall there is, of course, resorting to half-truths, poorly formed agreements, deception, out-and-out lies, or infidelity, all of which are the opposite of consensual and ethical nonmonogamy. Also, there are times in any relationship when you can't gain access to your partner for co-regulation or soothing. Everyone has moments when they don't have the emotional bandwidth or willingness to set their own agenda aside and help with yours. At times like that, self-regulation has to be the order of the day.

Any time one person notices that another is distressed and throws them a lifeline of some sort, they are co-regulating. A long hug or snuggle is co-regulation. Reaching out a hand when your friend is crying is offering co-regulation. Petting your cat is co-regulation of a different kind. Telling your partner you are struggling and asking them to help you turn your thoughts to a more positive direction is asking them to help you regulate.

Co-regulation is gorgeous, transcendent, and extremely powerful. It has the ability to heal deep and old wounds. But the downside of co-regulation is that you can't do it by yourself. You need a willing partner or friend (or pet) to achieve it. It's wonderful when it happens, but I want my clients to have access to techniques that make them feel happy, calm, and grounded even when they don't have someone else around who's willing and able to help them get there.

Writing in your journal, meditating, going for a run, or taking a warm bath are examples of self-regulation. Doing an exercise identifying thoughts that lead to feelings and deliberately changing your thoughts to get to a new emotional experience is a powerful strategy for self-regulation (see the "Daily Practice Identifying Thoughts and Feelings" worksheet in appendix B and the "Creating Personal Change" worksheet in appendix E). Anything that helps you feel calm and grounded is self-regulation. Whenever you engage in an activity for the purpose of shifting your emotional state, you're self-regulating.

Exercise: Holding Steady Self-Coaching

Most people, myself included, did not get a good early education in self-regulation strategies or ways to help ourselves calm and get grounded during times of stress. Instead, most of us have a hefty repertoire of punishing self-talk, self-blame, self-indictment, and self-sabotage. If this describes you, or your client, a new repertoire is needed. When reaching toward a new skill, for instance, staying calm and getting curious when your partner tells you something that is important to them but difficult for you to hear, you will probably need a good internal coach to help you achieve your objective rather than freaking out or shutting down (see the "Holding Steady Self-Coaching Worksheet" in appendix B).

THE RELEVANCE OF ATTACHMENT

Secure attachment, whether developed in childhood or created later from reparative experiences, cultivates a number of important relational skills. Some examples are as follows:

The ability to tolerate differences
The ability to understand multiple viewpoints without letting go of
    our own
The ability to empathize with completely different perceptions than
    our own
The ability to self-soothe during a separation or disappointment
The ability to trust that the other person will return
The ability to get curious about and understand someone else's
    meaning-making
The ability to feel safe enough in a relationship to risk disagreeing
The ability to feel someone else's love for us even when we are apart
    from them
The ability to feel love despite disagreement, anger, or disappointment
An awareness of safety at home base, allowing exploration, risk-
    taking, and recovery from life's disappointments

When therapeutic interventions or personal attempts directed at increasing differentiation aren't working and the "holding steady" skill set is wobbly, it will probably be necessary to attend to developing an increased sense of security in the world, both independently and relationally, to have the necessary foundation for tolerating discomfort and interpersonal differences, as well as identifying and expressing unique viewpoints. This might include mending attachment wounds, healing past trauma, and/or reworking beliefs or coping strategies that may have been developed in childhood to good effect but are not serving relational goals in adulthood.

There are four attachment styles: secure, anxious, avoidant, and disorganized. The secure attachment style might have emerged from childhood experiences of connection and security, or it might have been developed later as a result of reparative experiences, in which case it is described as "earned secure." This is important to understand, because it is certainly possible to create reparative experiences in a relationship, and/or as a result of therapy, that result in an increased sense of internal security. There is a lot written about attachment and its importance in a relationship; a quick internet search will get you as much information as you could possibly want. I particularly like Stan Tatkin's books (see bibliography) for learning how to help clients understand different attachment styles between partners and co-create reparative experiences for themselves and one another.

I think it bears mentioning that a person may have had a relatively happy childhood and still have developed coping strategies that create relational problems later. Some people, of course, also have deep wounding from loss, trauma, and so on, that may create issues later. Everyone experiences challenges in childhood, whether large or small, and we all have developed strategies for managing those challenges. Our child selves developed coping strategies from the perspective of a child's mind and a child's skill set, and the powerlessness of a child who is dependent on others for their very existence. Kids are smart and develop ways of solving their problems that generally work very well. But then we grow up, have adult relationships, and discover that many coping strategies we developed as youngsters are ineffective as adults in adult relationships. Most people can benefit from developing new, more empowered, and collaborative relational stances. This results in the ability to feel emotionally safe and balanced in stressful interpersonal situations, for instance, when discussing distressing topics.

Imagine a client who is too distressed to stay within their window of tolerance with a given topic. Or perhaps this describes you on occasion. When someone is highly distressed, the first order of business has to be helping them heal internally just enough to feel safe on the planet so they can tolerate the discomfort of having significant differences of opinion with their partner. By the way, this used to describe me and occasionally still does, so if you find yourself having difficulty holding steady, you're in good company. Don't beat yourself up about it, but know that it is possible to feel *so much better*! I wish someone had helped me put all the pieces together, including issues of attachment, differentiation, and neuroscience when I was much younger. In particular, it would have been helpful to know that emotional groundedness during times of stress is possible, that even shutting down is a kind of ungroundedness, and that achieving internal balance is possible and has many amazing benefits, all of which actually accrue to me, not primarily to my partner or anyone else. This empowering stance is one I hope to communicate to everyone I work with.

This can sometimes be a complicated course of therapy: working deeply with family-of-origin issues, healing trauma, and cultivating resilience. With luck, there might be a partner with more highly developed skills at holding steady who can help create reparative experiences. It isn't productive to try to discuss a topic when the participants are not within their window of tolerance, and of course the project is particularly challenging if everyone involved is having difficulty holding steady simultaneously. I strongly believe in the resourcefulness of human beings and our strong drive toward personal growth and healing. If you find yourself wanting extra support, help, or guidance, working toward feeling more secure in the world is a situation where a therapist should be able to help quite a lot.

For therapists, it is important to understand how to conceptualize cases where there are high levels of distress. Clients may tell you they won't stay in therapy if they can't discuss the topic they came to you for, for instance. But if they can't stay in their window of tolerance, they are going to experience something like trauma as a result of the dysregulated discussions, whether from a sense of abandonment because the distressed party is shut down or disassociated, or the attack and defensiveness of hyperarousal. It is extremely distressing as a therapist to witness this, let alone condone and be a part of it. And, of course, it is even more distressing to be the one who is that upset and unsettled. In fact, if the relational therapy is focusing on a stretch goal, meaning something that requires some growth and development to achieve, this level of distress can be a contraindication to discussing that topic. The topic at hand may be better tabled and the relational therapy adjusted to having the goal of stabilizing and creating safety and security relationally. Or it might make sense to shift to individual therapy with the goal of healing residual issues from the past and increasing skills associated with self-regulation and resilience in preparation for being able to tolerate hard conversations about the hot-button issue. But it won't work to have relational therapy that involves being outside of the window of tolerance for a majority of time either in session or at home. When differentiation is too distressing, attachment-based interventions are in order.

DEVELOPMENTAL STAGES OF RELATIONSHIP

Many times it helps just to normalize the challenge. An emerging awareness of differences is normal in relationships and often accompanied by relational distress. I let my clients know that it is normal and expectable for relationships to progress through stages, not unlike the stages of development we go through as children. This is the underlying concept of Bader and Pearson's Developmental Model of Couples Therapy. It can be very comforting to know that the bumps people face in their relationships are not necessarily an indication of a fatally flawed relationship. According to Bader and Pearson, the first relationship stage is symbiosis, in which couples establish a strong bond, focus on their similarities, and often make an effort to minimize differences. Creating this foundation of unity is an important developmental task and provides the stability and sense of security needed to navigate the inevitable challenges ahead.

But in the normal course of a relationship, symbiosis passes and, in an often-bumpy path, gradually gives way to differentiation. Partners go from being tightly bonded and focused on their similarities to be-coming increasingly aware of their differences and unique, sometimes divergent viewpoints. This can create a lot of tension and is a common time for couples to seek relationship help from a counselor, coach, or therapist. If the partners don't know this is a normal and expectable stage, they might think it is a bad sign or indicates something dire is wrong with the relationship. Explaining the tasks associated with dif-ferentiation is very helpful. I also highlight the deeper intimacy that comes when we successfully navigate differentiation and can move on to other stages of relationship, including exploration (increased independence without fear of losing connection), reconnecting (mov-ing easily between more togetherness and more independence), and synergy (where strengths of both are readily accessed, teamwork is strong, both function independently, and the whole is much larger than the sum of the parts). It is also not uncommon for a person or couple to be strongly differentiated in many areas of life, including their relation-ship, but then experience some situational challenge in their relation-ship and need to refocus on strengthening differentiation again.

EMOTIONAL CONTAGION FOR THE FORCES OF GOOD

One sign of differentiation is knowing how you feel and maintaining some control of your own internal state even when others are quite upset. We have all experienced getting upset because others are upset or feeling anxious because we are in a situation where a lot of people are feeling upset or anxious. Getting control of our own emotional state despite whatever other people are experiencing is a great skill to develop. It can be extremely liberating.

The great news about emotional contagion is that positive emo-tions can be contagious, too. This means that a strong self-regulator and communicator can stabilize the system, simply by holding steady. Sometimes this involves setting their perspective aside and getting deeply curious about another person's perspective, even to the point of expressing empathy for an opinion or viewpoint opposite their own.

Sometimes it involves resisting the impulse to change one's viewpoint in a conflict-avoidant reaction to a partner's discomfort. If this sounds like the job a therapist does every day, you're right. But you can also do it in your personal relationships. It is a superpower well worth cultivating, and that is accessible to everyone and of benefit to all.

When I used to be a midwife, I used my own emotional state to regulate others on a regular basis, and quite deliberately. Before I entered the house or room where the birth was taking place, I would pause and adjust myself internally in preparation for whatever was about to happen. I would intentionally down-regulate, so that when I entered the situation, I could set a calm tone and bring down the anxiety of anyone who might be feeling a little wound up. My speech was soft, calm, and grounded, and I was very conscious of cultivating and sharing that calm with those around me. I use the same skills as a therapist, and also a partner and friend. When things are feeling tense, I get as grounded as possible. I do what I can to stay calm and communicate my calm, without minimizing anything that is being said. As a therapist, you get plenty of opportunities to practice these skills, and I'll bet you're already pretty great at them.

The next step is to let your clients know it is possible for them to do this too, and practice it in your own relationships. I tell my clients that *no matter* how badly their partner is behaving, they always have choices to make about their own behavior and emotional response. They always have the ability to shift the course of the conversation toward the light. They can choose to be a leader and turn the tone of the conversation toward generosity of spirit, curiosity, calm, and validation. In extreme examples, they can choose to take a time-out in a loving manner to end the toxic interaction. In the words of Peter Pearson,

> It's easy to be considerate and loving to your partner when the vistas are magnificent, the sun is shining, and breezes are gentle. But when it gets bone-chilling cold, you're hungry and tired, and your partner is whining and sniveling about how you got them into this mess, that's when you get tested. Your leadership and your character get tested. You can join the finger-pointing or become how you aspire to become.

EXERCISE: TIME-OUT, OR EMOTIONAL REGULATION FOR DIFFICULT CONVERSATIONS

Having a time-out strategy in place is crucial for managing escalation in difficult situations and hard conversations. We all have a limbic system and a lizard brain, the parts of the brain Dan Siegel describes as the "downstairs brain," or "thumb," and brainstem, or "palm," in his hand model of the brain. These are the parts of the brain that store emotional memory; scan for danger; and cause us to immediately fight, freeze, or flee when something potentially life-threatening happens. These parts of our brain are responsible for the survival of our species; they motivate us to save ourselves at the expense of others, if necessary. Without this lifesaving capacity, our ancestors would have been eaten by predators long ago, and we wouldn't be here today. When our self-protective brain perceives threat, it dumps a cascade of stress-related chemicals into the bloodstream so you can outrun a tiger or lift a boulder off your foot. This part of the brain is not smart, just reactive. It has no logic and no empathy. It's not interested in being polite.

In the 21st century, we don't have nearly as many saber-toothed tigers, but our self-protective brains are still fine-tuned for life-threatening danger. Remember, your lizard and limbic brain's jobs are *not* discernment. They will respond in less than a millisecond to anything that might in some way resemble a memory of trauma, embarrassment, disappointment, or pain. So, when your spouse snaps at you, you get a dump of stress hormones that makes you respond as if they were a guy with a machine gun coming at you fast. Your self-protective mechanism doesn't discern between an embarrassing moment and a life-threatening one. It helps you avoid all perceived threats.

When triggered, you can no longer access the parts of your brain that use logic or, possibly more importantly, empathy. The thinking, connecting, and processing parts of your brain are disconnected in this stressed-out state. It takes quite a bit of time to metabolize all those stress hormones and once again become able to access logic, curiosity, and empathy. In a relationship context, the pivotal moment is the one when a discussion turns into a fight. Voices are raised, fingers pointed, and doors slammed, and you see your partner as "them" rather than "us" and go to war. You or your partner are likely to say hurtful things that you will later regret.

Later, if you try to remember exactly what happened during the fight, you're going to remember every bad feeling and every hurtful thing that was said. So will your partner, but they will be remembering the things *you* said, and the two of you probably won't be able to agree on the sequence of events that led to this situation or exactly what happened. Once that discussion became a fight, your self-protective brain took charge of focusing on every negative feeling or perceived slight, and the logical and connecting parts of your brain couldn't establish a coherent sequence of events and store it in an orderly fashion. This is why it is not productive to go back over an old fight blow by blow.

When you get triggered during an argument with your partner, anything you say or do is likely to damage your relationship. When you're triggered, your choices boil down to fight, flee, faint, fawn, or freeze. If you fight, you will say hurtful things you can't take back. If you shut down or leave the scene, your partner will perceive it as abandonment, which may be less dramatic but is just as damaging.

Because you love your partner and don't want to say or do hurtful things, or create a messy tangle that is hard to unravel later, everyone concerned must agree on a strategy that reminds you to stop talking, interacting, and causing damage, and start self-soothing, dialing back the stress, and getting some calm under your feet. This is much easier said than done, but I can't stress enough how important it is not to continue fighting once triggered. Damage is the only possible outcome, and once caused, this type of damage is difficult to mend, because we are so brilliant at hurting those we love in exactly the ways that will do the most damage.

I created a handout describing the time-out exercise in detail, including the aforementioned information and going much further, including the actual steps to take to come to a full stop and get grounded again, and reengage in the discussion at hand. I give this handout to clients who struggle with taking breaks, slowing down, and controlling difficult conversations or anyone who recounts a story of a fight, rather than a productive discussion (see "Time-Out Exercise" in appendix B).

CHAPTER 9

Using the Initiator/Inquirer Process to Support Differentiation and Move Toward Decisions

THE INITIATOR/INQUIRER PROCESS

Relationship therapy relating to polyamory is a combination of providing information and debunking myths; facilitating conversations; and, eventually, supporting decision-making. Ideally all of this happens seamlessly, while increasing understanding, deepening connection, and increasing security between partners even as they explore their differences. Hopefully as this unfolds, partners discover new and richer layers of love and respect for one another, many times as a direct result of better understanding one another's unique perspectives, challenges, and strengths. Sometimes, you will find that clients awaken or reawaken sexy connections between them in the process; after all, the world wouldn't be very exciting if we were all the same. Sometimes the spark flickers and almost goes out from years of avoiding difficult conversations or molding ourselves to be as similar as possible; once you start exploring differences, particularly with some depth, the spark can revive as a beautiful and semieffortless side effect of curiosity, good attention, and deeper exploration.

It is helpful to have some tried-and-true strategies for managing difficult conversations in increasingly differentiated ways and helping others do so. The therapeutic tool I use most often for this is the initiator/inquirer (I/I) process from the Developmental Model of Relationship Therapy. On the surface, it is a structured way of communicating, much like active listening, but with a few crucial twists that take it to the next level. It's one of the most powerful tools in my kit, serving simultaneously to support differentiation and take note of where specific skills are in need of strengthening. Since most people could use some help building the complex skill set of differentiation, I end up using the process frequently, personally, and professionally. For many of my clients, the bulk of their sessions are spent using the I/I. If you are doing a self-help skill-building project, I think you will love the I/I. Without a facilitator (coach or therapist) present, you will have to self-monitor to discover where you are experiencing challenges or getting stuck, but it is helpful to be able to identify where to focus your efforts. Most of us can make significant changes but not all at once. Focus your efforts on building one skill you would like to develop that will make a difference to you and your relationship. Eventually that skill will become easier, and then it is time to add another.

While some of the components of the initiator/inquirer process seem simple, they actually require substantial development, so be patient with one another, your clients, and yourself. Take note of small, incremental progress, and celebrate the successes.

I'm deeply grateful to Ellyn Bader and Peter Pearson for developing this tool and generously permitting me to share it with you.

Setting Up the Initiator/Inquirer Process

When I introduce the I/I in therapy, I start by explaining the two roles, which I do with support from the handouts in appendix D. First, I give each partner the handouts that describe the roles (one for initiator, one for inquirer) so they can follow along as I explain the particular tasks and challenges associated with each role.

The Initiator

The *initiator* is the person who has something about themselves or their experience, preferences, or feelings that they want their partner(s) to understand. They will try to take their communication to a deeper level than they have previously by talking about themselves, their perceptions, their emotions, the meanings they are making of the situation, how it is getting under their skin, and where they are stuck. This is quite different from blaming or finger-pointing; it is a complicated project that starts with figuring out what you think, feel, and prefer separate from what anyone else might want from you. Then it moves into sharing that information with a partner, as the initiator.

I want the initiator to have the experience of feeling heard and feeling like their partner "gets" them. For this to happen, the inquirer has to be able to stay present with difficult material. The initiator has a role in making that more likely; if they make it clear they are expressing their perceptions, it will be easier for the inquirer to hold steady and hear what they are saying. If they blame, shame, or indict the character of the inquirer, it will be more challenging for the inquirer to hear what they are saying and access curiosity and empathy. I encourage initiators to do the following:

Get clear on what they want their partner to understand about their own thoughts, feelings, and perceptions before they start talking.

Focus on one thing at a time.

Use language that will make it easier for the inquirer to hear them. For instance, they should avoid exaggerating or using words they know will distract or upset their partner.

Talk about themselves and their feelings, perceptions, and meanings, rather than their partner.

Express themselves in a way that isn't intended to make their partner feel bad about themselves.

Manage their tone of voice, intensity level, body language, and facial expressions.

The Inquirer

The *inquirer* is the person who is listening to the initiator. The inquirer is focusing their attention on understanding their partner in a new way. Their goal is to figure out what to say, ask, and do to encourage the initiator to keep expressing themselves, increasingly deeply and honestly. When this goes well, the inquirer learns a lot about how the initiator sees the world. When it goes *really* well, it is magical, because the initiator also learns more about themselves. I encourage the inquirer to do the following:

Focus on hearing what their partner is trying to express to them.

Stay in their own psychic space, meaning engaging in whatever self-talk is needed to stay clear that their partner, the initiator, is talking about their own experience and perceptions, and not take it personally even if it sounds personal.

Cultivate curiosity about their partner's perspective.

Stay focused on the partner's experience.

Avoid defensiveness, leading questions aimed to convince, and other reactivity.

Manage their body language, facial expressions, and tone.

Once I have described both roles and answered any questions, I ask the partners to identify where they think they might get stuck with a really tough issue and reinforce their motivation by going over whether they want to get past that, and why. Then I ask for permission to coach them if they seem to be taking a wrong turn on the way to their goal. This makes more room for me to be directive, which is often necessary. I want them to invite me to coach; that way, my frequent interruptions and clarifications can be framed as helping them reach their goal, rather than challenging or controlling them or saying they're wrong.

Everyone in the conversation is encouraged to express what is true for them, even if it is difficult for the other to hear. They do this while still remaining relational, by which I mean fostering connection that doesn't depend on agreement. The inquirer is challenged to access a deep curiosity about the initiator's perspective, as well as tap into their empathy and express some understanding of the initiator's viewpoint.

This is a pretty radical move for many people, because many people think that expressing empathy or validating someone's perspective implies agreement. In the initiator/inquirer process, it is made clear that empathy does not require or even imply agreement. This process has nothing to do with compromise or even decision-making. Instead, it is about exploring the world through someone else's eyes and allowing someone you care about to help you explore your own world more deeply than you otherwise might have by asking great questions and really leaning into curiosity.

However, the ability to hold two perspectives with love, curiosity, and respect, when one of those perspectives feels scary or unwelcome, is a very sophisticated developmental task. By that I mean, you have to develop the capacity to do it, rather than just following some easy steps. This is what makes it a growth process, an adventure, and a personal challenge. The rewards are many. One big one is the sense of personal empowerment that comes from knowing you can discuss anything without coming unglued. Another is the incredible feeling of expansion that comes from really showing up as the kind of person you want to be in a relationship—curious, loving, and a good listener, perhaps. And it is also wonderful to know you will be able to follow through on your agreements, because deep in your bones you know you can disagree with your partner openly and not have to go underground to avoid disagreement.

A lot of shifting can happen as this process unfolds, as empathy and increased depth often lead to new understanding and new possibilities. There is no way to predict the outcome, but in my experience it is crucial to postpone any decision-making until the issue can marinate and be nurtured by this process.

The I/I is a brilliant intervention, because it directly addresses every aspect of differentiation of self. You can immediately identify where each partner becomes challenged and see what ineffective coping strategies they use in times of stress. You can help them develop the three parts of differentiation separately, as well as the "holding steady" piece, and help them build skills in situ in your office so they have a new experience and a clear idea of effective next steps.

In the previous chapter, I discuss each part of differentiation of self in depth. The I/I is the primary tool I use to identify where each partner is struggling in terms of differentiation. As the partners discuss their concerns, I can coach them and help them avoid the pitfalls they have habitually fallen into, and learn new ways of being. I want them to begin to have a new experience; theory won't build the neural pathway. But actually doing it in my therapy room will begin to create the new way of being that they can then strengthen in subsequent sessions and between sessions.

Skill-Building Using the I/I

When working with someone using the I/I, I want to help them to sharpen a number of skills and experience some increased awareness. If you are using it yourself in your own relationship, you can use the following list to guide you:

Accepting difference. Each partner is a unique individual, and their differences don't make one right and the other wrong. There can be multiple perspectives, each of them valid, and partners don't have to agree or share the same perspective to understand and empathize with one another's perceptions.

Maintaining emotional boundaries. When Sally expresses something about her perceptions, feelings, and thoughts, she is saying something about herself. Even if she is saying, "It drives me nuts when you go out on a date with someone else, and I wish you wouldn't do that," she is saying something about her own preferences and desires. Dave gets to decide what, if anything, to do with it, but his first step is to understand her perspective, feelings, and experience more deeply.

Holding steady, or self-regulation. You will see if Sally has a difficult time staying calm and grounded when expressing herself. Notice if she is clear or fuzzy; does she choose one thought to express, or does she wander around and pile on a bunch of tangential stuff? Is she able to state her perception as such, or does she put it as if it were an indictment of Dave? You will also notice if Dave listens easily and calmly or if he tends to get defensive, rush to a solution, argue with her perception that he went on a date, etc.

Accessing curiosity. If Dave is able to access curiosity about what Sally is saying, he will be able to ask questions that help her go deeper and further describe her experience. For instance, he might ask, "What is it about me going on a date that drives you nuts?" or "What do you experience when you feel driven nuts?" or "What aspect of me going on a date gets under your skin so much?" Any of those questions will help Sally go to a new level with her communication and also help Dave gather information about how she experiences him dating other people.

Tolerating the discomfort of not knowing how things will be resolved. Can the partners stay in the tension of their conversation, accessing curiosity and exploring their feelings and thoughts, without rushing to relieve the tension by "solving the problem"? This is also challenging for therapists, so I'll ask them the same question: Can you hold the space for tension, potentially for many weeks, while the clients work with the complexity of their dilemma and responses to one another? Can you help them manage the tension and reach for curiosity and empathy rather than allowing or encouraging them to rush to solve the problem? Imagine acknowledging that things feel unsettled and uncomfortable, and that there is a lot of energy in the room, with much uncertainty, and all of that can exist and the partners can still love and respect one another, and choose to connect deeply with one another, even without knowing how they will eventually resolve the issue.

Deepening the conversation. Both roles, the initiator and the inquirer, can take the conversation to a deeper level. If one partner is really struggling, the other can take the lead and contribute a lot of depth and calm, stabilizing the situation and creating emotional safety by accessing and expressing curiosity. Together, they will need to go deep and cover not only what happened or is happening, but also their emotions, the stories they told themselves about it, the meanings they made about the situation, and how it affected them.

Co-regulating. Do they help one another when things feel difficult? Do they comfort one another? Are they emotionally gentle with one another? Do they reassure one another, complement one another, and thank one another for sharing? Are they able to do those things without giving up on their point of view or minimizing their personal concerns?

Empathizing even without agreement. Even if the conversation is stressful, it is possible for partners to empathize. It does require understanding enough about the other's experience to actually *feel* for them, so curiosity is a first step. The goal is to have to an ah-ha moment, like, "Oh! I get it! I wouldn't have put it together like you did, but I can see how you arrived at that. I can see how that makes sense from your perspective."

Delaying gratification. The inquirer will need to hold back their desire to get a word in edgewise, voice their disagreement, be the center of attention, etc. It takes a lot of grit to get curious about one's partner's perspective for a nice, long time. At first, couples might not be able to tolerate staying in one role for more than a few minutes. But as they build skill, they will be able to sustain tension and attention on someone else, and delay the gratification of voicing their opinion or feeling heard or getting validated. Eventually there might be one initiator per session. As they build skill, I challenge them both to stay with just one role for a little bit longer.

Listening deeply. A big reason the initiator/inquirer works is that it gives partners the experience of feeling deeply heard and understood. If you feel that your partner has truly listened to you and, better yet, actually "gets" you, it doesn't matter as much if you don't come to an agreement. Feeling "gotten" makes differences much easier to tolerate.

Creating emotional security. There is nothing as amazing as being in a relationship in which your partner makes the effort to manage themselves sufficiently to truly understand your perspective and emotions, even when in deep opposition to their own experience or preference. This is the foundation for security. Without this, we all have to agree with one another to feel emotionally safe, and obviously that's not going to happen. You are helping your clients build the skills needed to have peace, safety, and connection even with diversity. You are creating world peace, on the individual level.

Practicing the Initiator/Inquirer

Depending on the level of reactivity the clients have, it can be helpful to have them try this out for the first time on something easy. This gives everyone a lower-stress topic with which to grasp the assignment, both in terms of what they will have to do to accomplish it and what it feels like when they are able to do it. Here are some examples of how I help clients practice the process:

I may suggest the initiator share some positive feedback with the inquirer and have the inquirer get curious about what that was like for them, what it meant to them, and so on. Then they try switching roles.

I may ask the initiator to describe to the inquirer exactly how they like their first beverage of the morning. The inquirer can get curious about details, why this is important, what the experience is like for them, and so on. Then they can switch.

I might ask the clients to pick a topic that is maybe a 1 or 2 on a 10-point scale of intensity, where 1 is low and 10 is very high. One couple I worked with discussed gun control, which was about a 2 for both. They empathized so easily with one another's perspectives that they chose to switch perspectives and stand up for the opposite side of the issue as well, and they ended up having a lot of fun with it. If you try this approach, watch out for switching topics midstream or piling other issues on top. If you're not careful, you can find yourself dealing with a level 8 issue before you know it, and before the clients have built the ability to access curiosity, focus, or self-control.

I might ask the clients to share something about a dream or desire they have, or something they particularly love doing.

Supporting the Initiator/Inquirer Process

One important way to support this process, whether in your own relationship or in therapy, is to give lots of positive feedback, complimenting progress along the way. Perfection is not the goal; all progress and sincere effort deserves acknowledgment. Look for and compliment anything that represents getting clear about their thoughts, feelings, and perceptions; holding steady; saying something difficult; or accessing curiosity or empathy, regardless of how their partner receives or reacts to it. The self-protective brain has a strong tendency to hyperfocus on the negative to the exclusion of the positive, and no one feels good stretching their skills if they think their efforts are not being noticed and appreciated.

Either partner can turn to me at any time and ask for help, and I suggest they do this early and often, rather than getting upset, flooded, angry, or reactive. Taking lots of short breaks is much better than es-calating or shutting down, either of which might necessitate a full-on time-out, which is time-consuming. I might help a client formulate the next thing they want to say. If either partner asks me for coaching help, I will engage directly with them about where they feel stuck. The other partner will probably learn something as they listen to their partner getting refocused, becoming grounded, grappling with defensiveness, struggling to get clearer about what they want to say, experiencing vulnerability, and/or staying with what they are trying to communicate.

It is so important to remember that each partner has the ability to im-prove an interaction, even if their partner is not making it easy for them. No matter how their partner is acting, I want both to figure out how to respond from their best self. The handouts for initiator and inquirer in appendix D can help them figure out what that might look like. For this to work, the conversation must move slowly enough so that everyone has time to choose their words and responses rather than merely react to one another. This can be counterintuitive to say the least, when you are the one in the hard conversation. Consider setting a timer for five minutes and then pausing for a three-minute guided meditation, for three deep breaths, or to hold hands and smile at one another or give and receive positive feedback. Or set a timer for 10 minutes and then hug until both of you are completely calm and laughing. Anything to keep the pace slow and stop escalating automatic reactions.

If someone does become reactive, the success of the project depends on their ability to either slow down, take small breaks, take larger breaks, or go on a time-out depending on the intensity and depth of the triggered response. If you are coaching, you might help clients get calm by breathing with long, slow exhales; taking a break; or doing a mindfulness exercise. If they are able to catch it early, I might just help them breathe, refocus on how they want to be in this situation, and try again. I might ask them what other options they see for themselves, aside from reacting to their partner. If they can remember what kind of person they aspire to be in a stressful conversation, I might ask them how that type of person would respond in this situation. Tossing a ball back and forth between them can help as well, in a somewhat magical manner. For more suggestions, refer to chapter 8, in particular the sec-tions "Holding Steady: Differentiation Glue" and "Regulation."

If the inquirer feels stuck and asks for support from me, I might ask, "What can you ask that will help your partner talk to you about this more deeply?" or "What can you ask that will keep your partner opening up to you about this?" or "Does what they just said make sense to a part of you? Are there questions you have that might clarify what you're not sure about?" This looks easier than it is, and when you practice it, you will see what I mean. The self-protective brain really does not want to slow down right when things are looking dangerous. Stopping to ask more questions about the thing that hurts is extremely counter-intuitive, and when you learn how to actually do it, it is also extremely empowering. Once people experience that empowerment once or twice, progress speeds up because the process has its own obvious reward. Until then, it can be slow going. Often in the beginning, when people are still building the capacity to do this, I might offer the inquirer questions they could ask the initiator. For instance:

How does that get under your skin?
Can you tell me more about how you feel when that happens?
What do you think I'm still not understanding about this?
Is there something specific I do or say that contributes to this problem for you?

Any time the inquirer is having a hard time thinking of a question, I recommend they say back what they are hearing and check to see if they are understanding what the initiator is trying to express. This is helpful because it invites the initiator to go deeper without the inquirer having to come up with a good question. It also is good practice for checking rather than assuming, and slowing down to get more detail rather than running away or changing the subject.

If the initiator is struggling, I might help them take a few breaths, get grounded, and remember what they wanted to express to their partner. I might remind them they can express anything about themselves and their preferences, desires, or beliefs, and trust that their partner will be okay. I might create a little time-out and do a sidebar with the initiator to help them figure out what they want to say and how they want to express it. Slowing things down is often helpful to give the initiator time to think before they speak, which helps set a calm tone for the communication. If you are working with a client who struggles with figuring out what to say and getting it all out, they may benefit from the "Preparation for Communication Worksheets," which you will find in appendix C.

If the partner in either role shows some vulnerability or emotion and the other partner does not respond with warmth, I am likely to slow things down to see if I can help them build other-awareness while still helping them say what they intend to say and hold steady. This is a great moment for building differentiation. Many people collapse emotionally when their partner starts emoting. I might ask if they can hold steady even though their partner is experiencing emotion. "Can you express warmth and caring for them, and still express what you are trying to say?" "Can you let them have their reaction and emotion without it changing what you are saying?" "Can you reassure them or help them get grounded and then continue without going off course?"

I encourage them to avoid the word *need* because it tends to invite reactivity. "I need you to . . ." is a near-cousin to an ultimatum and is likely to get a problematic response. Unless they really are talking about a true need, like food, water, shelter, or safety, I think the word *want* is more likely to be helpful in keeping the conversation going in a connected, constructive way. "I want you to . . ." or "I would prefer if you . . ." are a little easier to hear and respond well to. For more on this, see the information in chapter 8 about needs versus desires and the accompanying exercise in appendix B.

I let partners know agreeing is not necessary, and problem-solving is a different process. This is about really hearing, disclosing more deeply, and holding steady while exploring the territory. This is the time for learning about the landscape and gaining a much deeper understanding of one another, not making decisions. Everyone gets to decide on actions and responses later, and no amount of distress expressed by the partner is a mandate for change on the part of the other. For more on decision-making, see the section entitled "Moving Toward Decision-Making" later in this chapter, as well as chapter 11, "Negotiating Polyamory: Forming Good Agreements," and chapter 12, "Negotiating Polyamory: Talking Points for Partners.

Using the Initiator/Inquirer with Threesomes or Moresomes

Sometimes you will have more than two people in your office at one time, and the therapy will still be about having deeper, more connecting conversations that encourage empathy and understanding. When this is the case, there are a number of ways to handle it, but my preference is to have one initiator at a time, and everyone else works together as inquirers. This works well because it gives a family group a strategy for deep conversations that doesn't involve one taking the role of peace-keeper, mediator, observer, or coach. Ideally, I want everyone working together equally, and, at the same time, I want to hold everyone to a high standard and support everyone's growth edge.

If you have, for instance, a triad trying to make a decision about some aspect of shared living, each one would take a turn in the initiator role, with the other two functioning as inquirers, to explore the territory thoroughly before approaching a decision-making process. Usually, I think it is helpful to have the person who is experiencing the most emotion or distress at the moment be the first initiator. As each initiation is coming to a close and everyone is getting clear and saying back what the initiator is expressing, one person might write down some notes about the important aspects of the situations for that person. Then the next person initiates, then the third, and so on, depending on how many partners are present. At the end of that process, there will be notes about the most important aspects of the situation to each participant in the conversation.

Moving toward Decision-Making

I include the preliminary steps toward decision-making here because I want to make it clear that this is a sequential process. Gathering information about each partner's unique perspective and preferences must come before anything that might look like decision-making. Additionally, I think people often make the mistake of making decisions while in stressed-out mood rather than a creative, generative one.

Imagine that you have been working with a couple trying to decide if they want to open their relationship. It may have been emotionally difficult for both, but you have used the I/I process and now your clients are both able to express and say back to their partner what they understand about one another's perspective. Everyone feels like their partner understands their point of view. The conversations have gone deep, and it is clear that each person has enough understanding of the entire situation to begin working toward making a decision.

Decisions, or Experiments?

As the partners approach making a decision, there is a key distinction to be made between a decision that is here to stay and an experiment that is intended to be run and reevaluated, adjusted if necessary according to the needs and preferences that are revealed through the doing of the experiment, and run again. Starting out by seeking the be-all and end-all of decisions is usually a mistake. In most situations, it will work much better to seek a first experiment for how to move forward. This is because we learn by doing, not theorizing. No matter how great your first experiment seems, you won't know how it actually plays out for everyone concerned until you live your way into it. Also, knowing this is going to be your approach can reduce anxiety significantly; no one has an easy time agreeing to something that might trap them in misery if it doesn't work out as anticipated. It is much better to know that your evolving needs and preferences will be honored and taken into account, and adjustments made. I envision a long-term relationship of any kind as a long series of experiments, ever-evolving throughout the years and allowing for the kind of flexibility that results in deeply satisfying relationships with emotionally secure, satisfied partners.

To create a first experiment or action plan of any kind, it is important to have the following things in place:

Clarity about everyone's unique perspective, opinion, meanings made, thoughts, feelings, struggle, etc. This is achieved using the I/I process discussed here.

An idea of what strengths those concerned bring to the table, including positive information about dreams and desires

A creative spirit for problem-solving that is not limited by negative beliefs or emotions and moves into a generative place

An array of options far beyond what is immediately apparent

Strengths and Validation Shower

A strengths assessment involving everyone concerned is fun and generally results in a nice shift in mood toward the positive. What are everyone's strengths with regard to the issue at hand? Help them make a list for each person involved. For instance, what gifts did they show in their communication with one another? Access to feelings? Courage? Resilience? Clarity? Honesty? What are they really good at? What do they bring to the table? Collaborating on a strengths assessment like this is a great way to generate some hope and elevated emotions before you shift to practicalities; have the partners shower one another with validation, as well as identify for themselves what they bring to the table. I often wrap up an I/I process with a strengths/validation shower to consolidate what each partner brings to the relationship and this particular situation.

Exercise: 30 Ideas, No Matter How Silly: Brainstorming Process

The creative spirit and elevated emotion are crucial for effective problem-solving. Without them, your clients are likely to create something just as problematic or limited as their original situation. For this reason, I like to move toward problem-solving with a large brainstorming list of everything anyone involved can imagine as a possible solution, even if not realistic, and regardless of agreement. I use this brainstorming process in my own life any time I feel stuck or could benefit from expanding my perception of options. It can be used for everything from how to have more fun together to what to do on your own when your partner is out of town. It can be used by just one person or an entire family. If there is an idea that hypothetically could solve the problem, put it on the list. Don't stop until there are at least 30 things on the list of possibilities, and feel free to put silly things on the list. If the list gets to 45 or 60 items, so much the better. This process should feel free and fun (see the "30 Ideas No Matter How Silly: Brainstorming Process" worksheet in appendix D).

Going from Brainstorming to Experiment 1

Once you have your brainstorming list, you can use it to choose a first experiment if you feel ready. Everyone with a stake in the game should pick three to five items on the list that feel manageable and see where there is overlap. Together, partners should come up with a hypothesis regarding what a good first experiment would be. Then they should create a plan for putting the first experiment into effect and pick a date not too far in the future to reevaluate. Each person involved in the experiment should write down specifically what the experiment is, what their own action steps are, how running this experiment will benefit them, and why it feels important to them to give it a try. Partners should also decide on a plan for how to handle it if things go wrong; anyone should be able to bring up any problems sooner than the reevaluation date if needed, while still respecting that each might need to practice holding steady a little bit, too. There is a tender line between, "I'm working hard to make this work, breathe in, breathe out, sticking with it moment by moment" and "Abort mission! This is not working!"

CHAPTER 10

Getting Polyamory Therapy off to a Strong Start
Understanding the Change Process

With any relational therapy, coaching, or self-help project there are some decisions you need to make early in the process to set it up for success. When relationship goals include polyamory, however, there are a few specific considerations you'll need to keep in mind at the beginning of the process.

First of all, because there are often more than one or two people whose interests are relevant to the course of therapy, you will need a way to decide who should come to the first session or first phase of therapy. Sometimes it will be intuitive—for instance, if you're working with a solo polyamory practitioner, it will probably be pretty clear that individual therapy will make most sense, or with a couple that is considering nonmonogamy but hasn't yet embarked on the experiment, in which case relational therapy for a dyad will make sense. But often it can get pretty complicated, with multiple partners and partners-of-partners involved, and many people invested in the outcomes. You will need a way to think about this and take the lead in how to set up things for success, particularly for times when you and your client might not be on the same page.

In this chapter, I explain how I make the decision about who should come to therapy and present a variety of examples to illustrate the complexities. I discuss how to sort through the unique and often imperfect situations clients may bring to you, and deine quickly who to invite to the first session. I also discuss a strategy I learned from Peter Pearson for starting the change process before the first session that I have found makes a huge difference in the success of the early stages of therapy, and include a handout about this. Lastly, I discuss laying the ground-work for effective change by careful assessment of goals, including a worksheet to guide this process.

If you are using this book to guide your own personal growth, this chapter has some important concepts that can help you lay good groundwork. While I'm discussing therapy strategies, including how and why I use them from my perspective as a therapist, the purpose of these strategies is to help clients who want to create some sort of change in their lives, making them very relevant to self-help. Feel free to skim the parts where I address therapists if they aren't relevant to you, but don't miss the handout and worksheet I present at the end of the chapter.

THE CONSULT CALL

I always have a phone conversation or videoconference with a potential client before I set up the first appointment. I know not everyone does this. If you don't, you will need to figure out which aspects of the following system will fit into your practice and which won't.

I do my own screening, in large part because I want to figure out if I feel comfortable with the client and want to work with them before committing to the therapy and setting up an appointment. My consultation has a basic screening role, because I don't want to go further with someone who is outside of my scope of practice. If, in the course of the screening, I discover that, in fact, someone is out of my scope or won't be a good fit for the way I practice, I'll make a referral on the phone.

Of course, in the initial consultation, I also want to give my clients the opportunity to ask me any questions they may have, so they can get an idea of who I am and how I work. I want us all to feel like the chances are good that we will have a good fit and work well together.

In the consultation call, I learn about the presenting problem, which involves getting an idea of how the client(s) have set up their relationship and how it is functioning. I ask questions that help me understand how they make decisions about their relationship. This is key to my process of determining who should come to the first session: I want to know who has the decision-making power with regard to the issues that are bringing them to therapy, because I probably want the decision-makers in the therapy room at the start of therapy. I expand on this topic more in the next section.

In addition to this, in the consultation call I assess and discuss individual motivation for change and set up the direction of the first session. This is a technique I learned from Peter Pearson, and it has made an enormous difference in how my first sessions go, because it empowers my clients to start thinking about how to create their change rather than hoping that either their partner will change first or I will somehow magically change them. When I do it well, clients start thinking differently about the problems they want to shift before they arrive in my office, which saves us all a lot of time and frustration, and delivers a lot of value to the client.

This consultation call serves a few functions, acting as the following:

a screening tool
an assessment
an opportunity for clients to ask questions about treatment
an opportunity to figure out who to ask to come to the first session
a way of setting up the therapy for success, even before the first session

This entire process takes anywhere from 15 minutes to a half-hour, unless I'm planning to do a longer session, like a one-day intensive or longer, in which case I take an hour to do my screening. Sometimes I gather the basic information by e-mail and then set up a one-time 90-minute assessment to determine if we are going to continue to work together. I think it is crucial to get enough of the right information so I can be intentional about who attends my first session. The entire therapy goes better if I lay good groundwork.

WHO SHOULD COME TO THE FIRST SESSION?

Determining who should come to first session of therapy with polyamorous clients isn't as simple as "who's in the relationship." There are a few reasons for this; first of all, because polyamorous people have multiple cooccurring relationships, with other people who may also have multiple cooccurring relationships, it can get pretty crowded and complicated very quickly, with layers upon layers of how important any given topic is to everyone concerned. A goal of trying to include everyone who might potentially have a stake in the therapy would certainly result in a lot of chaotic first sessions and, in my opinion, limit the potential for growth and progress.

In addition, the power dynamics of each polyamorous relationship are unique, with many possible structures. It is possible that some people are much more empowered than others in determining the structure of the relationship and the agreements surrounding it. Consider, for instance, a primary/secondary structure, in which a dyadic pair may have outside partners but both members of the couple have agreed to give one another certain rights. They may have agreed to give one another the right to veto partners, cancel date nights, or close the relationship at any point if it seems like polyamory isn't working out. My point is not that primary/secondary relationships always include these specific agreements, but rather that they may include these, or any other agreement, and some agreements have a big impact on everyone concerned.

Whatever the issue is that brought the client(s) to therapy probably doesn't involve each partner equally. If the real issue is an interpersonal dynamic between two people, it may be that having anyone other than those two people in the room will just add confusion without adding value; however, I can also imagine a situation in which it would be extremely relevant to have a third partner in the therapy room in such a situation, for instance, in the case of a triad. If a triad makes decisions as a family and part of the family dynamic is that when there are tensions between two the third takes a mediator or peacemaker role, it will be helpful to have all three partners come to therapy. In fact, undertaking that therapy without including support for managing the triad/triangulation dynamic in ways that work well would be overly limited and probably result in relapse.

The biggest pitfall I have come across is the temptation, and sometimes the client's desire, to bring in more people than I really want or need to have at the start of therapy. This is the pitfall I would like to help you avoid.

Relationship therapy can be challenging in the best of times. Imagine having several people in your therapy room who are distressed and have a stake in the game but no power to make decisions. Now imagine that they're there alongside the decision-makers, who are also distressed, and who are feeling pulled in multiple directions, additionally complicated by having partners with differing desires sitting right there next to them. If you think this sounds like a recipe for disaster, I completely agree. Identifying the decision-making body before the first session is my way of avoiding a volatile and painful situation like that one. Confusion and unnecessary conflict are the last things I want at the start of therapy. Instead, I want my clients to feel hopeful; I want them to feel that their situation is manageable and their problems are solvable. I can facilitate that by organizing the therapy to support healthy emotional boundaries and good decision-making from the start.

With this in mind, at the start of therapy I almost never want anyone in the room who isn't empowered to make decisions about the relationship. In the early stages of therapy, I'm learning about the relationship structure and agreements, and the individual partners, and beginning to understand their strengths and challenges. Often, as I gain an understanding of these foundational aspects of their relationship, they will be learning right along with me. Together, we may discover that they aren't clear on their agreements, an inadequately repaired breach of trust is shaping the current situation, or there is some past trauma that is living forward in unhelpful ways. I've rarely seen a situation where it wouldn't be helpful to see the smallest possible decision-making body at first.

The decision-making body may be a pair, an individual, a triad, a quad, or any other arrangement; it's defined only as the person or group of people that has the authority to make decisions about the structure of the relationship. Every polycule has a decision-making body, or possibly several. If you understand who makes decisions primarily, and more specifically who will be making the decisions that are relevant to the specific agenda of the therapy, then you know who the decision-making body is.

Keep in mind, however, that things may very well evolve throughout the course of therapy, and it may become important to bring in other people. That may be because new people become part of the decision-making body or simply because you become more confident that including other partners in the room will not derail the course of therapy. Sometimes it is helpful to invite "guests" to support the therapy; with polyamory, that might be someone else in the polycule who is involved in some aspect of the issues that form the goals of the therapy. Sometimes with a triad or quad, the middle or end stages of therapy might be spent working with various individuals or dyads as they work through particular challenges that mostly affect smaller subunits, once the family therapy goals have been met.

IDENTIFYING THE DECISION-MAKING BODY

In the consultation call, I ask a few questions to determine who the decision-making body is in this relationship. If I'm talking to one or two people on the phone and they are describing something that sounds like a V to me, I will ask, "Do you have a primary/secondary structure to your relationship? (Or does one relationship take precedence over all others?)" If the client is describing a triad or quad, or some other type of family structure, I will ask, "Do you make decisions as a family?" If the answers to these questions are clear and simple, the decision is usually also simple. That takes care of the vast majority of cases. Occasionally the answers will not be clear or simple.

Once in a while, for instance, there will be a triad or quad who is in transition from a primary/secondary V or N but who have restructured their relationship. For instance, they may have moved in together, aspiring to make decisions as a family. This is a situation where my therapy guidelines will need to be assessed on a case-by-case basis. Two options that spring to mind are:

1. Invite the whole family, because I want to strengthen their skills for getting where they want to go, which is a family decision-making structure. After all, I will eventually need to help them build tolerance for a direct discussion of where each is blocked about sharing decision-making, so why not start out as we want to continue?

2. Invite the original primary decision-makers, because I want to help them sort out what is getting in their way when it comes to

sharing decision-making power with the third before involving the third in the conversation. Once the original dyad gets some traction, invite the third, and help the triad navigate the challenges related to the evolution of their relationship power and decision-making.

This is an example that highlights the importance of the consultation call or visit. I usually try to get a sense of where differentiation is breaking down for each party and make my decision based on that. If everyone functions pretty well as a team and has some skill with tolerating differences, I will probably err on the side of supporting their growth by inviting them all, because I think they will be able to tolerate the difficult conversations. But if it is clear that there are some foundational problems having to do with understanding or forming agreements, or if one or some of the people involved are experiencing a lot of emotional dysregulation, with a shortage of skills, emotional safety, or internal security, I will probably err on the side of inviting fewer people to begin with.

WHAT ABOUT NONHIERARCHICAL RELATIONSHIPS?

Things look a little different with clients who have a nonhierarchical structure to their polyamory. With nonhierarchical polyamory, there is no primary/secondary power structure, which means that I can't make my decision based on who is empowered to make decisions, except in the case of a triad or quad where everyone is involved in making decisions, equally; therefore, I instead focus on whose interests are most relevant to the issues we'll be working on in therapy. I determine the presenting problem and then begin asking questions to help me understand who will need to be involved in solving it. I rely on the clients to help me understand this and choose to have the first session attended by the smallest number of people that make sense given the presenting circumstances. Remember, as the therapy evolves, you can always include other partners, depending on how the therapy proceeds and who is involved in the presenting challenges as they evolve.

There are some additional ethical issues to consider when it comes to making decisions about seeing polyamorous clients and their entire polycules; I address those in chapter 20, "Ethical Considerations."

WHEN MIGHT OTHERS BE INVOLVED IN THE THERAPY?

Imagine a primary/secondary V. The primary dyad is the primary decision-making body, as in any primary/secondary relationship. As such, that dyad would be the logical place to start therapy; however, some issues and challenges will of course be between the hinge person and their secondary partner. Occasionally, issues between the partners in that dyad will be the focus of the therapy.

In that case, I will only spend enough time with the primary dyad to make sure I understand their agreements, so I don't work at cross-purposes unintentionally. That might be accomplished in just one session with the primary dyad or even just a consultation call, and then the bulk of the therapy would be with the secondary dyad. Alternatively, if the hinge person makes decisions themselves after taking into account the preferences of their partners, that is a nonhierarchical situation more like solo polyamory, and I would be perfectly comfortable seeing the hinge with whichever partner they want. In that situation, I might want my first session or consult to involve just the hinge to determine if it will be individual or relational therapy.

Occasionally, issues between metamours (that is, the partners of the hinge person) could be the focus of the therapy. If the presenting problem involves the relationship between metamours and at first glance doesn't seem to involve the hinge person, I would still want to understand the decision-making dynamics, strengths, challenges, and agreements before undertaking the therapy between the metamours. This might be a situation where it could make sense to have all three at the first visit or in the consultation. Helping clients get clear on agreements and decision-making will allow us all to work together to strengthen their relationship(s). Also, the hinge has a lot of influence on the systemic dynamics between metamours; it is hard to imagine a situation between metamours that doesn't in some manner involve systemic dynamics with the hinge. For more on this, see chapter 17, "Role-Related Challenges and Benefits: Primaries, Secondaries, Hinges, Etc."

HOW IS THIS DIFFERENT FROM THERAPY WITH MONOGAMY?

When I see a monogamous couple, my strategy for deciding who should be in therapy is much different. I often hear from potential clients who aren't sure if they want individual or relational therapy. In the absence of violence or emotional abuse, my advice is almost *always* that if they think they might want couple therapy, they should start with couple therapy. This is my logic: If I see an individual, there will be a join there. Then, the other partner is likely to have difficulty joining the therapy at a later date because they're likely to perceive uneven alliances. I've heard from a lot of clients that they didn't feel safe or heard by their partner's individual therapist when they attempted to transition into couples therapy with them. I don't want to undermine the couple therapy in that way.

There are also some other reasons I tend to recommend relational therapy over individual therapy. I find that relational therapy moves faster and has less room for artifice or hidden agendas: I get to see what is going on right in my office, including the good, the bad, and the ugly. People regularly expose their partner's secrets, so I get more information up front, even if it might emerge in imperfect ways. Also, when I start with a couple in the room, I save a lot of time that might otherwise be spent with me not understanding the relational dynamics. I know that when I hear an individual's description of their partner's behavior and beliefs, I'm only seeing it through their eyes, and their interpretation is always skewed—often negatively, if they are having relationship problems. Ultimately, I find it much easier to do one or a few couple sessions and then determine that individual therapy would be more efficient, rather than try to do it the other way around.

With polyamory, I approach it differently. As you have seen, I usually try to get the smallest relevant group in the room first, clarify some foundational things, and then branch out from there according to the challenges of the various people involved. Upon reflection, I think this is because of a fundamental difference between monogamous relationships and polyamorous ones: With monogamous relationships you can assume that, if you have both partners in the room, you're addressing the decision-making body. You won't fully understand the power dynamics without discussing them, but you're probably not missing a major player and they probably aren't uncertain about how they make decisions.

Not so with polyamorous relationships. You could have two people in the room, neither of whom have any decision-making power, or you could have a room full of people and none of them knows who makes the decisions and how. Plus, when you're working with polyamory, you're likely going to be discussing some aspect of how your clients make decisions, prioritize time or resources, and make and keep agreements.

Still, I can think of a situation in a monogamous relationship where decision-making issues might arise. Imagine a situation where you are seeing a couple who is monogamous, and after a time in therapy, maybe a few sessions or a few years, you have the sense that something is "off." You begin to wonder if there is an aspect to the situation you aren't seeing. Maybe one of the partners is having an affair and not disclosing it. Or maybe someone is on the brink of leaving and isn't discussing it. It feels like there is an elephant in the room, and you are just spinning your wheels and waiting to find out where the missing piece is before anything useful can happen. This is a little bit like not having the entire decision-making body in the room. If someone is having an undisclosed and major affair, they may be taking another person's preferences into account and making plans around someone who isn't in the room and isn't being discussed. If you've ever been in that situation as a therapist, you know how it feels. It can be quite challenging, because not only is there the betrayal to contend with, but it's also very difficult to have productive therapy when major aspects of the relationship's dynamics are hidden from view. If you've experienced that feeling, you have an understanding of why you want the entire decision-making body in the room and also why you don't want anyone else, at least at first.

Examples

Here are a few imaginary but not uncommon examples of situations in which it takes a little extra thought to determine the decision-making body. Read them and answer these questions for yourself:

Who is the decision-making body?
Who do I want to see in the first session?
What questions would I ask the client to clarify the decision?

Then read on, to see my thoughts on each case.

Example 1: A potential client calls you and says, "My name is George. My wife Sue and I are in a polyamorous triad with Brad. We're having some problems, and I want us all to come in for relationship therapy together." You ask what kind of problems they are experiencing, and George tells you, "Sue is having some problems accepting my relationship with Brad. We got a bit of a rough start because it started with me having an affair with Brad, but she says she is open to polyamory, and I know they will hit it off if they just spend some time together." You ask, "Does one of these relationships take precedence over the other for you?" and George tells you, "Absolutely. I'm not leaving Sue, no matter what. I just want us to work it out, and ideally, I'd like to end up having Brad move in with us." Who is the decision-making body? Who do you want to have come to the first session?

Example 2: A potential client calls you and says, "I'm polyamorous and I have a few different relationships going—one longer-term one and two newer ones. But I'm struggling because one of my newer partners wants to be exclusive, and I just don't know how I feel about that." You ask, "Do you have a primary/secondary structure with any of your relationships?" The client says, "No, not really. I don't believe in hierarchy." You ask, "It sounds like you are trying to figure out how you feel about being exclusive with one partner; ultimately, who is going to make that decision? You? You and a partner?" and the client tells you, "I'm going to make the decision, but first I have to figure out how I feel about it." Who is the decision-making body? Who do you want to see in the first session?

Example 3: A potential client calls you and says, "Hi, My name is Claire, and I've been dating a woman named Mary for a few months. Mary lives with Jo, and they are committed to one another, and I'm really struggling with always being second place. Mary and I want to have relationship therapy so we can work through this." You ask, "So, am I understanding correctly that Mary and Jo have a primary/secondary relationship and you are Mary's secondary partner, and you are finding that to be difficult?" Claire says, "Yes." Who is the decision-making body? Who do you want to see in the first session?

My Thoughts on Example 1

In the first case, although George refers to himself, his wife, and his lover as a triad, they don't make decisions as a family. In fact, it sounds as if George and Sue haven't formed any cohesive agreements about opening their relationship. Additionally, they may not have repaired sufficiently from George's infidelity with Brad. It sounds like George and Sue have a primary/secondary structure, meaning that they make up the decision-making body. In my opinion, inviting Brad to the therapy too soon could be a big mistake.

I might hypothesize out loud that George and Sue could benefit from sorting out a few things between the two of them, to create a more solid foundation for opening their relationship in ways that work for both of them. Because George has come to me already with an idea of what the therapy would look like and that idea includes both Sue and Brad, this might be a hard sell. If indeed he wants to preserve the relationship with Sue, she will need to have a voice in the decision-making, and George will need to hear how she feels and what she wants, even if that is hard for him. I would ask him if that agenda interests him. If so, I would invite George and Sue to come in for therapy.

Another option might be to have George come to individual therapy. But from the little I know in this scenario, there is probably some significant unfinished business between Sue and George, and relational therapy will be a much more direct way to help them recover from past infidelity, explore both partners' opinions about whether to open the relationship and how to go about it if they decide to move in that direction, and support both partners in having a voice and building every aspect of differentiation.

Another option is to decline taking the client at all. This is not, at first glance, the simplest presentation of polyamory. There seem to be a lot of loose ends and some major gaps in the story; it would be understandable if it felt overwhelming to take it on. Moreover, although I have a lot of experience and confidence working with polyamory, if George insisted that he, Sue, and Brad needed to attend the first sessions, I would decline to take the client. I'm not interested in setting up Sue for an ambush, nor do I think that will support George's stated goal of preserving that relationship. I would let him know that, if his goal is strengthening his relationship with Sue to the point that they open their home to include Brad, the best chance of success would be to start by getting some clarity with Sue. If he didn't like that idea and wasn't interested in taking my advice after I explained my thinking in terms of helping him achieve his stated goal, I think I would probably assume we wouldn't have an easy or effective time working together, and would decline to work with them. If I thought I might be missing something important and might really want to work with George, I would suggest we start with an individual session and see how it feels.

My Thoughts on Example 2

In the second case, the decision-making body seems to be the individual client, who has a nonhierarchical relationship structure with several partners. This client sounds like they are making decisions on their own terms about their relationships. I would invite this client to come alone to therapy. Once they have some clarity about their feelings about exclusivity and their various partners, it might make sense to invite another partner to come as a guest to therapy. Oftentimes, that isn't necessary at all. In fact, I generally prefer to avoid it, because the partner can feel ganged up on, particularly if the original client has something difficult to share. Instead, I might choose to spend some of the individual therapy sessions using two chairs to rehearse difficult conversations with partners, build skills for nonreactive communication, and get clear on how the client wants to respond in a variety of situations. For more on this, see the exercises "Preparing to Communicate," and "Rehearsing Tough Conversations" in appendix C. If the client really wants to do that communicating in a therapy session, I might suggest they start with a new relationship therapist, who can build a more even join by getting to know them together from the start.

My Thoughts on Example 3

In the third case, although Claire wants to come into therapy with her partner Mary, it seems that the decision-making body is Mary and Jo, and the potential client, Claire, is a secondary partner. If that is the case, it might be best to see the client individually; as a secondary partner, they are a decision-making unit of their own. In individual therapy, the focus could be on increasing the aspects of differentiation for Claire, to support improved communication in Claire's relationships. If the primary presenting problem and goals have to do with Claire managing the complexities of a secondary relationship, individual therapy would make a lot of sense. This is another case where the exercise "Preparing to Communicate" might be helpful, as well as the other handouts for chapter 8, "Conceptualizing the Case: If Polyamory Isn't the Problem, What Is?" Mary could be invited as a guest to Claire's individual therapy in the future, if needed.

There are some other ways this could play out, and they are more complicated. I can imagine a situation where I might see Claire and Mary together from the start, but my ideal scenario for that would begin with a phone call from all three, Mary, Jo, and Claire, or at least two, Mary and Jo. If Mary and Jo, the primary dyad, were in agreement that all of the relationships would benefit from Claire and Mary working together better, I could get on board with that; however, if the presenting problem has to do with allocation of Mary's resources of time and energy, it is hard to imagine how that wouldn't affect both Jo and Claire. I would probably want Jo to be part of the therapy in some manner, even as an occasional visitor, so Jo would have a voice in my therapy room and I wouldn't be operating on anyone else's interpretation of what Jo wanted. I would feel most comfortable having Mary and Jo at the first visit, possibly with Claire present. This is an example of a situation where I might not be able to adequately assess the situation and make a recommendation for therapy without seeing all three, even though they are in a primary/secondary V.

I can also imagine an uncomfortable situation in which Claire and Mary want to come in for therapy but Jo does not want to participate for some reason. That reason might be simple, or it may be complicated; for instance, maybe Jo's not happy about polyamory, despite obviously living in a polyamorous relationship that is functioning reasonably well. This is a thorny gray-area zone and one that I would navigate carefully on a case-by-case basis.

The interesting thing about polyamory is that it can look so many ways. There's no rule book to refer to. If you find yourself in a complicated situation like this, think about the emotional boundaries of those involved. Are there conversations that should probably be happening? Do all the stakeholders have a voice in the matters that concern them? If not, is it by their own choice (as in a don't ask, don't tell agreement), or is someone else making the decision to leave them out of the decision-making process, either inadvertently or intentionally? Consider who makes decisions in the relevant relationships and who came to you as a client. Consider role-related challenges. For more on those, see chapter 17, "Role-Related Challenges and Benefits: Primaries, Secondaries, Hinges, Etc."

Most importantly, make a decision that feels right and good to you. Don't put yourself in a situation where you can already tell you are going to feel bad about the work you are doing. Don't take on a client or situation just because they want you to, when your internal guidance system is screaming *no*! But don't walk away from working with a situation that is complicated just because it is complicated, either. Many of the best functioning polyamorous relationships I know of started out with situations that were not ideal, sometimes in fairly dramatic ways.

Sometimes, after a consult call, I'm still not certain who to invite to therapy, or what the therapy would look like, or, in some cases, whether I want to work with the client. When this is the case, rather than engaging in therapy in a usual manner, I will instead do a 90-minute, 2-hour, or 3-hour one-time-only session as an assessment. I make sure the clients know there will be no obligation on my part, or theirs, to continue on to therapy. I tell them that at the end of our time together I will make recommendations for how to move forward, and those recommendations may or may not include working together. I set it up so I can be as creative as needed. If I'm not sure I want to work with the client but I know who would be in the room, I keep it on the shorter side because I will know by the end of 90 minutes if I want to work with them. This determination usually has to do with whether they have some insight into self-motivated goals (see the "How to Get the Most Out of Relationship Therapy or Coaching" worksheet in appendix D). If, on the other hand, I have no idea who ideally would be in the therapy, I will invite all contenders, and shift between group, individual, and dyadic configurations as needed for me to have it sorted out by the end of the session. In a situation like that, I might have chosen a three-hour format.

Another way to do this is a four-part assessment, involving a relationship/family session, followed by individual sessions for everyone involved, followed by another family session to make recommendations. This is a common assessment strategy for dyadic therapy and will also work with polyamory, but I personally prefer the three-hour, single-session strategy because I don't want to set up myself or my client for a long, unruly relational session with the wrong people present. I'd rather have more flexibility than that and feel free to send some of them to the waiting room or a nearby cafe while I help one or two sort out their agreements, or do whatever is needed to identify who the client should be and what type of therapy will serve best.

UNDERSTANDING THE CHANGE PROCESS AND STARTING IT BEFORE THE FIRST SESSION

Now I'm going to shift gears and share some more general guidance for getting therapy off to a good start. These techniques were developed by Ellyn Bader and Peter Pearson, founders of the Couples Institute, and creators of the Developmental Model of Couples Therapy, and they are equally applicable to monogamous and polyamorous relationships.

Have you ever seen a situation like this? A couple comes into your office for their first therapy session. You say, "What brings you here today?" Immediately, one partner launches into a tirade about how their partner did this or that thing, or has this or that character flaw and must change for them to be happy and have a good relationship. The other partner pipes up with their version of the story, and now you learn all about the first partner's character flaws and the reasons they need to change for their partner to be happy and have a good relationship. They both look at you expectantly, waiting for you to pick their side and start whipping their partner into shape.

This common scenario arises from a common misapprehension: that one person can define what they want the relationship to be like and expect their partner to change to match it. And a secondary misapprehension that taking sides with that agenda is a therapist's job.

Much as everyone wants their partner to change, the only realistic or helpful goals are those we develop for ourselves, about ourselves. That's because the only parts of a relationship anyone can control are their own: how they react, respond, and engage. No matter how badly behaved your partner is, the only thing you can change is how you, yourself, show up, moment by moment. This is just as true for therapists as for anyone else; I cannot change anyone other than myself, no matter how much I might want to.

Compare that to a client who tells you something like this:

> I've identified something I'm doing that is getting in my own way, and my partner doesn't like it either. I can see how my life would be better if I changed that, and my relationship would be better too. I'd like you to help me figure out how I'm getting stuck so I can achieve my own goal of being more the person I want to be in this relationship.

How refreshing. I love working with clients who take personal responsibility for their own growth and behavior, and recognize that how they show up in their relationship has an effect on their partner's choices and reactions.

Exercise: How to Get the Most out of Relationship Therapy or Coaching

Peter Pearson has developed a strategy for getting his clients headed in that direction before the first session, involving a handout and homework given to clients before the first session, and I use his strategy regularly. Using his version as a jumping-off place, I created a handout for my clients that I give them when I first schedule their visits. It's called "How to Get the Most Out of Relationship Therapy or Coaching." I ask them to do the homework exercises it contains before their first visit. I've included a copy of this handout in appendix D, and you're welcome to adapt it for your own purposes. Please attribute the concept to Peter Pearson of the Couples Institute. If you are engaging in a relationship self-help project, I strongly recommend starting with this handout, as the exercises included in it are the strongest jumping-off place I can offer for creating change in your relationship.

GOAL-SETTING: FOUNDATION FOR CHANGE

Every therapy or coaching endeavor involves the art of goal-setting, whether individual, couple, or family. Every personal self-help process should also involve a careful goal-setting process, some of which might be somewhat counterintuitive. For some, this process is fairly straightforward, in which case the exercises in the handout "How to Get the Most Out of Relationship Therapy or Coaching" may be sufficient; however, for many the process of goal-setting is quite challenging, and more support may be needed. I cannot stress enough how important effective goal-setting is. Without it, the change process won't be sufficiently fueled by individual empowerment and relevant personal motivation.

Exercise: Getting Clear on Your Goals

Goal-setting involves multiple parts, including the following:

Getting clear on what you want for yourself, in your own life, for your own reasons.

Translating goals you may have for others into action steps for yourself, so you can actually create change in your life effectively. Remember, you can only change yourself. If you want your partner to change something about themselves, you can tell them what you hope they will do, but ultimately it is up to them to do it, and they may not. To support your own happiness, you will have to figure out how you yourself can make a change that is meaningful to you. Happily, any change you decide to make yourself has the potential to make a difference in the gridlock between you.

Once goals are clear, there are more aspects of the change process to work through, namely the following:

Getting clear on what is getting in the way of change, in you and perhaps also in your partner.

Identifying motivation to change, in other words, why you would bother and how you will benefit.

Making the rubber meet the road with one or more action steps, over and over, without losing focus, until you have a new way of being. Depending on the change you are seeking, this might take a few weeks, a few months, or longer. The more focus and consistency you have with follow-through, the quicker the change will take root. In my personal experience, the process is not linear; it feels very difficult for the first block of time, maybe 10 repetitions, and then becomes quite a bit easier. When it finally becomes congruent, easy, and automatic, or nearly so, I look back and wonder why I waited so long.

The "Getting Clear on Your Goals" worksheet describes a step-by-step process to support the crucial, foundational work of effective goal-setting (see appendix E).

THE CHANGE PROCESS: WHERE THE RUBBER MEETS THE ROAD

Once you have carefully considered goals from the viewpoint of what you (or your client) would like to create in life and in relationships, the next step will be to work with the change process itself. Action steps are an important aspect of change, and they get a lot of attention in books and articles about forming habits. Since actions move you closer to your goals, this makes a lot of sense. But behavioral goals, or simple actions, may or may not be as simple as they look or effective on their own. There is an intricate relationship between intentions, behaviors, thoughts, uncomfortable feelings, automatic responses, primitive emotional self-protection, elevated emotions like love and gratitude, and desire itself. Effective change is a creative process and involves working with all of these aspects, a little like a dance with many steps, each of which depends on and forms the basis for the others. Making the rubber meet the road is an art form, creative pursuit, interesting experiment, challenging exercise, and very exciting project rolled into one.

Exercise: Creating Personal Change

Creating a desired change in your life is not an automatic occurrence. In fact, it is quite the opposite. A surprising amount of what we think, feel, and do is *truly* automatic, and it will continue to unfold on autopilot until we decide to do something different intentionally, and consistently. Developing a new way of being requires creating a change in your brain; new connections must form between neurons in something like a new path in the woods, and old superhighways of much-used automatic responses will gradually weaken as you use them less. Throughout time, with consistency on your part, the new path will become ever clearer and stronger, and easier to find and use, until you have a new way of being that feels normal, reliable, and easily accessible.

This process of creating a new neural network in your brain is surprisingly possible, and I'm sure you have done it many times. Think of some examples from your own past experience; what are some goals you have identified and then tackled with some success? Notice what has worked for you in the past to help you accomplish your goals. Also, take note of where you have gotten tripped up or stuck in pursuit of goals. You might also consider big personal changes that happened as a result of a change in external circumstances. Since thoughts, physical feelings, emotional feelings, and actions intertwine, when something shifts how we think or what we believe, or we get a huge reframe or "wake-up call," it is easier to create behavioral shifts. For instance, perhaps you developed some new and positive habits in the aftermath of a breakup, after a health or family crisis, during quarantine for Coronavirus, or after a move to a new location. If so, consider what contributed to any positive change and what tripped you up or blocked your success when you wanted to create a change and weren't quite able to.

You don't need a huge crisis to make a change, thank goodness. You can create change just because you want to. For instance, you can make your own shift in belief system by gaining information or insight. You can create enough repetitions of a new action that your thoughts and feelings change, and you can choose to accelerate the process by intentionally shifting thoughts and feelings. Or, you might change your self-talk with a lot of focus to generate new feelings that then lead to new actions. You could also develop a mindfulness practice focused on intentionally creating such positive, elevated emotions as love, appreciation, and gratitude, which will make the actions and thoughts shift more easily. Wherever you start, the pieces interlock.

While the process is quite simple, it definitely requires a lot of focus and repetition, as well as some grit and determination, to help you turn away from the superhighway of automatic responses. My main message is this: You can do it, just because you want to, and your body and brain were made for this work. You deserve the changes in yourself that you desire, and you can achieve them. I know because I have done it, and I continue to experiment with the process of change all the time. It is fascinating, empowering, and fun.

For an insight-building deep dive into your current thoughts, feelings, and actions, and the ones you would like to create, plus a few other important aspects to consider, check out the worksheet "Creating Personal Change" (see appendix E). I learned it from Vann Joines, and it is a brilliant exercise for a coaching or therapy session, and equally applicable to self-help.

Exercise: Creating Change Action Plan

Once you are clear on your goals, have crafted goals that are truly within your ability to reach, and have taken a careful look at the thoughts, feelings, and actions that support your current experience, as well as the outcome you want, you are ready to create an action plan to make the change happen. As with all change, if you frame your action plan as an experiment, you are likely to encounter less internal resistance than you would if you frame it as a vow. Being a warm and positive coach for yourself is also important, since no one ever had much success with lasting change by beating themselves up for being a failure.

When you're ready to craft an action plan, refer to the "Creating Change Action Plan" worksheet (see appendix E). In it, I will walk you through the process of deciding on an experimental change for yourself, identifying your motivation to do it, and keeping your attention on the project so you can succeed in creating a new neural network. This is a process of experimentation regarding *personal* change; this is about creating a habit that is important to you, responding with more warmth or less defensiveness in a tough conversation, or some other way in which you would like to create a new way of being that is more in accordance with the person you want to be.

Part III

POLYAMORY IN THE THERAPY ROOM
Common Presenting Problems

CHAPTER 11

Negotiating Polyamory
Forming Good Agreements

Some people read an article, talk to a friend, or watch a show about polyamory and decide to jump right in and give it a try. Others do extensive research, read lots of books, and engage a therapist to help them lay a solid foundation for opening up before taking any other action steps. Some slide into polyamory sideways. For instance, a partner's infidelity can evolve into an awareness that they don't see themselves as monogamous, leading them to open their relationship while simultaneously working on repairing damage from past deception or broken agreements. Some open their relationship into polyamory, while others become monogamish, or swing, or develop some other nonmonogamy; sometimes those nonmonogamies evolve into polyamory and sometimes not. Every relationship and situation is unique, and there are many paths to polyamory. Still, whatever the relationship style, everyone who opens their relationship will at some point have one or, more likely, many conversations discussing their preferences and outlining their agreements.

I love it when I get to help early on in the process of opening up, because I think having an intentional process is part of what sets up polyamory for success. Actually, I think having an intentional process, rather than just diving in and hoping for the best, will set up *any* relationship for success. You could think of this careful process as somewhat similar to premarital counseling. The conversation revolves around figuring out what each partner wants; identifying areas of agreement and disagreement; and coming to some decisions about how to move forward in important areas of life, especially areas where there is some tension.

In this chapter, I discuss what you can do as a therapist, friend, partner, family member, or helping professional to support the crafting of good agreements when someone is beginning to explore polyamory. First, I talk about some common pitfalls that I often see, so that you can get a sense of what problems to be on the lookout for, and I share some strategies I often use to shift them. Then I talk about how you can support a good agreement-making process and what that looks like. In the next chapter, I provide a list of topics that anyone who's looking to embark on a nonmonogamous relationship should consider, which you can use to guide your clients' conversations or your own.

PITFALLS IN AGREEMENT-MAKING

Oftentimes the reason agreements get broken is because they're not made well in the first place. It's not easy to make good agreements. It takes a lot of grit to sit with the discomfort of disagreement and hang in there long enough for a real resolution to emerge. But it pays off in the long run, with deepened trust and strong agreements built to last.

Pseudo-Agreements

Giving up; giving in; exploding; getting melodramatic; attempting to convince, coerce, or manipulate; becoming exhausted or overwhelmed: These, like any response that stops or derails the conversation, are ineffective strategies people turn to when the discomfort of disagreement gets intense. None of those strategies leads to connection. None of them advance the discussion in a productive direction. But worst of all, they often result in a sort of pseudo-agreement offered under duress: "Okay, have it your way, I'm too tired of this conversation to argue anymore." That *sounds* like an agreement, but it isn't really. It's a tactic for avoiding discomfort. It comes of giving up on the conversation, rather than sticking with it until everyone concerned comes to a considered decision.

Here's why that matters: A pseudo-agreement is a setup for betrayal. The person pseudo-agreeing might already know they just want the hard conversation to end and have no intention of keeping the agreement.

They might hope for the best and tell themselves they will be able to follow through despite their concerns, but when they find themselves challenged to keep the agreement, that resolution won't hold for long. Or they might feel resentful and blame it on their partner when they don't follow through, because they felt coerced into giving way, not seeing that they gave up their power in the moment by folding too soon.

That doesn't mean that partners' desires must be in perfect harmony. I would be happy with, "Okay, I see that this is important to you, and it might work. Let's try it for two weeks and then discuss it again," or even, "I need a break, I'm exhausted, let's take this up again on Wednesday," but not, "Okay, have it your way." The key difference is whether the person making the agreement is taking responsibility for their choice.

Rules and Their Complications

People who are just launching into an open relationship (polyamorous or otherwise) often want to talk about what rules they're going to put in place. It's important to discuss agreements, but sometimes a focus on rules is marked by misconceptions that set people up for failure. When I have clients who are early in the process of discussing opening their relationship, I like to give them a gentle caution about the dangers of rules and how they don't necessarily always work as expected. Here's a rundown of a few common misapprehensions that sometimes lead people astray when deciding how to structure an open relationship.

Rules Can't Protect You from Feelings

People often assume that if they just put enough rules and agreements in place, they'll feel less jealous, scared, and threatened. But you can't legislate your way around an emotion. Oftentimes partners spend weeks setting up the rules that they expect to protect them from discomfort, only to discover that they still are struggling with uncomfortable feelings. What they need is not more rules, but more strategies for holding steady through discomfort, more sources of support (rather than just their partner), and a flexible and accessible approach to renegotiating agreements as things come up. No matter what agreements anyone might make, they will probably still experience some jealousy and other forms of emotional discomfort sometimes. The good news is, it's completely possible to strengthen the ability to self-regulate and co-regulate around these emotions, and doing so will likely strengthen their relationship and make them happier, healthier, and more flexible in the long term.

Poorly Made Rules Can Open the Door to Deception

It may seem counterintuitive, but setting rules can open the door for deception. If there are agreements that are poorly made, too many agreements, or confusion about what the agreements mean, people tend to end up breaking the rules. Then they have to deal with their partner's anger, disappointment, and sense of betrayal, or go underground and compound the betrayal by lying about it. Neither is an appealing option.

The solution is to make agreements that the partners want to keep. Good agreements reflect values and are in accord with beliefs, or at least are in alignment with stretch goals. They stay "top of mind" because the partners actually believe in them; even if they're a challenge to keep, the partners feel that their agreements are in accordance with the kind of person they aspire to be. Ideally, everyone concerned should have a voice in every agreement, and agreements should be made from a genuine, personal place, with insight and concern for the preferences of everyone involved.

Sometimes someone will make an agreement and then just sort of forget about it. That's a hint that it probably wasn't a very well-made agreement in the first place. Other factors that can affect follow-through include difficulty with focus, lack of motivation, memory impairment, ambivalence, or avoidance. Carefully made agreements require attention to carry out. If you agree to something you don't really believe in, it's going to be hard to keep it at the top of your mind when you are making choices, especially when it's competing with your strong desires and the pressing demands of your busy life. People who struggle with focus or memory will encounter trust issues in their relationships, and this is worth delving into with a lot of energy if they aspire to have multiple secure relationships. At the point when they decide they want to open their relationship, they are also deciding they want to take on the project of becoming trustworthy. If they seem to be a little fuzzy on that concept or weak on follow-through, it is entirely appropriate for you to make a strong, challenging statement about what is needed to be successful at polyamory. Some external supports, for example, calendars, habit trackers, or lists, might be helpful, but the important point is to address the issue head-on rather than ignore it and imagine it will go away.

Rules Can Have Loopholes

Many people rush through their conversations about opening up the relationship, in particular skipping over discussion of the nuances of the agreements they are making. The inevitable result is agreements that are riddled with loopholes. Partners may come away from the conversation with very different assumptions about what was meant or agreed to. This often happens when the partners are impatient to come to a resolution. Perhaps they're uncomfortable sitting with tension, fatigued from a string of difficult discussions, or simply so eager to get their experiment underway that they don't want to take more time in the discussion and planning phase. But if they rush through this process, without fully spelling out what they're thinking and without discussing all the permutations, variations, and exceptions they can think of, they will end up with loopholes.

Loopholes create space for something that feels like deception. Imagine a couple that has decided to try opening up their relationship. They decide it's okay for them each to date other people but don't have a deeper discussion about what they're each comfortable with or what information they want to disclose to one another or when. One partner strikes up a connection with a mutual friend but feels a little awkward and uncomfortable about it, and doesn't mention to their partner who the connection is with for a while. When they finally do, their partner feels angry, embarrassed, and betrayed. They're sure that their partner should have known better, but their partner was just acting on their understanding of the rules (and perhaps avoiding a conversation they intuitively knew would be uncomfortable). At the very least, loopholes like this create big misunderstandings that can undermine trust and emotional safety.

Unfortunately, loopholes tend to cluster around the topics that freak out partners the most. This makes sense if you consider the role of avoidance. Loopholes happen when partners feel too anxious to dig into the topic that's worrying them. Oftentimes people don't want to get overly specific about their agreements, in part because of what it reveals about themselves, and in part because of what they fear about the topic at hand. But the most anxiety-producing aspect of their situation is *exactly* what they need to discuss beforehand or else it will reveal itself, disastrously, down the road. This fact is a great example of why it can sometimes be so helpful to have a skilled therapist or coach guide the process of making agreements.

Helping clients close up loopholes involves helping them learn how to recognize what they're avoiding, hold steady through a stressful conversation, and move right into the scary details. You'll need to encourage your clients, or your partner(s), to get very specific.

No amount of discussion can predict every eventuality, so don't worry that you have to talk for decades before taking any action; however, some loopholes are glaring and can be seen a mile away. You will be able to spot them because they are the ones with emotional load. If someone prefers to avoid conflict, they could get frustrated with all the processing they are doing with regard to agreements, while still not discussing the elephant in the room, whatever that is for them. Helping them focus their efforts on the hardest, most relevant topics will have to be balanced with their developmental ability to hold steady and discuss difficult things effectively. If someone is highly motivated to open the relationship, hopefully they can apply that motivation to developing skills with the various aspects of differentiation of self. If a person has difficulty holding steady talking about a hypothetical difficult situation, they are certainly going to have difficulty discussing it after there has been a misunderstanding or breach of trust.

Problems with closing loopholes in agreements is not a special issue for polyamorous relationships, by the way. I think people in monogamous relationships are at least as prone to forming implicit "agreements" or making assumptions about what their partner thinks, in part because there isn't nearly as much of a cultural expectation about agreement-forming with monogamy as there is for polyamory. For instance, monogamous partners often do not really spell out what each of them means by fidelity; instead, they assume they agree with one another (despite probably sensing it might be a fraught conversation to have). But down the road, they may feel betrayed when it turns out their partner had a different definition. For instance, is watching porn okay when you're in a committed relationship? What about flirting? What about having a crush on someone else? Friending your ex on Facebook? These are things that people often don't spell out when they embark on a monogamous relationship, and it can cause tremendous distress later on if it turns out there is disagreement.

I think that discussing these things in some detail would benefit people in every kind of relationship. That's what premarital counseling is all about, after all. But premarital counseling doesn't always get couples there. It is understandable that, in the flush of excitement that comes with an engagement, many couples don't want to pause, take up the hard work of developing their differentiation of self, and suffer through hard conversations that could be put off until later (hopefully, never). After all, when you speak up about difficult things that you and your beloved disagree about, you have to face the possibility that the relationship might not make it. Who wants to do that in the first blush of new love?

It takes a lot of grit and endurance to make good agreements. A therapist can help a lot by outlining the skills that are involved in differentiation and helping clients build them, so that conversations about differences can become creative, engaging, and interesting, instead of frightening. Agreement-making discussions are often very accessible as a self-help project, particularly for people who have cultivated an ability to have difficult conversations in a productive manner, and without getting either bogged down or skipping over important details. If things get tense and fraught, and you are having trouble making headway, either find a good helper or refer to the nuts and bolts of differentiation and holding steady in chapter 8, or both.

There Are Some Things Rules Can't Change

Your partner is who they are, with their own values, preferences, character, and beliefs. They may make an agreement to do something (or not do something) because it is more comfortable for you, and they may follow through on that agreement, but there is no reason to think they will then become a person who thinks that is a preferable way to be. Sometimes, however, I get the sense that one partner thinks that putting external guidelines on their partner's behaviors will turn them into a person that makes decisions more in accordance with their values, preferences, or beliefs.

If you approach things in this way, you run the risk of creating rules that your partner perceives as limiting their autonomy or ability to be themselves, rules that end up feeling like bars on a cage. I've never seen someone show up as their best self when they feel trapped. For someone who gets rebellious when they feel trapped, rules can exacerbate an already complicated situation. Some people feel trapped easily; some have a lot more tolerance for following rules that they don't particularly love. Consider this when you are helping clients form agreements or in forming agreements of your own.

Counterintuitive as it might be, I tell my clients if they are hoping their partner will change in some significant way, they are much more likely to get what they want by getting curious about how they see things, how they make decisions, and what they want, and by giving them a lot of room to explore a broad range of options than by imposing a lot of rules.

Rules Made under Pressure Don't Work

Oftentimes people make agreements that they don't really believe in or they know they won't keep. This might be because they want to give their partner what they're asking for, based on a sense of guilt and obligation, or to avoid or shorten an unpleasant interaction. That's an extremely common avoidant behavior and a form of people-pleasing. The solution is for them to get better at managing their emotions and speaking up about their thoughts, beliefs, and preferences. As a therapist, you can keep an eye out for this dynamic and intervene when you see it. When it emerges, it's a good opportunity to offer specific support for the conflict-avoiding person. Look out for situations in which one partner has a history of telling avoidant lies or lies of omission, or "forgetting" about their agreements. They may feel, in the moment, that they are helping their partner by agreeing to what they want, but no one's relationship is strengthened by broken agreements.

In these situations, I slow down the conversation and deliberately make space for the client to look inside and identify what they think, feel, believe, and prefer (the first aspect of differentiation). I give them explicit permission to say only what is true. I ask them to take care about what they are agreeing to, because following through on agreements is so important to building trust in relationships. I remind them that, just because their partner wants them to agree to something doesn't obligate them to do so. Their partner is an adult and can manage their disappointment or whatever feelings arise if they don't get what they want. *The most important thing* is to show up honestly. This is because keeping (or renegotiating before breaking) agreements is an absolute requirement for building a trusting, collaborative relationship. If this is to be a relationship in which *everyone* thrives, it is important that no one agrees to something that they actually don't want to follow through on.

This can be a little bit of a hard sell for the other partner, who may be really looking forward to hearing what their partner will agree to do (or not do), and who may have a lot of distress related to the topic being discussed. The more distress there is, the more likely the partners are to try and force a resolution. It's your job to stop that from happening, whether as a therapist, or in your own relationship. In fact, the more distress there is concerning the discussion of any particular rule or agreement, the slower the process needs to go and the more carefully both partners need to look at what they actually think, feel, believe, and want. I take these moments of decision-making about rules very seriously and go very slowly, even if it makes everyone extremely uncomfortable.

Here are some ways I might do this, as a therapist:

I can see you are reading your partner right now, and you know what your partner wants you to say and do. I can see that you care about your partner's feelings, and a part of you wants to give them exactly what they want. Before you speak up, I want you to take the time to read yourself as well. Look inside and identify what you are feeling. Can you identify your own thoughts, preferences, and desires? It is in your partner's best interest for you to take the time to get clear about what you think and what agreements you want to make. Take your time.

I have too much respect for your partner to want you to rush into this agreement. Your partner doesn't need you to make an agreement you don't plan to keep, because that is going to undermine trust, which is the last thing your partner needs or wants. I'd much rather you had a difficult conversation about something true than agree to something you don't intend to do. Your only job right now is to be completely honest with yourself about what you are willing to agree to. Only make an agreement you can keep.

To the partner who is asking for the agreement, I might say the following:

I know you want the truth and only the truth. After all you have been through, you know you are strong, and you can handle a lot. I don't want you to have to handle any more broken agreements. But that means you might have to hear some very frank thoughts from your partner, about what they are and are not willing to agree to and actually follow through on. Are you ready to have a real discussion about real agreements with this real person beside you who intends to follow through on their agreements from now on? Are you ready to hear what they are interested in following through on and what they aren't ready to agree to yet?

I see that it is hard for you to hear that your partner isn't ready to agree to what you want them to right now. I want you to know that, as difficult as this is, you are doing great. I can promise that forcing an agreement or rushing into it won't work. I can't promise that going slowly like we are doing right now *will* work, but I can promise that rushing into an agreement without getting really honest about it will absolutely *not* work.

To make a good agreement, there has to be room for everyone to look deeply at what they think, what they feel, what they prefer, what they believe, what they intend, and what they want to build. It's also helpful if they can identify how difficult keeping the agreement is going to be for them, so that we can discuss putting some supports in place. I want to support them, but they will need other supports as well. That often can be their partner but not always. Do they have friends or family they can get support from? Becoming a person who only makes agreements they can keep is a big project, and an honorable one.

RULES THAT ARE MADE TO BE BROKEN

There are a few specific agreements that, for whatever reason, people tend to break much more frequently than others. Be on the lookout for these and double down on careful agreement-making processes if negotiating rules like this:

> *"You can see anyone you want, except this one person."* Why does this agreement get broken? Well, there's usually a reason that *this particular person* is being excluded. Perhaps there has been an infidelity with that person before or a flirtatious vibe that the partner has picked up on. Alternatively, it may just be the allure of the forbidden. Naturally, what happens is that after this rule is put forth and the other partner agrees to it, they *somehow* end up in the arms of the forbidden person. What would help the partners more would be having a robust conversation about *why* this person seems threatening to the relationship and what attraction they might hold before deciding on a ban. That conversation, however, takes a significant level of differentiation of self.
>
> *"You have to use a condom or a barrier method every time."* To me, this seems like it might be the most important rule to honor. With good reason, it's one of the most common rules nonmonogamous people establish. Yet, people break it all the time. It drives me crazy. My suspicion is that it has something to do with the heady, fluttery, crazy feeling of an early crush, which often leads people to make careless decisions they wouldn't otherwise make. It may also be tied to low levels of differentiation. Another possibility is substance use in intimate situations, leading to poor decision-making, memory, and follow-through. In any case, if opening your relationship is important to you, take my word for it, this is

not an agreement you want to break. As a therapist, I wonder, in a sexual situation, is the partner able to assert, "No, we need to use a condom, and if we're not using a condom, we're not having that kind of sex (or whatever the specifics of the agreement were)," to someone with whom they're completely infatuated? If not, apparently it is not yet time to open the relationship, *or* it is not a good idea to agree to use a condom. If someone is strong enough to admit, "I'm not confident I will be able or willing to use a condom every single time," I commend them for it, and this is a fine example of a hard yet honest disclosure I would reward with honest praise. It is so much better to have this conversation now rather than after a condom is not used and chlamydia or pregnancy is diagnosed. This is already going very well, compared to other possible outcomes. Then I wonder if the partners can work together to come up with a backup plan for if a condom is not used. What would feel safe and respectful to the other partner?

"I have to be able to contact you when you're out with another person in case there's an emergency." This is another extremely common agreement—and for good reason. When it gets broken, it's usually due, again, to the heady power of new relationship energy. You're gazing into the eyes of that special someone and don't notice that you have 40 texts and five missed calls. Or you turned your phone off even though you agreed not to or forgot it was on silent from your last business meeting. Or it ran out of battery and you didn't bring a charger. Sound weak? There is no way to explain away a broken agreement that doesn't sound weak. The only strong response is a sincere apology and leveling up in the ability to either form a good agreement in the first place or follow through. It can be deeply distressing when this agreement is broken. Even though generally it's just a matter of being distracted and not checking your messages, it can feel like abandonment or outright aggression. When your clients want to hammer out this kind of agreement, help them think through the complexities that will be involved when it comes time to follow through. Sometimes batteries actually do die. What is the backup plan?

"Don't fall in love." "Multiple loves" is a key component of polyamory, so this kind of agreement is much more common with

people who are in an extradyadic consensually nonmonogamous relationship but don't consider themselves polyamorous. This agreement invites breaking perhaps more than any other. How many people can actually control whether they fall in love? How many people, who are in the early stages of falling in love, have the emotional wherewithal to break off the new relationship because falling in love wasn't part of the agreement? In fact, one of the most common reasons that people end up pursuing polyamory after a broken agreement is that they were originally in an open relationship and a romantic component emerged. If you are thinking of making an agreement like this one, I would like to draw a distinction between feelings, like love, and actions, like hooking up. You probably can't control what feelings develop, but you certainly can control your actions. For instance, you can discuss newly developing feelings with your partner right away rather than putting off that discussion. And you can choose not to act on the romantic feelings in any number of ways, all of which involve quite a bit of self-control. More discussion of details leads to more ability to follow through on agreements, as long as you keep it clear and concise.

HOW TO MAKE AGREEMENTS THAT CAN BE KEPT

Making good agreements requires differentiation of self and flexibility. If you or your clients are new to polyamory, there are a million things to think about in the beginning and a lot of ideas and questions to consider. Having a coach or therapist guide this process can make all the difference. Tackling it on your own requires patience, patience, and more patience. The tips for therapists that follow are also relevant if you are guiding your own process.

The process of opening a relationship is often charged and complicated, and it can feel overwhelming for clients and therapists alike. When you or your clients experience that overwhelming feeling, it is an opportunity to notice what's going on inside and come up with strategies for managing those feelings. The following are some general guidelines for supporting the process of developing agreements for a polyamorous relationship:

Slow it down. Make sure everyone takes sufficient time to really look inside themselves and understand what they want, and are also able to listen with curiosity to their partner. Revisit chapter 9, regarding the initiator/inquirer process, for some useful structure for these discussions. Encourage asking questions of one another and investigating all the possible loopholes anyone can imagine. Ask, "What might go wrong? What is the backup plan?" This kind of thorough discussion can be fatiguing and time-consuming, especially if the participants need to take a lot of breaks or time-outs to manage difficult emotions. But, almost certainly, there is no deadline they have to meet, and they can afford to take the time to come to a good agreement. Also, hopefully, not every topic will be equally fraught. If the partners in question are still developing emotional management or communication skills, consider starting with discussion points that are not overly stressful. If partners seem to be driven by a sense of urgency, help them free themselves of any imagined deadlines. If decisions really must be made quickly, see if they can both agree to a short-term experiment and support them each in gathering data about how it goes so they can have a fuller discussion in a week or two when they integrate lessons learned and come up with a new experiment.

Be thorough, and go slow, but don't stall entirely. On rare occasions, I have known someone to filibuster to stall a decision or action they are opposed to, for instance, their partner dating someone else. I'm not opposed in theory to more discussion before taking action, but the partner who wants to take the action may get frustrated to the point of infidelity if the situation gets out of hand, particularly if they are reacting to a passive aggressive tactic or thinking they are being manipulated. Of course, ideally, everyone concerned would manage their emotions, speak up about their frustrations, and challenge themselves to hold steady and help their partner get comfortable by creating safety, rather than making threats of escalating action. And you can certainly point out what you observe and make suggestions along those lines. But don't forget that the filibustering partner is also having difficulty with emotional regulation. Without a doubt, the dynamic I'm describing here is a challenging one. But here is the wild card:

Emotional security is an interesting thing; intuition would suggest that it always arises from increased predictability, and it often does. It seems on the surface that postponing opening the relationship will confer safety to the frightened partner. But I've also seen situations where someone goes from being the worst possible monogamous partner to becoming the most reliable and dependable polyamorous partner. For someone like that, their partner won't experience their reliability until they feel free to express themselves congruently in an open relationship. The "experiment" construct can be a useful way to work with this type of situation. Each partner might choose one small action to try, which is their personal experiment, and gather data on how it goes for both, assessing again after an interval.

Make sure they hear each other out. Frank discussions about having sex and romance with other people can become uncomfortable, especially for people who are just starting to consider nonmonogamy. This can also be tough for therapists, or clients may imagine it is uncomfortable for their therapist and avoid frank revelations. You can debunk that myth by letting them know they don't have to protect you in their discussions. It can be tempting for people to edit their truth to avoid hurting their partner's feelings or get reactive, resulting in a shut down in their partner if things get tense. These dynamics are what keep people from having the deep conversations they need to create good agreements. Do your best to hold a space in your therapy room where difficult truths can be spoken and heard. Help everyone hold steady, listen well, and speak frankly. Of course, there is a fine line between topics that need to be discussed and "too much information." Use your best intuition to discern the difference, as you would in any relational therapy, and watch out for situations in which one partner is oversharing due to anxiety or shock or wound.

Embrace flexibility. Your clients aren't going to know what works and what doesn't until they try. Experience teaches; theory does not. This is one of the most difficult things about opening a relationship. The best-laid plans will not prevent missteps and mistakes. When things go awry, it's an opportunity to learn more about what does and doesn't work for each partner. Most agreements will probably have to be renegotiated as new situations arise, so make sure your clients know that these early discussions are just the beginning of a relationship-long process; they should expect evolution. This is good news: They don't need an ironclad set of rules that covers every eventuality; it will serve better to nurture a sense of teamwork, a willingness to flex with new developments, a sense of humor, and a spirit of adventure. Without some guidance, a first experiment with polyamory can easily become a painful training in the school of hard knocks. Set up your clients to expect some surprises, some of which will not be pleasant or easy, and let them know you are confident that they can navigate the challenges that arise with grace, humor, and flexibility.

RULES, OR EXPERIMENTS?

It's often helpful to frame rules or agreements as experiments: "I'm willing to try this experiment for a month or two and set a date to re-evaluate." This approach supports ongoing conversation with periodic check-ins, keeps partners from sweeping difficulties under the rug, and supports flexibility throughout time and through changing circumstances. It also helps partners learn to have fuss-free discussions about tough topics, because practice makes perfect. The more often you discuss something with curiosity and flexibility, the harder it is to get melodramatic about it. Hearing your partner say, "Sure, let's try it that way for a month and see how it goes. I'll be curious to see what we both think after we watch it play out," can go a long way toward defusing tensions and minimizing polarization. It implies teamwork, attunement, and responsiveness, as well as a can-do attitude that breeds goodwill.

In life, there are no guarantees. All anyone can do is take a good guess. Oftentimes, I've seen clients who are terrified that something about polyamory will be very hard for them, but when it unfolds, they discover, to their shock, that it's actually easy for them, or if not easy, it's manageable. I've also often seen the opposite, where someone doesn't think something will be challenging for them and then it brings them to their knees. Your clients aren't going to know what feels hard and what feels manageable until they live their way into it. You may not know what the focus of therapy will be until things start to unfold in real life.

That said, it is helpful to acknowledge the possibility of an emotionally overwhelming outcome that would benefit from immediate intervention, as well as the possibility of a very successful experiment. That's why I prefer the frame of "experiments" rather than plans. I think it is less extreme language and less likely to be perceived as a trap. And these are, by definition, experiments that will certainly need to be evaluated and modified, probably multiple times, throughout a lifetime, with changing circumstances.

THE POSSIBILITIES ARE ENDLESS

If you're seeing a couple that's thinking about embarking on an open relationship of some kind, offer them free rein to discuss the wide-open field of possibilities. There are infinite ways to structure a nonmonogamous relationship, and your clients have complete freedom to experiment and consider and discover the structure that works for them. Monogamy? Monogamish? Polyamorous? Swinging? Open? Friends with benefits? Kinky play only, no sex? Sex but no kissing? All of it, but not in our bed? No overnights? Dates only once a month, or once a week? Whatever you want my love, as long as we get to connect every weekend? Whatever you want as long as I'm out of town, or you are? It's all fine as long as I don't know much about it? Seriously, I've seen it all. I've seen every possible variation succeed, and I've seen every possible variation fail. It's not the structure itself that makes or breaks the experiment.

Your clients are, presumably, looking for a relationship style that works for them specifically. The discussion shouldn't be limited to "polyamory: yes or no." Instead, the question is this: In the vast and infinite world of possibilities, what kind of relationship do *they* want to create? Maybe together you and your clients can think up an entirely new kind of open relationship that no one has heard of yet but that will be a perfect fit for them. My perspective is that anything you can imagine has the potential to work, if the partners are up for it, committed to working as a team, comfortable talking about what does and doesn't work well for them, and flexible enough to make adjustments and roll with the punches.

Here is an important question for someone who is considering opening their relationship, whether they are just trying it for the first time or have tried it in the past but encountered problems they don't want to repeat: "Imagine a situation in which an open relationship of some sort works well for you. What are you doing? What is your partner doing? What are other people, partners, and family members doing? How do you feel? How does your partner feel? How are you thinking about yourself, your partner, and other partners? What kind of support do you have? What kind of situation is it?"

A WORD ABOUT VETOES

It's pretty common for people in primary/secondary relationships to have veto rules: "If, at any point, I start to feel like that person you're seeing is a threat to our relationship, I can tell you to stop seeing that person, and that's what you'll do." Vetoes are a controversial topic in the polyamory community, and many argue that it's better to avoid putting them in place. One of the big problems with vetoes is that people often don't follow through on them. As you can imagine, a person might exercise their right to veto when they're feeling threatened because they've noticed that their partner is getting really close to the other person they're seeing. Naturally, it's pretty hard to break up with someone specifically *because* you're getting close to them.

Sometimes partners respect the veto rule, which can be quite painful as they break off a relationship that was becoming important to them; sometimes that resolves quietly, and other times it blooms into resentment. Sometimes they refuse to end the newer relationship, which only validates their partner's feeling of being threatened. Most damaging of all, they may pretend to break off the connection but go underground with it, turning polyamory into infidelity. Using a veto in this type of situation also prevents what can be important character-testing and skill-building opportunities that potentially can be important to increased emotional safety. As an example, if Mary enforces a veto when James gets deeply emotionally connected with Rosie, Mary won't get to find out how James would have handled the situation, including possibly finding new and important ways to connect and strengthen their relationship to balance accommodating a newer connection. There is a growth curve there, and it can lead to important healing, potentially including Mary realizing that all is well and polyamory will work for her. Or it can lead to James and/or Mary realizing that there are some important things they want to add to their relationship or their routines to better manage James having two romantic relationships simultaneously in ways that strengthen both.

That doesn't mean that veto rules can never work. One of the biggest benefits of vetoes is that they can provide a feeling of security as a couple embarks on an experiment with nonmonogamy. Veto rules work better when people really believe in them, so if you are working with clients who are considering a veto rule, it might be relevant to discuss what those involved believe about fidelity and having multiple loves concurrently. In what circumstances do they believe that giving up something important to them to further the comfort of their partner is the right thing to do? What do they believe about potentially causing some emotional pain to another partner to make their primary partner more comfortable? Would the veto agreement go both ways or just one way? How will they engage in a meaningful learning curve that will strengthen their connection if they end relationships that get challenging?

Veto agreements are complicated, and they can backfire spectacularly if they're not kept. Keep a sharp eye out for any indication a veto agreement is being offered up reluctantly. Look out for loopholes that haven't been discussed and any signs that either partner perceives it as a cage or trap.

Also, know that polyamory often evolves for the couples who engage in it. A couple might put a certain set of agreements in place in the first three months of their open relationship and then change them significantly many times. By the time someone is in their second decade of successful polyamory, they may have significantly altered the original rules or done away with many of them completely. The veto often falls into this category. Consider suggesting that it be an experiment or a time-limited agreement rather than a forever rule.

For some cautionary tales about specific agreements that often backfire, see chapter 14, "Infidelity, Broken Agreements, and Building Trust."

AGREEMENT STYLE: DON'T ASK, DON'T TELL

While we're discussing controversial relationship styles within polyamory, "don't ask, don't tell" deserves a mention. In this relationship style, partners agree that one partner prefers not to know details about their partner's other relationship(s). The specifics vary, from, "I don't want to hear the play-by-play, or I'll get jealous," to "I don't even want to know if you have any other partners." Don't ask, don't tell (DADT) has a generally negative reputation in the polyamory community, and it does certainly have some significant drawbacks. That said, I have seen it work well for years on end, and I hate to argue with success.

Because I'm closely acquainted with some well-functioning DADT relationships, I've given it a lot of thought. Why does it work sometimes? What doesn't work about it? What are the pitfalls? What are the benefits?

People get nervous about DADT for several reasons. It is sometimes perceived as an indication that one or more of the people making the agreement are not entirely comfortable with polyamory. It is also sometimes seen as implying a lack of consent: If you don't know what your partner is doing, how can you consent? Plus, the pseudo-secrecy associated with DADT makes a lot of people very uncomfortable— sometimes even the partners in DADT arrangements who would be comfortable sharing much more information but agree to hold back disclosures based on respect for their partner's wishes.

I see DADT as a request for co-regulation. Oftentimes this is what it sounds like:

Honey, I just seem to lose my mind when I think too much about you being with that other person. Once I get a grip and start thinking about something else, I'm more or less fine. I think if I knew less about what you are doing exactly, it would be easier for me to stop obsessing about what you're doing and focus on my own interests. I'm not asking you to lie to me, but I think it would be easier for me if I didn't know where you go when you go out or which friend you hang out with. Just tell me you're going to see a friend, okay?

This is an example of co-regulation, because it is one partner asking the other to change a behavior to help them manage their emotional state.

Of course, as a strategy for emotional regulation, willful ignorance has its pitfalls. Still, when I'm being honest with myself, I have to admit that I use it in my own life, and so do a lot of other people. Imagine a situation in which one partner is in charge of paying the bills. Is that only because they are good at it and want to do it, or does it also serve the purpose of allowing the other partner to put potentially troubling thoughts about money to the side, knowing their partner is handling it well? When you decide to send your partner to the emergency vet with your dog, while you stay home because it's just too much for you to bear, it's not like you don't know the dog is sick. You just don't want to watch it all unfold, and you trust your partner to handle it and keep you informed about important decisions. These are common, everyday versions of something like "don't ask, don't tell."

Consider how this compares to common, everyday forms of secrecy. For instance, I hear things like this all the time: "I didn't mention to my partner just how much my new shoes cost, because, well, they don't really need to know that," or "I'm hoping they don't notice how many new books I bought this month; I doubt if they would approve." That is quite different from DADT, in which the person who is not getting the detailed information actually requested that they be protected in that manner.

Like any relationship structure, DADT works best when partners discuss it in detail beforehand and put some time into crafting robust agreements. This is not always the case; I've seen some fairly imperfect DADT that still works well enough for everyone concerned. Ideally, however, it should be clear what types of information will and won't be shared, and in what circumstances the partner who's not getting all the information would actually like to be consulted or updated more fully. I also think it is important that there be some sort of regular check-in strategy, because if the agreement is simply, "Go do your thing, and don't tell me about it," the partner who has agreed not to bring it up will be left without an approved way of discussing changes *they* may want to make in agreements. This is a loophole that again can lead to lies, secrecy, or broken agreements. At minimum, I think it is important that DADT include a clause for how a partner who wants to discuss changing or updating an agreement will feel freely able to do so.

If your clients are considering a DADT arrangement, it is important to remember that it doesn't mean never discussing polyamory. Rather, it's a way to *limit how often partners will talk about certain aspects of polyamory*, based on the individual needs and preferences of the partners involved. They will need to have at least one robust discussion about agreements for DADT to work at all; having no agreements is likely to backfire.

Furthermore, they will need to make a plan for when or in what circumstances they should check in. Regular upkeep is worth the effort. Refer to chapter 12, "Negotiating Polyamory: Talking Points for Partners," for a robust guide to the topics partners should consider as they decide how to structure their relationship.

THE POWER OF CONSIDERATION

There's a personality trait that a lot of people who are in happy, healthy polyamorous relationships share. I call it "good manners," but you could also refer to it as "kindness" or "consideration." In essence, it is the ability to take other people's feelings and preferences into consideration without losing track of your own.

If you have a client who is naturally considerate, it will be a huge asset in their project of opening the relationship. If not, I recommend they spend some time and effort building the skill, because it makes a meaningful difference in the day-to-day functioning of a polyamorous relationship.

Many people are taught that good manners are simply about smoothing things over and not rocking the boat. The good manners that training produces are built on a foundation of conflict avoidance and people-pleasing. If that's what you or your clients are used to, finding the balance between being kind and being honest can be quite a challenge. But good manners can also be built on empathy, which requires that a person develop some skill at managing difficult emotions gracefully to be able to tolerate the emotions of others while also acknowledging and managing their own.

True consideration also requires the participation of both partners. That's because, for you to take another's emotions and preferences into account, they need to be forthright with you about what they feel and believe. You will need to work systemically to get to a place where everyone involved can be both frank and kind, thoughtful about one another's desires without neglecting their own.

Consideration can appear in many different ways. Here are some common examples of considerate behavior in polyamorous relationships:

Never being rude or mean when frustrated or angry.

Honoring a partner's preferences about what to share and not share about other partners or dates.

Being meticulous about getting home on time or calling well ahead of time if plans change.

Never texting other lovers when in a conversation or at dinner with another, with the exception of making yourself available to your primary if that is the agreement, or in specific other agreed-upon circumstances.

Never being sarcastic or mean when choosing to give up something for someone else's comfort. In other words, if you decide to break a date to spend the evening with another partner because of some extenuating circumstances, live the choice generously, rather than reluctantly. Don't agree to it if you can't be nice about it.

Taking personal responsibility for your own decisions, rather than blaming it on your primary partner: "I'm sorry, I would love to spend the evening with you as we planned, but I really want to be home with [my primary partner] because they are having a really hard day," rather than, "I need to break our date because [my primary partner] needs me to be home with them."

Keeping your phone charged, turned on, and with you, if you have agreed to make yourself available to a partner.

While some of this might seem obvious, I've seen breaches of good manners often enough that I've given some serious thought to how to cultivate the relevant skills. Much of it comes down to excellent follow-through, which ultimately depends on having made good agreements or valuing your own integrity enough to be willing to follow through with agreements that you don't 100% believe in until such time as they can be renegotiated.

Much of it also comes down to generosity of spirit, which is more complicated than it appears. I believe that, at its core, generosity of spirit is based on good emotional boundaries. It requires you to be clear that you are in charge of your own life, choices, and decisions, so you don't blame them on anyone else. Similarly, it requires understanding your own goals and motivation, holding yourself to a high standard of behavior (even in less-than-ideal circumstances or times of stress), and discerning when you are experiencing enough distress to discuss a topic that troubles you (as opposed to being slightly annoyed but choosing not to sweat the small stuff).

I'd like to share this personal account, which serves to illustrate the powerful impact that even small acts of consideration can have. It also highlights the creativity that can be brought to bear when it comes to crafting strategies to work with difficult emotions.

> My wife was okay with polyamory in principle but had some reservations about it. So we discussed it a lot and worked out some agreements that made it more comfortable for both of us. A key point is that these agreements were negotiated until we were both okay with them—an agreement that feels too unfair to one partner is likely to be not honored or to cause resentment and other problems.
>
> One such agreement that my wife requested was the mikvah, or ritual bath. After I had a date with someone else I would take a bath or shower, which included a small ritual to mark the dividing line in time and attention—a bit of meditation or quiet thought: "Now I am thinking about my wife and reentering my life with her."
>
> This felt reasonable and easy for me to do, and it helped my wife feel good about our arrangement, so I was happy to do it for her.

I'm so impressed with these partners, who not only demonstrate a beautiful example of a highly differentiated, thoughtful agreement-making process, but also found a way to harness the power of consideration into a deeply meaningful ritual that helps them honor their commitments to one another and keep their aspirational selves front and center.

WHEN IT WORKS, IT WORKS

At this point, you've probably gotten a good sense of the things that can go wrong in polyamorous relationships when the agreement-making process is rushed, forced, or neglected. Without a robust process of negotiating and development agreements, the bogeymen of relational therapy threaten our clients: broken agreements, deception, resentment, etc.

I hope that you've also gotten a sense of what it looks like when things go really right. Imagine considerate partners, engaged in deep discussion that honors all of their perspectives in full nuance and detail— honestly striving to come to creative agreements; running experiments with flexibility, imagination, and grace; and working toward crafting a relationship that is uniquely suited to their beliefs, preferences, and desires. When it works, it's a beautiful thing, and it often does work.

I also want to leave you with the awareness that a polyamorous relationship doesn't have to be absolutely ideal to function well enough. How many monogamous relationships have you known to be truly ideal? Why should polyamory be any different? Less-than-ideal circumstances, unique personalities and personal challenges, and the inevitable learning curve of being a relational human being tends to throw a curveball into relational functioning, whether in monogamous or polyamorous relationships. Of course, as therapists, we help our clients understand what goes into creating secure functioning, good agreements, and so on. But I don't want you to think well-functioning polyamory always looks perfect. It doesn't. The key, as with monogamy, is whether there is enough—enough safety, enough progress in the right direction, enough connection, enough excitement . . . just . . . enough. Is there enough of what everyone needs and wants in their relationship for everyone involved to stick with it? If there is, you have an example of a well-functioning relationship.

CHAPTER 12

Negotiating Polyamory
Talking Points for Partners

The issues facing people who are considering opening their relationship are many and varied. There is so much to discuss. This chapter offers exercises designed to help guide some of those discussions. I hope this chapter can help anyone who is considering opening their relationship cover the ground they need to cover. This will probably involve exploring lots of topics, some of which will be more comfortable than others. It will also involve going deeply enough into conversations to more fully understand what is at stake for everyone concerned, hopefully avoiding problematic loopholes coming to light later on down the road.

There is no rulebook regarding what topics need to be discussed; that varies and is very individual. I have offered suggestions of topics to consider, but you may not need to discuss them all, and there will be some that don't feel immediately relevant. I recommend going with your intuition. Skip what isn't important to you right now, and use your energy for the more immediately relevant topics. Polyamory tends to evolve, so keep in mind that discussion points that aren't important now might emerge later on, in which case you can revisit them. If you sense that a particular topic will be difficult for you or your partner to handle, that may be an indication that the topic is important and should not be skipped.

You might use these exercises and talking points early on in the process, perhaps when just beginning to consider embarking on a polyamorous relationship. Having a series of thoughtful, differentiated discussions about a broad variety of issues that might arise will dramatically increase the chances of success, while building some important relational skills. These worksheets and exercises may also come in handy with people who have been in an open relationship for some time but may have skipped over some important discussions or left loopholes that are showing up now, or whose relationships have evolved in such a way that they are now facing new challenges.

You and your clients are free to use these worksheets in whatever way they will be most helpful; you can use the questions in session as the need arises and/or use them for homework between sessions or a self-help project.

Because differentiated conversations start with self-awareness, the exercises I have developed guide participants through an internal investigation of their own unique thoughts, feelings, opinions, and beliefs. Of course, this is intended to lead to deep and productive discussions between partners, as self-knowledge naturally gives way to sharing aspects of ourselves and our thoughts with one another.

The initiator/inquirer (I/I) process is ideal for many of these conversations; for an in-depth discussion of how to use the I/I, see chapter 9. With practice and encouragement, everyone gets better at figuring out what they think and feel, as well as speaking up about difficult topics. The more difficulty partners have discussing these topics, the more structure they will need. People with higher levels of differentiation will have more fun with the process, and want and need less assistance, support, and coaching. If there are topics on the list that feel more manageable, I recommend starting with those, rather than beginning with the most difficult material. If someone is really struggling with the concept of polyamory, remind them that discussing is not the same as deciding. The "Holding Steady Self-Coaching Worksheet" might be helpful (see appendix B). I would also encourage them to take the initiator role in an I/I discussion, with their partner as inquirer to help their partner get curious, ask good questions, listen carefully, and come to understand what is distressing them and why. This might also help them come to know their own thoughts, feelings, and reactions more fully.

As I discuss in the previous chapter, "Negotiating Polyamory: Forming Good Agreements," you'll want to keep your eye out for the topics your clients seem to *avoid* discussing and support them in managing the difficult thoughts and feelings that lead to avoiding those topics. Helping clients, and one another, have the detailed and specific conversations needed to close any loopholes will avoid serious complications down the line. Even though no one can predict with total accuracy where future challenges will arise, gaining an understanding of how their partner(s) feel about various situations now will make it a lot easier to bring things up later if challenges develop.

TO OPEN OR NOT TO OPEN: THAT IS THE QUESTION

The first discussion partners will probably have is about whether to open their relationship. Sometimes that discussion will have happened years before you meet the clients. Other times it is the focus of therapy. You will notice that some of the exercises I present in this chapter are also presented in chapter 6, "The Therapist: Bias, Strengths, and Challenges," and chapter 7, "What Makes a Good Relationship?" This is because we all have thoughts and experiences, dreams and desires, that form our beliefs and longings about relationships, and we all make assumptions based on them. People who work professionally with clients who are in open relationships will probably benefit from taking a look at their thoughts, beliefs, and formative experiences about relationships, and people who are considering being in an open relationship would also benefit from that exploration. The exploration is the same, the angle of perspective is just a little different. Whether you are a therapist or client, working on a self-help project or just reading this book out of curiosity, thinking more deeply about multiple aspects of a relationship is likely to be useful.

I present these exercises as I would to a client. Feel free to include them in session, give all or parts of them as homework, or do them yourself if you would like to.

Exercise: My Relationship Ideas: Reflection Worksheet

When beginning to think about opening a relationship, it is natural to come up against beliefs, experiences, emotions, reactions, fears, and biases, some of which may be subconscious. If they remain uninvestigated and unspoken, they can cause mischief by influencing our reactions and responses while remaining invisible or semivisible.

We all have the power to influence our own emotional experiences through choosing which thoughts to dwell on and which to give less attention to. If someone is either idealizing or pathologizing any particular type of relationship, or worrying that a negative situation they experienced earlier in life might repeat as a result of taking a particular action now, it is well worth exploring this.

A belief system is just a thought we think a lot, not necessarily an indicator of a truth. Some of the thoughts we have maintained for the longest time arose early in life and just never got reexamined. There is no right or wrong relationship structure, just the relationship structure that is a good fit for any particular individual at this time. If someone is thinking about whether they might want to open their relationship, I think it is important to take a look at beliefs and experiences that form their ideas of what a relationship is or can be. Getting some sunshine on unexamined thoughts through noticing and discussing them will help prevent mysterious blocks from emerging later on. For an exploration of the origins of your ideas about relationships, see the "My Relationship Ideas: Reflection Worksheet" in appendix A.

Exercise: Examining Assumptions about Relationship Structures

As always, I draw a crisp distinction between thinking about and considering a topic and making a decision about one's life choices. Even feeling positive feelings about polyamory doesn't mean you have to choose to have an open relationship. Take one step at a time, with decision-making being the last step.

The "Examining Assumptions About Relationship Structures" worksheet (see appendix A) will challenge you to think about what the benefits and pitfalls might be for a wide range of relationship styles, beyond your own personal experience. The exploration in this worksheet then moves to questioning whether assumptions about benefits and pitfalls are accurate or if it might be possible to create those specific benefits, or encounter those specific pitfalls, with any relationship structure. Keeping this thought exercise light and fun, and far outside of any decision-making process, is recommended. Let the worksheet guide a process of internal exploration or spark an interesting conversation with a friend or partner.

Exercise: Dreams and Desires

Whatever you long for in life, and in a relationship, I want you to have it. Unless you have taken some time to think about this, you might not be completely aware of what you long for in a relationship. Or you might have given up on some things that are really important to you because you didn't think you would get them.

Because dreams and desires are the juice, energy, and passion of life, ignoring them is likely to lead to an existence that feels a little (or a lot) dry. Take some time to really think about what excites, energizes, and wakes you. Thinking (and feeling) about dreams and desires lends itself well to creativity and fun. Consider doing the "Dreams and Desires" exercise (see appendix A) in writing or by making artwork, a collage, or even a vision board.

Use the I/I framework to support sharing between partners about dreams and desires. As a therapist, it is invaluable to have ways your clients can practice the I/I skills with topics that are generally easier to keep positive, and the "Dreams and Desires" exercise is great fodder for less fraught, more fun conversations between partners.

CRAFTING YOUR UNIQUE OPEN RELATIONSHIP

The next set of exercises assumes that your clients are actively discussing how to make some form of consensual or ethical nonmonogamy work for them. Again, they begin with self-reflection as a necessary precursor to a differentiated conversation. No matter what kind of open relationship your clients are thinking about crafting, the questions here should help them explore the possibilities and discern their preferences.

Exercise: Imagining Many Forms of Open

"Imagining Many Forms of Open," which can be found in appendix F, was designed to expand the ways we tend to limit our thinking about relationships as a result of being raised in a culture that only discusses monogamy. A failure of imagination is easy when our cultural narrative is as limited as it is. This worksheet consolidates thinking about the qualities you seek in a relationship, and the kinds of relationship experiences you want. This worksheet makes a foundational assumption that you are planning to try some form of open relationship, distinguishing it from the "Relationship Concept Worksheets," which support thinking about types of relationships before making a decision to move toward opening up. When considering various forms of open, it can be helpful to revisit definitions of various structures and broad concepts presented in chapter 1, "Consensual Nonmonogamies: What Are the Options?"

As you think about and discuss your options, keep in mind that open relationships tend to evolve, as experience teaches much more effectively than theory. You are unlikely to come up with the be-all and end-all of relationship structure plans that will suit everyone concerned forever more. Start from an assumption that life will be your best teacher, and plan on modifying your plan as things unfold.

Exercise: Discussion Topics for Intimate Relationships

Discussions about individual partner's preferences with various aspects of open relationships might overlap with decision-making about opening up, come after the decision, or more likely both, in addition to being revisited again and again as circumstances change, time passes, and more is revealed. Therapists often ask me for a list of topics clients should discuss before or in the process of opening up their relationship. The problem with creating such a list is that situations and circumstances vary so much. Some partners have shared households and responsibilities, while others do not. Some have a hierarchical structure, while others do not. The list goes on; variety is the spice of life. No list is going to cover the ground and simultaneously be totally relevant for everyone. The result of careful consideration is "Discussion Topics for Intimate Relationships," located in appendix F. It is a fairly comprehensive list, divided into eight realms: fidelity; connection; safety; primacy; visibility; time, money, and other resources; disclosures; and negotiation. I think this covers most of the ground I often encounter when working with open relationships, and a fair amount of it applies equally to monogamous partnerships. It is possible that you will think of other realms, and likely other questions as well, in which case please add them. As always, my handouts should be treated as a jumping-off place.

My hope in arranging these discussion points according to realm is that it will be intuitive to stick to one realm at a time. One surefire way to get overwhelmed by difficult material is to pile a lot of stuff on one discussion. If the material is difficult, tackle just one or two of the smaller questions at a time, and make sure they are from the same realm. Take lots of breaks, and be kind to one another. Some topics will be easy, and some less so. Consider limiting time spent on discussing the finer points of opening your relationship to help everyone stay fresh, engaged, and untriggered. If anyone starts yawning or shutting down, it might be time to take a break.

This list might seem overwhelming in itself. Not everyone needs to discuss all of these things. The people involved in the discussion should decide what to discuss. I think it is also helpful to remember that for some people, these conversations might be fun and exciting, and for other people, they might be overwhelming, extremely difficult, and require a lot of emotional management, care, and focus. If anyone experiences discussing these topics as being a lot like work, please don't make talking about this stuff the entirety of what you do together. Make time to do other things together just for fun, and take time for refreshing and nurturing solo activities, too. Remember, you are crafting a relationship you both (or all) want to participate in; no one wants to participate in a relationship that is all work. It is important that the pacing of the discussions respects the emotional needs of everyone involved.

The I/I process is ideal for these discussions and can create some helpful structure outside of therapy sessions. Revisit the "Time-Out Exercise" (see appendix B) if needed. And remember, you can always expand options for any topic by using "30 Ideas No Matter How Silly: Brainstorming Process" handout (see appendix D).

TYING IT ALL TOGETHER

Now that there have been some deep discussions and your clients have given thought to many issues that arise in open relationships, it may be time to start making some decisions, running some experiments, and discovering how everyone feels and responds as things actually begin to unfold. The following are some guidelines for the decision-making process:

Expect that you and your partners' preferences will differ. It is not necessary to create a tit-for-tat balance to have a well-functioning open relationship. I have seen many relationships in which only one partner has other partners, and all is well. I have seen situations in which one partner enjoys romantic connections and the other prefers friends with benefits or hookups. I've seen lots of situations in which one partner enjoys lots of sexual adventure and the other prefers to have just one or two long-term, stable relationships, or none. Rather than shooting for "even steven" across the board, partners should strive to represent their preferences honestly and craft something unique that fits them. In fact, far from being necessary for success, in my experience, an "even steven" setup is incredibly rare.

Experiment, experiment, experiment. Don't make a "rule book" and expect to follow it for the next five years. Instead, craft an experiment that feels workable as a starting point, and check in frequently about how things are going. Investigate the beautiful and delicate balance of emotions, responses, feelings, preferences, choices, and decisions as it evolves throughout time. Nurture the evolution with frequent conversations and readjustments.

Practice holding your emotions (and your partners') gently and without judgment. There will probably be plenty to hold. Expect that your emotions will evolve; sometimes, one partner starts out feeling challenged, and then circumstances change and the other partner is suddenly the one being challenged. So don't be too quick to judge your partner; remember that there will almost certainly come a time when you will want and appreciate extra consideration and patience yourself. In fact, one of the huge strengths of polyamorous relationships is the frequent role reversals. There is a lot of empathy to be gained by shifting circumstances, as you're likely to discover.

Stay flexible. You don't have to revise your entire plan every time someone has an emotion. Still, tweaking a little here and there in response to shifting circumstances is a great idea. Once in a while, of course, you may need to do a major reshuffle, and that's fine. Keep track of the delicate balance of emotions and notice how your tolerance for difficult emotions increases as you continue to challenge yourself; keep adjusting things to better fit everyone involved.

Don't jeopardize the emotional safety of your relationship on a whim, for fleeting pleasure, or to make someone else comfortable. Here is my most forceful relationship advice: Do not break your agreements. Instead, renegotiate. If you're going to be late, call with plenty of notice. Every successful relationship depends on emotional stability and security, but when it comes to nonmonogamy, you're expecting your partners to be next-level relationship champs. For goodness' sake, make it as easy on them as possible, either by keeping your word or initiating the conversation about changing an agreement.

Be kind. Whether or not you have a hierarchy in your relationships, everyone involved is a human being, and they all deserve to be treated with consideration, decency, and respect. I hope this goes without saying, but sometimes people lose sight of how being a decent and caring human being helps complicated relationships work well. Polyamory requires being with the one you're with, which can make those you *aren't* with at any given moment feel the gap in your attention acutely. A secondary or non-nesting partner may struggle when your other commitments take you away for a while (for instance, if you're trying to keep your primary relationship stable in a crisis). Another typical situation that creates stress is when a non-nesting or secondary partner has a crisis in their life. Be prepared to show a lot of grace when you're in this situation and not the one in crisis, because the tables often turn and, eventually, you're likely to be in the other person's place.

Exercise: Consolidating Information, Working toward Action

As discussions occur, information flows, ideas emerge, and differences reveal themselves, partners will begin to get clear on some potential action steps to take. It is time to make some lists, consider which action steps to take first, and identify areas where more information would be helpful to move forward with confidence. Refer to the "Consolidating Information, Working Toward Action" worksheet in appendix F. It can be used individually if you are trying to set things up for yourself, as in solo polyamory, and is equally relevant for couples, throuples, or any other group. It includes a list of topics that frequently come up in the "need to learn more about it" category.

WORKING WITH DIFFERENCES

Holding tension with differences is a challenging and exciting task. Oftentimes, people feel a strong urge to jump to a premature "resolution" to relieve the discomfort and sustained vulnerability of disagreeing. Don't do it. Clients need to get comfortable letting the tension exist and developing strategies for showing their love and affection even when they're in the midst of disagreement. They can take lots of breaks, stretch, or toss a ball back and forth to manage tensions and lower reactivity so they don't give up on important topics prematurely. Therapists need to get comfortable with tension, too. When relationship therapy clients disagree about something big, the best thing a therapist can do to help is make a space for tension, help clients tolerate the tension, and assist them in continuing to figure out what they want to express, and then say it and hear one another with curiosity. Help clients reach for empathetic understanding, which is not the same as agreement or sharing the same viewpoint. Gradually a solution will begin to emerge. Premature "resolution" always comes back to bite you, and your clients, later.

We frequently talk about resolving disagreements by coming to a compromise. When clients come to me with an impasse, they tend to expect me to side with one or the other of them, or broker a compromise in which they both give a little and get a little. So it might surprise you to hear that, in most circumstances, I do not believe in compromise.

My first issue with compromise is that it conceives of differences between partners in a completely linear fashion. If I'm at point A and you're at point Z, a compromise means that somehow, we are both supposed to give up half of our concerns or desires so we can meet at point M. Everyone loses to some extent, and no one is fully satisfied. That might not be such a problem for small issues, when the stakes aren't particularly high. But when it comes to the bigger issues, the ones that have deep implications for the partner's lives, futures, and identities, it may not be possible to "just let go of it" to meet in the middle without building a deep reservoir of resentment.

Instead, I believe in holding the tension and taking the conversation to deeper levels, with each partner helping the other explore their thoughts and feelings much more deeply. It's amazing how, when you nurture curiosity, depth, and empathy, a certain magic happens. As we come to understand our partner(s) deeply, we become able to think about the problem from multiple viewpoints—at a minimum, ours and theirs, and something greater than the sum of the parts. This becomes a powerful force for good, a generative space of creativity where potential solutions begin to materialize. When two or more partners are unlocked from battle, moving freely in their creativity and love for one another, holding one another's perspectives with respect and care along with their own, the solutions that begin to present themselves are new; they are not the same limited and linear solutions that were apparent at the beginning of the process. This is why the I/I process comes long before decision-making and also why holding tension so the I/I can develop and mature is so important. Something has to unlock for beautiful and creative solutions to begin to present, and when they do, it truly is magical.

When I am guiding my clients in the process of holding tension with differences and they are struggling, I often ask them this powerful question, which I got directly from Ellyn Bader and Peter Pearson: "What do you do that makes it hard for your partner to give you what you want?" This question is just as powerful when framed as a direct question from one partner to another, for instance, "My darling, what do I do that makes it hard for you to give me what I want?" (fill in the "what I want" part with the specific item). Similarly, this question can be framed positively, as in, "What could I do that would make it easier for you to give me what I want?" There is an important fine point here; the goal is not to come up with a trade, as in, "I'll do the dishes, if you make the bed." My goal when I ask this question of someone I love is to get honest feedback about how I'm getting in my own way, and in the way of my partner, possibly subconsciously.

This question, and the concept behind it, almost always stops people in their tracks. Most people are used to turning their attention to their partner and what they are doing wrong, rather than looking at how they are getting in their own way. This question invites us to see things in a new light, one that challenges but also invites us to take back our own power.

Ask your clients, yourself, and your partner(s) that mind-bending question and watch what happens. Ask for honest feedback about how you are getting in your own way, because often we can't see it for ourselves. We all hold in our hearts a tender dream of how we want to be loved. But we all have the ability to make it almost impossible for our partners to respond to us in the ways we most strongly desire. Identifying this and changing it is the most powerful way I know of to resolve a major dilemma. When we figure out what we are doing to block ourselves and our partners, and stop getting in our own way, very often the dilemma clears itself up.

CHAPTER 13

Understanding and Addressing Jealousy

Whenever I teach about polyamory and jealousy, I hear this: "Wait. I thought polyamorous people didn't get jealous." Or this: "If you're jealous, why do polyamory? It's inevitably going to crash and burn." Let me start out by debunking these myths. *People in polyamorous relationships get jealous.* If you're working with polyamorous clients or relationships, you're going to be working with jealousy and a variety of other uncomfortable emotions. And if you are exploring polyamory yourself, you are very likely to run into jealousy, either in yourself or in your partners. In fact, jealousy and its close cousins—envy and negative self-comparison—are by far the most common issues I see with my polyamorous clients.

Yes, there are those rare people who truly don't seem to experience jealousy. But they're few and far between, and even those people who think of themselves as not experiencing jealousy can occasionally be blindsided by uncomfortable emotions. Almost everyone sometimes finds themselves preoccupied with what their partner is doing or thinking about with other people or making comparisons between themselves and another partner.

It's common in our culture to assume that if you feel jealous, your partner must be doing something wrong or something hurtful *to you*, and that they should change their behavior to free you from your jealousy, whether that means no longer chatting with that attractive coworker, cutting ties with exes, or not cultivating friendships with people of your gender. It's even more common to assume that if your partner is seeking out a relationship with another person, you are more than justified in feeling jealous. Heck, it would be weird if you weren't.

Indeed, if you're feeling jealous, your partner could decide to change things about their behavior, and that might ease the jealousy; however, what if your partner isn't interested in limiting their friendships to make you feel better? Or what if they do make changes and you still experience jealous feelings?

What if there's another way to respond to jealousy—one that doesn't require your partner to manage your emotions for you? Perhaps it's possible to take a look at why those emotions are coming up right now, what thoughts and stories are coming along with the feelings, and make an attempt to shift your perspective. Maybe some of the distress is based on past experiences or cultural narratives. The narrative your jealousy is spinning for you is not necessarily an accurate reflection of the current circumstances. Maybe your partner can love and choose you, and also love and choose someone else, without taking anything away from you.

Thinking about jealousy in this way requires that we assume it is possible to feel secure, safe, chosen, and loved when our partner is with someone else. For many people, including many therapists, this is quite a reach; however, my work with the polyamory community has driven this point home over and over again: *It is very possible to have a securely attached open relationship.* I've seen it many times. In fact, this is *the* goal of relational therapy for people in polyamorous relationships. Polyamory doesn't in any way preclude security. Happy polyamorous people have found the ability to feel loved, honored, and chosen in the absence of exclusivity. I've seen this in mono-polyam situations, primary/secondary relationships, and nonhierarchical structures.

But how do they actually do it? And how do we, as therapists, help?

JEALOUSY IS AN EMOTION

As therapists, we're in the business of helping people manage all kinds of emotions. It is well understood that emotions come and go, have more to do with the past than the present, and stick around longer and with more toxicity if we dwell on or obsess about them. Much of the distress associated with uncomfortable emotions comes from not the emotion itself, but rather the meaning made about the emotion or situation.

As therapists, we discuss self-regulation of emotional responses frequently in an effort to help clients experience less unnecessary distress. For instance, we are great at helping clients understand that anxiety is an automatic response that is often out of proportion to the current circumstances. When someone is in a state of high anxiety, they are less likely to make good decisions and more likely to respond in ways that are overly reactive.

That's easy enough for us to understand when we're talking about anxiety. But what about jealousy? My view of jealousy is that *it is an emotion like any other*. I help my clients learn to self-regulate with jealousy just as I do with anxiety. In fact, jealousy and anxiety are close cousins. Your toolkit for working with anxiety is exactly the same one you will use for working with jealousy or any other negative emotion:

Pausing and breathing before reacting
Taking long exhales to soothe the nervous system
Self-soothing by warm and positive internal coaching
Practicing mindfulness to build the muscle for choosing thoughts and feelings
Being fully present in the reality of the moment
Investigating meaning-making
Checking assumptions
Communicating about fears/vulnerabilities
Seeking effective co-regulation strategies
Cultivating effective distractions
Down-regulating or up-regulating to return to the window of tolerance (For a review, see chapter 8, particularly "Understanding Automatic Responses and the Self-Protective Brain," and the exercise "Holding Steady Self-Coaching" in appendix B.

Sounds familiar, right? The only *new* tool you need to be able to work effectively with jealousy is the perspective that *it's possible to work with jealousy*. And not just possible but desirable: Whatever your perspective on polyamory, by helping your clients to regulate and work effectively with their jealousy, you will be helping them feel happier, make better decisions, and create better relationships. They are also likely to get better at regulating other uncomfortable emotions. And if it is your own jealousy, emotions, and relationships that are the focus of your efforts, I call this is the Happiness Project. There is no more important goal than your happiness.

WHEN DOES JEALOUSY ARISE?

Jealousy can show up at any time. Some common situations in poly-amorous relationships that are likely to evoke jealousy include the following:

At the beginning stages of opening a relationship

When a partner meets someone new or is in the early stages of a new connection

When a partner's outside connection starts to deepen and take on new emotional weight

When a relationship ends or goes through a rough patch

When outside stressors (job anxieties, financial woes, lack of fulfill-ment, etc.) increase stress and decrease resilience

When a partner seems to be choosing another connection over you

When swiping on dating apps or texting another partner gets in the way of focusing on high-quality time together

When a lack of consideration is perceived

When a partner breaks agreements or lacks good follow-through

Becoming effective at helping jealous partners handle the emotional upheaval and feel better is the focus of this chapter. But challenging partners who are engaging in behavior that will predictably make jeal-ousy worse is a closely related project.

For this situation, I like the question, "What are you doing that makes it hard for your partner to give you what you want?" It helps everyone concerned take a look at the system of interlocking ac-tions and responses between them, from a perspective that includes acknowledging that they may be doing things that make their own life, and their partner's, considerably more difficult.

You can also use the aforementioned list as a guide for figuring out what might be most helpful. If the jealousy is arising as a result of a stage or phase of relationship, that is one thing. In that situation, helping the partners function as a team will probably be the primary objective. This will likely include helping them co-create as much flexibility and security as possible while also managing automatic reactions, making sure there are positive and connecting moments and special time together, working well with concerns that arise as events unfold, and so on. But if someone involved is also engaging in some of the inconsiderate behaviors on this list, or others like them, they can take some actions that are likely to make a big difference to their emotional state, as well as their partner's. It is not reasonable to expect your partner to feel mellow and relaxed when you are with another intimate partner if you are breaking agreements, constantly checking your phone, or giving all of your attention to a new love. If you, or a client, is struggling with managing new relationship energy (NRE), see chapter 18.

JEALOUSY IN MANY FLAVORS

Jealousy, as I use the term here, is an umbrella term for an entire range of difficult and painful emotions, thought patterns, and anxieties, any of which might arise in any relationship but certainly in polyamorous relationships. It's often helpful to sort through exactly what kind of jealousy your client is experiencing and how it manifests. This may include, but is not limited to, the following:

Classic possessive jealousy ("I don't want anyone else to be with my partner.")

Envy ("I wish I was out having fun dates, like you.")

Jealousy about a partner's time ("You're always out with so-and-so, and we haven't had a date in months.")

Jealousy about the emotional dimension of the relationship ("You're totally crushing on so-and-so, and our relationship feels so settled and domestic now—I miss when you were all hearts and flowers over me.")

Self-comparison of body, sexiness, sexual skill, level of success, etc.

Preoccupation with what a partner is doing when not with them

Preoccupation with what a partner is thinking about when they are with them

JEALOUSY AS A NARRATIVE

Human beings make sense of the world through the lens of narrative. This is particularly true when it comes to negative emotions. When we feel angry, lonely, disappointed, resentful, and so on, we look for a reason or make up a story to explain our pain. Looking for a reason somehow feels better than sitting with our discomfort, even if that reason may be flawed and clouded by our reactive, emotional state. Jealousy is no exception. So here's another tip for working with jealousy: When your clients tell you about their jealousy, *look beyond the situation itself and help them identify the narrative they're creating.*

Let's take a look at an example. Imagine Lisa is alone on a Saturday night when her partner, Dan, is with Margo, another lover. Lisa feels lonely and sad. She misses Dan and wishes they were together. She feels jealous of Margo for having Dan's attention that night. Here are some examples of stories Lisa might tell herself in this situation in an attempt to make sense of her feelings:

"Dan decided to go out with Margo tonight rather than be with me, and that can't be a good sign. He's probably more attracted to Margo than he is to me. I have put on some weight lately, and Margo is probably much more beautiful." This story can easily spiral in several different directions, damaging to Lisa's self-esteem and the connection she experiences with Dan. This story attempts to explain her negative feelings in the context of fears and beliefs she has *about herself and her own attractiveness.*

"Dan has been kind of distant lately. How could he be with her tonight? He knows I'm lonely and should have taken my needs into account and put me first. He's probably thinking about leaving me for her." This story attempts to explain her feelings in the context of fears and beliefs she has *about Dan and his connection to her.*

"Margo is really seducing Dan. She is so annoyingly popular and perfect, and really makes me look bad in his eyes. I'm worried about what they say about me when they're together. Probably Dan told her all about our fight over breakfast, and now she really dislikes me and she's probably encouraging him to leave me. I wish he would stop seeing her." This story attempts to explain her feelings in the context of fears and beliefs she has *primarily about Margo and, to some extent, also Dan.*

"This is a perfect example of why polyamory won't work for me. I feel lonely tonight, and I told him so, but he had a date with Margo, and he chose her over me. How can anyone live like this? When I'm upset, he should be with me or at least not put some other woman before me. Polyamory is just not going to work for me." This story attempts to make sense of feelings in the context of fears or beliefs she has *primarily about polyamory and possibly some differences of opinion with Dan as well.*

Let's unpack this from the perspective of a therapist. If you were Lisa's individual therapist, you would have no way of knowing which aspects of her point of view, assumptions, and story have a grain of truth, are completely accurate, or reveal significant vulnerabilities or erroneous thinking. In my experience, barring cases of emotional or physical abuse, gaslighting, and deception, the most therapeutic option is to assume stories that emerge from difficult emotions are flawed in some significant ways.

No doubt Lisa would like it if Dan could simply reassure her and wipe away her fears. That would be wonderful. Unfortunately, it's not a sure bet. As Lisa's individual therapist, you would have no idea about Dan's level of emotional intelligence, availability, or relational skills. You wouldn't know if he would be good at, or even capable of, co-regulation.

Hopefully the partners have a reasonable amount of emotional connection; are able to attune to one another sometimes; and have some interest in helping one another feel peaceful, safe, connected, and positive. But it wouldn't be surprising if, during an emotionally difficult interaction, both were upset and neither particularly emotionally available for the other.

I hate to set my clients up for failure, so I tend to focus on helping clients *build skills for self-regulation first and foremost*. Co-regulation is like icing on the relational cake. It's fabulous, but if it's the foundation instead of the topping, the cake might collapse. You can't count on co-regulation. So when you really need some help, start with the surest bet: Bet on yourself.

MANAGING JEALOUSY AS AN INDIVIDUAL

Managing story and meaning is important to mental health and happiness. Jealousy and jealousy-related feelings invite meaning-making at least as much as any other emotion, so my first and most effective strategy for helping clients work with these feelings is to do the following:

1. Interrupt the assumptions.
2. Identify and question the story.
3. Look for alternative explanations.
4. Help the client develop their emotional GPS.

It is not always easy to separate thoughts and feelings, and it is self-protective and natural to search memory banks of past experiences for "proof" of negative intentions and focus on and amplify the negative stories and feelings. Recognizing that this process is self-protective *and also optional* can be quite challenging. It can also be incredibly liberating.

Therapeutic interventions that open the door to a discussion of the problematic nature of meaning-making require challenging the client to think about their emotions differently. Let's unpack the list of treatment steps one by one.

Making a Therapeutic Challenge to Assumptions

Challenging self-protective thought patterns and meaning-making is part of our job as therapists. If we don't do it, we are implicitly reinforcing self-defeating thought loops and behaviors; however, making therapeutic challenges is not the easiest part of our job, and many therapists understandably shy away from it. This is because no one finds it easy to release tried-and-true self-protective strategies, no matter how self-defeating they may be. Remember, the amygdala is not discerning and is not concerned with being relational or fostering interpersonal connections. Making therapeutic challenges and still maintaining a warm, safe environment for therapy is an art form but one I hope you will practice.

In this instance, I might listen to Lisa and then say something like,

> I really hear how awful Saturday night was for you, and I see you're suffering. Dan went out with Margo, and you felt lonely, and then it seems like you're saying what happened for you internally was that you made up a lot of stories that were extremely painful, about your body, his love, Margo as a betrayer, and polyamory as a flawed construct. It really sounds like it was just awful for you. Did I get that right?

Then I might say, "Are you aware of how much of your pain on Saturday night was the result of stories you told yourself that may or may not be true?"

Another approach would be,

> You are suffering a lot. I care too much about you to feel good about the amount of suffering you are experiencing. Some of what you experienced on Saturday night was sadness and loneliness, which is hard, but the real *suffering* seems to be attached to feeling bad about yourself, fears about your connection with Dan, fears about what Margo and Dan might be doing or saying, and hopelessness about making the relationship work. That's understandable. Those are extremely distressing stories. I do not want you to suffer unnecessarily, so I'm going to suggest something that might feel pretty challenging. Is that okay? The stories you told yourself on Saturday night were optional, and they may not be true at all.

It might be possible to tell yourself something different, and as a result, feel a different feeling.

Identifying, Questioning, and Expanding the Narrative

A good strategy for managing meaning-making is to coach the client in *generating alternate explanations for the current situation* that might be as true as or truer than the narrative that is dominant in the client's imagination. Done well, this can be a game-changer.

Your client is likely to find this challenging at first, because once core fears are activated, they feel like "truth," not "story." Starting by walking the client through the process in therapy is useful, because you can provide support for stretching outside of the problematic narrative. Once your client learns this practice, it can become part of their self-soothing toolkit, and they can use it on their own when difficult feelings arise.

I might ask Lisa what story she is telling herself and then ask her to think of several other stories that are at least as likely to be true. Let's imagine that Lisa is telling herself that Dan choosing to date Margo is evidence that he is more attracted to Margo than to her. In that case, I might ask Lisa to generate some other possible meanings that could be made from Dan choosing to date Margo. This requires a shift in thinking, and often a client needs some coaching to do it. Ideally, Lisa would think of some possible stories that are more about Dan than Lisa.

For instance, Dan might not feel like he is a monogamous person and instead believes that he will always want to be dating more than one person. This might be a pattern that has played out throughout his life and not have anything to do with Lisa, or Margo, or how attractive either of them is. Comparing and finding ourselves lacking is a common and painfully ineffective way of thinking about interpersonal attractions. That doesn't make the comparison true.

Exercise: Challenging the Thought/Feeling/Meaning Spiral

Lest this sound easy, let me be perfectly clear: *This is not at all easy.* The activated brain doesn't know it is activated. When activated, most people aren't aware they are telling themselves a story that may not be true. Instead, it feels more like noticing the brutal, painful truth once again after having forgotten it or set it aside for a little while. It almost feels more real, and certainly more compelling, than the calm, rational, curious, empathetic, relationally connecting ways of being that we have access to when we are not activated. I created a worksheet to support this process, step by step. This worksheet is specific to managing jealousy and related narratives, but the techniques are equally applicable to any emotion and story/narrative. (See the "Challenging the Thought/ Feeling/Meaning Spiral" worksheet in appendix B, which is part of the "Emotional Balance Worksheets" set.)

The steps I recommend for challenging a painful narrative are simple. Yet, they can be difficult to implement. They get easier with practice, and the effort is so worth it, with a huge payoff in happiness. Because this is such an important skill, I'm going to apply the steps in the handout to the example of Lisa and Dan. If Lisa were to use the "Challenging the Thought/Feeling/Meaning Spiral" exercise, she might write something like this:

1. Feelings: jealousy, anger, resentment, loneliness
2. Thoughts and story: Dan is more attracted to Margo than he is to me, and ultimately he will choose her over me.
3. Opposite story: Dan is not more attracted to Margo than he is to me, and ultimately he will not choose her over me. Or, Dan is just as or more attracted to me than he is to Margo, and ultimately he will choose me.
4. Possible alternative narratives:

   Dan is simply not a monogamous person. He would be interested in dating other people no matter who he was with. It's not about who I am; it's about who Dan is.

   Dan is simply curious about what it would be like to be with other people, and he will always be curious no matter how good our relationship is. Maybe I can empathize with that curiosity— have I ever felt that myself?

   Dan is courteous, and he believes in keeping dates. He had already made plans with Margo when I told him I was feeling lonely, and he believed it would be wrong to break the plan with her to comfort me. He has enough faith in our relationship to know that it will be able to survive this kind of situation. I wish he had made a different decision, but it is somewhat understandable, knowing him as I do, that he made the decision he did.

The point of this exercise is not to uncover the "right" explanation, but simply to show that there are alternative ways of interpreting the situation that don't paint it in such a dire light. Lisa doesn't have to accept any one of these explanations right now. But simply recognizing that they also exist, and that the situation she faces is not a guaranteed recipe for disaster, is a big step.

A further step in this process would be to encourage Lisa to let Dan into her internal process by communicating with him in some way. Checking her assumptions by asking him about his thoughts, feelings, and motivations would be one way to accomplish this. Another option would be to ask Dan or a friend for some positive strokes for her struggle and success at challenging her negative thinking.

Developing and Responding to Emotional GPS

When someone is just beginning to explore the way thoughts, feelings, and meanings interact with one another, they may have difficulty parsing out what is a more negative thought versus a more positive thought and using that determination to guide them toward happiness. Tuning in to emotions is the way to begin the journey. But when most people tune in to their emotions, they follow the emotions to negative thoughts, begin to spiral, and go straight down the rabbit hole of negative thoughts, even more negative emotions, and so on, until they are in a deeply miserable state of being.

This is not the only choice. The ultimate goal is happiness, so an important turning point is learning how to learn to follow emotions *toward more positive-feeling thoughts* rather than heading toward the negative. A crucial distinction is this: What you feel emotionally does not need to guide what decisions you make. You can feel good about apples and still decide not to eat apples. It will work much better to learn to follow your sensitive emotional GPS toward happiness and *then* decide what you want to do, according to *what you want to do*.

I think it is helpful to start tuning the emotional guidance system by inviting awareness of emotions that are attached to thoughts and making choices accordingly. If we use the example of Lisa and Dan, Lisa identified this story: "Dan is more attracted to Margo than he is to me, and ultimately he will choose her over me." This story represents a number of thoughts: Dan is attracted to Margo. Dan is more attracted to Margo than to me. Dan has a ranking system about attraction. Dan will make relationship choices based on ranking about attraction. Dan will prioritize Margo over me. Dan will leave me. Dan will choose Margo over me, which will be why he leaves me.

These are all distinct thoughts, and I might ask Lisa to feel and rate her feelings when I repeat some of these thoughts to her. We could use a scale of 1 to 10, where 1 is feeling bad, 5 is feeling neutral, and 10 is feeling great. I would imagine that "Dan is attracted to Margo" is less distressing than "Dan is more attracted to Margo than to me." If that is true, and Lisa can feel it and then follow the emotional guidance with a goal of feeling better, she could decide not to head in the direction of comparison and instead play with thinking thoughts that help her feel a tiny bit better than "Dan is attracted to Margo."

You can see that this treatment plan, which involved challenging assumptions, identifying and questioning the narrative, expanding the narrative, and developing and responding to emotional guidance, is simple yet quite challenging to implement. Happily, this learning curve will pay off in every sphere, not just with jealousy, polyamory, or any other single situation. Emotional dysregulation is universal, and learning to manage it with skill will make a huge difference in mental health and happiness, regardless of relational circumstances.

In this vein, I'd like to share a wonderful story that illustrates what can happen when a person, rather than clinging to their jealous narrative, decides to open themselves up to another kind of story about themselves, their partner, and their partner's partner:

I'm a member of a V-shaped polyamorous family. That means my partner is the "hinge," and he has another partner who forms the V with me. They've been together 10 years, and we're going on three.

Needless to say, I have a lot of experience working with my own jealousy. I have what's known as an anxious attachment style (basically my mother wasn't terribly soothing so it's hard for me to trust other humans deeply). So it's no surprise I have struggled to be in a relationship that looks like none I've ever been in: My partner and I live together half of the week, and he lives with his other partner the other half of the week.

In the first few months of my relationship, I noticed a secret desire to one day get my partner to dump his other partner and just be in a relationship with me. I found the idea of sharing unbearable, even though I had agreed to it from the first date. When I noticed this territoriality, I had this image of myself as almost a caveman who owned his human. I didn't like that.

So here's how I worked on the thorny phenomenon of jealousy.

One grueling day my gut-wrenching jealousy was tormenting me. So I sat down and wrote what I was jealous about, what the other person offered that I didn't. And I realized it was all directly grounded in my own insecurities, my old dark angels. Everything about the other partner that made me nervous were things I didn't feel secure about in my own life.

Soon after that, I asked my partner, "I really would like to understand what it is about this man that makes him so essential to you that you would fight to keep the relationship alive."

He balked. He'd already seen how the mere mention of his other partner could make me tense up so I imagine he was afraid of hurting me. Ironically, I had to do a lot of encouraging to get him to tell me about the intimate positive qualities of the person I kinda wanted to see calmly sucked into a quicksand pit.

So we got comfortable, made eye contact, and he slowly explained how this loving relationship was central to his life, how this person was kind and thoughtful and open. In the course of hearing this potentially really uncomfortable stuff I was surprised to feel myself relax. I realized this guy, my partner's partner, a) was not going away and b) was full of loving intention. Thus, if I wanted to create a family with my partner it had to include his other partner.

This last holiday season the three of us hosted three generations in my home. Now no one bats an eye.

To me, this story is an illustration of how difficult polyamory can be and how beautiful and transformative the associated personal work can be when someone rolls up their sleeves and strives for a deep change in perspective. That is polyamory at its very best.

IDENTIFYING ROOT NARRATIVES

It is often helpful to discuss and understand where a core negative story arose. For instance, when and how did Lisa learn she is less-than, unattractive, unimportant, or "not enough"? If there is a core to the narrative about jealousy that can be identified, consider when it arose in the client's understanding of who they are and how others relate to them.

Understanding the origins of these beliefs can help shake the feeling of "truth" that comes with them. A deep piece of work can be done to help the client heal the original wound as well, through any number of therapeutic strategies, including but certainly not limited to Gestalt chair work, transactional analysis, inner child work, Internal Family Systems, redecision therapy, or EMDR.

I want to share a vivid personal account that relates a turning point in a polyamorous relationship. In this story, one partner, at first overwhelmed by jealousy driven by long-standing personal narratives, learns how to challenge those narratives and rewrite them.

Unlike some polyamorous people, I am no free spirit. It has always been difficult for me to trust that I am unconditionally loved and have the confidence to loosen my emotional grip on the people I care about. I have known my beloved husband for more than half of my life. My relationship with him is central to my sense of safety and well-being. On so many levels, I know that he will love me no matter what—and that his interest in other women is simply natural, fundamentally human, and has no bearing on his feelings for me.

However, in practice, it can be hard for me to remain in touch with that understanding. I tend to catastrophize. And the fear that arises when I commence my "What if . . ." thinking leaves me reeling. For example, once when my husband returned from a simple date (dinner, making out), I felt like I was encased in a block of ice. I found it hard to even sit next to him at a function at our child's school. Even though he was being extremely kind and solicitous, I was filled with an inexplicable anger and hurt. I couldn't exactly trace what it was about, but it was not a pleasant evening for either of us.

After about an hour of that, something did shift, however. I could no longer bear his pain and discomfort. Compassion softened my heart, loosened my tense shoulders. What the hell was I doing? He had done nothing that violated any of our agreements, and he had been trying to reassure me, only to be rebuffed again and again. I was ashamed of myself. The ice began to melt.

All I could think of to do at that point was cry. And apologize. I tried to explain that I was stuck in an ice block of my own creation, and I thanked him for his patience in waiting for me to chip my way out.

When he offered to stop dating entirely, my reaction surprised me. I knew that the relationship with this woman, which involves once-a-month dates, in many ways nourishes my husband's soul. It offers him a kind of validation and a novel experience that I simply cannot provide. I am just too close to him to do that—much as one's mother is not the best character witness in a court of law. To my surprise, I told him that I wanted these experiences for him. I could see that the problem rested entirely with me, and I wanted to grow.

Throughout time, it has gotten much easier for me to cope when my husband goes out on dates, even though they have gotten more elaborate and potentially triggering. But the difference in the way it feels for me is profound. Although icy blasts occasionally swirl around me, I have tools now to warm myself up. First, I have the gift of experience that tells me that he will come back and that I will never be abandoned. Each time he leaves, after all, is also a time he returns, by choice, home, to me.

Second, we have the understanding that we will reassure one another, without fail, whenever and however it is needed. We have code ways we do this, and it never fails to help ground us both. Third, I enjoy his gratitude and pride in me that I can give him this extraordinary gift (which is, by the way, also a gift he gives me). He is a happy guy, and we enjoy each other's company more than ever, despite the fact that we both have other partners. Lastly and most importantly, I am inspired by my own vision of the person I want to become. Sometimes I have glimpses of the woman I am trying to grow into—a woman so confident and loving that she worries little about loss or abandonment. Why would she? She is so badass and fun to be with that she draws people to her—her husband especially. I am not this woman yet, but I can see glimmers of her now and then, urging me on, smiling reassuringly as I live boldly, surrendering to the crazy truth of big, big love in this world.

ALTERNATIVES TO MEANING-MAKING

Once a client is aware that thoughts aren't necessarily accurate reflections of the truth and that narratives arising from difficult feelings are generally flawed, and once they have some understanding of where their core narratives may have arisen, it will be helpful to develop a repertoire of things to do instead of thinking, storytelling, or meaning-making. Many people don't know this is an option, so they may not have strategies for doing this already. Or, sometimes people have excellent skills they use in other contexts, for instance, at work, but may not realize they can use those same strategies when they experience difficult emotions in their relationship. Does your client have strategies for self-care, distraction, compartmentalization, or self-soothing that can be applied to relational distress?

I might say,

> You can feel sad and lonely, and not tell yourself anything about it at all. Instead, you can pour a cup of tea, or draw a bath, meditate, or do an art project, or go for a run—anything that is a self-loving act, a way of taking good care of yourself and your vulnerable, raw feelings. You could also distract yourself from the situation and emotions. Try removing your attention from what Dan is doing and instead focus on something you love to do. The key is to intentionally calm yourself. What are some things you love to do? Whatever you choose to do should feel like a relief, a break from feeling bad and thinking about feeling bad. So, writing in your journal, calling a friend, or going to the gym won't work if you're rehashing how upset you are, going over the details, and involving your friend, your mind, or your journal in a rant. Those things will only work if you use them deliberately with the intention of getting calmer and happier. For instance, you could make a gratitude list in your journal or ask a friend to distract you by talking about themselves, telling you about some good news, or engaging you about a project you are excited about. See the difference? What have you done in the past, when you have felt upset, that has worked to either take your mind off of it or nurture yourself in spite of the emotions?

From here, we can create a list of strategies to start experimenting with when difficult emotions arise.

ATTACHMENT AND SECURE FUNCTIONING

Jealousy is a powerful emotion. It gets right down to the core questions relating to attachment: "Am I safe with you?" "Can I trust you?"

"Will you be there for me?" "Will you choose me even when I'm not at my best?" "Are we okay?" When these questions arise, they are so massively uncomfortable that most people will go to great lengths to avoid them. Typical emotional avoidance strategies include looking for someone to blame; shifting the topic by throwing out a juicy, sure-to-trigger lure; throwing up a smoke screen in the form of dramatic emotions—I could go on.

Most ineffective relational behaviors have the effect of masking vulnerability, often subconsciously. When you see defensiveness, attack, nagging, blaming, patronizing, stonewalling, and name-calling, look for the vulnerable emotions underneath these responses. When the emotional material is as challenging as jealousy, one common defense strategy is to bail out: "This relationship isn't worth it; I'm done."

This is why it is so important for people who are in polyamorous relationships, and therapists who work with polyamorous relationships, to know that *polyamory can and does work, very often, and for a lot of people*. It is easy when hearing a story resulting from hurt feelings that probably includes blaming the partner(s), to feel a lot of empathy for the person with hurt feelings and conclude that the only reasonable decision is for their partner to end any extradyadic relationships that are contributing to the emotional distress. I strongly encourage you not to fall into that trap. If you are struggling with your own challenging feelings about your, or your client's polyamorous relationship, ask yourself the following questions:

> Have I ever seen this type of emotional response come up for someone who is in a monogamous relationship?
> If so, how did I think they should handle it?

This line of self-inquiry can be helpful because most of us don't see a monogamous relationship that isn't working and jump right to asking, "Why don't you solve your entire problem by ending the relationship?" We might instead ask questions like these (a tip of the hat to Ellyn Bader and Peter Pearson, creators of the Developmental Model of Couples Therapy, for formulating these questions):

> What do you get out of this relationship?
> Why do you stay, when things are so hard?

What is your contribution to the dynamics that are so difficult right now?

Of the things you contribute, are there any you would like to explore changing and, if so, why?

What kind of partner do you aspire to be in this relationship? How far away are you from that right now? And what small step could you take to get closer to being the partner you want to be?

WHAT IF IT IS JUST A BAD RELATIONSHIP?

We all know that sometimes relationships end, and sometimes the end of a relationship can be the best possible outcome for everyone. Of course, anyone who is in a relationship should feel empowered to make the decision to end it if it is just too hard, and, in fact, I think knowing this can help a person find the strength to really challenge themselves to grow; after all, if the experiment fails beyond what you can tolerate, you can always decide you've had enough. But there is nothing about polyamory that makes a relationship more or less viable than a monogamous relationship.

There are some truly horrific polyamorous relationships. There are some truly horrific monogamous relationships. Things that undermine trust tend to create deeply flawed relationships, and some of those are hard to mend. If this is the case in a polyamorous relationship you are working with, I would suggest that lack of trust is the problem, not polyamory. There are other types of situations that tend to make for problematic relationships: self-absorption, conflict avoidance, not following through on agreements, emotional dysregulation, gaslighting, emotional manipulation and abuse, projection—I could go on and on. In none of these cases would polyamory be the problem. The trick is being able to identify and make effective challenges and confrontations *about the actual problem*, not about polyamory.

Ask your client (or yourself) why they (or you) are in the relationship and about their feelings about polyamory. Many people have mixed feelings or reluctance about being in a polyam relationship, but if they were clear that they did *not* want to be in this relationship, they would have broken up rather than come to couples therapy. Your job, as with a monogamous client, is to help them figure out the puzzle they currently find themselves in.

If you happen to believe polyamory is never (or rarely) viable or adaptive, or usually results in one or more people being victimized, you're working at a considerable disadvantage whether the topic at hand is your own relationship or that of a client. If, on the other hand, you know polyamorous relationships work well sometimes, for some people, and can be happy, healthy, and long-lasting, you will have a better chance of questioning faulty assumptions, identifying where a narrative might be skewed toward negativity, and working with the vulnerabilities underneath reactive responses. Ultimately, this will lead to the clients becoming able to discern whether the relationship is sufficiently workable and fulfilling or if a breakup is the right choice.

I tell my clients I'm all for them deciding to break up, but I think it would be better to make that decision from a place of rational thought rather than during a period of time where tempers are running high and judgment is clouded by self-protective mechanisms and negative meaning-making.

CLOSING THOUGHTS ABOUT JEALOUSY

Jealousy is a natural, common, and near-inevitable part of life and relationships. But like any other emotion, it shouldn't have the power to rule our lives. Working effectively with jealousy (and other difficult emotions) will help you take control in session and defuse the unproductive, time-consuming spirals of negative meaning-making that uncontrolled emotions tend to evoke.

Your client's growing ability to self-regulate will pay off in every relationship in the future and every sphere. And since every relationship is guaranteed to present interpersonal conflict, difficulty self-regulating or managing negative meaning-making will come back and haunt the next relationship and the one after that, whether monogamous or polyamorous.

It can be tremendously heart-wrenching to see someone you care about afflicted with the pain of uncontrolled emotion. As empathetic helpers, it is tempting to try to solve the problem for the sufferer to alleviate their pain. When the emotion is jealousy, it can seem like the obvious solution is to either encourage ending the relationship or push for a behavior change in the partner. Those might indeed be useful steps, but they carry the risk of sidestepping personal growth. Better to stay steady in the stream of emotion and learn to challenge and shift damaging and disempowering narratives, check assumptions, and move toward connection and truth. It's a beautiful thing to watch self-confidence and inner peace grow as someone you care about learns to work through a jealous moment without spinning out.

A final thought: I've spent most of this chapter talking about addressing jealousy in the context of polyamorous relationships, but these skills will come in handy in any kind of relationship. Jealousy is not reserved for people in open relationships; plenty of people in monogamous relationships experience it, too. Any progress a person can make toward being happy and feeling grounded and balanced within themselves will pay off in every relationship and in many contexts. It's all part of what I call the Happiness Project.

CHAPTER 14

Infidelity, Broken Agreements, and Building Trust

INFIDELITY BEFORE POLYAMORY

Sometimes the entry point to polyamory is infidelity. We all know how damaging the lies and betrayal surrounding infidelity can be. With that in mind, I think the most fascinating thing about the transition from infidelity to polyamory is that it often works very well—after, of course, a significant process of rebuilding trust, shedding old conflict-avoiding habits, and building differentiation of self. It amazes me when I consider how many cases I've personally seen in which partners rebuilt the wreckage of an affair, or multiple affairs, into a beautiful, loving polyamorous relationship, demonstrating truly impressive courage and compassion in the process. I want to share a story with you from someone whose personal experience illustrates how dramatic this transformation can be.

I have extensive experience in both polyamory and infidelity, and I can tell you without a doubt that they are incredibly different. You see, I started cheating on my partner while she was pregnant with our first child. Yes, I'm one of those assholes, and I will never be able to undo the things that I have done. During the next four years, I proceeded to cheat on my partner with multiple women, multiple times, and while I will never make an excuse for my behavior, there were reasons why I did what I did, which can be boiled down to two main themes: I was transgender, and I was way too ashamed to tell anyone that I was trans. My resentment and my fear of vulnerability created the perfect storm to seek fake connection elsewhere. In short, for me, cheating happened when I feared vulnerability.

Polyamory, on the other hand, will fail miserably if everyone involved doesn't embrace vulnerability. And not just once at the outset. It is a conscious and necessary intention every single day because feelings of jealousy or hurt or anger can crop up at any time.

I am thankful that my partner and I were able to work through a lot of hard things so that we could completely restructure the relationship we thought we were committing to when we got married. We both now have multiple fulfilling romantic relationships and have had an open relationship for almost 10 years.

Stories like these are not uncommon. Clearly, polyamory provides a path for people to fulfill desires that might otherwise be met through infidelity, while still acting with integrity, compassion, and respect for their partner. But I don't think that explains how someone can go from being an incredibly unreliable monogamous partner to becoming an extremely reliable, dependable polyamorous one. I think this comes down to an identity issue. In our culture, many people have no idea that polyamory exists, and certainly not that it is a viable relationship option. Perhaps this is changing now, as polyamory and other consensual nonmonogamies are showing up in the media more, but until perhaps five to 10 years ago, most people had never heard of polyamory.

Imagine being someone who has always thought of yourself as having more than one partner. In your imaginings growing up, you pictured yourself with two or more partners. Then you find yourself grown and longing for deep connection. You get married or form a committed relationship. But a part of you is still not fulfilled, and you don't have language for it. Then you meet someone other than your spouse to whom you are deeply attracted. This is what you always imagined for yourself; it just makes sense. But you didn't, and still don't, have language for it.

I think this is one common way in which infidelity can be the entry point to polyamory, and polyamory not only provides a missing piece, but also opens the door to an ethical, values-based way of expressing a lifelong identity. It makes sense to me that, once a person is expressing important parts of themselves in ways that are respectful, ethical, and honest, and that are not based in secrecy and shame, they could become much more dependable and reliable relationally. When internal chaos settles down, external chaos settles down, too.

As you can see, the discovery of infidelity may result in a discussion of polyamory. Compared to the other possible moments you might discuss polyamory with a partner—for instance, in the early stages, before the relationship even commences, or later on, once the relationship has progressed quite a bit—this seems like it would be the least likely option to result in success. While it's arguably the least ideal, the most traumatic, and dramatic, I have often seen it succeed nonetheless. Oftentimes, partners successfully move past the infidelity and create a well-functioning open relationship. Maybe the bombshell disclosure of a desire for polyamory gets obscured somewhat by the bigger and more damaging bombshell of infidelity, or maybe the pain of the affair is perceived as being less than the pain of the lies, making a natural entry point for a discussion of consensual nonmonogamy.

It seems to me that an early, up-front discussion is the easiest and most likely to result in successfully opening the relationship, and I have seen it work extremely well, and with considerably less drama, than other approaches. Perhaps that's because early in a relationship partners are still discovering multiple aspects of one another, and perhaps it's because the new relationship energy can help partners stretch outside of their usual comfort zone and try new things. Also, without years of water under the bridge, it might be easier to use good manners, be truly considerate of one another's preferences, and make a good repair, which makes a big difference. Unfortunately, this ideal approach requires that a person already be aware of polyamory as an option or have the foresight to know they might at some point in the future want another relationship concurrently and have the courage to bring it up early on.

Infidelity that leads to polyamory can look a lot of different ways, but here are a few situations I have seen fairly often:

Someone knows they are not interested in monogamy but is afraid to bring up polyamory to their partner. They may be deeply people-pleasing or conflict avoidant. Instead of having the tough conversation, they have multiple relationships and hope it works out. Oftentimes, of course, one partner will discover another partner.

If they thought there was an agreement to be monogamous, this will be a discovery of infidelity.

Someone has a lot of internal confusion about what they want or who they are in multiple spheres. They just sort of stumble through relationships without a lot of internal clarity about themselves. As their partners confront them about broken agreements, they begin to figure out more about themselves, and the discussion of polyamory emerges.

Someone thinks they made an agreement with their partner to have the option of extradyadic relationships, but the discussion was vague and the agreement was never formed and confirmed. They think they are free to consider having other relationships, and their partner does not think they agreed to that. Fast-forward to the crisis when a new relationship is either disclosed or (worse) discovered after nondisclosure.

Someone has one or more experiences of infidelity. In the process of mending, recovering, and rebuilding trust, they engage in therapy or some other personal growth process, focusing on issues related to making and keeping agreements. They get better at figuring out what they want and expressing their desires and preferences to their partner. Sometimes it turns out that what they actually want is to have more than one intimate relationship at a time. What started out as therapy to heal infidelity turns into therapy to discuss one partner's desire to have a polyamorous relationship.

Someone has been married for decades and stumbles into a romantic attraction to a coworker or friend. They act on the attraction. This leads to a realization that they don't want to give up the new relationship or that they want to continue to be able to experience new love/new relationship energy on occasion. At the same time, they don't want to give up their long-term relationship. One way or another, they learn about polyamory and open the discussion, either right away, much later, or after attempting to open the relationship on their own and encountering problems.

The transition from infidelity to polyamory is challenging. It requires both partners to take an honest look at their desires and goals as individuals and partners. This kind of work is also an opportunity for a therapist to really test their polyamory-related cultural competence, because infidelity is certainly a rough start. Additionally, this therapy involves making a repair, and for most people the process of initiating, and allowing, a solid and compassionate repair that results in a stronger relationship is quite a stretch.

When I work with an infidelity case, I always wonder in the back of my mind whether the partners are aware that polyamory is an option. The existence of an extradyadic relationship suggests that at least one person is or has been interested in at least one extradyadic relationship. I'm curious to discover how they decided to engage in that relationship, how they decided to lie about it or keep it secret from their partner, and which aspects of the situation they would do differently if they had it to do over again. Would they choose not to act on their attraction for the other person? Would they act on it but choose to be transparent about it? Both?

If either or both of the partners are interested in discussing poly-amory, I think that, as a therapist, it is important to be able to engage in the conversation. Considering that there are so many examples of suc-cessful infidelity-to-polyamory transitions, I think it's important that people be aware of their entire slate of options, so that they can make a fully informed choice. Plus, as a therapist, you're ideally positioned to debunk myths and provide resources to support their learning. Your clients probably won't get that anywhere else.

FACILITATING HEALING AND BUILDING TRUST

Naturally, this might sound a bit challenging. One partner is reeling from a betrayal—how are you supposed help them hold steady for a discussion about the option of an open relationship? Polyamory is no more effective as a way to mend a broken relationship than adopt-ing a pet, getting pregnant, moving overseas, or adding any other huge stressor. Even in the best of circumstances, the transition into polyamory tends to be a big deal. It's an undertaking that challenges many people's sense of feeling chosen, emotionally safe, and secure. As you can imagine, recovery from infidelity is far from the ideal circumstances for beginning that process. Ideally, partners opening a relationship would start from a place of strength and connection, rather than woundedness and lack of security.

Many therapists would say that healing and repairing from the infidelity has to come first, before a discussion of opening the relationship. While I don't disagree in theory, I have also seen successful polyamory evolve from circumstances that are far from ideal. Plus, both of your clients in the couple may, in reality, want to discuss polyamory; in fact, I have only rarely worked with couples who are willing to completely table the discussion of polyamory while rebuilding from infidelity. It's completely possible to have the two conversations simultaneously, and that's often how it works in my therapy room.

LIES AND LIE-INVITING BEHAVIOR

Trust is an interactional system. It involves more than one person, like any other aspect of a relationship. Both partners have a role in creating an environment of trust between them. When an agreement has been broken or a lie discovered, it is easy to focus on the partner who had the lapse. But when we do that, we miss an important aspect of the solution, which is the relational system between partners.

In their book *Tell Me No Lies* (2001), Ellyn Bader and Peter Pearson take a deep dive into the systemic nature of honesty and lying. Bader and Pearson offer a taxonomy of lies, distinguishing between loving lies, conflict-avoidant lies, passive-aggressive lies, and felony lies.

Loving lies are told to make someone feel better: "I loved that dish you cooked. I didn't notice that the bottom was burnt." They're common and low-level, and usually don't cause damage in relationships; in fact, they can help build security and trust.

Conflict-avoidant lies, on the other hand, are told to avoid getting into trouble or sidestep a difficult or painful discussion. They're extremely common and systemic in nature. That means that the behavior of both partners is implicated in their existence; in other words, if one partner is telling conflict-avoidant lies, it's probably because they anticipate a conflict if they tell the truth.

Bader and Pearson illuminate this dynamic with a very useful concept: "lie-inviting behavior" (p. 37). If one partner responds to a difficult disclosure by blowing up, shaming, shutting down, or becoming otherwise emotionally dysregulated, their partner is likely to avoid conflict in the future by telling untruths, large or small. This is especially true if they are somewhat conflict-averse to begin with. Throughout time, this effect can compound if it isn't addressed.

I have often noticed lie-inviting behavior in real life and the therapy room. Many of us experienced it as children, myself included. For example, I have rarely met a preteen or teenager who doesn't engage in conflict-avoidant lying, usually in response to the lie-inviting behavior of parents and teachers who might overreact, blame, or shame rather than inviting honest feedback about preferences. If a young person has gotten in trouble for doing something they very much wanted to do, and they intend to do it again, they will certainly become increasingly good at lying, or at least avoiding the confrontation. Not many teens give a lot of deep thought to how to give up or reframe something they want simply because their parents don't want them to do it. Add a dose of age-appropriate impulsivity and I think it may be fair to say that, by the age of 21, we all have quite a bit of experience lying to get our way, cover our tracks, avoid getting in trouble, or make our parents happy.

I bet you've encountered lie-inviting behavior before. It tends to sound like this:

"How could you even *think* that, let alone say it to me?"
"Don't ever bring that up to me again!"
"Wow. Just wow. You're really going to go there?"
"If you ever do that again, there are going to be huge consequences."
"Oh my gosh, that's just disgusting. How could you?"

These are all examples of responses that could easily shut down a partner who has something to disclose. Most likely, the partner who is engaging in lie-inviting behavior has no idea that this could be the result of their actions. They don't necessarily want to be lied to; they're just blindsided by uncomfortable feelings and reacting in the moment. Understanding the concept of lie-inviting behavior helps people honestly evaluate what is at stake and what they might be contributing to the interpersonal dynamics of deception. Learning to invite the truth is very possible, and the alternative is to continue subconsciously reinforcing concealment; understanding this core concept is quite motivating, and can lead to a big shift in a damaging dynamic. Of course, this growth trajectory leads to partners needing to get good at holding steady, as some difficult truths may then begin to emerge.

This is the stance I strive for: "I value honesty highly, and I deeply want to know the real you, not some fake mask you think will be easy for me to see. I would love it if you would tell me the truth. I promise never to torture you for it or hold it against you. I might experience some emotions, but I won't blame them on you."

The final two categories of lying, as set forth by Bader and Pearson, are passive-aggressive lies and felony lies. These are more serious, and they reveal something about the character of the person doing the lying. These are big lies that compound and create major damage in people's lives. They are difficult to recover from. These include egregious infidelities spanning periods of years; multiple outright lies told directly to the face of the lie-ee; gaslighting; lies intended to create damage or harm; ongoing lying and lies upon lies; lying to gain power, push back, or punish; and lying that is so ingrained and habitual it isn't clear that the client is even aware they are lying.

Most therapists have had experience with clients who were extremely skilled and destructive liars. Working with a habitual liar is incredibly challenging. The person for whom lying is part of their character has a much larger project when it comes to changing that behavior, and their partner has some tough decisions to make as they watch their partner reveal their character, for better or worse.

Because of the cultural stigma related to polyamory, which is compounded by our larger culture of sexual shame, many people who habitually commit infidelity may not even know that it is possible to have multiple extradyadic relationships without lying, betrayal, and broken agreements. For this reason, I have seen some real miracles occur when the topic of polyamory is brought into the conversation. This is perhaps the best reason I can think of to mention the possibility of consensual nonmonogamy to people who have a history of infidelity.

Let's imagine you are working with a client who is a skilled liar and has engaged in felony lying and habitual infidelities spanning a period of years. Sounds like a rough case, right? But, in my experience, it is not at all uncommon for polyamory to become a solution that resolves their internal dilemma. I've seen people in this situation become highly principled, highly relational, caring, attentive, and dependable in consensually nonmonogamous relationships, whereas in "monogamous" relationships they were what I would describe as characterological liars with histories of multiple infidelities, sometimes with little remorse.

CO-CREATING TRUST

Trustworthy people are in touch with what they want and able to communicate about it. If a trustworthy person finds that their internal sense of congruence with themselves is in conflict with what their partner wants, they will bring it out into the open for discussion, even if it's an incredibly challenging discussion and even if it risks their relationship, rather than break an agreement. The underlying skill that makes them trustworthy is differentiation of self.

Let's face it, depending on the intensity and weight of the topic, that is a tough skill set, even in the best of circumstances. We have all seen plenty of partners who make it extremely difficult to choose the hard conversation over a little deception they will probably never discover. Again, the skill in question is differentiation of self; partners who engage in lie-inviting behavior display a lack of differentiation, as they are unable to hold steady and stay curious when their partner shares something that is not easy for them to hear.

Of course, we are ultimately responsible for our actions. No matter how badly behaved our partners are, we can choose to treat them with respect. Empowering your clients, and, for that matter, also your partner(s) to act based on what kind of person and partner they aspire to be, rather than based on a "tit-for-tat" attempt to give their partner as good as they get, can make a huge difference. Even though differentiation of self is relational, each partner can choose to be the one who raises the tone of the conversation by holding steady, listening with openness and curiosity, and responding with warmth and candor.

Some people prefer to do their processing internally, rather than externally with their partner. Sometimes the tendency to keep one's internal struggles, thought processes, and fantasies to yourself is related to conflict-avoidance, and sometimes it's simply a personal preference.

Regardless, transparency is a big part of building trust. I encourage everyone to make some of their internal process visible to their partner. If our partners only see our finished, polished thoughts and conclusions, they know something about where we end up but not much about how we got there. The story of how we arrived at the conclusions we did can reveal a lot about our character. If we can let our partners know we struggled and won the battle, that can help build trust in our ability to do the same in the future. If our partner has a lot riding on our ability to make a particular choice or decision but they never see us struggle and win the battle, it would be understandable if they were to wonder whether we're actually losing the battle and lying about it.

Counterintuitively, I think it even builds trust to hear a partner disclose that they struggled and lost the battle. Understandably, people don't want to disclose a slip during the process of "rebuilding trust," but it's still much better than a lie, if that's the alternative. Transparency is a muscle that fosters trust as it grows stronger.

Exercise: Co-Creating a Trusting Relationship

Having explored the systemic dynamics around truth-telling and creating trust in a relationship, you might feel ready to think more deeply about your own part in creating a healthy, trusting dynamic in your relationships. To this end, I created a worksheet. It brings up questions about how you would like to actively strengthen this aspect of your relationship. Some questions invite self-reflection, and others discussion between partners. As always, use it in any way that seems helpful. (See the "Co-Creating a Trusting Relationship" worksheet in appendix D.)

This, like many of my handouts, may lead to a desire to change something about the way you show up in your relationship. If you identify something you want to change, check out the "Creating Change Worksheet Set" in appendix E. This set of worksheets walks you through several important aspects of the change process.

THE AFFAIR PARTNER

Now I'm going to turn to a controversial and challenging topic, whether you are a therapist or other helping professional, or are yourself in a relationship that is grappling with infidelity: How to handle the relationship with the affair partner. Sometimes, the partner who committed the infidelity is eager to sever ties with the affair partner, but other times they might be reluctant or unwilling to do so. This can happen in a situation where the partner who had the affair has always been interested in polyamory, even if they haven't had the language for it. A discussion of polyamory in the wake of an affair can be a reasonable strategy for someone who is interested in preserving the affair connection without sacrificing the relationship with the original partner.

But occasionally someone will want to discuss *polyamory* in a context where it seems the term is being bandied about to buy time to decide whether to stay or leave, or legitimize broken agreements. I hope you are clear by now that polyamory is no way to legitimize or mask broken agreements. If the therapy project is making a decision to "stay or leave," that is not the same as making the decision of "polyamory or monogamy," although they may overlap.

If a person has a history of breaking agreements, they have a developmental process to undertake to become able to make better agreements, which will surely be necessary if they hope for a functional polyamorous relationship. Polyamory is not a shortcut, an easier path, or way out of being honest. It is, if anything, a trial by fire for differentiation, dependability, and trustworthiness. I cannot stress this enough. If you are considering opening your relationship in the aftermath of infidelity or other broken agreements, you have a very challenging project of personal growth ahead. You will need to take stock of what you want, take responsibility for broken agreements and promises, and learn how to be honest with yourself and your partners. Let relationships that are terminally incompatible go, and start showing up with your honest, true self—the self that can keep agreements or honestly discuss a preference to change the agreement before taking action that breaks trust. Your dream of having a polyamorous relationship depends on this skill set.

As a therapist, deciding how to help clients manage the relationship with the affair partner can be challenging. You may well empathize with the betrayed partner, for whom a continued relationship with the affair partner is likely to feel threatening and unfair. It may feel like laying down an ultimatum is the best move to alleviate the betrayed partner's distress and salvage the relationship. In fact, most couples therapists, including me, were taught that the extramarital relationship has to end for the couple to heal their relationship or even for couples therapy to proceed.

For a number of reasons, I don't agree. For one thing, the partner who had the affair may not be ready or willing to end that relationship but still feel pressured to agree with the ultimatum. Many people in that situation don't have a sufficient level of differentiation to have that complicated conversation, especially with the alignment between the therapist and partner pushing against them, combined with the weight of cultural expectation. This combination of pressures does not support a differentiated conversation, and it runs the serious risk of creating resentment and pushing the partner toward renewed deception.

As a therapist, I find it difficult to feel confident that a decision to break with the affair partner is coming from a differentiated place, rather than a conciliatory one, particularly if it came from me in the form of an ultimatum. If there is going to be a decision to end the affair, I want it to be crystal clear to everyone concerned that the decision came from the partner who had the affair. I think a conciliatory stance often backfires with resentment and rebellion, the very last thing needed in this situation. Of course, these same issues apply for the other partner. It is important not to make an agreement (for instance, to agree to having the third party involved for a time) without exploration of the thoughts, feelings, and desires associated with this choice. All in all, it is very convenient if the partner who had the affair chooses to take a break from the affair partner for a time while the original dyad sorts some things out, but it must be clear to everyone concerned that it is their decision for their own reasons.

This is a time in therapy when I like to slow things way down. I try to make sure all agreements are framed as experiments and that there are plans in place to revisit them. I want to make sure no one feels trapped into an agreement without having had multiple opportunities to voice a different opinion. It helps to get good at holding tension with a difference of opinion, which is a situation many therapists find difficult. I recommend sitaying out of the middle and facilitating a deeper exploration of all sides using the initiator/inquirer (I/I) process and/or chair work.

I also do some psychoeducation. I think it helps couples to know that infidelity is common, that most marriages recover from it, and that polyamory exists and can be a viable option. The entire treatment strategy leans heavily on supporting differentiation of self, because without the ability to make and keep agreements, which is foundational to emotional security, neither monogamy or polyamory is likely to work well.

If, after honest discussion, the couple decides to keep the relationship with the affair partner, that decision will test both partners' growth far more than simply pretending to drop it. They will each be challenged to be honest with themselves and their partner about an incredibly difficult subject that evokes strong feelings for both parties. Rather than hiding their actions or true self to preserve the relationship, they will have to show their entire, authentic self to their partner, including the parts that aren't so easy to accept.

Challenging both partners at their unique growth edges in a situation involving an affair is not Therapy 101 stuff. It's extremely challenging for the therapist, as well as the clients. But if you all can learn to keep steady and stay curious, it's possible for them to rebuild an honest relationship that honors their authentic selves.

THE STAY-OR-LEAVE DECISION-MAKING PROCESS FROM A POLYAMORY-INFORMED PERSPECTIVE

I'm sure every therapist, counselor, and coach has worked with people who are making a decision about whether to separate or stay together, and most people have personal experience with this dilemma as well. There are a million reasons to leave a relationship and plenty of relationships where everyone involved would probably benefit from ending it. I also discuss relationship transitions, including the stay/leave decision, in chapter 18, "Relationship Transitions: New Relationship Energy, Relationship Decisions, Shifting Between Partners, and Breakups."

However, here I want to discuss a particular situation that happens in the aftermath of infidelity. The partner who had the affair will need to decide whether they want to commit to a monogamous arrangement, in which case they will need to decide which, if either, relationship to stay with, or move toward an open relationship structure. Here are some of the possible choices:

Stay with the original partner monogamously, and repair from the infidelity.

Stay with the original partner, ending the affair relationship, but open the discussion of polyamory or another form of consensually open relationship with the original partner in hopes of forming a workable open situation in the future.

Leave the original partner *and* the affair partner, and be single; figure out their personal preference between monogamy and polyamory; and date in accordance with that preference when the time comes.

Leave the original partner and be monogamous with the affair partner; this still requires some repair from the infidelity, as both partners in the new relationship have to acknowledge that each has proven their ability to participate in infidelity.

Leave the original partner, stay with the affair partner, and start a conversation about opening up the new relationship.

Stay with both the original partner and the affair partner, and open the discussion of a consensually nonmonogamous relationship involving both partners.

I hope that this list calls attention to the complexity of the situation and also some of the specific challenges involved in each course of action. There is no simple solution, and there are pitfalls inherent to each of these possible solutions. Helping clients develop the skills needed to succeed in any of these courses of action is an exciting and complicated process.

Working with this kind of situation is interesting to me, because the partner who had the affair may never have had the opportunity to examine all of these options honestly. Most people haven't really considered polyamory as a viable option, most partners don't have sufficient support to seriously discuss it, and most therapists don't bring it up in this type of situation. I truly believe that the demographic of people who engage in infidelity should give careful consideration to what they believe about monogamy, transparency, agreements, reliability, fidelity, responsibility, and every other related and relevant topic. This population will have more successful relationships in the future if they carefully consider what they want in relationships and how they need to grow to create the life they want. I don't have a stake in the game and don't care which of the many available options a person chooses, but I do have a bias: I have a strong dislike of infidelity and would much prefer to support personal development toward relational connection. Even if someone decides they want to have no commitments, be a completely free agent, and only have lots of casual connections, at least they can be honest about it and find willing partners who consent on those terms.

A WORD ABOUT SERIAL MONOGAMY

I'd like to take a moment to discuss the cultural construct of serial monogamy. Serial monogamy is culturally condoned and very common, but it's also optional. If a person thinks they have to end a relationship to start another and frequently develops crushes they want to act on, they are unlikely to get the opportunity to develop long, deep intimate connections. To me, that's a little sad, especially if they would like to develop long-term connections. I often wonder how much serial monogamy would decrease if people knew that nonmonogamy was a workable option. If someone aspires to develop a long-term, committed connection, and also wants to experience new love periodically, they can probably figure out a way to do that.

Wanting to experience new love periodically does not make you shallow or incapable of commitment. Therapists are in a profession that highly values relational connection; shouldn't we be fostering it where we can? I'm just not ready to sell out this demographic. Instead, I want to help them craft a life with as much depth, connection, and dependability as they desire. I want them to know polyamory exists, as a strongly principled alternative to serial monogamy.

THE AFTERMATH OF BROKEN AGREEMENTS

The key to preventing broken agreements is making them well in the first place. I discuss this in great depth in chapter 11, "Negotiating Polyamory: Forming Good Agreements," so I won't repeat myself here. But it's worth taking some time to talk about how to deal with the aftermath of broken agreements.

Helping clients have conversations after broken agreements is a special art form, and having those conversations in your own relationships is even more challenging because your emotions are so close. In both cases, the key is understanding, from your partner's perspective, how they decided to do the thing that broke your heart and why they didn't feel comfortable sharing it with you at the time. That is one of the most difficult conversations partners can have and also one of the most potentially transformative. To create some structure for a conversation like this one, refer to the I/I process described in chapter 9. For a discussion of how to make a good repair, refer to chapter 16, "Recovering from Polyamory Gone Wrong."

INFIDELITY IN POLYAMORY

The culture of polyamory values transparency, consent, open communication, and respect for all partners; however, that doesn't mean individuals in polyamorous relationships are immune from engaging in deception or unethical behavior. Any broken agreement regarding interactions with another person can be considered infidelity in a polyamorous relationship. Because of the level of differentiation required to have hard conversations, broken agreements of all types happen along the learning curve, as people become more confident and competent holding steady, working relationally as a trust-building team, tolerating differences, and managing their expectations and desire to control outcomes. For more on the many ways polyamory can go wrong and how to help clients recover from it, see chapter 16, "Recovering from Polyamory Gone Wrong."

CHAPTER 15

Working with Mono-Polyams and Reluctant Polyams

WHAT IS A MONO-POLYAM?

A mono-polyam is a person who identifies as monogamous (meaning that they prefer to have only one intimate romantic relationship at a time), who finds themselves in a relationship with someone who identifies as polyamorous.

WHAT IS A MONO-POLYAM RELATIONSHIP?

This is how I refer to a relationship in which one partner considers themselves to be polyamorous, while the other considers themselves to be monogamous. The polyamorous partner may have one or several other partners, or they may simply be open to other relationships. But in any case, one partner has, pursues, or remains open to extradyadic connections, while the other doesn't.

This is different from a polyamorous relationship in which one partner doesn't currently have an extradyadic relationship. That's just a polyamorous relationship with a polyamorous partner who is currently single, whereas in a mono-polyam relationship, the monogamous partner is making a conscious choice to be monogamous.

IT'S A LITTLE CONTROVERSIAL

If you do a little reading about polyamory, you will probably read that mono-polyam relationships simply don't work. Polyamorous people are often advised not to expect things to work out with monogamous partners, and monogamous partners will probably hear discouragement from every corner—friends, family members, and even their therapists. As a result, when couples consider opening their relationship, they often assume both have to be polyamorous.

I disagree with the conventional wisdom. As far as I'm concerned, mono-polyam relationships are completely workable. This isn't just a theory: I personally know a number of happy, satisfied monogamous people who are in relationships with polyamorous people. From the evidence of my own experience, then, I can honestly say that this relationship structure exists in happy, healthy, adaptive forms that stand the test of time. I have also helped a lot of couples create this form of relationship and seen it work very well even with a rough start. I hate to think that people who love one another deeply would give up on their relationship just because one wants to have other partners and the other does not. At the very least, they should consider taking a deep dive into whether it might be workable after all.

Can a monogamous person feel deeply valued, chosen, appreciated, upheld, uplifted, and securely attached in a relationship that's not romantically and sexually exclusive? I think people who believe mono-polyam isn't workable tend to assume the answer to this question is "no." But clearly it can happen, at least in some instances, because I've seen it. The project boils down to each individual figuring out if they want to make that happen in their own relationship. As a therapist, I'm interested in helping people who want to do it find the tools and support for doing so. Ultimately, each person will have to assess for themselves if their relationship is workable.

WHAT DOES A HAPPY, HEALTHY MONO-POLYAM LOOK LIKE?

The people who make a mono-polyam relationship work well are often highly differentiated, strongly values-led, and deeply relational. They also tend to have impressive self-awareness. Ironically, I think this is part of why therapists tend to think this relationship style doesn't work: Many of the best examples I know of never went to relational therapy, because they didn't need to. By definition, therapists see the people who need help with their relationships; that means we miss out on the people who are in highly differentiated relationships, have shared values and secure bonds with their partners, and can sort out together what will work for everyone involved with relatively little fuss.

By definition, you won't see one of those successful-without-therapy mono-polyam partnerships in your office, so I want to give you a snapshot of what it looks like. This is a true account, from the monogamous member of a long-term, healthy mono-polyam couple:

> In the 25 years my (lesbian) partner and I have been together, I've had no real interest in being in another sexual or romantic relationship and don't imagine that will change in my lifetime. My spouse, however, has had another relationship—with a man—for more than a decade, with my knowledge, consent, and support.
>
> I think I always knew that nonmonogamy was a possibility in my spouse's mind. When I first expressed romantic interest in her, she was in the process of getting involved again with an ex-girlfriend—in fact, moving to another state to live with her and try to make a go of it—but as I recall, neither of us let that rule out the possibility of exploring whatever might develop between us. And what developed was at first a long-distance relationship in which I guess you could say I was her secondary lover. That had its uncomfortable aspects for me, mostly having to do with uncertainty about what our future would/could be and the particular relationship she had with the ex; however, there were also ways in which it was a relief to me that she was involved with someone else. I was worried about getting involved with someone who would want to be attached at the hip and not let me have the space I needed—and by then I'd dated a couple of people with whom I felt that. Not being her "everything" right from the start gave me a great sense of freedom and room to fall in love with her without those kinds of fears.
>
> Almost 20 years ago my partner first met the man who has come to be another significant partner/lover for her. At first it was a case of friendship and shared interests between them, and gradually it evolved into a sexual relationship. My partner was very honest and open about it from day one, and the fact that I was in the loop from the beginning certainly contributed to the success of our situation. I had plenty of time to get used to the idea that they might someday become more involved, and she has always made sure I know that her primary partnership is with me,

that she chooses me, lives with me, has made a home with me, is married to me, and wants to grow old with me.

In the early stages of her involvement with him, I believe she would have stopped pursuing that relationship if I had been truly unhappy and distressed by it. But I wasn't. In fact, I appreciated that she had someone else with whom to share interests I didn't share—and that aspect has continued throughout the years. She and I are very close, and she shares her vocational and personal processes and struggles with me, but I don't want or need to be her sole support. I appreciate that she has him to process things with.

Sure, I've had moments of annoyance or jealousy but nothing lasting. Actually, I think the times I've struggled most have been when it seemed like the two of them were struggling or she was unhappy with the situation with him; I've gotten mad at him on her behalf a number of times.

Our situation works well for us. He stays with us one night a week and is an active and positive part of our life but doesn't live with us. Sometimes he helps around the house or works with one or both of us on various projects. I like that when the two of them spend time apart from me in the house, I have the chance to focus on my own things, without distractions. Sometimes, when they are together, I come home late and dinner is ready.

I like to spend time around him as well—I can honestly say we're friends—and I enjoy having a little bit of male energy in the house; I was raised with four brothers. I think it has helped that I have known him all along and know without a doubt that he highly respects me and *my* relationship with her. He makes her happy, which makes me happy. They are considerate and don't make me feel like a third wheel when we're all together.

I sometimes go out of my way to make it possible for them to spend time alone together—on occasion they've spent part of a weekend together at our house, and I've jumped at the chance to go off and have a personal retreat somewhere else. Since I crave time by myself anyway, it's not a sacrifice, and they try hard to make sure it isn't an inconvenience for me.

Here, I see a strong, loving partnership, with warmth, a sense of community, and deep respect for each partner's unique self. Would this couple have been well-served, when they were first considering a monopolyam partnership, by being told, "It rarely works?" I don't think so.

Of course, in my work as a therapist, I've also seen mono-polyam couples that come to me with huge differences of opinion, entrenched impasses, and lots of conflict. Sometimes, after working with the relationship for a while, the partners decide to break up. Occasionally, they might decide to try monogamy again. Interestingly, I've also seen some of these pretty nonideal situations ultimately evolve into workable mono-polyamory. It's certainly not textbook, but it's still successful for the long haul. Go figure. If you want to help people in this situation explore their full range of options, you must develop some ways of thinking and talking about this that go further than our cultural script. They can find a zillion other therapists, friends, and family to tell them polyamory is prohibitively difficult or not workable. You will be able to help them much more effectively if you can have a frank conversation about belief systems, goals, challenges, and their ability to create what they are able to envision. They will probably have to build a lot of emotional muscle and stretch quite a bit, but they need a pep talk more than they need another detractor.

WHAT ABOUT COERCION?

I teach therapists to work with polyamory for many reasons, but one big reason is because I have a soft spot in my heart for the mono-polyams. They have even more difficulty finding good help and support than the average polyamorous person. Something about this relationship structure makes a lot of people nervous: Is the monogamous partner sure they know what they're doing? What are they getting into, and what's in it for them? Surely this can't work. Maybe they are being brainwashed, coerced, or taken advantage of. Maybe they aren't able to figure out what they want or are settling for less than they deserve due to low self-esteem. These concerns don't just come from monogamous people. Even within the polyamorous community it can be hard to find support for this relationship style.

Of course, in some cases, there might be reason to worry. Therapists often ask me, "How can I tell the difference between consensual nonmonogamy and something that is coercive, manipulative, or takes advantage of one partner?"

I think this is an important question. I also think it reveals some fears about polyamory. Let's start from the viewpoint that polyamory can be totally workable, just like monogamy. Let's also keep in mind that having a monogamous relationship doesn't ensure that there isn't coercion or manipulation, or that one partner isn't taking advantage of the other. Additionally, the idea that monogamy is the most natural or normal relationship setup is a belief system, not a universal truth. With those ideas as a foundation, I will ask a couple of provocative questions:

How can you tell the difference between a healthy, consensual *monogamous* relationship and one that is coercive, manipulative, or takes advantage of one partner?

Why do we assume it is potentially coercive for one partner to want polyamory but totally okay for another partner to require sexual exclusivity? Is it possible that demanding sexual exclusivity could be manipulative, controlling, or coercive?

I don't intend to be flip about this, nor am I trying to promote polyamory for everyone, or anyone. I'm not asking you to change your belief system, either. I'm just hoping to help you find effective ways to consider these important distinctions. Your clients need you to be able to help them achieve well-functioning polyamory. They also need you to be able to identify and help with icky, coercive dynamics that border on abuse.

Without a doubt, there are some polyamorous situations that are coercive, manipulative, or otherwise questionable and icky. If you are in a relationship yourself that involves a coercive, manipulative aspect, please engage a skilled therapist to help you figure out your next steps. You may be able to shift the dynamic in your relationship, or you may not, but a therapist can give you a reality check about what you are experiencing and perceiving. If you are in fact ready to leave your relationship, a therapist can help you figure out how to do so without having abusive relational dynamics go from bad to dangerous, or dangerous to deadly. If you are a therapist reading this book to help clients and others, you probably have good radar for detecting manipulation and coercion, as well as abuse. If you truly believe that polyamory *can* be workable, you will be able to tell the difference between healthy polyamory and coercion in therapy, just as you do with any other kind of relationship. Your intuition is your best guide when it comes to detecting coercion. When your gut says "ick," there is likely a problem, *unless* your gut says "ick" simply from hearing that someone wants to open their relationship. If you check your bias and honestly don't have a problem with a client choosing polyamory, I'm pretty confident that any "ick" you detect is actually an indicator of a problem. See chapter 6, "The Therapist: Bias, Strengths, and Challenges," for more on identifying and working with bias.

UNCERTAIN MONO-POLYAMS: DISCOVERING WHAT'S POSSIBLE

Let's imagine a monogamous person who is considering being in a mono-polyam relationship but finds the situation challenging. They love their polyamorous partner deeply, but there are serious challenges. Perhaps they experience a lot of jealousy; carry past wounds from a history of infidelity; lack necessary information about polyamory; or come from a family with conservative ideas about what relationships, commitment, and fidelity look like. Nonetheless, they want help figuring out if they can craft a relationship that works for them with the person they want to be with, who just happens to be polyamorous. This mono-polyam will probably need to take a deep look at their values and beliefs to come to terms with what they want to do. They might benefit from the following:

Accurate information and myth-busting about polyamory

Support for accessing an internal sense of knowing, so they can do a deep dive into what is most important to them

Support for stretching and working with internal dilemmas, with regard to emotional regulation, belief systems about fidelity, narratives, holding and tolerating tension about differences, and any other issues that might relate to this

Assistance with full and deep communication with their partner, including considering and sharing how this topic challenges them, exploring what they want in their intimate relationship, and getting really curious about what their partner envisions and why polyamory feels important to them.

In short, this is a mono-polyam who could use a good relational therapist. You won't know the outcome ahead of time, of course, and the therapy might not be entirely easy, but the partners themselves will work it out if you can help them avoid getting stuck in fearful responses, defensiveness, or other ineffective coping mechanisms. At the end of the day, this is a therapy that revolves around building differentiation; each partner must develop the skills to identify what they want, listen deeply to one another, and work together to build a relationship that works for them. For more about differentiation and therapy, see chapter 8, "Conceptualizing the Case: If Polyamory Isn't the Problem, What Is?"

RELUCTANT MONO-POLYAMS: WORKING WITH AN IMPASSE

Now, imagine a monogamous client who asserts, "I'm monogamous, I don't want to be polyamorous, and I didn't sign up for a polyamorous relationship. I want a monogamous relationship, period." At the same time, their partner identifies as polyamorous, and their position is, "This is what I want for my life, and it's an essential part of who I am." Yet, both partners love one another and are reluctant to break up. They are hoping therapy will help.

This, then, is a situation involving an impasse. An impasse is any situation where one partner has a strong opinion that they want one thing and the other partner has an equally strong opinion that they want something else. When there is an impasse, a therapist or coach can be extremely helpful in getting to a resolution, because the process can be tense and emotional. It is very tempting to ease all that tension by just making a decision, which in a polyamory versus monogamy dilemma would usually result in a breakup. I'm going to share with you my strategies for working with impasses as a therapist, all of which can also be applied to a self-help project. While I'll specifically be talking about working with a "monogamy versus polyamory" impasse, keep in mind that impasses are very common and a normal aspect of any relationship; these are the same strategies I use with any set of clients stuck on either side of any seemingly unresolvable difference.

Working with an impasse can be frustrating and emotional but also potentially very fruitful and rewarding. An impasse can be a crucible for each partner to look more deeply into themselves and also discover a deeper layer of the person they love. When I've worked with monogamy versus polyamory impasses, I've seen a huge range of results— from breakups, to formerly monogamous partners discovering that polyamory actually works really well for them, to people who aspire to polyamory deciding to table it and be monogamous. I never know ahead of time what the outcome is going to be, because it depends on the partners and what they discover as they engage in a deep process of discernment, but as long as they work together to come to a solution that honors them both, I'm happy with the result.

The key to helping effectively with impasses is staying out of the middle. My interventions are designed to keep me firmly in the role of facilitator, not arbitrator. I tell my clients,

> I don't get a vote in the decision you will eventually make, and I don't have a stake in the game. I've seen this work out any number of ways, and I'm confident you can work it out in some manner. But let's make sure you both really understand yourselves and one another, and consider all angles of the dilemma you face, before you start taking action steps that you might regret later.

This is how I approach helping with an impasse:

- *Normalize discomfort and slow things down.* If you break up every time you feel uncomfortable, you won't get to have a long-term relationship. I don't think it is likely that anyone can be with their partner for decades without coming up against some significant differences. When that happens, it is going to feel uncomfortable. This is a piece of attachment work: Strong, long-lasting relationships call on us to be able to disagree with someone and love them at the same time. An extreme difference of opinion (and the attendant discomfort) may *feel* like an emergency, but it isn't one. Lots of people weren't raised knowing this. If that's the case for you, realize it can make a huge difference for you. Help your clients take the opportunity to learn how to find stability internally, as well as relationally. Here are some strategies you or your clients might find helpful:

- *Find internal stability.* Notice that you are okay now. You will be okay no matter what happens. Take some time to do something that makes you feel good: Go to the gym, take a bath, read a book, spend time in the woods, or do whatever else comes to mind. Don't spend your self-care time simmering about the problem; use it to recharge, and learn to set aside the rumination.

- *Block rumination.* Circling back to the problem and making meaning about it won't help. That means no obsessing about the issue, no wondering "why me," no angry venting to your friends. Give your brain a break, so it can use its energy to actually think. If you are having trouble thinking about other things or blocking ruminations, try meditation. Try exercise. Try things that feel good. Pet a cat. Wrap up in a fuzzy, weighted blanket and have some tea. Sing. Remind yourself that emotions pass and that when you are experiencing lots of emotions is not a time for thinking.

- *Affirm your essential okayness.* Some people get a lot of relief from figuring out how they will survive the breakup, if it comes to that. Remind yourself that when you have had enough, you will leave the relationship. Make sure you are clear that you are making a choice to stay for now, and you are capable of making the choice to leave if you get clear that is the right thing. Another aspect of being "okay" is realizing you are strong enough to handle this conversation; talk won't kill you. Breathe. You're okay. Your partner is okay. You will work it out. Or, at some point, you will know for sure that the right step is to leave. Either way, you're okay now, and you will be okay in the future.

- *Challenge yourself to stretch, explore, and get curious.* Do not make a decision until plenty of exploration has happened. Plan to spend some amount of time—three months, six months, a year—exploring the territory, learning about yourself, learning about your partner, and learning about various kinds of relationships. Plan to explore with curiosity before expecting yourself to make a decision. Plan to figure out how to think about different kinds of relationships without freaking out. Remember, no one can make you choose to be in a relationship that doesn't work for you. This helps avoid the pitfall of taking every conversation or thought too seriously. It is easier to hear your partner's perspective if you don't think you need to react to it by making a decision. Don't make a decision yet.

- *Deliberately create positive interactions.* No one works hard to nurture a relationship that isn't fun and alive. Figure out how to table the stressful topic, and make time to snuggle, go for a bike ride, take a vacation, and talk about something else. Being able to deliberately create connecting, pleasant experiences together, in between discussions about the difficult topic, is an essential skill for a happy long-term relationship.

• *Make sure you have self-motivated goals.* Why are you still wrestling with this dilemma? I'm guessing it is because part of each of you wants this relationship to work. Maybe you are hoping that you will change your partner. That's common, and it wouldn't surprise me a bit. Oftentimes, when my clients come to me, one is hoping that I'll convince their partner that polyamory won't work, and the other is hoping I'll convince their partner to give polyamory a try. That's not my job, thank goodness. Even if I wanted to, I have absolutely no way of knowing if polyamory is a good fit for anyone, nor can I change anyone other than myself. The first order of business is to help everyone get clear on what they want to change about *themselves*, not about their partner. For more on this, check out the "Creating Change Worksheet Set" in appendix E, starting with "Getting Clear on Your Goals." This worksheet set will walk you through the exact process I use personally, and with clients, when there is something I (or my client) is unhappy about (and somewhere I/they hope to get with that situation). The following are some examples of good self-motivated goals:

  - "I want to show up with curiosity, rather than defensiveness, when my partner is telling me something about themselves."
  - "I want to figure out what I think and feel, and tell my partner about it."

- ◦ "I want to learn more about polyamory without getting wrapped up in fears about my future."
- ◦ "I want to create a loving, safe, and secure connection with my partner."
- ◦ "I want to make good agreements and follow through on them reliably."
- ◦ "I want to understand better why this freaks me out so much."
- *Avoid stonewalling.* "I won't talk about the thing that is important to you" or "I won't consider the thing that is important to you" are not relational stances, and they will not help you connect or further the success of the relationship. Sometimes people are afraid that if they get curious about their partner's perspective or experience empathy for their partner's viewpoint they will somehow have to adopt it for themselves. They will need to understand that considering or talking about something is not the same as agreeing to it. Hearing and empathizing with your partner's perspective might change you, and them, but it cannot force anyone to make a decision they don't want to make. Maybe their partner would be willing to acknowledge that discussing this is a separate process from making a decision and promise not to hold them to anything they might explore in the process of discussing possibilities. Consider putting that in writing. Consider reminding your partner that you appreciate them exploring the material and won't make any assumptions about actions they might take in the future. Remind your partner that you are not interested in coercing or manipulating them; you are interested in knowing them, and you respect their willingness to explore interesting material with you.
- *Remember the parts of differentiation of self, and work toward them.* It will take some developmental growth to have the robust conversations that lead to well-informed and sound decisions. A push to open a relationship can be a sign that one partner is differentiating—that is, expressing something about themselves, their preferences, beliefs, dreams, or desires. The process of differentiating inherently creates tension, but it is a necessary part of growth for both the individuals involved and the relationship as a whole. Chapter 8, "Conceptualizing the Case: If Polyamory Isn't the Problem, What Is?" describes how to assess your clients, or

yourself, to determine which areas of differentiation need special attention and cultivation. As you support your clients, yourself, or your partner through many conversations, keep an eye on which aspects of differentiation are slipping and build skills where they are needed. The growth edge will probably be a little different for each partner and shift throughout time.

- *Create space for nuance.* Oftentimes, in an impasse, people get stuck on their side of the playing field. As they argue around and around an issue, they dig in their heels and get entrenched in position A or position Z. Because they don't want to weaken their stance, they can't really have an authentic, nuanced conversation, which would wander through the entire alphabet. Consider a discussion about opening up the relationship in which both partners have gotten entrenched on their side. The partner who's all for opening up the relationship probably won't feel comfortable sharing that there *are* some things about the idea that make them nervous and some things they prefer about being monogamous, because they don't want their partner to seize on those arguments to "prove" that they're wrong. The partner who wants to stay monogamous, on the other hand, can't share that there are some things that intrigue them about the idea of exploring an open relationship, for the same reason. This entrenchment means that the partners are not really having a full, honest conversation—they're just holding down their respective forts. You can do your part to shift this dynamic. Create some wiggle room and space for everyone to express complicated feelings and nuanced opinions. See "Exercise: Resolving a Dilemma Using Two Chairs" later in this chapter for more on this strategy.

- *Open up the field of possibilities.* People sometimes don't have a lot of information about what a nonmonogamous relationship can look like, and they may make a lot of assumptions about what it would entail that aren't necessarily true. This is one of the unfortunate results of the lack of visibility of nonmonogamous relationships. The fact is (as you know from chapter 1, "Consensual Nonmonogamies: What Are the Options?"), polyamory can look like an *infinity* of different things. Among other things, many people don't know that a mono-polyam relationship is even possible. I think it's important for people to know that the field of options doesn't just include two opposite poles. It's a vast menu, and although you can't control what your partner wants, you have more options than just "exactly what they want, and I get nothing" or "exactly what I want, and they get nothing." I often recommend that clients read books that describe the vast array of variations of consensual nonmonogamies to enrich their sense of possibilities and shake up their entrenched positions. They might also expand their options using the exercise "30 Ideas No Matter How Silly: Brainstorming Process" in appendix D.

- *Use the initiator/inquirer (I/I) process.* When I work with impasses, I spend the bulk of therapy supporting every aspect of differentiation of self while the partners discuss their dilemmas using the initiator/inquirer process. The I/I is a tool for guiding partners toward deeper insight and empathy in their discussions of sensitive topics. It's especially great for times when you want to make absolutely sure you are not contributing your own opinion to the outcome: It keeps you out of the middle, because the conversation is between them. You coach the process but don't weigh in regarding content. Help them stay in the process and access curiosity, empathy, and depth, and they will resolve their dilemma. For much more about the I/I process, including guidelines on how to put it into practice in your therapy room, or your living room, see chapter 9, "Using the Initiator/Inquirer Process to Support Differentiation and Move Toward Decisions."

- *Consider using individual sessions or individual self-care time for skill-building.* This can be helpful when the partners are very reactive about a particular topic. I use individual sessions or even a referral to an individual therapist when I think there are specific skills that will help the difficult discussions move forward more productively, for example, self-soothing, communicating just one thing at a time, holding steady when hearing something difficult, rehearsing how they might want to handle it if their partner responds in the ways they fear, figuring out what they want to express, and accessing empathy for a different and possibly scary perspective.

Exercise: Resolving a Dilemma Using Two Chairs

A dilemma is a situation in which someone faces a choice between two or more options. This comes up almost every time anyone has a goal for themselves or a desire for something that doesn't come easily to them. If it were easy, it would already be decided and done. When someone is wrestling with a dilemma, it may appear that external circumstances have them stuck, but more likely they would be able to solve the problem and take action if it weren't for the internal conflict and the confusion the internal conflict stirs up. That is more likely what has them stuck.

What I am describing is the internal argument between the two parts, or viewpoints, within the person with the dilemma. Imagine a dilemma like this: "One part of me wants to stay in this relationship, and another part wants to leave" or "One part of me wants to try opening up my marriage, and another part is sure that is a bad idea." Just as you start thinking about the topic from one point of view, the other point of view interrupts with objections, fears, limitations, and dire predictions. Then emotions get a foothold and take control of thoughts, and it becomes hard to think clearly about anything.

To my way of thinking, the magic of chair work with a dilemma like these comes as a result of giving each viewpoint an uninterrupted opportunity to speak. This allows for an evolution of thought, and eventually some clarity. Using two chairs to give each of the two parts of the self their own space is helpful for the full experience, which can be quite powerful.

The other magical aspect of chair work is that it keeps the therapist and anyone else, including the other partner, out of the middle. Clearly every aspect of the internal conflict exists within the person experiencing the dilemma.

This is also a useful exercise if two or more clients disagree with one another about something, for instance, opening up the relationship. In that case, you can use the same two-chair strategy to help each partner, first working with one and then the other, identify both perspectives *within themselves*. Almost always, each partner can relate at least a tiny bit to each position, and helping them explore both is the most effective way I know to work with gridlock. Watching your partner grapple with both sides of a dilemma when you thought they only could see "their side" is a revelation, and then it is your turn to do the same. This strategy often leads to less tension, more empathy, and a lot more creativity when it comes to problem-solving. It is my favorite way to decrease artificial polarization and shake up impasses that have calcified in place.

This is a powerful exercise, perfect for individual therapy, relationship therapy, and self-help with or without a partner present. It has its roots in Gestalt therapy and can be done in many ways. I learned to use it in various ways from Ellyn Bader, Peter Pearson, and Vann Joines. For more examples of common two-part dilemmas and step-by-step details about how to use chair work to resolve a two-part dilemma, see the worksheet "Resolving a Dilemma Using Two Chairs" in appendix E. For more information and a different application, see chapter 18, "Relationship Transitions: New Relationship Energy, Relationship Decisions, Shifting Between Partners, and Breakups."

HOW MUCH TO CHALLENGE: A THERAPIST'S DILEMMA

Most of the therapists I know worry a lot about whether they did something wrong when a client decides to leave, and most consider very carefully before they decide to terminate or recommend a hiatus from relational therapy. Because this is something therapists take very seriously, and it happens more often in therapy that involves big disagreements or impasses—particularly in therapy situations that require the therapist to frequently challenge their clients—I want to address it here. In this context, I'm talking about the challenging situation of working with an impasse about polyamory.

In this situation, I aim to challenge both partners. I challenge the reluctant partner to consider how they might benefit from opening up. I challenge the polyamorous client to consider how they might create increased emotional security in their relationship. I challenge both partners to manage their reactions; consider what they believe; identify what they want to create and who they want to be; hear what their partner wants, thinks, and feels; express empathy for one another; and validate one another's perceptions and desires as being entirely valid. I encourage everyone to be honest about their willingness and desire to change, while also encouraging them to stretch outside of their comfort zone. I encourage honest self-reflection and communication. I give both partners a lot of information about what polyamory looks like in real life, with the goal of correcting misinformation and expanding their perceptions of what's possible. I also educate them about what goes into workable monogamy. We explore what the partner who wants to delve into polyamory is hoping to get from polyamory and if there might be ways other than polyamory to get it or light up that part of their lives. We do the same for the partner who wants to go with monogamy.

Once in a while I lose a client because they feel like I'm not impartial or I failed to convince their partner to agree to be monogamous or polyamorous. If a client terminates therapy because they are disappointed that I didn't change their partner's mind, I'm okay with that. They had a misconception about what to expect from me in therapy, and if that's their definition of successful relationship therapy, I'm certainly not the right therapist for them.

Sometimes a monogamous client or reluctant polyam will get the idea that the requirement of therapy is for them to give in and try a polyamorous relationship. That might be a requirement of their relationship or their partner's hope, but it is not my goal or a requirement of therapy. I go to quite a bit of trouble to prevent this misconception, but it still happens on occasion.

My goal is to support differentiation. If my client gets clear that they don't want to be in a polyamorous relationship, and are able to say so and have a conversation with their partner about it, I'd call that a success in differentiation and celebrate their clarity and ability to communicate it. As soon as they are able to do that, I will challenge their partner to be able to hear it, get curious about it, ask good questions, and express empathy and validation.

But if a client isn't ready to say that to their partner *and* they aren't comfortable with a therapy that revolves around considering polyamory, that puts me in a bit of a bind. I'm not willing to say polyamory won't work, because I don't believe that to be true, and I expect my clients to do their own communicating, with both one another and me. Once in a while, a client solves this problem of the massively uncomfortable conversation by firing me, rather than their partner.

For what it's worth, I don't think it is possible to be a therapist who never loses clients. To me, the question comes down to this: What kind of therapist do you want to be, and which clients do you want to lose? Personally, I'd rather be a therapist who challenges both partners and provides information about a marginalized relationship style than be a therapist who challenges less, takes fewer risks, and avoids the really gritty conversations about polyamory and monogamy as belief systems. Either approach will lose me a few clients. If I take the first tack, I might lose the clients who would prefer that I sort out the impasse for them by telling their partner to be monogamous, whereas when I take the second approach, I'll lose the clients who aspire to differentiate and relish the challenge of sorting through these complicated negotiations. At the end of the day, I'd rather hold on to the second group of clients, and I get lots of clients who come to me because their previous therapists didn't stay out of the middle and allow them to have the tough but meaningful conversations they needed to have.

CONCLUSION

You may have noticed that the tools I provide in this chapter aren't specific to mono-polyam relationships. That's because they don't need to be. To work effectively with mono-polyams and reluctant polyams, you just need the perspective that mono-polyam relationships can work and the skills to help your clients build differentiation and resolve impasses. If you have that perspective and those skills, you'll be more equipped to work with mono-polyam clients than the vast majority of therapists, because so few people realize that mono-polyam is workable. For this, your clients will thank you.

At the end of the day, only your clients know what is workable for them. Only they can decide what kind of relationship they want to build and what kind of partners they want to be. If you can help them hold steady as they explore the territory together and keep them from coming to a hasty resolution or becoming immovably entrenched in disagreement, you are completely capable of working with a "monogamy versus polyamory" impasse.

CHAPTER 16

Recovering from Polyamory Gone Wrong

Recently, I asked several thousand therapists what their most pressing questions about polyamory were. One of the top responses was, "What do you do when a couple has tried polyamory before but it went wrong and now they are coming to you to give it another try?" This question surprised me. Every therapist who works with relationships has lots of experience helping people repair their connections after things go amiss. Before I heard this question, it hadn't actually occurred to me that the project might look different with polyamory in the mix.

Honestly, whether the situation involves monogamy-gone-wrong or polyamory-gone-wrong, I'm still not sure it does look all that much different. That's good news; it means you probably already have the skills to work with these cases. Nonetheless, since I got this question so many times, I felt that I ought to put aside some space to address it. If you have experienced polyamory gone wrong in your own life and want to explore some ways to conceptualize the problem, accomplish a good repair, hit reset, or start again from a stronger foundation, I hope this chapter will help. If you encounter difficulty along the way, a therapist or coach should be able to help.

At this point, you've read about what goes into making good agreements and how to address the developmental blocks associated with differentiation of self. To avoid too much redundancy, this chapter focuses on some specific reasons polyamory may go wrong and shares some ideas for how to help people more forward and create something that works better for everyone concerned.

CONCEPTUALIZING POLYAMORY GONE WRONG

There are a variety of common challenges that can lead to problems in polyamorous relationships. I outline these challenges here. If you're working with a client with a history of polyamory gone amiss or have experienced problems seemingly associated with polyamory yourself, first ask yourself which of these broad categories are involved, keeping in mind there might be several.

- *Systemic dynamics that result from a lack of some or multiple aspects of differentiation.* Lack of differentiation of self is extremely common with all types of relationship challenges in all types of relationships. Chapter 8, on case conceptualization, will help you pinpoint the specific differentiation skills that need work. Oftentimes, a lack of relationship skills presents with broken agreements (or the perception of broken agreements). This usually happens when agreements are overly complicated, misunderstood, full of loopholes, or rushed in the creation. It can also happen when one or both partners are trying to please and resolve rather than have the difficult conversations that set up a relationship agreement for success. Refer to chapter 11, "Negotiating Polyamory: Forming Good Agreements," for more information on recognizing ill-made agreements and supporting a robust agreement-making process.
- *Systemic dynamics that result from a lack of secure attachment.* This is a common underlying difficulty and can show up in many ways: when one or both partners have trouble showing affection, showing up with emotional vulnerability or reliability, following through on agreements, soothing themselves or their partner effectively, having hard conversations well, bouncing back and reconnecting after disappointments, nurturing the positive aspects of their relationship, cultivating separate interests, remaining warm and connected when disagreeing, and so on.
- *Inadequate repair following a major disillusionment in the past.* I will discuss what goes into making an effective repair later in this chapter. These questions will help clarify what needs to be repaired and where to start:

○ Do the partners agree on what the fatal problem was? If not, giving each one the opportunity to explain what was so hard for them will be an important early step.

○ Do the partners know how the situation affected one another? Again, if not, this points to the opportunity for some deep and important conversations. Refer to the initiator/inquirer process described in chapter 9.

○ Are they able to acknowledge their emotions and vulnerabilities? Their partner's? These are skills to build in the aforementioned conversations, and it can take some time to get there.

○ Are they able to acknowledge their own role in the thing that went amiss? If not, progress will stop until this ability develops. See the "Getting Clear on Your Goals" worksheet in the "Creating Change Worksheet Set" in appendix E.

○ Is the situation likely to repeat? Sometimes the circumstances that caused problems may be unusual or involve a particular person who may be out of the picture now. In that case, it may be over and done with. More commonly, however, there's a risk of the situation repeating itself; in that case, resolution and repair won't be sufficient, and your clients will need to make a plan for how to do things differently next time. Making a good plan depends on deeply acknowledging how things went wrong in the first place and looking at choices made, potentially quite early on in a lengthy unfolding process.

• *The exposure of relational vulnerabilities.* Polyamory sometimes can put pressure on the relationship and reveal its weaknesses. It may highlight or reveal troubling relational dynamics that otherwise might have emerged more slowly or subtly.

• *The exposure of fundamental incompatibilities.* Occasionally polyamory reveals or highlights a core difference between partners that one or all are not interested in resolving. The key here is to discern how much interest each party has in staying together and why. Every long-term relationship has some significant and inconvenient differences between partners; if they have good reasons to continue to choose one another and show themselves to be capable of development and willing to develop, fundamental differences don't have to be deal-breakers; however, sometimes there is a fundamental incompatibility that is a deal-breaker. This might be a difference of opinion, belief system, way of being in a relationship, or character aspect that emerges.

• *Emerging identity issues* Polyamory may also emerge as the result of one partner discovering a new aspect of their identity—for instance, bisexuality or kinkiness. Exploring this through polyamory may lead to further discoveries, which can shift relationship dynamics in complicated and challenging ways.

HOW POLYAMORY EXPOSES RELATIONAL VULNERABILITIES

"Why is it," my clients sometimes ask me, "that being in a polyamorous relationship forces me to deal with exactly the relationship issues that are the hardest for me, over and over again?" It's true: Polyamory has a funny way of shining a magnifying glass on a relationship's weak points. Any stress that exists concerning communication, connection, security, and power is likely to rise to the surface. That stress is already there, but polyamory often forces partners to recognize and contend with it.

When polyamory goes wrong, it's often because polyamory-related stressors exposed preexisting personal, interpersonal, or relational vulnerabilities. Highlighting these vulnerabilities is a bit of a double-edged sword; it forces the partners into an uncomfortable and perhaps painful situation, but it also gives them the chance to confront the issues and work on them, potentially resulting in an ability to connect more deeply and happily than ever before.

Here are just a few examples of relationship or personal vulnerabilities that can cause polyamory to go wrong:

One or more partners are afraid of telling difficult truths.
One or more partners have difficulty holding steady when hearing difficult truths.
One or more partners tend to make assumptions and react without checking things out.
One or more partners have difficulty responding honestly and kindly when their partner wants to check their worst fears or most worrying assumptions.

One or more partners aren't comfortable with the decision-making or power dynamics in their relationship. That will show up as a vulnerability when they add another partner to the equation.

One or more partners struggle with insecure feelings when they are apart or have trouble thinking about someone or something else, or pursuing other individual interests.

One or more partners tend to withdraw attention after the honeymoon phase or get squirrely when intimacy deepens.

One or more partners develop crushes easily and tend to get tunnel vision about the new love. Managing new relationship energy well is truly an art form, and this is often a culprit when polyamory goes wrong. For more on this, see chapter 18, "Relationship Transitions: New Relationship Energy, Relationship Decisions, Shifting Between Partners, and Breakups."

One or more partners have a hard time putting someone else's needs first, especially in circumstances where there is something they really want (for instance, to go out with James on Thursday night).

One or more partners find scheduling or communication tedious.

Whatever relational issues happen to be your personal kryptonite, polyamory will provide you the opportunity to confront them, and then some.

EMERGING IDENTITY

We all evolve throughout our lifetime, discovering new elements of ourselves as we face new experiences. Being in a long-term relationship doesn't preclude huge shifts in identity. What happens, for instance, when a married heterosexual person is blindsided by a sudden same-sex crush and realizes they're bisexual? Or that they're kinky? Or trans? Consensual nonmonogamy in some form can provide some much-needed flexibility to people in long-standing relationships who don't want to lose their beloved partner as a result of discovering new aspects of themselves.

Revelations like these can result in some dramatic relational shifts. It can feel like an earthquake is sweeping through the relationship, upending old assumptions and revealing new ground. Therapy is a great place for partners to process surprising revelations, grieve past expectations, and devise experiments to explore the new territory. For more on navigating these challenges, see chapter 3, "Overlapping Marginalized Populations and Intersectionality," and chapter 1, "Consensual Nonmonogamies: What Are the Options?"

REPAIRING PAST HURTS

Every relationship involves disappointments and deep disillusionments, and many people never learned to make a good repair. People who have tried opening their relationship and encountered problems are likely to have some lingering pain, guilt, or resentment as a result. If they are going to forge ahead with a new experiment in polyamory or some other form of nonmonogamy, it is well worth revisiting the repair. Without an effective repair, unmended wounds will likely come back to haunt them.

For polyamory to work really well, everyone involved must feel emotionally secure. It's hard for partners to trust one another if the rift from the past is still open, especially if one or both partners don't feel heard or understood.

Say your clients are recovering from a past situation in which, although nominally polyamorous, one person was deceptive, breaking agreements and then lying about it. Their partner has good reason not to feel trusting. While I can certainly appreciate how difficult it can be to make amends and how frustrating it can be to want to move forward rather than delving into the past, it is very difficult to build deep trust if the wounds of the past are still smarting.

You can encourage your clients to make good repairs by reminding them that slights, both large and small, are part of interacting with others, which means that making good repairs is a lifelong relationship skill. It will serve them well, no matter what happens. A good repair is about taking responsibility for your actions, preferences, and choices; it is not about punishment, blame, or shame. An effective repair has many parts.

EXERCISE: MAKING A GOOD REPAIR

Repairing past hurts and taking responsibility for one's actions is incredibly powerful and a necessary relationship skill because everyone makes mistakes from time to time. Even if you don't ever make a mistake, I predict the time will come that you discover something about your partner's preferences by doing something that feels hurtful to them and that you didn't even see coming. Making a repair is a skill that you can use for hurts both small and large, and I think of it as part of any relational toolkit; everyone needs to make a repair from time to time, and most of us should probably do so more often than we do.

I created a handout outlining the steps called "Making a Good Repair," which can be found in appendix D. It begins with a sequence of action steps to help the person making the repair get grounded and in a strong frame of mind. These preparatory steps are just as applicable to the other participants, as it takes grit, grace, and endurance to discuss past or current hurts. This is especially true if either partner is still very upset. Getting grounded is important because a repair attempt will not be nearly as effective and may fail entirely if either partner finds themselves emotionally drowning in guilt or shame, resentment or blame, or any other toxic emotion. If ever there were a situation that warrants getting grounded before jumping in, making a repair is it.

I also recommend taking some time with the repair process. This is too important to be rushed. If anyone involved experiences a strong impulse to gloss over any of the steps, it is better to take a break and come back to it again later. Getting emotionally flooded will just lead to shutting down or firing up, neither of which will help. Take your time.

PROBLEMS CAUSED BY NEW RELATIONSHIP ENERGY

New relationship energy (NRE) refers to the overwhelmingly compelling and delightful experience of falling in love. It's a powerful, wonderful feeling, and it can also lead people to be incredibly rude to and inconsiderate of their partners. Lack of consideration, bad manners, and the inability to put someone else's comfort before one's own desires are character traits that will be quickly revealed as soon as NRE comes into play. The first time people experience NRE, they tend to behave badly. It's almost inevitable. Occasionally, I have seen it handled well with people who have a lot of experience subverting their own desires in favor of higher values or a lot of access to empathy. Handling NRE badly is the cause of a lot of pain and suffering, and damaged trust that can be very difficult to repair.

Imagine a situation in which a couple, Elisa and Zelda, has decided to explore polyamory. Soon into the experiment, Zelda falls hard for a new partner, Justin, and is completely swept away by NRE. Elisa was initially excited about the experiment, but Zelda's behavior starts to get more and more annoying: She often half-listens to what Elisa is saying, while she stares at her phone, waiting for Justin to text back; she changes plans at the last minute to meet up with you-know-who; she becomes unreachable for hours on end when she's out on dates. Elisa feels neglected and sidelined. Ultimately, the very mention of Justin becomes triggering for Elisa, and she asks Zelda to break off the relationship.

Situations like this are pretty common, and they're often what's behind rules like, "You can see anyone, except this one person." When NRE creates havoc in a polyamorous relationship, the sidelined partner often identifies their partner's lover as the problem and seeks to solve it by having their partner end that relationship and establish a rule to keep them from reconnecting.

There are a couple of problems with this approach. One is that, at one point at least, their partner and this other person shared strong romantic and/or sexual feelings. Those don't just vanish overnight. If the people involved don't get clear on why they themselves wanted to end that relationship, it can end up actually increasing the desire, rather than decreasing it. That can be a setup for deception in the future.

The larger problem, however, is that in truth, the dynamic that resulted in one partner feeling unchosen, unimportant, or disrespected isn't really about the other lover at all. It is about their partner, their partner's choices, their partner's manners, their partner's vulnerabilities, their partner's character—it is about their partner. But that makes it much more challenging to deal with than simply blaming it on the other person. To deal with a problem having to do with your partner's consideration of you, or vulnerability to compliments and praise from someone else, or anything else that might be going on, you will need to have some difficult conversations that are very direct.

In a polyamorous relationship, it is not an effective strategy to lose your mind and expect the world, and your household, to revolve around your needs and desires every time you fall in love—particularly if that involves you standing up your long-term partner, breaking agreements, failing to return home on time, mooning around extolling a new partner's praises, or smelling like someone else's perfume (or bed) when you do come home. If your clients have suffered from badly handled NRE in the past, they will need to make a sincere and meaningful repair, acknowledging their mistakes and taking responsibility for poor choices and skewed priorities. In addition, they will need to make a plan to handle NRE better next time, because NRE is unavoidable. Happily, it seems that it gets a little easier to manage with practice. For more about managing NRE well, see chapter 18, "Relationship Transitions: New Relationship Energy, Relationship Decisions, Shifting Between Partners, and Breakups."

CONCLUSION

There are many entry points to polyamory, not all of them ideal. Additionally, people often embark on a polyamorous relationship with the best of intentions, only to find all of their relationship's unresolved tensions quickly rising to the surface. Even when it unfolds in an orderly, respectful, and considered manner, polyamory inevitably puts partners in challenging situations, for instance, acknowledging and openly discussing romantic or sexual feelings for other people. On one hand, that can make the relationship much more tense and difficult; in some cases, the relationship doesn't survive the strain.

On the other hand, exposing the relationship's weak points makes it possible for partners to work on them. They may end up building a much stronger relationship than they would otherwise—sometimes stronger than they even knew possible. In any of these situations, having access to a skilled relationship therapist can be the difference between saving the relationship and losing it.

You may have clients who come to you looking for support in the process of embarking on a polyamorous relationship. In that case, you can help them prepare for the challenges that are likely to arise and guide them in the process of differentiating, thereby reducing (although not eliminating) the chances of that experiment going amiss.

However, it's far more likely that your clients will come to you *after* things have already started to go wrong. Rather than looking ahead and anticipating the potential difficulties, they may only realize they need the support of a therapist once the problems have started to crop up. For that reason, it's important that you be prepared to help your clients make repairs. You'll need to be able to anticipate common problems that arise in polyamorous relationships, recognize their underlying developmental causes, and skillfully navigate the challenge of increasing differentiation and a secure connection through the emotional tension and vulnerability caused by whatever issues brought the clients to your therapy room in the first place.

Polyamory can be very challenging. So can monogamy. In fact, intimate relationships give us unlimited opportunities to connect deeply but also to learn and grow, develop our character, and gain skill navigating challenges we could never have seen coming and may have preferred to avoid. Ideally, as we encounter a lifetime of relational challenges, we allow them to strengthen us, rather than tear us down. Ideally we embrace the opportunity to continue to more fully become the people and partners we aspire to be, differences, mistakes, and all.

CHAPTER 17

Role-Related Challenges and Benefits
Primaries, Secondaries, Hinges, Etc.

Based on hierarchy and relationship structure, each member of a poly-amorous relationship may have different roles and responsibilities, and experience different challenges and benefits. In this chapter, I discuss a variety of common roles in turn and describe some of the unique issues associated with each position. I also discuss some situational relational challenges, like nesting and non-nesting challenges, and challenges related to relationship length. Of course there is a lot of overlap in roles, since many polyamorous partners are in more than one relationship, hence more than one situation and role. This chapter is intended to start you thinking in terms of roles and situational dynamics; it is not a comprehensive document covering every possibility.

When we talk about role-related challenges, we're getting into some challenging aspects of polyamory. I explore it in detail here because I think it is crucial that therapists, counselors, and coaches have ways of thinking about these issues so they can be of service and help their clients craft relationships that feel respectful of everyone involved. And for people who are crafting their own polyamorous relationship, it might be helpful to have a heads up; the way you structure your relationship creates particular roles and dynamics, and each has its own challenges and benefits.

PRIMARY/SECONDARY: NOT AS
CUT AND DRIED AS IT SOUNDS

Many polyamorous relationships are structured with some form of primary/secondary hierarchy. Although primary/secondary structures vary widely in terms of agreements, rules, and expectations, they do inherently create different roles for different partners: Some will be primaries, and some will be secondaries. A primary partner will likely have different challenges, benefits, and concerns than a secondary.

But hierarchy isn't as simple as it sounds. While a primary/secondary structure attempts to reduce complicated relational dynamics to a rubric that determines who should be prioritized in any given conflict, things are often more complicated than the labels imply. Like any aspect of a relationship, it can go extremely well, extremely badly, or anything in between, depending on how the people involved see things, make meaning, and behave.

Since polyamory tends to bring out strong feelings about attachment, primacy, security, reliability, and so on, it is possible for an expression of primary/secondary hierarchy to feel or actually *be* extremely dismissive of secondary partners. At the same time, some primary/secondary structures are less rule-bound or functionally hierarchical than even some nonhierarchical structures. At the end of the day, experience and perception are more important than labels. In other words, if a person has a perception that someone else's needs or desires supersede theirs, this will result in a certain type of tension or challenge, regardless of whether they think of themselves as a primary or secondary partner and whether their relationship has an inherent hierarchy built into its structure.

Listen to what your client, or your partner, is telling you about their experience in terms of whether their thoughts, feelings, and experiences are honored, seen as important, validated, and taken into account when it comes to making decisions. Regardless of role or hierarchy, it is possible for everyone involved to feel important. If someone feels that their feelings and preferences don't count, it will create some fundamental problems, no matter what labels they use to describe their relationships and agreements. There is also a distinction to be made between taking into account a partner's feelings and preferences in general, and doing so when it comes to making decisions. If a partner generally feels validated and important to their partner, that's wonderful, but if that validation and importance doesn't extend to decision-making, problems are likely to arise.

As you read the descriptions of role-related challenges, keep in mind that many people have more than one role. A hinge might also be a primary and, in another relationship, a secondary partner, and so on. And some challenges, for example, experiencing NRE, apply to anyone in a polyamorous relationship, although different roles might have different challenges with the experience.

EXAMPLE: HYPOTHETICAL POLYCULE

Because these concepts are hard to grasp without examples and can be a little convoluted, I'm going to describe a hypothetical polycule and diagram it for you. These imaginary partners will assist me throughout the chapter as I describe various role-related challenges.

We'll start by meeting a hypothetical couple, Sam and Anne. They have been married for five years, share a home and a mortgage, and are in a primary/secondary relationship, meaning that both of them put the needs of one another before the needs of any other partner they might have.

Anne has another partner, Ralph. Ralph is Anne's secondary partner. Ralph identifies as polyamorous but doesn't currently have another partner. Sam also has one other partner, Jill. Jill is solo polyam; she doesn't believe in hierarchy and makes her own decisions, after taking her partners' preferences into account. Jill is dating several other people, one of whom is a nesting partner, Ramona. Ramona isn't dating anyone other than Jill and considers herself to be monogamous.

So, Ralph and Sam are metamours, Jill and Anne are metamours, and Sam and Ramona are metamours. As you consider these imaginary people, start to imagine the challenges they might face in their various relationships. As you consider what problems they might face, also challenge yourself to consider the benefits of polyamory that each of the people involved might experience.

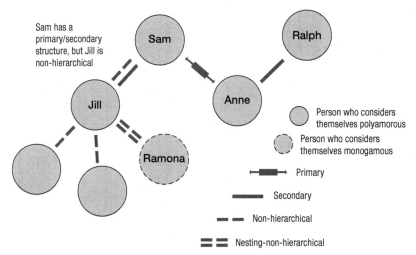

Sam has a primary/secondary structure, but Jill is non-hierarchical

Person who considers themselves polyamorous

Person who considers themselves monogamous

Primary

Secondary

Non-hierarchical

Nesting-non-hierarchical

Hypothetical Polycule.

PRIMARY PARTNERS

Because primary/secondary structures often arise out of monogamous relationships, many primary partners have gone through a process of opening up their relationship. When everything goes well and everyone involved does a careful job with putting their primary partner first and following through on agreements, there will likely be little or no lasting negative fallout from the process. But often the road to polyamory is far from ideal. If there are still wounds to repair from the process of opening up, everyone will benefit from taking the time to make those repairs carefully and form plans for how to move forward with care (see chapter 16, "Recovering from Polyamory Gone Wrong," and the "Making a Good Repair" exercise in appendix D). Additionally, some primary partners are less than delighted about their polyamorous situation or in early stages of working things out, running experiments, or bouncing back from difficulties with previous attempts to open up. This is not specific to primary partners, but to anyone with a history of rough bumps along the road to polyamory.

Another potential challenge for primary partners is managing changing circumstances that are outside of their direct control. Depending on the relationship habits and preferences of their partner, there might be an ever-changing parade of partners, or there might be just one. In either case, the partners may or may not like their metamours.

As you are imagining the kinds of challenges primary partners face, carefully consider how people in those roles also might benefit from polyamory. For instance, I've seen situations where a primary dyad is experiencing a lot of stress, perhaps from a health crisis or a pivotal point in a career, and other partners have chipped in to help. I've often been impressed by how metamours can show up, with great generosity and kindness, in just the moment they're needed.

Imagine not having to worry so much about your partner's emotional well-being and mental health during a tough patch, because you know they are supported by another partner or two. Imagine how having a roster of "aunties" or a circle of friends in a community might potentially benefit the children. They'll always have someone they care about at their school concerts and soccer games.

I encourage you to use your imagination and flesh out this list with ideas of your own or from your own experience either personally or clinically. Thinking through potential challenges, strengths, and solutions will make you a helpful support when your clients are trying to navigate the complexities of polyamory.

SECONDARY PARTNERS

Some people are very uncomfortable with such hierarchical structures as primary/secondary. For some, this is a values-based concern having to do with the foundational primary/secondary concept of privileging one partner over another, or all others. For others, it is because hierarchy can take a shortcut around being careful and considerate of the unique preferences and humanity of every participant. As I discuss earlier in the chapter, I believe that what matters in practice is not the label, but whether each partner is acting from their best self, with warmth, curiosity, openness, and generosity of spirit. That said, it's certainly true that secondary partners can be shortchanged by primary/secondary setups and often are.

Being a secondary partner comes with its own unique challenges. At worst, secondary partners may feel like they're in a constant power struggle with the primary partner, wrangling for time with their beloved and constantly afraid that the relationship is about to be vetoed out of existence. Many people don't go looking for a secondary relationship per se. The most common reason I see people choose to become secondary partners is simply that they fall in love with someone who has a primary partner. In that case, they aren't necessarily choosing to become a secondary because that's their preferred relationship style, but because it's the option they have for being in a relationship with the person they love.

That said, being a secondary partner can be a great situation for someone who wants a relationship but not a full-time primary one. Maybe they have an intense, time-consuming job, hobby, or spiritual practice. Maybe frequent travel is an important part of their life. Maybe they just don't see themselves as a "marriage person" and like to have a lot of freedom and independence. Also, many people choose to be secondary partners because they already have a primary partner. It is a misconception that no one would choose to be a secondary partner or that there are no benefits. The following is a description of a well-functioning secondary relationship to serve as an example of what is possible.

> I was in a secondary relationship of 20-plus years. We supported one another through some big life transitions. We both knew we could not live together—we'd drive each other nuts in a week. A long weekend together was about all we could handle. She would say, "We have a great time, and he packs up his dirty laundry and goes home." I would say that our polyamorous arrangement allowed us to appreciate and enjoy the ways we got along well, while not stumbling much over the ways we did not.

This example points to a nice feature of polyamory. There are many people, like the ones in this account, who love one another and enjoy one another's company but whose compatibility wouldn't survive getting married, or living together 24/7. Polyamory enables those relationships to find their own shape and function in their own unique way.

Let's return to our imaginary polycule. Ralph, Anne's secondary partner, isn't seeing anyone else at the moment, and that may lead to some challenges. No matter how egalitarian and warm the primary partners in a polycule are, there will be occasions when Anne cancels something at the last minute that Ralph was looking forward to, and this will happen for reasons that are entirely out of his control. Furthermore, he may or may not know the circumstances of the change in plans, and even if he did, he might not agree with the decision or how it was made. This sets up the possibility that Ralph might feel resentful, sidelined, and a lack of control. Depending on what Ralph's strengths are, he might thrive with this arrangement. Much will depend on how reliable and dependable Anne is in her relationship with Ralph, and how skilled she is at managing the challenges of being a hinge.

There are a few ways people can set up themselves to better handle the challenges of a secondary relationship. For instance, having a lot of other interests can be a huge help. For some secondary partners, dating other people gives them plenty to do. For someone in Ralph's situation, who doesn't currently have another partner, much will depend on how much time he likes to spend alone, how strong his other social supports are, how prone he is to taking schedule changes personally, and how he handles rumination and negative thoughts when his feelings get hurt. If he is dissatisfied with the amount of time he spends with Anne and wishes for more, that will make things harder.

Secondary partners will need to contend with the agreements their partner has made with their primary, and those agreements may have been designed specifically for the purpose of limiting the amount of time they spend with their secondary partner and how. For instance, primary partners may agree to have no overnights with secondaries, limit the number of dates they have in a week, or break off the connection if the other partner ever starts to feel threatened. If Sam and Anne have agreements of this kind, Ralph may be challenged to manage some complicated feelings about both the agreements and the fallout from them.

Jill is also a secondary partner, in her relationship with Sam. But Jill has several other partners, including her nesting partner, Ramona. I wouldn't want to suggest that Jill will *certainly* struggle less than Ralph, because it is still possible to struggle with difficult emotions and negative thoughts even if your other commitments keep you busy. Nonetheless, many secondary partners find that it helps to have plenty to do, including having other partners with whom to be intimate. Again, much of what Jill experiences will depend on the quality of connection and security of the emotional bond between Jill and Sam, and how Sam handles the role of hinge.

It's easy to fall into the trap of imagining what might have been: If only we could have a few more nights a week, or if only we could go on that trip together. Rather than getting caught up in these fantasies, secondary partners will need to take a clear-eyed, pragmatic look at how it benefits them to be in a relationship, exactly as it stands, and without any "if onlys."

If someone has difficulty controlling their thinking, they might collapse into anger and resentment, or they may obsessively fantasize and ruminate about the positive points of the relationship. The following are some examples of things a secondary partner might tell themselves about their secondary status and situation. You will notice that some of these messages are likely to contribute to feelings of dissatisfaction, and others are likely to help them stay grounded and soothe themselves.

> I wish Anne and I could spend more time together. It's so unfair how Sam can just call her up any time and she'll do whatever he wants. I feel so good about myself, and her, when we're together, and I want more. I wish my entire life were more like the time we spend together, and I really resent that she divides up her time the way she does. It is a little easier to bear the time I spend away from her if I let myself get a little annoyed with her. Why does she put up with all those rules anyway? It's not fair.

> I love spending time with Anne. Sometimes I wish we could spend a night together, but honestly, I don't know for sure that would be as much fun as it sounds. There are some real advantages to limiting the time we spend together, as frustrating as that can be. For one thing, it keeps things hot; we don't see enough of one another to get bored. For another, we don't have to manage a lot of business. We can just play. If we spent more time together, it would be a lot less like a mini-vacation. I'm sure I'd start to notice some of her shortcomings; after all, everyone has them.

> I wonder when I'll have spent enough time with Anne to begin to really see her more negative side. Right now, we're squarely on the honeymoon. It's blissful to be together, but I know she's human. If I think about it, having some limitations on how much time we

can spend together probably serves us well. Actually, when she stayed a little longer last time, I did notice it was a little hard to think up things to talk about after dinner. Plus, if we spent more time together, she might start to notice some of my shortcomings, too. I guess it's not all bad that we don't have to go there.

I did okay without Anne up until now; what did I used to do with all my time? I think I'll make a list of the things I enjoyed doing before we met and start doing them again. I've gotten a little overly focused on having fun with her, but I know there is more to life. I don't like how I feel when I'm waiting for her to have time for me. I'm going to get busy doing other things and just enjoy it when I'm able to see her.

When secondary partners feel powerless, it can be hard to avoid getting reactive. They may issue ultimatums, for instance, to try and regain some control: "If I can't see you at least once a week, this isn't going to work for me." Unfortunately, issuing ultimatums from a power-down position is a losing proposition, and of course, we don't always get our way, so while I support the differentiation it takes to figure out what you like and do not like, turning it into an ultimatum for someone else often ends in disappointment. When I have a client or friend who is considering issuing an ultimatum because they believe their situation is untenable, I'm also curious to know if that's actually true. New love can make us feel desperate, and that desperation doesn't ever feel good. But what if, instead of issuing an ultimatum, you sat with it a little bit and tried to discover what you can actually tolerate. You might find out that, if you can get enough focus on your own life and your own interests, you actually don't need to see that partner once a week.

You could also decide to share your feelings, thoughts, and preferences with your partner so they are aware of what you are experiencing, and what you would prefer; it is surprising how often secondary partners don't take the risk of expressing their desires, or do so only when they are upset. Discussing things honestly and from a position of internal personal empowerment will certainly result in learning something about your partner. They may show warmth and understanding regarding your experience, in which case even if they choose not to accommodate your preferences, you might feel connected, supported, and satisfied with the relationship. Of course it is also possible that you might realize you don't have much respect for your partner's way of responding when you discuss your feelings and preferences. This could result in a realization that you're not interested in being in this relationship with these particular challenges, in which case you may decide to end the relationship on your terms. In any number of ways, and oftentimes, I've seen huge personal breakthroughs come as a result of sitting with discomfort, communicating honestly, and letting things evolve. So often, in fact, that I highly recommend the project of challenging your assumptions and really working on finding ways to hold steady.

Nonprimary partners often have to deal with a lot of uncertainty. That works best for someone who is good at rolling with the punches, releasing attachment to particular outcomes, and not taking things personally. Sometimes the primary partner asserts their primacy with lots of rules, vetoes, emotional emergencies, and sudden and/or dramatic changes of plans. This can end up being pretty painful, even untenable, for the secondary partner. Polyamorous people have a term for this dynamic: *couple privilege.* Couple privilege describes a dynamic that privileges the primary relationship, often to the point of discounting or minimizing the personhood of the other partner(s). Veto rules, for instance, are often identified as a sign of couple privilege. A veto rule allows the primary partner (at least theoretically) to veto the relationship with the secondary partner if it starts to make them too uncomfortable: "If I start to feel like that person you're seeing is a threat to our relationship, I can tell you to stop seeing that person and that's what you'll do."

Primary partners often use their veto power when the secondary relationship is beginning to become too serious and emotionally involved in their eyes. Maybe they're not threatened by their partner having sex with someone else, but they are threatened by their partner starting to fall in love with someone else. On the other hand, sometimes the veto gets used as a last-ditch effort to get a besotted, badly behaved partner to keep agreements, come home on time, and stop texting their lover at the dinner table. I hope it is obvious at this point that the veto rule is not the main problem in this scenario.

Naturally, the use of a veto can lead to a number of problems. On one hand, it's going to be pretty hard for the partner to respect the agreed-upon veto if they are, in fact, falling in love with their secondary partner. That's frequently a recipe for resentment or broken agreements, or both. On the other hand, if the veto is respected, that leaves the secondary partner in a very painful place—the rug is pulled out from under them just as they were getting so close, precisely *because* they were getting close.

I can understand the desire to have a veto rule. It can provide a feeling of emotional security in the face of vulnerability and uncertainty. Sometimes, they are somewhere between useful and benign, and sometimes they are desperate attempts to create order in an emotionally chaotic situation. In any case, the mere existence of a veto rule will inevitably make the secondary partner feel endangered and vulnerable.

I want to share a personal account from a person in the "hinge" position in a successful long-term primary/secondary relationship. The partners in this relationship had a veto rule at first and later reconsidered it:

When I first developed a crush on a close friend, long before I actually acted on it, I told my husband of eight years about it. At the time, it was important to me that he knew that I wouldn't act on my attraction to my crush unless he felt comfortable with it; opening our relationship wasn't a totally new concept for us, but this would be the first time either of us had acted on it. I wasn't interested in risking my marriage, and I felt like his comfort and happiness would make or break the success of the mission. I don't know what would have happened if he had exercised his veto; he didn't, and so I can only speculate. But for months, as the other relationship developed, I continued to reassure myself that my partner was okay with it, and I occasionally checked in with him about it to make sure. Every time I checked in, he told me it was fine.

One day, as things in the new relationship were heating up and we were about to take it to a new level, I think I wanted to reassure myself, as much as my husband, that I was in some kind of control of the situation; again I told my husband that I would end it if he felt threatened. Much to my surprise, he said, "I'm not sure that's actually true, and I'm not even sure I think that would be a good idea; you two have a pretty big relationship, and I don't think it would be good for *our* relationship, or even *right*, for me to say you have to end it, even if you would, or could." That was a real turning point for me; my husband called my bluff, in a way, by acknowledging the reality that it isn't a simple thing to end an important relationship.

Now, years later, I don't think of it in those terms at all; if my husband told me he felt uncomfortable about some aspect of my other relationship, I would want to know why and how to help him feel comfortable, and I certainly might change something about how things were going to help smooth out any problems. But ending the other relationship isn't something I would offer up as a solution. I learned that from my husband, who was principled enough and smart enough to know that making me choose wouldn't make us any stronger, even when I didn't know it myself.

HINGES

A "hinge" is someone who has two or more other partners. Most often, this is something akin to a V. Take our example polycule. Both Anne and Sam have more than one partner, so both of them are hinges in primary/secondary structures: Anne is a hinge between Sam and Ralph, and Sam is a hinge between Anne and Jill. Jill is also a hinge because she has more than one partner, but she doesn't have a primary/secondary structure. Jill is a hinge between each of her other partners, one of whom is her nesting partner, Ramona.

Being a hinge can be quite complicated, particularly in a primary/secondary structure or with a nesting partner, because both of these situations involve sudden changes in plan due to shared responsibilities or agreements that are in place. Being a hinge requires you to simultaneously hold *your* needs and desires, the needs and desires of your primary partner, and the needs and desires of your secondary partner, and successfully negotiate between all of these potentially conflicting interests. It's not really possible to be a hinge without occasionally letting someone down or telling someone you care about something you know they don't want to hear.

How a person behaves and makes decisions when they are in touch with their highest and best self is one thing, and how they make decisions when they are anxious or triggered is quite another. Once again emotional management comes into play. Someone who is often in a decision-making role, for instance, a hinge partner, will be more likely to thrive if they cultivate emotional management skills so they are able to stay in their window of tolerance most of the time, notice when they are not, and cultivate skills to take breaks and bring themselves back effectively.

You can see that for many reasons, being a hinge requires a high level of differentiation of self. A hinge might feel like they're constantly being yanked back and forth, trying to balance the differing desires and expectations of their partners. This is especially true for hinges that have trouble with the idea that they can't fulfill everyone's desires and will have to let some people down at least some of the time. A hinge can exhaust themselves running between their partners and trying to make sure everyone feels sufficiently comfortable, valued, and loved at all times. They will need to get used to experiencing other people's disappointment without collapsing. They will need lots of practice holding steady through feelings of anxiety and guilt, and they will need to get accustomed to the hard truth that you can't please all of the people all of the time.

Imagine a situation in which Anne is at home with Sam on the weekend and Sam tells Anne about some difficult feelings he is grappling with. They have a great talk, and Anne decides the best course of action is for her to cancel her date with Ralph later in the week, because it will help stabilize and solidify things at home. In the moment, it is clear to Anne that Sam's feelings are valid, and the sacrifice she will make regarding seeing Ralph later in the week is minimal compared to the benefit that will result from increased stability.

Then imagine that Anne has lunch with Ralph during the day on Monday and tells him she needs to cancel their date for Thursday night. If Anne's emotional boundaries are not clear, she might say something like, "Sam is having a hard time, so I can't see you on Thursday night," or even, "Sam doesn't want us to see one another on Thursday night, so I have to cancel." The problem here is that Anne is pinning the responsibility for cancelling on Sam, which might understandably result in Ralph feeling like his interests are being pitted against Sam's, even though it's ultimately Anne's decision to cancel. A better way to frame it would be, "Last night, I had a conversation with Sam about some feelings he's been struggling with. It's important to me to be there for him this week, so I've decided to cancel my date with you on Thursday night." This more appropriately boundaried approach requires that Anne take responsibility for the decision and handle any emotions Ralph might have about it herself, rather than blaming the situation on Sam.

Many secondary partners have told me that they feel much more stable and secure when the hinge is strong enough emotionally to have a real conversation about their own choices and responsibility, even if the secondary partner is unhappy about the decision. After all, they care about their lover's emotions; if it feels important to Anne to connect with Sam, Ralph might be disappointed, but he's likely to understand where she's coming from, particularly if she talks about why it feels important *to her*. On the other hand, if Anne blames the canceled date on Sam, she sets Sam and Ralph up as adversaries. Sam probably wouldn't like being cast as the villain, and Ralph doesn't get to have the benefit of empathizing with Anne to help him manage his disappointment.

Let's imagine that, after her conversation with Sam, Anne decides not to change her plans with Ralph. Here again, she can choose how she frames her choice. She can take responsibility, saying, "I'm sorry, Sam, but I made a commitment to spend time with Ralph, and it's important to me to honor that commitment," or she can pin it on Ralph, saying, "I'm sorry, honey. I wish I could stay home with you, but I promised Ralph, and he'll be so upset if I cancel." Again, I have noticed that the entire situation usually goes better if the hinge person takes full responsibility for their choice. This is one advantage solo polyamory or relationship anarchy has over primary/secondary, at least in theory; in nonhierarchical situations, it is a little easier for everyone to see that everyone is making their own decisions and ideally taking responsibility for those decisions.

Unlike primaries and secondaries, hinges exist in both hierarchical and nonhierarchical structures. Every polycule has at least one hinge, and sometimes several. Because of their position, hinges can make or break relationships between metamours, which affects the dynamic of the entire polycule. Because of this, whenever there are difficult relational dynamics, I strongly recommend looking to the role of the hinge. Hinges carry a lot of responsibility, because they are in direct communication with all of their lovers, some of whom may not be in communication with one another. A highly differentiated hinge can stabilize an entire polycule, and a hinge who is a bad communicator, overly avoidant, or lacking in emotional boundaries can brew a lot of bad blood and stir up a lot of chaos.

As a therapist, the effort you give to helping the hinges will pay off immensely for everyone involved. If you are a person in a polyamorous relationship, consider if the hinge(s) in your polycule are sufficiently supported, and if they are not, this would be an area where any investment will probably pay off very well. The more the hinge can understand their own thoughts, feelings, and desires; make good agreements and follow through; take responsibility for their opinions and choices; and stay steady in the face of others' emotions the more their partners will benefit from their clear communication and strong boundaries. Consider the difference between a relationship ending because a primary partner enforced a veto rule and a situation where a strongly differentiated hinge made a decision to break up, took responsibility for their choice, and had the hard conversations associated with that decision without passing the buck.

METAMOURS

Every relationship between metamours is unique, but here are some possibilities:

The metamours have never met.

They have met but aren't friends and feel neutral about one another.

They have met and don't like one another.

They have met and one of them doesn't like the other, but the other does and would like to hang out together sometimes, or a lot.

They are casual acquaintances and see one another socially.

They like one another but rarely see each other.

They are close friends and see one another often.

They live together and share household responsibilities.

Imagine all the ways these various situations might have come about and the potential implications of each.

The relationship between metamours may have evolved organically and without any real planning. For instance, metamours might never meet if they live in different cities or have vastly different interests. Alternatively, the status of the relationship between metamours may be determined by a primary/secondary agreement or set of rules. For instance, a primary partner who's uncomfortable with the idea of knowing their partner's lovers might ask to never meet their metamours or put a rule into place that their partner can only get involved with people they don't know and will never meet. On the other hand, the primary partner might have made a rule like, "I want to meet all your lovers at least once." In that case, they might have met, even if they have nothing in common and don't like one another. The relationship dynamics surrounding metamours, primaries, secondaries, and hinges can be quite convoluted and complex, and each configuration carries its own challenges and strengths.

Metamours often suffer from triangulation. Many metamours don't have direct communication with one another, making the hinge the messenger. Aside from the inherent liabilities of having someone else do your communicating for you, tons of unnecessary drama can result if the hinge lacks boundaries or good manners.

That said, I've also seen situations in which someone in the polycule insists on direct communication between metamours, even when it makes no sense at all. I think the dilemma boils down to this: What decision is being made, and who will be making that decision? If the decision is being made by an individual or dyad, I see no reason to force a summit with everyone around the same table. But if the decision is being made by consensus and it's going to affect everyone, everyone definitely needs a voice in the negotiations. Figuring out how to hear every voice when metamours don't speak to one another is a special challenge. It is important to note that some polyamorous relationships with noncommunicating metamours do quite well.

Frequently, the hinge is the person gathering votes and hearing opinions. That can be entirely appropriate and healthy, as long as they are able to take responsibility for their own decisions and choices. But if there is a lot of "he said . . . she said . . . they said . . ." in the conversation, either their emotional boundaries need clarification or the decision affects enough people that they should consider bringing everyone into the room to express their own opinion.

TRIADS, QUADS, AND OTHER FAMILIES

Triads and quads generally make decisions about things that affect the entire family together. The same principles apply: Use consideration, good manners, and clear communication, and take responsibility for your own preferences and choices. There may be more people around the table than most of us are used to, but the decision-making process is otherwise similar to that of any other family.

The most common challenges I see in family structures involve triangulation, peacemaking, and coalition-forming. For instance, if a dyad is having a conflict, it is tempting and common to debrief that fight with another family member, simply because everyone in the family is close friends, and often lovers, with everyone else. Unfortunately, that can result in an uncomfortable us/them dynamic. That's not always the case; if the listener is able to stay boundaried and avoid the "fix it" pitfall, they may do just fine. But the risk is that they feel internal or external pressure to go to the other partner and try to sort it out second hand. This is often ineffective and, additionally, usually results in everyone's feelings getting hurt in some manner. Better to listen and empathize, and leave it at that, or encourage direct communication.

Similarly, it requires a lot of self-control and restraint to avoid becoming a mediator for your partners in a triad, quad, or moresome, but it is an effort worth making. "I'm sorry you are having such a hard time with Joe; I think you are making some important points about what you want; why don't you go have a conversation with Joe and share your thoughts and feelings directly? I know they would want to hear your concerns."

It is also easy for two partners to form a coalition "against" the third—to stage an intervention regarding cleaning the kitchen or some other shared complaint, for instance. This dynamic can be problematic if they come off like critical parents, because that will almost certainly be met with rebellion, and the coalition-forming can feel hurtful. Ideally, each partner should make a deliberate effort to avoid manipulation and game-playing that becomes circular or mimics patterns from imperfect families of origin.

When I have worked with triads and quads, I have started the therapy with each partner present. I try to get well underway with skill-building and identifying everyone's self-motivated goals and developmental growth edges before dividing up into smaller groups. Once I feel like the skill-building is sufficiently established, if it seems like it would be helpful, I might work with various dyads, individuals, or threesomes on issues they want to shift between them. Sometimes those sessions might have the fewest number of people possible, and sometimes the other partners might be present to support the deeper work and practice discussing issues without triangulation or coalition-forming. I like to use the initiator/inquirer process in family sessions by having just one initiator at a time but multiple inquirers. This helps partners in family groups learn a great strategy for teamwork that doesn't involve inducting one partner as either a critic, advisor, or mediator.

SITUATIONAL RELATIONSHIP ROLE CHALLENGES AND BENEFITS

Nesting Partners

Nesting partners are partners who share a home, regardless of whether they have a primary/secondary or nonhierarchical structure to their relationship. The challenges and benefits nesting partners experience revolve around shared space, shared responsibility, and the challenges of long-term partnership.

Many primary partners are also nesting partners, but some are not, and there are plenty of nesting partners who practice nonhierarchical polyamory. Let's imagine a pair of nesting partners, Nour and Crystal, who practice nonhierarchical polyamory. Nour and Crystal have a mortgage and household together, and pool their finances. That means that they probably will prefer to be available to one another in certain ways. Shared resources result in shared responsibilities; even though Nour and Crystal don't have a primary/secondary structure, the fact that they have commitments to their shared household will affect their priorities and choices.

For instance, what if the basement floods when Crystal is out on a date? What if the dog becomes frighteningly ill? By the way, who is going to make sure the dog gets walked tonight if they forgot to discuss it at this week's family meeting? Who will cancel their date to be home for the washing machine repair person? Is it okay to bring a date to the shared home? How about into the shared bed?

Situations like these arise more often than you might imagine, so it is important that nesting partners discuss the circumstances in which they want to be available to one another. I've seen trust erode between nesting partners based on a decision to shut off their phone on a date, either unconsciously or deliberately to get a break from tension at home. Naturally, that's when emergencies crop up. Lack of follow-through when there are substantial shared responsibilities results in broken trust, often on a spectacular scale. Keep in mind how this relates to people who are newly opening their relationship, are nesting partners, and are perhaps a little conflict avoidant. Nesting partners, whether primary/secondary or not, who prefer not to make many agreements or avoid having discussions about agreements, will certainly encounter problems when life's twists and turns happen with regard to shared responsibilities.

Nesting partners will need to discuss whether other partners can come to the shared home, sleep in a shared bed, interact with the children, or benefit from shared resources. These are going to be important conversations. These issues will probably need to be revisited periodically, as circumstances, people involved, and comfort with polyamory shift.

Non-Nesting Partners

Some of the challenges non-nesting partners face are analogous to those experienced by secondary partners, and, of course, the two categories often overlap but not always. If a crisis arises in your partner's shared home and they decide to rush away to deal with it, you may feel sidelined; as always, the more differentiated, flexible, and gracious the partners can be with one another, the less likely troubling power dynamics are to arise.

On the other hand, there are certainly advantages to not being nesting partners. It probably means fewer conflicts about household chores, shared finances, and living arrangements. If you happen to be a messy person and your partner is neat as a pin, not living together can be what makes the relationship work. Not being nesting partners likely means more time apart; people may find that having ample time apart gives them the opportunity to bring their best selves to the occasion whenever they spend time together, rather than slipping into a "room-mate" dynamic, as sometimes can happen with nesting partners.

Long-Standing Relationships

Jealousy is a common issue for polyamorous people of all stripes, but long-standing partners may be more likely to suffer from the "old news" kind of jealousy. Let's return to our earlier imaginary couple, Sam and Anne. Say that Sam has just started seeing Jill, and he's got stars in his eyes. He makes plans for exciting dates with Jill, and they stay up all night discovering new things about one another; the excitement of the new relationship makes them want to shine in one another's eyes by being their best, most generous, most interesting selves. Then, when Sam gets home to Ann, he's tired out and comfortable enough to just throw his socks on the floor and flop down on the couch, remote in hand.

Anne knows Sam loves her deeply, but she can't help but feel jealous that he hasn't put aside time for a romantic date together any time recently. Although she deeply values the stable home they've managed to build together, she also remembers what it was like when she and Sam first fell in love and wishes she could have a little of that romance and infatuation back.

There is nothing like new relationship energy to motivate people. The worst problems arise when people feel like they're entitled to new relationship energy and their partner is "getting in the way" by asking them to honor their commitments, make themselves available to handle shared responsibilities, and offer their attention and support. That kind of attitude creates all sorts of mischief. Experiencing new love while in a long-term committed relationship with someone else is a privilege. By enabling them to have that experience, their long-term partner is giving them a beautiful gift. They can keep the love flowing by honoring and appreciating their partner, and making sure all positive benefits accrue to everyone involved.

When you're working with this kind of jealousy, it helps to highlight how consideration and creativity keeps the spark alive in long-term relationships. Ask your clients how they can consciously choose to honor and feel honored by one another. Long-term polyamorous couples often work quite deliberately to keep their connection alive. When I see that, I am impressed by the gifts that can result from open relationship structures. It seems that the very stressors that could spell disaster are turned into significant strengths. How many people in long-term, stable marriages could benefit from their partner becoming highly motivated and creative about going on extra-fun dates?

New Relationships

New relationships carry a special challenge: handling new relationship energy. New relationship energy (NRE) has the power to make or break relationships. It is a force of nature, and like any force of nature, it tends to shake up things quite a bit, sometimes by creating a powerful impetus for growth, sometimes by leaving a path of destruction in its wake. Oftentimes, it's a little bit of both. NRE tends to result in a certain amount of impulsivity in even the most responsible and reliable people, and that impulsivity can easily lead to broken agreements and inconsiderate behavior. Refer to chapter 18, "Relationship Transitions: New Relationship Energy, Relationship Decisions, Shifting Between Partners, and Breakups," for an in-depth discussion of NRE, including strategies for handling its challenges well.

Aside from the excitement of NRE, there's an entire slate of challenges that come with having a relationship of relatively short duration. First of all, in a new relationship, everything feels a little insecure. That newness is invigorating partly because you are on high alert and nothing is really settled. It can be challenging to manage all of that intensity and uncertainty in any circumstances, and doing so in a polyamorous relationship adds a layer of complexity. Imagine being newly involved with someone who has a stable relationship that has lasted a decade or more and is deeply connected with their partner. Feelings of insignificance and competition can easily complicate the new love experience, as well as fears about measuring up or destabilizing something amazing.

One big pitfall of a new relationship is that the intensity and rose-colored glasses of NRE can result in a new partner fantasizing about being an *only* partner, particularly if they aren't experienced with poly-amory. This happens for lots of reasons, but I suspect the main one is that most of us grew up and formed our ideas about relationships in a culture of monogamy (and serial monogamy). A new partner may not yet have realized that falling in love with a polyamorous person doesn't have to lead to their beloved choosing between relationships.

If you are noticing desires to supplant a longer-term partner in the life of your beloved, you are likely to be disappointed. If, on the other hand, you are dating someone who is dropping hints about wanting to be your one-and-only and you have a long-term partner at home, the conventional wisdom is to run from that relationship. I don't necessarily disagree, but I think that before dropping your new lover completely, it's worth having a frank talk about what polyamory means to you and the importance of your long-term relationship in your life. Don't be wishy-washy or waffle. It is your job to make it crystal-clear to your new love that you are not looking for a monogamous relationship with anyone, no matter how attractive that person may be.

HANDLING IMPERFECTION

Every role in a polycule will benefit from increased differentiation of self and nonattachment to specific outcomes. Flexibility is key, as is tuning in to partners, showing good manners and consideration, and using good boundaries. There will always be problems. Negative feelings will arise. People will make mistakes. Partners will express themselves imperfectly. The key lies in responding with as much flexibility and grace as possible when it happens, and continuing to challenge yourself to be the partner you aspire to be.

I think differentiation is a moving target, not a static state. The skills of differentiation develop throughout time, usually in response to discomfort that spurs growth. Helping people deal with relationship challenges requires helping them respond to their own difficult emotions by striving for growth, rather than collapsing into escaping, attacking, controlling, or shutting down. That said, you can't know if growth for the client will result in them staying in the relationship or leaving it. Only the client can figure that out, so I see it as my role to help them respond to their challenges proactively, rather than falling into reactivity, and see where it leads them.

A person may be able to say what feels tolerable and easy for them today, and they may be able to say what feels uncomfortable, but most of us don't actually know what we really and truly cannot tolerate. When it comes to tolerating the imperfect behavior and choices of someone we love, it can be very complicated to balance the ongoing decision: Is it good enough for this moment, today? Do I want to leave today? I've helped a lot of people ask themselves, sometimes multiple times a day, "Do I want to leave right now?" If the answer is no, the next questions include the following:

What sounds like fun right now?

How can I best take care of myself?

What can I do to break my thought pattern and focus on something else?

What thoughts would I like to think that would lead to some positive emotions?

What activities would lead to positive feelings, and what thoughts go with them?

Is there an action I need to take to feel good about how I handled this situation? Would I take that action now, tomorrow, or some other time?

What supports could I add to my life that would make a difference in how happy I am with this situation? If I had two more close friends and another hobby, would this be closer to an ideal situation? Are those things I'm interested in having anyway, for my own reasons?

In my opinion, unless someone is ready to leave the relationship right now, "I cannot tolerate this" is not a particularly useful or helpful statement. "I am having trouble tolerating this today" is more useful, because it suggests the possibility, or even probability, of relief. My question for clients in this situation is, "Where do you want to get with this?" This is my strategy for helping clients figure out if they want a change of their experience or their circumstance. It will also help me see if the client has a goal of their own or if they are hoping for their partner to change. If the answer is, "I want to end this relationship," that is a pretty clear direction for therapy. If the answer is, "I want my partner to stop behaving like this," that is a goal that is not within their control. They will have to figure out something that is in their control, which might involve a shift in their response or distress about their partner's actions, or it might be a desire to communicate with their partner about their experience or something else. For more on how to work with the change process, see the "Creating Change Worksheet Set" in appendix E.

Relationship Transitions
New Relationship Energy, Relationship Decisions, Shifting between Partners, and Breakups

Transitions are part of any relationship. When you are in more than one relationship, there will be more transitions to handle. When your partner is in other relationships, there are also *their* relationship transitions to weather. And when you're in a marginalized group like polyamory, you may have difficulty finding supportive friends and family to lend an ear and a shoulder to cry on.

It is not uncommon for someone to want support, feedback, or help navigating the inevitable and sometimes quite complicated circumstances of shifting relationships in a polycule or family dynamics related to those shifts. This might involve handling their own new relationship energy or a partner's, figuring out how to best handle imperfect circumstances in a relationship, discerning whether to end a relationship, managing emotions concerning a partner's breakup, or managing a breakup of their own. Polyamory also comes with a unique kind of transition: the openly acknowledged transition from one partner to another or one household to another.

TRANSITIONING FROM ONE PARTNER'S SPHERE TO ANOTHER

Imagine you're in a polyamorous relationship. You have one nesting partner who you live with, and you also frequently spend long stretches of time in another partner's home. Think about the challenges that come with being all-in in more than one relationship. There are unique relational dynamics that come with each separate relationship. You may have very different roles and different agreements in each household. You might have a lot of responsibility with one partner and much less with the other. Maybe in one household you have a weekly routine that involves many tasks of daily living, while in another household or with another partner you just play. Maybe you have one relationship that is based on shared interests and you attend a lot of social events together, whereas you are more of a homebody with another partner. With yet another, you might be a parent, coparent, or fun extra adult who plays with the kids. You have pillow talk with more than one person. You catch up on the news with more than one person. You do your best to be considerate and take into account the desires and preferences of many people, both your partners and their families.

Many polyamorous people move from one household to another or one partner to another on a regular basis. Some partners spend sustained periods of time together, and some spend only brief times together. Sometimes partners see one another frequently, sometimes rarely. Some relationships are conducted primarily online or via phone, whereas others involve sharing a household. The specific challenges partners face depend on the unique agreements each relationship has and the natural form each relationship takes.

This can create a kind of dual life. It's not quite the same as the kind of dual life people experience with infidelity, because everyone who is directly involved is aware and consenting, yet there are some similarities. For instance, partners may choose to exercise restraint and privacy in public, to avoid the appearance of infidelity in front of people who don't know about the polyamorous relationship. Many polyamorous people are completely out in one household and completely closeted in all others. Some take close neighbors into their confidence, to curtail potential gossip about infidelity.

There's a particular kind of duality that arises from the balancing act that hinge partners have to perform to be considerate of their different partners in their distinctly different relationships. Sometimes this can lead to a kind of decision-making inertia on the part of the hinge. When they are with one partner, in that partner's household, everything they say and do with that partner fits with the culture of that household. It makes perfect sense in the context of that environment. Then they go to their other partner's house and experience a totally different culture, context, and set of expectations and ways of being together.

I'd like to illustrate this by means of an imaginary example. Let's say we have a hinge named Ravi, who has two partners, Lisa and Belinda, each with their own household, and Ravi shares their time about equally between the two.

In Lisa's household, the culture is very relaxed, free-flowing, even a little loosey-goosey. She's not a big planner, and she tends to go with the flow. Let's imagine Ravi is spending the night at Lisa's house and then planning to meet Belinda in the morning. Ravi and Lisa wake up at 8 a.m., and they have a little time before Ravi plans to go over to Belinda's, so Lisa decides to make a tasty breakfast of French toast. But French toast takes much longer than either of them thought, and then Ravi's socks have gone missing in the general chaos of the household, and then a neighbor knocks on the door and comes inside for a bit of coffee and a chat. What with one thing and another, Ravi ends up arriving 30 minutes late at Belinda's house.

Belinda tends to live her life in a much more structured, scheduled manner. She thinks Ravi's lateness is an indication that either Ravi or Lisa doesn't care much about her or respect her time. Lisa, on the other hand, is late all the time and would never be upset if someone was late to meet her. When Ravi is in Lisa's household, all the chaos just seems warm, funny, and full of life, but when Ravi is in Belinda's household, it makes sense that she would take Ravi's lateness as a sign of disrespect. Ravi doesn't know how to explain Lisa's world in a way that would make sense to Belinda or explain Belinda's concerns in a way that would make sense to Lisa.

Imagine that Ravi, recognizing Belinda's perspective and their own desire to partner her well, decides to promise her that they'll do their best to never be late again. At the moment Ravi tells her that, it makes perfect sense; it doesn't feel like a difficult agreement to make. Ravi wants to be on time and understands why it is important to not only Belinda, but also Ravi. But when Ravi explains this commitment to Lisa, while she may respect that it's important to them, it doesn't fit with her world or priorities through her own lens, and so it's difficult for her to keep track of it. It doesn't come naturally for her to ask herself, "Is this breakfast going to be too elaborate to finish in five minutes?" It's hard for Ravi to keep track of their commitment, too, because when he's in Lisa's household, they're immersed in Lisa's culture.

This challenge points to an opportunity for growth with the first part of differentiation, which involves identifying one's own thoughts, feelings, beliefs, and preferences, separate from anyone else's. If the hinge person is getting swept up in the different cultures of each partner and each partner's household, it can be hard for them to keep track of their own internal compass. Staying relationally connected with integrity with two or more different people, each of whom has their own priorities and beliefs, is quite a complex project. But it can look just like plain, ordinary conflict-avoidance or lack of follow-through from the outside, for instance, to a therapist, or even a partner. In this type of situation, I think it is important to acknowledge the deeper developmental project the person faces, beyond simple conflict-avoidance. The hinge is being called on to display immense congruence and integrity, as well as cultural sensitivity and a high level of personal flexibility. They also have to develop a high level of reliability with follow-through, even with different styles in different households. For many people, this requires a level of intention regarding actions and agreements that doesn't come naturally.

MANAGING NEW RELATIONSHIP ENERGY

New relationship energy (NRE) refers to the overwhelming new-love obsession that tends to define the early stages of a new relationship. Every train of thought gets rerouted to refer back to the person you're crushing on, every song reminds you of them, and every five minutes you check your phone to see if they've texted you back yet.

NRE can be a wonderful thing. The world would be a duller place without it. For one thing, it feels amazing, and missing it is one of the reasons many people want to open their relationship. Also, it helps you bond closely to your new partner, so that, once you start to notice one another's flaws, you already have a strong foundation of closeness to build on.

Sometimes, however, it's a dangerously powerful force. NRE can make you obsessed with your new partner. It drives you to think about them constantly, contact them, and try to be near them as much as you can. Oftentimes, people don't know how to control that impulse, and it can be difficult to *want* to control it because it feels great. As you can imagine, this can cause some problems in polyamorous relationships.

Imagine you're in a committed polyamorous relationship, and your partner has just started seeing a new person. They're head over heels, completely obsessed. In the ideal version of events, they have incredibly good impulse control and excellent manners. They maintain a clear vision of the kind of considerate, reliable partner they want to be in their longer-term relationships in the forefront of their mind, even in the throes of new love. They know that showing up with integrity, energy, passion, love, and consistency in all of their relationships will benefit them and all of their partners. Handled well, NRE can be an asset to both new and older relationships. For new relationships, it allows partners to connect deeply and creates a solid foundation for staying connected and working as a team with the challenges that all relationships eventually face. For longer-term partners, it brings a lot of energy, motivation, and willingness to try new things, all of which can be leveraged for the good of all, not just the new relationship.

In the less-than-ideal version, however, they might get caught up in new love, lose sight of the larger picture, and let important responsibilities fall by the wayside because they are dying to spend as much time as possible with their new crush. When that happens, NRE can lead to all kinds of damaging behavior. To be fair, to some extent, it's beyond conscious control; our very neurochemistry changes when we fall in love. Plus, our culture idealizes new love. Imagine feeling those new-love feelings after being in one relationship for 10 or 25 years. It's an extremely difficult time to exercise self-control.

But NRE is not so much fun if you're the one back at home, holding down the fort with several small children, a complicated household to run, a broken water heater, an absent partner, and a lukewarm relationship that's getting buried in an ever-growing stack of obligations and broken agreements. In that situation, it's pretty understandable when long-term partners become annoyed and begin to lose patience with the "whole polyamory thing."

Most polyamorous relationships go through a huge learning curve with the first experience of NRE. Both partners will make mistakes; hopefully, they will also make effective and deeply healing repairs. Ideally, the relationship gets much stronger and more enjoyable for everyone concerned as a result of lessons learned, and the energy and passion NRE brings, but the path to get there is usually winding and littered with obstacles.

Inconsiderate behavior during NRE does some of the most egregious damage to polyamorous relationships. If a person has any personal challenges involving selfishness, power imbalances, or impulsivity, those growth areas are immediately going to show up as liabilities when they get involved in a new relationship. If you have a client who is thinking of opening their relationship and you notice personality traits that might get highlighted during NRE, now is definitely the time to address them. A therapist can help with effective structures to contain or manage impulsivity, lack of focus, and lack of follow-through that will predictably bloom into total disaster when NRE occurs.

Exercise: How I Plan to Handle New Relationship Energy

If you have the opportunity, you can help your clients inoculate their relationship against NRE before it happens. The partner who is experiencing new love will benefit, and their partner who is holding down the fort will also. After all, they too are having a uniquely challenging experience and could probably use some support. Having clarity about intentions helps with follow-through, particularly when temptation is strong or tempers run high. Getting clear on what you have to lose, and gain, is important because in the throes of NRE, logical thought will probably be considerably impaired for everyone concerned. The prescription also calls for adding fun and excitement to their day-to-day life, as well as mini-vacations with no stress, deeper conversations during dinner once in a while, and maybe a few adventures. It won't prevent NRE, but it will help avoid a toxic, polarized dynamic when it happens. The worksheet "How I Plan to Handle New Relationship Energy" is intended to guide a process of self-reflection to clarify intentions and provide a visual record to strengthen follow-through (see appendix F).

If you need some extra support with NRE, you can also turn to your peers for help. If you know someone who has an open relationship and has handled NRE well, ask them about it. How did they work together as a team? What skills did they need to develop? How did they manage the intense emotions that go with NRE from all sides?

Therapeutic Approaches for NRE-Related Complications

Working in therapy with someone who is behaving badly during their experience of NRE (or their partner's) is quite a challenging project. Systemic dynamics are complex; both partners bring something to the dynamic, but it can be hard to see how to disrupt the ineffective patterns, particularly if there is one-sided bad behavior that would be legitimately distressing to anyone. Emotions run high. This is a situation where I think a good therapist can be invaluable. Partners probably need someone who understands both systemic dynamics and polyamory to take a leadership role and help them find a path to sanity.

Oftentimes, people make significant mistakes in their first NRE experience. The partner in the throes of new love may break agreements, come home late, text their lover at the dinner table or in bed, fail to use a condom, talk about their new love constantly, or obsess out loud about some (or every) aspect of the relationship. If the new relationship is a little fraught in some way, they may want to process their romantic challenges with their longer-term partner, which can get quite tiresome.

These behaviors range from rude, ineffective, or self-defeating to out-and-out damaging. If you are wrestling with these challenges in your own relationship, some of the following thoughts and strategies may help you avoid pitfalls or craft more effective responses in difficult situations. But if you are in a relationship with egregious acting out, please get yourself some help. This can be a lot to handle on your own.

If you are a therapist helping clients who are struggling with NRE-related challenges, this section is for you. When you see clients, or partners, acting with little or no consideration for one another, it can be pretty tempting to deliver a well-deserved smackdown. As a therapist, you'll have to ignore this temptation and work to create an effective challenge with therapeutic value. It's a tough line to walk: Somehow, you will have to figure out how to challenge ineffective and self-defeating behavior without coming from a critical or parental place. The last thing you want is for them to respond by moving into a rebellious stance. They know their behavior is bad, and they are braced for criticism. One whiff of criticism and you will be in a psychic wrestling match with a rebellious teenager.

It's much better for you to stay out of the middle. Avoid delivering lectures, and make sure that they are doing the work themselves. Do they have a part of themselves that wants to honor their commitments to their partners? That understands that it will ultimately benefit them to tend to their long-term partner, no matter how swept up they are in new love?

Even if the conversation between the parts of their dilemma takes place squarely between parts of their internal self, leaving you out of it entirely, they might very well take a critical or parental stance with themselves. Generally, that's not much more effective than you taking the critical parent stance. Remember, they are having an adolescent experience: new, obsessive, all-consuming, hormone-soaked love. Someone experiencing NRE may very well respond to everyone in their life from an adolescent part of themselves, particularly if that part hasn't gotten a chance to come out and play much in recent years. That's not a bad thing in itself; the danger is that they may get trapped in a push–pull cycle of criticism and rebellion with themselves, their other partner(s), or you. Once someone takes a rebellious, defensive stance, their "F-you" energy may fuel increasingly bad behavior. This is especially unfortunate if their *partner* behaved badly with NRE in the past; in that case, they can claim, "Well, you did it first!"

Adolescent and other child-like parts really like having fun. In my opinion, most adults don't have nearly enough fun. No wonder NRE wreaks havoc—it's a *lot* of fun! Your client may be having more fun than they have had in years. In different circumstances, the choices they're making—to prioritize fun over obligation—might actually be very adaptive. Your job is to help them restructure this entire situation into something that can succeed and supports their long-term goal of nurturing happy relationships that last a lifetime.

In this vein, you might consider focusing on increasing the ways your client can have fun and experience freedom, as well as connection. Perhaps they are just now getting in touch with some important aspects of themselves that have been shoved aside for far too long. That's good news. But it is also news about *them*, not about their glossy new partner, their stale marriage, or any other person or circumstance in their life. What are they discovering about themselves? How can they live that out, in their daily life, with or without this new person, and, ideally, while strengthening their original longer-term relationship(s)?

With polyamory, no one has to be everything to anyone. This new person can be perfect for some activities, without taking anything away from the strengths and gifts that other relationships offer. The key is remembering that the other relationships have their own strengths and shine with their own beauty, even if they don't seem quite as glossy at the moment.

It can also help to channel some of that overflowing erotic and romantic energy back home to the longer-term partner(s). Encourage your clients to cultivate gratitude and appreciation for this amazing opportunity. Their longer-term partner is giving them an amazing gift in the form of this opportunity to experience NRE. Few people are freely given the opportunity to experience the excitement of new love and the stability of long-term love at the same time. It's helpful if they can see their longer-term partner(s) as completely amazing rockstars of relational intelligence and generosity. It's also worthwhile to find a way to deeply honor and uplift anyone who is at home managing the duties of daily life, which is, after all, an honorable practice with or without NRE. Partners who feel honored and appreciated don't experience as much difficulty with jealousy or resentment during NRE.

In a way, this relationship stage is an opportunity. It can highlight the need to develop more ways to appreciate partners, as well as include more play in the "responsible" relationships. If those relationships have fallen into a pattern of just managing the dull, onerous tasks that move things forward in an otherwise unexciting or somewhat overwhelming life, they stand to benefit tremendously from the shifts partners can make now and the infusion of passion, energy, and sexual mojo that can be leveraged for the greatest good of everyone concerned.

NRE cuts both ways. Some of your clients will be struggling to manage their feelings, thoughts, and reactions to their *partner's* NRE. For the partner who is not currently in love, it can be a very trying time. Even when NRE ends up benefiting both partners, the NRE-fueled growth spurt can be annoying to a preexisting partner. Imagine wanting to try something new sexually for many years and meeting resistance from your partner, and then they fall in love with someone new and suddenly they are doing exactly the thing you have wanted for years, and possibly telling you all about it as if you had never mentioned it. This is a huge benefit, if partners can manage to keep their eye on the prize, rather than getting wrapped up in who caused what, and why, and making a lot of meaning out of the "idea" coming from somewhere else. A lower-desire partner experiencing NRE might bring home a significantly increased interest in sex, which is a classic benefit of NRE, but only if their partner can stay focused on the positive outcome and not get wrapped up in jealousy concerning how it happened. Helping partners leverage the strengths of NRE in ways that accrue to every relationship, not just the newest one, is very important.

Lessons Learned from NRE

In my experience, the first round of NRE is usually the most challenging, and it usually ends with many lessons learned. Hopefully, next time, the learning curve won't be so steep. I think the intensity of the first NRE mostly has to do with our monogamous mindset as a culture. Whether or not we are consciously aware of it, our culture gives us a very limited idea of what is possible in relationships. Figuring out how polyamory actually works is a process. It involves living your way into something that was previously theoretical and discovering that some things that our culture thinks are impossible are actually both possible and quite amazing.

Some of the things people learn during, as well as before and after, NRE include the following:

It is possible to have multiple relationships without lying, hiding, sneaking, or cheating.

It is possible to follow through on agreements reliably even when you are in love (or lust) with someone new.

It is possible to manage a lot of emotional intensity without actually coming unglued. It gets better with practice: Each time you survive your partner going out on a date with a new person, it gets easier to handle.

The lust doesn't go away because you canceled a date with your new crush; instead, absence makes the heart grow fonder.

It feels good to be a strong leader and take responsibility for your choices, agreements, and commitments, rather than passing the buck.

Rules that limit what you can do with your new love make things hotter in the long run. The less you see the new love, the longer the NRE lasts. In the same vein, the more you limit what your partner can do, the longer their NRE lasts. Similarly, the less drama there is concerning NRE, the quicker it ends.

Pushing your partner past their comfort zone makes their comfort zone smaller. Helping them feel comfortable and secure is what makes their comfort zone expand. If you want them to allow you to do something you really want but they're not so sure about it, increase their feeling of security proportionately to how challenging your request is for them before you even ask.

Your partner(s) knows what makes them feel secure. If you're not sure, ask.

If following through on your agreements with your long-term partner results in your new partner breaking up with you, that relationship probably couldn't have endured the challenges of polyamory anyway.

A new crush who talks about running away together, stirs up drama, or pushes you to choose them over your previous partner may not understand how polyamory works and may not actually fit into your life. Speak up about what works for you, and observe their responses carefully to make sure they are actually a candidate for a position in your life. If not, there are other fish in the sea.

Polyamory really is a way to experience NRE as a regular part of life, or at least occasionally. Once this sinks in, everyone behaves better because the scarcity/extreme novelty aspect goes away.

The drama and long-term consequences that come with broken agreements are not worth that one date that seemed so compelling at the time.

What goes around comes around. Polyamory is a recipe for role reversal, so treating your partner(s) with the same respect you will want when you're in their position will pay off.

Similarly, if you were an ass during NRE, you will get to hear, "Well, you did it first," shortly, in a smug tone, and it will sting.

There is no guarantee that spending more time with the new person will actually be better. Each relationship has its sweet spot in terms of time spent together, and more is not always better. This is a realization that comes from learning that you can date someone just because you like something about them, rather than as part of a monocentric long-term-mate-seeking agenda. Once you discover your new love isn't perfect, you can decide to just do the part that works best, rather than trying to make them into someone they aren't or turn the relationship into something it isn't meant to become. This is one of the biggest lessons of polyamory. It not only helps the person who is doing the dating make better choices about priorities, but also relieves their longer-term partner(s) of some anxiety associated with feeling threatened by new relationships. New relationships don't have to replace older ones; they can coexist. Most new relationships aren't any kind of competition for a stable, long-term, well-functioning nesting partnership. There is really no need to freak out about every crush.

Most relationships don't stand the test of time, and longer-standing relationships often have a deeper, richer flavor than shorter ones. Making fatal mistakes that destroy your long-standing relationships during NRE is not a bet that is likely to pay off, because, honestly, the new relationship isn't that likely to stand the test of time.

NRE doesn't last forever. If your clients are debriefing NRE from the past, help them assess the following: What did each of them learn about themselves? What vulnerabilities were revealed, either personally or in their relationship? What can they learn from NRE about how to strengthen their relationship?

When multiple relationships can coexist, any need for comparison or competition between partners or relationships is made obsolete. While not everyone who is in an open relationship is able to wrap their minds and hearts around that concept, it is worth heading in that direction intentionally. Every relationship is truly unique. Focusing on the unique strengths of longer-standing relationships can help manage common fears about a partner's new partner replacing you. You are irreplaceable, and so is your relationship.

RELATIONSHIP DECISIONS

Relationships aren't static. Once in a while, people have to make a hard decision about whether to stay, go, or make some kind of major adjustment to the relationship. More relationships means more of these decisions. Furthermore, in a polyamorous relationship, it might not be just one person's decision. People who are in multiple relationships are inherently opening themselves to the influence of multiple intimate partners. Plus, depending on the decision-making structure of the relationships, multiple people might get a vote in any major change. Consider the complexities of a breakup in a triad, or quad, for instance.

Ultimately, helping a client make decisions about polyamorous relationships is not much different than helping anyone with any relationship decision, with an added twist of the importance of differentiation sufficient to identify their own preferences separate from anyone else's, even with multiple stakeholders, and speak up about them. You may be called on to deal with specific challenges that are related to roles within polycules, and you'll certainly have to help your clients work through uncomfortable emotions and parse out difficult decisions with many variables; but aside from that, you will be using mostly the same strategies and techniques you use with any client who is struggling to resolve an internal conflict about a relationship. (For information about the issues related to specific roles within a polycule, refer to chapter 17, "Role-Related Challenges and Benefits: Primaries, Secondaries, Hinges, Etc." For more on handling jealousy, refer to chapter 13, "Understanding and Addressing Jealousy.")

Resolving Relationship Dilemmas with Two Chairs

Ultimately, the decision to leave a relationship rests with an individual, and usually the dilemma is relatively simple, even if the decision feels fraught. I almost always use chair work to explore this particular impasse in therapy, so I'm going to revisit this powerful strategy for helping one person explore a dilemma within themselves (see the "Resolving a Dilemma Using Two Chairs" worksheet in appendix E, originally presented in chapter 15). This can be used in individual therapy or relationship therapy; in the latter case, although the work is with one person, the others might be involved as witnesses or supports.

A dilemma is a situation in which you have choices or options and you don't yet know which direction to go. A part of you wants one thing, and another part wants something else. Often when we have a dilemma, we get gridlocked and tangled in our thinking, as the various perspectives wrestle for center stage. We experience an internal argument that doesn't advance effectively toward resolution because we switch viewpoints, lack clarity, often become confused, and don't have a structure that can facilitate the discussion.

Oftentimes people use therapy to help them make a decision, but the pitfall for the therapist is arguing one point or the other, or switching between them, in an effort to help the client think more clearly. This generally creates something that feels like resistance and frustration to both therapist and client, as it encourages projection of one viewpoint, or alternately both viewpoints, onto the therapist. I find it much more expedient (and more fun) to make it explicit that both viewpoints exist in the client, and my job is to facilitate the discussion between their viewpoints, not take a voice myself. This exercise is fun, creative, and extremely effective, and keeps the therapist out of the middle. What's not to love?

Resolving a dilemma using two chairs is a strategy with its roots in Gestalt therapy. Many different therapy models use chair work in various ways, and many more use variations on parts that are closely related. But the simplest way I know of using two chairs is to resolve a simple, two-part dilemma, such as is common when considering ending a relationship. In this case, the two parts might be "one part of me wants to stay in this relationship" and "another part of me wants to leave this relationship." Chair work separates these parts with their opposing perspectives and encourages each part to go to a deeper level, stay on topic, and identify deeper desires, feelings, and blocks.

It also facilitates a discussion between parts that reveals one part's aspirations or hopes for a brighter future, and the fears and other protective mechanisms (usually developed in early childhood) that another part holds, and which block risk-taking. Together the parts can work out an experiment (or a series of experiments) that will allow the adult ego state to both decide to take a risk, and also safeguard from harm in ways that allow stretching toward desired outcomes.

This is hard to imagine if you have never done it or seen it, but trust me here. This strategy is fun, results in a lot of depth, and is also a certain measure of magic. It is very effective in a therapy session and also effective as a self-help tool. If it feels forced or odd when you do it on your own or it doesn't seem to work, have a therapist do it with you the first few times. Once you see how it works, you will be able to use it any time you want help understanding your own multiple perspectives about a challenge or decision you face.

This strategy, in that it enables a deeper exploration of the internal landscape, results in either a congruent decision or a next action step or experiment to run. As a therapist, it keeps me out of the middle while helping clients move very quickly through their blocks. For step-by-step guidance in using two chairs to resolve a dilemma, see the worksheet by that name in appendix E. For an alternative strategy using the technique, see chapter 15, "Working with Mono-Polyams and Reluctant Polyams."

POLYAMORY AND BREAKUPS

The more relationships you have, the more potential for breakups. And in polyamorous relationships, breakups can be very complicated. Imagine being in a triad, where you and two other people are involved with one another, live together, and make decisions together. Perhaps you are raising children together and sharing finances and a mortgage. But a lot of tension starts to develop between you and one of the other partners in the triad. You decide you need to end the relationship, but you don't want to end both relationships just because you want to leave one of the partners. Instead, you want to transition your triad into a V. Unfortunately, that is a decision (and a transition) involving two other stakeholders, who may or may not agree about the breakup, and may or may not agree about transitioning to a V.

Imagine being in a quad, in a similar situation. You want to leave one partner but not all three. Or you want to leave two but not three. Imagine the complications if the one you want to stay with is not the one you were with originally, before the quad formed (if your quad formed from two couples joining).

Even if the person breaking up is not in a family structure like a triad or a quad, breakups can involve a lot of people. On one end of the spectrum, the person breaking up might be part of an active polyamory community. In that case, they will probably have to navigate the complications that come with being in a small, deeply entangled community; many of the people they might turn to for support could also be involved with their partners, or their partners' partners, or they could be one another's exes, or involved with partners' exes, and so forth. Sometimes polyamorous friends, rather than being reliable supports through a breakup, can be less than helpful—for instance, they might tell your client "I told you so" if they foretold a bad outcome due to some less-than-perfect aspect of the relationship. Or they might have you and/or your relationship(s) up on a pedestal and discourage you from breaking up because of their own discomfort or disillusionment. It is stressful to be in a secretly crumbling relationship that represents successful long-term polyamory to an entire community of people hungry for a role model.

On the other end of the spectrum, if your client isn't part of the community and isn't out to their friends and family, they might not have any support whatsoever for their polyamorous relationship challenges. Worse yet, some family or friends may know about the relationship but discount your client's struggles or say "I told you so" because they don't approve of nonmonogamy.

It is incredibly painful to endure a difficult breakup and not feel able to talk about it with your closest people. It's just as bad to try and reach out for help, only to be reminded, "I told you this could never work; what the heck were you thinking?" or "Are you kidding? Your relationship is perfect!"

There is one potential upside to polyamory when it comes to breakups: It can mean that the grieving person has access to additional emotional support, either from the larger community or other lovers. In some cases, mourning the loss of one partner in the presence of another lover can greatly ease the pain of the breakup, as long as that person has the patience for it, and assuming the relationships weren't tense and fraught. Still, this dynamic has a flip side as well: Sometimes it can be hard for people to grasp that having other lovers doesn't mean that breakups don't hurt.

Another aspect of a breakup in polyamory has to do with relationships between metamours. While deciding what relationship to have with an ex and how to get from here to there, and what relationship to have with an exe's extended family if those relationships were close, a polyamorous person is likely also figuring out what relationship to have with a metamour. The metamour may have become a friend, or there may be a lot of tension between metamours, or anywhere in between, but they are probably still involved with the ex. You can start to see that with the infinite shapes of polyamorous relationships; breakups are complex and the challenges related to them are exponentially more complex than with most monogamous breakups.

REDEFINING THE "END OF THE RELATIONSHIP"

Some polyamorous people, particularly those who consider themselves relationship anarchists, argue against the cultural tendency to prioritize romantic and sexual relationships over other kinds of relationship, like friendship. For those people, a breakup may not be seen as the end of a relationship, but rather a shift to a different stage—different but not necessarily less important or meaningful. This doesn't mean the transition will be painless, but it is a way of making meaning out of a breakup that can help prevent it from feeling like a "failed relationship." It can also help navigate the continued entanglements of community relationships that often come with polyam breakups. This reframe can also be effective with LGBTQIA+ people, some of whom don't have an expectation of distance from exes but instead will want to find the most painless path through a transition to friendship. It is worth asking your client what a breakup means to them and what their goals might be rather than assuming everyone wants maximum distance and no contact with their exes.

It is also worth mentioning that with polyamory, you don't have to break up with someone to be with someone else, and your partner doesn't have to be the be-all and end-all of perfect partners; if you don't want to be with them 24/7, you don't have to be, and you could simply downshift the intensity to fit what seems like the best fit. Sometimes you will see a polyamorous relationship shift from being hot and heavy to something more like friends with benefits, or just friends, as a result of any number of circumstances; it may feel like a breakup but not look much like a breakup from the outside.

CHAPTER 19

Polyamorous Families with Children and Coming-Out Issues

Sometimes polyamorous people in long-standing relationships decide to have kids, and sometimes people who are already parents decide to explore polyamory. There are many different ways that a polyamorous family can be structured, from a triad or quad that raises children together as a group to a couple of parents with a primary/secondary structure, whose kids may not even be aware of their parents' polyamorous relationships. Parenting issues related to polyamory include when and how to come out to kids, sharing responsibility for children, and how to help children prepare for the difficult conversations they might find themselves having if they discuss their parents' relationship style with others who may be quite unsettled by the news.

Reasonably enough, therapists worry about the children: Does it harm children to be raised in polyamorous households? What challenges do the children face? How about the parents? In this chapter, I discuss what the research tells us about polyam families. I also share my observations, gathered from years of interacting with polyam families inside and outside of the therapy room, and offer some stories from real people in diverse family situations.

This chapter provides a broad overview. If you want more detail about how polyam families with children function, I highly recommend Elisabeth Sheff's book *The Polyamorists Next Door*, as well as her more recent research. Much of the information in this chapter is drawn from Sheff's work.

WHAT THE RESEARCH SHOWS

Scheff interviewed children raised in polyamorous families. She noticed that their experiences could be broadly categorized by age groups: 0 to 8, 9 to 12, and 13 to 17. Each of these groups has slightly different needs, different levels of perception of what's going on in their family structures, and different levels of awareness about sexuality.

Sheff found that the children younger than eight simply take their parents' relationships at face value. If they feel loved and safe, and the family feels stable, then it's simply normal. This is congruent with what I have observed as well.

However, Sheff found that, as children get older, things can get a bit more complicated. They start to become more aware of their peer groups and recognize the differences between their family and their peers' families. If their peers notice these differences, they may be put on the spot and have to answer uncomfortable questions or be exposed to judgment.

Nonetheless, this is a problem that parents can prepare their children for. When you're in a marginalized population, it makes sense to help prepare your kids for the challenges that come with being different. Parents who are in same-sex relationships, for instance, learn how to do this, as do people of color. At some point, a polyamorous parent might want to have a conversation with their child: "This is not how everybody rolls, and some people are going to have a problem with it. Let's talk about how you feel about it, what challenges you might face, and how you want to handle it." As therapists, we can play an important role in this process by helping parents plan for this conversation and develop strategies they can use to help their children understand their unique family structure, manage questions friends might have, and understand marginalization.

PERSONAL ACCOUNTS FROM PARENTS AND CHILDREN

This is a story of one parent's perspective on raising kids within a polyamorous family; it sheds some light on the complex negotiations parents may have to make as they decide how much information to share with their children:

My partner and I have two children, ages 13 and 10. One of my girl-friends has an 8-year-old. One of my wife's boyfriends has two kids, ages 10 and 8, and her other boyfriend has one kid who is 10. What I find fascinating is how varied each respective parent is with their kids regarding polyamory—and they are all valid. My belief is that the most important aspect of being polyamorous and a parent is being intentional about the decision of how much to tell your kids and revisiting that deci-sion occasionally to see if it is still the best approach as the kids grow older and situations change. My partner and I are sort of in between regarding being out to our kids. We have not explicitly told them that we are polyamorous and date other people, but we also do not hide the fact that one or the other is going out with "so and so." Our reason for not telling them yet is that we rely on our grandparents for childcare (who we are not out to). They are religiously conservative, and we do not want to put our kids in an awkward position of accidentally being the ones to break the news to them. But as the kids are getting older, we are more comfortable with the idea of being out to them and have been working on sitting down with them to discuss it. My feeling is that they will not be surprised and likely won't think it's a big deal.

The following personal reflection comes from someone who discov-ered by mistake that her mother was polyamorous. For context, at the time of this story the narrator was familiar with the concept of poly-amory but did not yet know her mother was polyamorous. By handling the revelation with warmth and grace, her parents turned a potentially awkward or distressing revelation into an affirming experience.

When reflecting on finding out that my mom was polyamorous, I had to stop and think for a while because it wasn't something that stuck out in my brain. I think I was in middle school, but I don't remember it as a traumatic or negative event, but instead as my parents trusting me. I vaguely remember crying, but not because I was sad, just because I tend to cry often. While they hadn't planned to tell me when I learned of it (it was slipped by a relative at the breakfast table on Christmas morning), I remember it as a moment in which my parents trusted me and took the time to have a conversation with me about something that was important to them. Additionally, the person my mom was in a relationship with had, for years and years, shown me that he supported and cared about me. I knew he was someone I could trust and loved me long before I learned about their polyamory.

For comparison, here's the mother's side of the story.

> We had been talking for several years about when to tell our daughter that the friend of the family who came over frequently and sometimes spent the night was actually my other partner. We were worried about how she would handle finding out that this lifelong family friend actually had a larger relationship with me, and so we had put it off. Then it came up by accident, of all places at the Christmas breakfast table, via an extended family member. I was sitting next to my daughter and reached over and took her hand, and said something like, "I think you might have just learned something about me that you didn't know before." She told me she was okay, and we decided to talk about it after breakfast, when we could get some privacy and really talk.
>
> It was actually kind of humorous, in an awful kind of way. She didn't seem particularly traumatized by it, maybe because our family does talk about things pretty regularly at the dining table or maybe because she knew and loved some other polyamorous people. My main concern was how she would feel supported, or not supported, if and when she shared it with other people close to her who didn't know. I told her I would never ask her to keep a secret for me and she could tell anyone she wanted to but that not many people knew and so she might have to handle some questions if she did. She handled the conversation and the aftermath amazingly well, and there has been no negative fallout as far as I can tell, thank goodness.

In late middle school and high school, a new factor comes into play: As children age to the point where they might start dating or thinking about dating, they may start to wonder what form of relationship they would want to engage in. How do they see themselves relationally? Compared to when I was young, there are a lot more options kids can openly consider. Do they see themselves as polyamorous or monogamous? Gay, straight, bi, pan, asexual, or something else? Are they cisgender, transgender, or nonbinary?

I've heard this from a number of teenage kids raised in polyamorous families: "No way, I could never be polyamorous, because I'd be way too jealous." From a developmental perspective, that makes perfect sense to me. It will be interesting to see what happens for these kids as they get older, because they know they have options and that polyamory can work. For most people who are in polyamorous relationships today, neither of those things was true when they were growing up. For this reason, I would guess that throughout time, some of the kids who are currently growing up in successful polyamorous households are going to be successfully polyamorous, simply because they know that it's possible, and also because they've got advisors in their parent group.

Here are some thoughts from a young person who was raised in a polyamorous household:

> I haven't had a relationship yet, so I don't feel qualified to say if I would want an open relationship; I don't think so, but I don't know. I think, however, if a partner came to me at some point and said let's open the relationship, I might take it a little personally for a few days, but I'm pretty sure I'd eventually come back with okay let's talk about it. I'm definitely accepting of the idea that this (polyamory/open relationship) can work.

By the way, I've certainly never heard of any teenager raised in a polyamorous family feeling in any way pressured to be in an open relationship. The examples I've seen personally have featured careful, concerned, open-minded, and supportive parents who want their children to feel free to express themselves in ways that feel congruent to them.

The following are some thoughts from a young man who was raised in a polyamorous household, reflecting on what contributed to his overall positive experience of his father's polyamory.

> The amount of influence polyamory has had on me is hard to quantify. When I was really young, I didn't know the word for it, it was just like having an aunt, someone who was closely involved in my life. Overall, it has probably been a positive thing, particularly when someone Dad is dating has their own relationship with me, like reading together or something like that. At one point, he and I had a conversation where he said if you feel like one of my girlfriends isn't valuing or respecting you, tell me, because they are not as important to me as you. It was clear to me that I had some say in how things were going to go. That was a good moment for me and a pivotal moment for how I felt about the concept of polyamory; it was good to know that I was able to voice any displeasure I might have

at something that was happening. There were a couple times when I was unhappy and made it clear to him, and he made changes that helped.

This personal account points to some protective factors that I think are important to take into consideration. The father in this account ensured that his child felt that he had a voice in his household and situation, which translated into him feeling chosen, important, and protected.

Essentially, this account describes a secure attachment in a household with polyamory. Some things might not be ideal, but this young person doesn't feel alone, nor does he believe himself to be a victim or without recourse if he isn't happy. He expects his father to take his preferences and needs into account, both because his father said he would and because he followed through on that promise.

POTENTIAL NEGATIVE INFLUENCES ON CHILDREN

I worry about children who are raised in chaotic emotional environments. It is always deeply concerning if children are exposed to fighting, abuse, or excessive tension between their parents, or if they don't feel protected, safe, or chosen. These problems can emerge in any kind of relationship, monogamous, polyamorous, or otherwise.

Of course, polyamory is one issue that parents might fight about. I have seen some pretty contentious disagreements about polyamory, and I would be gravely concerned if I believed that any client of mine was exposing their child to such arguments; however, when that happens, I don't think polyamory is actually the problem. Rather, the issue is about parenting skills, emotional boundaries, safety, privacy, and regulation.

PROS AND CONS OF POLYAMOROUS FAMILIES

This is one huge potential upside of a polyamorous family: The more parents you have, the more resources may be at your disposal. If you have a blended family or a polyamorous family structure with kids there may be more financial resources to draw on and more people to lean on. We know that raising kids takes a village. Having a polyamorous family can be a way of creating that village. Every family has times of crisis: financial struggles, illness, loss, and so on. Being part of a larger family as a result of being in a polycule can make all the difference in getting through difficult times. I know of many situations in which having a larger family unit, whether in the form of a conventional blended family or a polyamorous family configuration, has provided some stability and security in times of stress or crisis.

But there are also some serious downsides, mostly due to marginalization. Many polyamorous people are in the closet. That can be a strange and jarring experience for kids if either they are enlisted to keep the secret or aren't told and only discover this aspect of their parents' identity and relationships later on. If children are unprepared for complicated conversations about polyamory with biased friends, teachers, or other community members, and find themselves in those conversations, it might be difficult to unpack the layers of difficulty they experience, particularly if they don't have someone safe and polyamory-knowledgeable to postprocess with. Societal prejudice can also do serious damage: People can lose jobs, friends, and family members if they come out (or are found out) as polyamorous. That's a painful thing to go through and would certainly have a profound effect on children involved in the process.

THE POLYAMORY CLOSET AND COMING-OUT ISSUES

I have worked with many clients who were grappling in one way or another with coming out. If you work with polyamorous clients, you will, too. It is not easy to withhold important aspects of your life and identity from family members, friends, colleagues, neighbors, and children. Much thought goes into these decisions, often for quite some time. Coming out as polyamorous can be risky. Sometimes it goes fine, and sometimes people suffer meaningful losses. I think the most important thing as a therapist is to validate that the client may suffer negative consequences of coming out. It's not helpful to suggest this doesn't happen or minimize the risk; however, there are also some significant downsides to *not* coming out that are worthy of consideration.

It is hard to keep secrets. There is a certain kind of grief that comes from not being able to share your authentic self with people you love. Neighbors, friends, and acquaintances may suspect infidelity if they see you or your client kissing a lover or otherwise being closer than friends generally are. Deep, longing looks at the table at a restaurant can be intercepted by curious onlookers and misconstrued. Then rumors spread, particularly in tight-knit communities or if the polyamorous person is well known.

It is hard to know where to turn for help during major transitions like new relationships and breakups if your closest support people don't know that you are in an open relationship. This adds a layer of complexity to every aspect of relationship transitions.

Secrecy and shame go together. It can be pretty icky to feel like you're sneaking around, particularly if you value transparency and openness. It's also very toxic to fear that people might abhor you, your partner, or your relationship choices if they knew the truth.

For people who are in family relationships (for instance, triads or quads), planning family visits can become weirdly convoluted. Do you bring your "friend" along? Do you leave your "friend" home? If you will be sleeping in separate rooms, does everyone pack separate toothpaste or pass it back and forth in the hallway? This is particularly difficult in situations that started with one or more preexisting dyads, like married couples. The potential for the nonmarital partner(s) to feel left out or less important is high.

People who otherwise haven't experienced marginalization can find the experience to be quite jarring. Sometimes I've worked with a white, heterosexual, cisgender person who has been in a monogamous married dyad for some time and doesn't have much experience with overt marginalization. Coming to terms with disclosing something many people find totally unacceptable can be a big learning curve and extremely unsettling. Some layers of privilege have to fall away to really embrace their own relationship choices and stand up for those choices to others who may not understand.

COMING-OUT STRATEGIES

I'd like to share some strategies that can be helpful in the process of coming out.

If there is a preexisting dyad, have both partners present for the coming-out conversation. This helps dismiss any fears that one partner may be unwilling or unaware.

Take care in selecting who to come out to. It's completely fine to come out to one or a few people first, before deciding whether to come out to everyone. You can choose by considering who in your family or friend circle tends to be open-minded in other areas, but it's equally important to consider who is good with confidentiality. The gossip mill is not kind to anyone, and this is the kind of secret that can cause a lot of harm if it gets out.

Some people test the waters by coming out in smaller ways. You can try disclosing other somewhat challenging information as a kind of test to evaluate how the person will respond. Observe whether those you want to come out to are able to get curious, ask good questions, be supportive, and keep confidentiality. On the other hand, if they are judgmental, leap to conclusions, and gossip to other friends you have learned something important about their character.

Resolving a Coming-Out Dilemma with Two Chairs

Coming-out decisions are a type of dilemma that might benefit from some two-chair work. Perhaps a part of your client wants to come out to their mother about their polyamorous relationship and another part definitely does not think that is a good idea. On the surface, there is no way to tell which part is aspiring for adaptive change and which part is protecting from an outdated position, given that coming out may or may not actually yield a positive relational outcome. Taking the conversation deeper using two chairs will certainly help surface the nuances of the decision, including blocks. For more on this, see chapter 18, "Relationship Transitions: New Relationship Energy, Relationship Decisions, Shifting Between Partners, and Breakups," specifically the section on relationship decisions, and chapter 15, "Working with Mono-Polyams and Reluctant Polyams," specifically the section on resolving an impasse. Also refer to the "Resolving a Dilemma Using Two Chairs" worksheet in appendix E.

Part IV

PROFESSIONAL CONSIDERATIONS

CHAPTER 20

Ethical Considerations

Polyamorous communities tend to be small and tight-knit. Oftentimes polyamory communities become a complex web of concurrent relationships, exes, and metamours. This is because, while some polyamorous people have just one or two relationships that last many years, others either have more concurrent relationships or shorter-term ones. Some people will continue to date after a breakup, and others will not. While polyamorous relationships are quite diverse, and polyamory certainly is not synonymous with promiscuity, it is still true that polyamorous people, in general, tend to have multiple relationships; therefore, the more polyamorous clients you have from the same region, the higher the chances that some of them will be linked somehow.

Another complication is the fact that, in marginalized populations, most people find culturally sensitive therapists via word of mouth. That means there is a fairly high likelihood that the new client you have a consult call with today is a lover, ex, or best friend of one or some of your current or past clients. This means that, if you're working with polyamorous clients, you're going to need to give some thought to how you will handle dual relationships.

If you are polyamorous yourself, you'll also have to give some thought to how many degrees of separation you need to have from your clients to practice ethically. If that is the case for you, I highly recommend you get someone who has a lot of experience with both polyamory and ethics to consult for you privately as you work through the complexities of your specific situation. Similarly, if another therapist who is associated with your practice is polyamorous, it will probably be helpful to discuss dual relationships with them, so both your colleague and your clients are comfortable. Neither your colleague nor your clients will want to bump into exes or current partners in your waiting room.

DUAL RELATIONSHIP STRATEGIES

I encountered the issue of dual relationships quite early in my practice, because my first polyamorous client told her friends about me. Shortly after that I got a number of calls from her friends. The following is a list of some of the ethical questions I considered:

How close is too close a friend to my current client?
How close might any of the potential new clients be to current clients?
How close might they be to past clients who could want to return to therapy at some point?
How close might they be with one another?

You will have to make your own determination of how close is too close using the code of ethics associated with your particular license. If you are not sure, I recommend hiring a consultant who has a lot of experience in this area.

Once you decide how close is too close, the rest of the aforementioned issues center on how to assess for the information without breaking confidentiality, how to turn the client away without breaking confidentiality, and to whom to refer.

Assessing for Dual Relationships

My strategy for avoiding dual relationship tangles is to ask some specific questions in the initial consultation call that are likely to lead to the potential client disclosing the information I need.

I always ask how they heard about me, which at a minimum helps me schedule them so they won't bump into their acquaintance in my waiting room, and sometimes leads to me deciding the relationship is too close for my ethical comfort based on information they disclose without prompting, or information I have about them from a current or past client.

I usually ask them to identify their partners by first name at least. If I'm still not sure, and think they may be closely involved with current clients, I ask for last names.

I always ask them to tell me briefly about their relationship concerns, which generally leads to specific disclosures about sticky tangential connections. This is an example of a situation where I will ask for names if they haven't offered them. I really want to know if the potential client happens to be the metamour my current client is in a contentious relationship with.

I might ask about their living situation; I consider a roommate relationship to be too close for comfort.

The last thing I want is to spend several months in therapy with a client only to discover that they are currently involved with (or just broke up with) a long-standing client. If that happens, you'll have to make a referral, but it's a lot easier to have that conversation before you meet, in part because you will need some way to accomplish the referral without disclosing that you are the other client's therapist. Since you can't identify your clients to anyone, in any circumstances, your potential clients will have to identify themselves to you with sufficient detail and specificity to prevent this unfortunate outcome. If you see a potential conflict of interest, you can say something like, "For reasons I can't elaborate on, I won't be able to be your therapist. Here are the names of several other polyamory-friendly therapists you can call."

Making a Referral

Once you have made a name for yourself as a polyamory-competent therapist, you are certainly going to need to make some referrals to avoid dual relationships. In an ideal world, there would be many polyamory-competent therapists in your region, so you could refer your client to another therapist without hesitation if you felt even a tiny bit of concern. Depending on where you are located, that may indeed be the case. But all too often, there aren't nearly enough polyamory-competent therapists to go around, particularly if you live in a small town or socially conservative region. Oftentimes I let potential clients know I would be happy to consult for whichever other therapist they choose to see, which frees them up to work confidently with someone who has little or no experience with polyamory but wants to learn.

As a therapist, supervisor, and human being, I always err on the side of both caution and privacy, and I strongly recommend you do the same. It is a trap to think you are the only person who can see any given client. As a therapist who works with marginalized populations in a small community, I've certainly felt the pressure to bend the rules or go against my own best judgment, particularly if a client really wanted to work with me or was having trouble finding a therapist who was a good fit. Tempting as it is to bend ethical rules, it is still a trap, and I would hate for it to cause problems for you, your clients, or your community. Word of mouth in tight-knit communities cuts both ways. Just as word of your ethically unimpeachable behavior will spread, so will word of any uncomfortable situation your client experiences or, heaven forbid, unethical behavior on your part. In fact, that is a big reason why I'm writing this book. Now you can hand copies of it to your five favorite local therapists. Once they've read it, you can refer potential grey-area dual-relationship clients to them.

SCOPE OF PRACTICE: IS THIS FOR ME?

Now that you're coming to the end of this book, you are ready to give some serious thought to whether you want to work with polyamorous clients. If you are certain of the answer, whether yay or nay, that's great. Read no further. I mean that sincerely. If you're clear that you want to get started working with polyamorous clients, welcome to a growing community of polyamory-competent therapists. Move on to the marketing chapter.

If, after reading this book, you're certain that you *don't* want to work with this population or if you believe that polyamory can't or shouldn't work, please do yourself and your clients a favor and just say no to working with polyamorous clients. You should work with the clientele that is a fabulous fit for you, with your unique skills and gifts.

But if you are still unsure and are left wondering about your next steps in discernment, the following are my suggestions for some ways to work with that dilemma:

Do a cost–benefit analysis. List the pros, cons, concerns, and benefits. See what comes up as a result of that inquiry.

Try out the exercise "Resolving a Dilemma Using Two Chairs" (see appendix E). You can frame your dilemma in these terms: "Part of me is interested in working with polyamorous clients, and part of me is not so sure" or any other way that accurately reflects the dilemma you face.

Discuss your dilemma with a consultant, therapist, or supervisor.

Ask yourself under what kinds of circumstances you feel uncomfortable, or think you will feel uncomfortable. Make a list. Are there any common themes? Then consider how you might work with your discomfort. Do you have a knowledge gap? An experience gap? What steps might you take to help you resolve any deficit and get clear on how to move forward?

Read on to the next section, where I offer my responses to some questions from other therapists who have grappled with the same questions.

QUESTIONS AND ANSWERS FROM THERAPISTS

Q: I worry working with polyamory is out of my scope. How can I know if I'm qualified to work with polyamorous clients?

A: This is such an important question. I'd like to reframe a bit. You've asked whether you're qualified to work with polyam clients. I think the more relevant question to ask, however, is this: Do you want to? As therapists, we are constantly refining the shape of our practice. Ideally, our refinements move us continually closer to the kinds of therapists we aspire to be. We are constantly learning. If you don't want to work with polyamorous clients, you don't need to expand your scope of practice in that direction; instead, you can expand in areas that really bring you joy. But if you do want to work with polyamorous clients, I don't see any reason why you wouldn't expand your scope to do so. You've already taken a terrific first step: If you read this book, you'll already know *much* more about working with polyamory than I did when I started seeing polyamorous clients. I say if you *want* to do it, go for it. And if you don't want to, by all means give yourself permission *not* to.

Q: If I identify myself as a polyamory-friendly therapist, will I alienate my more conservative clients?

A: I grappled with this question for a long time. I think there are ways you can identify yourself to the polyamory community without really registering on the radar of people who will be upset by the idea of polyamory. See more about this in chapter 21, "Marketing Yourself as a Polyamory-Friendly Therapist." I certainly haven't destroyed my entire practice as a sex therapist by having it become known that I specialize in polyamory, and I do have some fairly conservative clients. Some of them come to me to discuss how to open their relationship, so I want to acknowledge that social or political conservativism and interest in open relationships are not mutually exclusive. Your own personal decision about identifying yourself as a polyamory-friendly therapist might in part depend on where you are in your practice and what your professional goals are. At this point in my practice, I turn people away, so I'm not worried that some clients may never call me to begin with. Of course, that wasn't always the case. My sense is that I've gotten far more clients as a direct result of word of mouth from one polyam person to another than I've lost through making it known in various ways that I work with polyamorous clients.

Q: I'm worried that if I see polyamorous clients, people will assume I'm polyamorous.

A: I think there are two reasons you might be concerned about this, and by the way, I think it is a valid concern. Maybe you're not polyamorous and you're uncomfortable being lumped in with a marginalized and misunderstood group, or maybe you are polyamorous and you're concerned about being outed. Either way, it's a valid question. This is my answer: there are far more polyamorous clients who need and want therapy than there are polyamorous therapists to see them. This is true for every marginalized population and probably always will be. Give your hecklers a lesson in the demographics of marginalization. Explain why it is important to you to serve every population and leave it at that. If you find this doesn't come naturally, prepare it ahead of time and rehearse it so you are not caught off guard. Your personal life is no one's concern but your own, and there is no need to feel cornered into giving a personal answer. While you're thinking about this, if you're not polyamorous and your impulse is to just tell people you're monogamous so they don't have to wonder, notice how it feels to worry about how others perceive your relationship style.

Q: Some of this material is quite a reach for me, and I'm worried I will offend someone by my ignorance.

A: My colleagues and friends, Atala Mitchell and Madeline Barger, did a lovely piece of research on what polyamorous clients are looking for in a therapist. They found that full knowledge of every aspect of polyamory was not on the list of things polyam clients are seeking. Mostly, they just want a therapist who is open to learning and willing to get some of their information from sources other than their clients. If you say something that offends a client, thank them for telling you about their feelings, apologize, and move on. If a deeper repair is needed, that's okay, you can do it. If you lose a client after a solid attempt at repair, that wasn't the client for you.

Q: I feel pretty comfortable with polyamory, but I'm not all that comfortable with kink/BDSM and worried that will become a problem due to the overlap in populations.

A: That's a valid concern. I will say, however, that the vast majority of my kinky clients have never had any issues related to kink come up in the course of their therapy. I think you should be transparent up front so clients who are grappling with issues about kink have the opportunity to go find a therapist who is more comfortable with the subject. The majority of them will probably decide to stay with you. They now know that kink isn't your area of expertise and won't be blindsided by the need to find another therapist to help if something kink-related does come up. Incidentally, if that happens, you can probably find a kink-aware therapist to either consult for you or collaborate so you and your client don't de facto have to end the therapy work you have been doing together.

Q: There are so many details to remember, and the lingo is so unique. I'm worried I'll get it wrong and seem clueless.

A: I think you can let this one go. The language is evolving fast, and it's so regionally unique that I almost always ask my clients for clarification anyway. As long as you have the basic concepts down, don't sweat the details. Your clarifying questions will reflect that you understand the concepts involved, which is probably more important to most clients than having a shared vocabulary.

Q: I'm worried these relationships are too messy and I won't be able to keep track of everyone's partners.

A: I hear your concern. Weirdly, this has never come up as a problem in my experience. Even people who have many partners are mostly in therapy by themselves or with just one. If someone's situation is quite convoluted, draw a map with them to clarify. I've had a few clients draw me a relationship map; one that includes friends, coworkers, roommates, etc., can be very helpful. I can't imagine that they will think it is odd that you need help sorting it out.

Q: I don't really understand polyamory from within myself and have never experienced it, so how can I relate?

A: I realize it might seem confusing. After all, you're holding an entire book about the complexity of polyamorous relationships in your hands right now. But when it comes right down to it, we're talking about a real person sitting in your office discussing their genuine concerns. I think that the first and most important thing is to honestly identify if you want to work with this population and can truly believe it is workable for many people. With those things in place, I suspect that as soon as you start to connect with a unique individual and feel like you know and understand some aspects of them, including their struggles and strengths, it will become somewhat less prominent that they are in a polyamorous relationship. Let your empathy and humanity take over. You've got this.

CHAPTER 21

Marketing Yourself as a Polyamory-Friendly Therapist

Once you decide you want to work with polyamorous clients and get the training and information necessary for cultural competence (this book is an excellent starting point), you're ready to get started. That raises an entirely new issue: How do you find your audience? How do you let polyamorous people know that you're a polyamory-friendly therapist? And how do you accomplish that without alienating your other clients, if you see clients who might not be polyamory-friendly themselves?

WORD OF MOUTH

The number-one way that many therapists find their polyamorous clients is through word of mouth. The polyamory community tends to be small and close-knit, so word gets around. If you have one polyamorous client and they like how you work, you'll probably have more in short order. In fact, that's exactly how I got started working with polyamory.

After all, one of the biggest reasons I decided to write this book in the first place is the fact that there continues to be a real dearth of polyamory-competent therapists. If you let it be known, even fairly quietly, that you are a polyamory-competent therapist, you'll probably quickly become a rare and desirable commodity. Even though I hope there will soon be zillions of new polyamory-friendly and knowledge-able therapists, I suspect there will also be an increasing population of people who explore polyamory and might want therapists to help guide them as they try it out. As polyamory gets to be better known and understood, the demand for polyam-friendly therapists will only increase.

Although the relative rarity of polyamory-competent therapists can be a boon in some ways, it can also be a big inconvenience. Making referrals for your polyamorous clients can be quite challenging if there aren't many polyamory-competent therapists in your region. I recommend that you think this through before you get too far into your expanding practice; your first polyamorous client will tell their friends about you, which means the second wave of polyamorous clients who call you are pretty likely to be closely connected to previous clients, and you'll need to be careful about who you take on. See chapter 20, "Ethical Considerations."

SIGNALING YOUR INTENDED AUDIENCE

There are many ways to convey that you are comfortable working with polyamory. Some are subtle and quiet, while others make a bigger splash. One of the quietest and most effective ways I know is to adjust the language you use with *all* clients, colleagues, supervisors, and supervisees, and in all of your marketing materials, including your website and blog. Marginalized populations have ways of finding like-minded people, and monitoring language use is one of those ways. There are probably polyamorous people around you and you just don't know it; by using careful language, you may be able to let them know it is safe to come out to you.

The following are my language tips:

Don't assume monogamy. Use the word *relationship* rather than *couple* whenever you are speaking generally and whenever you are talking to someone who hasn't already used the word *couple*.

Don't assume heterosexuality. Use the words *partner* and *spouse* until your client clarifies, and any time you are speaking generally.

If there is a place in a conversation where the option of polyamory or open relationships would fit, go ahead and say it.

React well when nonmonogamy comes up. If someone says something derogatory about open relationships, don't miss the opportunity to say, "Well, it may not be for everyone, but it seems to work out pretty well for some people."

Similarly, when talking about infidelity, keep your sights squarely on where the problem really lies, which will probably include not only extradyadic intimacy, but also broken agreements, lies, secrecy, and deception. Avoid implying that having more than one sexual or romantic partner always means cheating or in itself is the problem in a failed relationship.

The next somewhat-subtle step might be to go through your website and other online listings and adjust your language to be more inclusive of nondyadic relationships, LGBTQIA+ populations, and such alternative sexualities as kink and consensual nonmonogamy. Of course, this is only ethical if you are actually qualified to work with these populations. Whatever language you choose should be accurate for your areas of interest. It's certainly possible to create a practice that's focused on nonkinky, non-LGBTQ people in nonmonogamous relationships, if that's what you want to do. But there's enough overlap between those populations that, if you're qualified and willing to work with all of them, it makes sense to either mention them all or use language that is inclusive for all.

A less subtle option is to identify "alternative sexualities" or "alt sex" in your list of specialty areas. Alternative sexualities refers to anything that falls outside of the hetero-cis-mono-normative cultural understanding of sexuality. Common usage implies kink and consensual nonmonogamies, in particular. Adding LGBTQIA+, if applicable, will also help the polyamory community find you. Please note, if you are not prepared to work with potentially complicated cases involving kink and BDSM, don't use the term *alt sex* to describe your practice; however, if you have decided you want to work with kinky clients, in particular, and just don't have much experience yet, doing some reading and finding a good consultant or supervisor who specializes in that area is the ethical road to expanding your scope of practice.

The term *alt sex* is still a bit subtle, in the sense that people who don't identify as having alternative sexualities generally don't know what it means, and they might just skip over it without registering the term. In fact, I use this term in my marketing materials. It feels right to me and helps my target audience find me. For what it's worth, in my therapy practice I still do have clients who aren't in the alt sex demographic, some of whom are a little on the conservative side. Somehow, they still manage to find me and choose me; apparently, they aren't too put off by my use of the term *alt sex*.

I also use the term *alternative family structures* to describe an area of my expertise. As far as I know, it's not a particularly well-known keyword, but I use it anyway, because it's descriptive without being pathologizing. This would be a good choice if you don't want to use alt sex for any reason or you want to be as descriptive as possible, since not everyone who has a consensually open relationship will think of themselves as having an alternative sexuality.

Of course, you can simply go ahead and write "polyamory-friendly" on your website and in your listings. That's a perfectly good and very direct solution. I know therapists who work mostly with polyamory and talk about polyamory openly on their website. The advantage of this is that they quickly develop a relationship in the community, as they are easy to find. If you're comfortable putting yourself out there as a therapist who works with polyamory, that's a great solution.

PUT THE WORD OUT IN THE RIGHT PLACES

Another good option is to advertise yourself as a polyamory-knowledgeable therapist in a place where polyamorous clients are likely to find you, either in addition to or instead of putting it right on your website. For instance, for a long time I ran an ad in a local LGBTQIA+ magazine, because there's a lot of overlap between polyamory and LGBTQIA+, and I also love working with LGBTQIA+ populations and have expertise and experience in related areas. If you're interested in pursuing this route, you might consider listing yourself with the website for the National Coalition for Sexual Freedom (NCSF), which has an online therapist locator for alternative sexualities. If you list yourself with NCSF, however, be prepared for kinky clients to find you there as well.

If you are ready to put it right out there, by all means, write some blog posts about polyamory. For me, that was a big, public step. I had to take a deep breath before I did it. I also had to think for about a year before I put speaking engagements on my website, because I was hesitant to mention the talks I gave on polyamory. To my relief, there has been relatively little negative fallout. For the most part, the net result has been positive: A lot of clients have been able to find me as a result of my blog, website, and speaking engagements. The fallout I have experienced has certainly not destroyed my practice, and there is the added benefit that clients have a more accurate impression of my expertise before they call me. It is surprising to me how often consensual nonmonogamies come up in conversation with most of my clients, monogamous or not. Apparently a lot of people have questions and want to discuss the topic.

The advantage of blogging is that you can get noticed for being polyamory-aware and friendly, while still deciding exactly what you want to say. Contrast that to, for instance, using the term *alt sex* on your website, which refers to not only polyamory, but also kink/BDSM. If you chose to blog instead, you could easily write about polyamory specifically, without involving kink in the conversation, if that were your preference.

There is always a way to get the word out, but the most important factor will probably always be word of mouth. However you decide to get the word out, gather a community of therapists around you with whom you feel comfortable giving and receiving referrals, identify a consultant or two in case you need them, and enjoy building a team of colleagues to serve the diversity of polyamorous clients in your region.

And let me extend a very warm welcome to the community of polyamory-friendly therapists. I'm so glad you are here, because the world needs you to express your gifts.

Relationship Concept Worksheets

Together these worksheets support an exploration of beliefs, biases, hopes, and dreams about monogamy, polyamory, and any other relationship style you can imagine, while honoring each individual's life aspirations and supporting the ultimate goal of a joyous life. They are equally relevant to a therapist exploring their biases about polyamory or monogamy, or a couple considering the pros and cons of various relationship styles. They can serve as a guide to self-exploration or discussion topics for interesting conversations.

This set of worksheets includes the following:

- My Relationship Ideas: Reflection Worksheet
    - Explores life events and perceptions of different types of relationships and how they have formed your ideas about fidelity, romantic connection, and many other aspects of relationships.
- Examining Assumptions About Relationship Structures
    - Guides consideration of the pros and cons of different relationship structures from a theoretical level and invites thinking about the degree to which the things you want in a relationship are related to the type of relationship you are in.
- Dreams and Desires
    - Invites thinking about what you desire, long for, and would like to create in your life, and your relationships, and how you might bring those aspects of joy into your life in your relationships, as well as in other ways.

MY RELATIONSHIP IDEAS: REFLECTION WORKSHEET

Think back to the romantic or committed relationships you witnessed when you were a child: parents, grandparents, aunts, uncles, neighbors, community leaders, older siblings, etc.

- How were these relationships structured? Monogamous? Open? Other? How did you know?
- What were you raised to believe about fidelity? Do you have memories of learning about infidelity? Did you witness any of the adults in your life dealing with the impact of infidelity? What was it like?
- What were you raised to believe about relationship agreements? Were they negotiable? Set in stone? Made by people? Made by God? Did you witness any adults in your life renegotiate relationship agreements?
- Did the adults in your life discuss things, generally? What happened when there was a disagreement? Did you have role models for positive experiences of coming to agreement or achieving resolution? Was collaboration and creative problem-solving valued and supported?
- Were you raised to follow a rule book or come up with your own solutions? Were your parents independent-thinking rebels, rock-solid upholders-of-convention, or somewhere in between?
- Were you raised in a faith tradition? What did your religious tradition teach you about marriage and relationships?
- Did anyone in your community have an "out of the norm" relationship (by your community's standards) that you were aware of? How did you know? How did people treat them and talk about them?
- Was sex discussed in your family and/or community? If so, how was it discussed? Did you grow up thinking sex was a positive thing, secret, shameful, or something else?

Think about the time when you began to have romantic feelings, and intimate relationships.

- In your earliest relationships, what ideas did you have about what was normal and acceptable in a romantic relationship? Where did you get your ideas about what was and wasn't okay? Did you discuss fidelity and other agreements with your partner(s)? If so, what were those conversations like?

- Did those ideas change in later relationships? How and why?
- What kinds of relationships did you witness your friends having? How were those relationships structured? How did you know about their structures? How did people talk about other people's relationships? How did your friends talk about fidelity, infidelity, agreements, monogamy, and nonmonogamy?
- Have you had experiences with infidelity? How about broken agreements of other kinds? Were you on the giving or receiving end? Did your beliefs about relationships change as a result of either infidelity or broken agreements? Do you think the wounds associated with those breaches have healed? If not, what do you think would be needed to mend the wounds? Is there something you could do from within yourself that would make a difference in your healing?
- Have you ever been in a nonmonogamous relationship? If so, what was that like for you? For your partner(s)? If not, what is the first thought that comes to mind about whether you would ever choose to be in a nonmonogamous relationship?
- Have you ever found yourself in a situation in which a previous relationship agreement is no longer working for you? Did you initiate a renegotiation of a relationship agreement with one of your partners? Have you ever lied about something rather than discuss it? Have you tended to give up something important to you rather than discuss it and renegotiate? How did you decide what to do? What happened as a result? How do you feel about it in retrospect?
- Do you think of yourself as being a little conflict-averse or are you more on the side of volatility? How willing are you to initiate a difficult discussion? How able are you to make a soft landing place for someone else to tell you something difficult?

Think about your friends, mentors, and role models. These might be actual people you know and love or fictional characters from a book or movie.

- Do you have role models for positive long-term monogamous relationships? If so, what do you admire about the people involved and their relationship?
- Do you have role models of positive long-term open relationships? If so, what do you admire about the people involved and their relationship?
- If you don't have role models for either monogamy, open relationships, or both, what do you make of that?

Now that you've written down a few notes about each of these questions, take a minute to write down any thoughts that pop out for you after having reflected on these questions. What do you think your current beliefs are about fidelity, nonmonogamy, relationship agreements, polyamory, and related issues? Indicate which of your *current* beliefs you want to keep and which you would prefer to change. Next to the ones you would prefer to change, write a brief statement about why you want to change them.

EXAMINING ASSUMPTIONS ABOUT
RELATIONSHIP STRUCTURES

This exercise will challenge you to consider the potential benefits and pitfalls of a wide variety of relationship styles. You'll be challenged to think beyond your personal experience and consider the reasons why someone might choose a specific relationship structure for themselves.

- Why might some choose a monogamous relationship? List as many reasons as you can think of. Think about reasons that relate to belief systems, preferences, fears, dreams, desires.
- Why might someone choose to have multiple concurrent sex-only relationships? List as many reasons as you can think of. Consider people you have known, thoughts or feelings you or your partner(s) have had, and books you have read. Why might someone want to hook up, swing, or otherwise have sex with more than one concurrent relationship or person?
- Why might someone choose to have multiple concurrent love/romantic relationships? List as many reasons as you can think of. Again, reference people you have known, thoughts and feelings you or partners have had, books you have read, and anything you can imagine.
- What do you think are the potential pitfalls of monogamy? List as many as you can.
- What do you think are the potential pitfalls of open nonromantic relationships? List as many as you can think of.
- What do you think are the potential pitfalls of polyamorous or romantic open relationships? List as many as you can think of.

Take a moment to consider whether the things you listed under reasons to choose various relationship types actually correlate with the desired outcomes. For instance, say you answered "to feel secure" when considering why someone might choose monogamy. You would then ask yourself if monogamy actually provides security. You might also ask yourself, "Does opening a relationship preclude security?"

Next, move even further into the exploration. Ask yourself, "How could a person structure a monogamous relationship to create emotional security? How could a person structure a nonromantic open relationship to create security? How could someone structure their polyamorous relationship to create security?"

Let's look at another example. Say that, under reasons for having an open re-lationship, you put "sexual adventure." Ask yourself, "Does an open relationship actually provide sexual adventure? Does monogamy prevent sexual adventure? How could a person structure a monogamous relationship to support sexual adventure? How could a person structure a nonromantic open relationship to enable sexual adventure? How about a polyamorous relationship?"

For each answer you gave, take some time to question it. Remember, this is not really about any choice or decision you will eventually make; it is about questioning your assumptions and getting clear on how you are connecting thoughts or ideas.

If you proceed from the assumption that all of the benefits—and all of the pitfalls—that you listed are possible in any type of relationship, with any relation-ship structure, what difference might that make in your life and relationships? In your ability to support others in their relationship?

DREAMS AND DESIRES

What is important to you in life and in a relationship? Consider things you deeply desire. What do you long for? What would make your life feel juicy, exciting, and magical? This list will vary from person to person, but here are a few examples of the kind of things that might show up: emotional security, financial security, fun, great sex, deep emotional connection, sexual adventure, long-term stability, creativity, joy, travel, deep conversations, great teamwork—you get the idea.

- Now make your own personal list of things that are important to you in life and in your relationship.
- Go through your list and think carefully about these questions:
  - For each item, can you see a way that you could bring that into your life without depending on any other person to do it for you? For instance, if you listed emotional security, ask yourself, "What do I do to make myself feel secure?" If you listed sexual adventure, ask yourself, "How do I express my sexually adventurous nature?" If you listed deep conversations, ask yourself, "What do I do to take conversations to a deeper level?"
  - Which of these desires do you imagine being met by one partner? Can you imagine some of these desires being met by a platonic close friend or friends? Community members? Another partner in a purely sexual relationship? Another partner in a romantic relationship?

The idea here is to empower you to enrich your life with the exact aspects of life that feel the juiciest and most important to you. Think of desire as the fuel that powers joy and see how much joy you can create in your life and relationships.

Feeling the exciting feelings associated with your juiciest dreams and desires is good for you. You don't have to wait for them to actually happen to enjoy feeling them, and you probably can also make a lot of parts of them happen as a part of your regular life without much else changing. Consider getting playful or creative; write poetry about your dreams and desires; or make a vision board, artwork, or anything else you can think of.

You might also enjoy sharing some of your dreams and desires with your partner(s). Telling them how exciting you find these ideas should be fun and is a great way to get to know one another on a deeper level. It will also give you practice talking and listening in turns and accessing depth and curiosity with some topics that are exciting, hopeful, and positive.

Emotional Balance Worksheets

This collection of worksheets can be used together in sequence or individually to help build a strong repertoire of skills for managing emotions. Included are the following:

- Daily Practice Identifying Thoughts and Feelings
  - Guides the exploration of not only the difference between thoughts and feelings, but also how your own unique thoughts and feelings strengthen one another, for better and for worse, so you can begin to work with them in ways that help you feel more positive emotions.
- Needs Versus Desires
  - Helps build awareness of how you talk to yourself and others about your preferences and needs. This supports strong communication with others.
- Holding Steady Self-Coaching Worksheet
  - Guides a process for self-coaching during a tough conversation and will support the ability to stay in a conversation longer and stronger, even when things don't entirely go your way.
- Time-Out Exercise
  - A necessary part of anyone's toolkit, this detailed guide explains how the functioning of the self-protective brain works against your ability to stay in a hard conversation and how to work with your brain's function rather than against it. Includes a step-by-step guide for taking a time-out, including what to do during the time-out and how to reapproach, and why.

- Challenging the Thought/Feeling/Meaning Spiral
  - A robust guide that explains how emotions and thoughts work together to create meaning, narrative, or story in our lives, and how to increase happiness and balance by taking control of this process in a powerful way. Equally applicable to any emotional experience, this handout focuses on jealousy.

DAILY PRACTICE IDENTIFYING THOUGHTS AND FEELINGS

For the purposes of self-awareness and clarity of communication, I'd like to invite you to practice identifying thoughts and feelings, and keep the two categories separate in a deliberate manner. For example:

- Several times a day, as a regular practice, ask yourself, "What do I feel right now?" Jot down a few notes. Just make sure the words you write down are feeling words. Examples include happy, sad, excited, worried, fearful, etc.
- Then write down some thoughts you are thinking that enhance those feelings, for better or worse. For instance, if you identified a feeling of worry, look for the thoughts that enhance worry for you right now. Examples might include thoughts like, "I'll never get this project done" or "my partner doesn't love me like they used to." Whatever the thoughts are that match the emotion, write them down.
- Start noticing the difference between thoughts and feelings. Notice how the thoughts strengthen the feelings and the feelings invite thoughts that support them. But thoughts and feelings are not the same thing; noticing the difference is very important.
- Once you can tell the difference between a thought and a feeling, you can start playing with these ideas, and if you do, I suspect you will notice you have more control than you think you do when it comes to emotional experience. For instance, if you would prefer to feel a different feeling, practice writing down the thoughts that go with the new feeling and see if you can shift your emotional state deliberately. This takes some practice but is extremely liberating. For example, if you would like to experience a feeling of happiness, ask yourself what thoughts would create happiness for you. Lying doesn't work, so you will need to look for happy-making thoughts that are also true. Here are some thoughts that support happy feelings for me to give you the idea: I love the feeling of sunshine on my face. When I look around me, I notice beauty (list the beautiful things) and take joy in that beauty. I love the feeling of my cat's fur and his purring. I love cooking some yummy food and then eating it. You get the idea; find things that bring up happy feelings, and focus on them. Notice your ability to generate happy feelings on purpose.

- If you have difficulty thinking up thoughts that generate emotions you would like to experience, ask someone else what they think about to generate that emotion in themselves. Then see if you can do it the way they do. Another way to investigate this is to imagine or remember a time when you felt the emotion and ask yourself what you were thinking in that scenario. You might also imagine watching a movie in which someone is experiencing the emotion you would like to experience; what are *they* thinking?
- Ask yourself, "What would I enjoy right now? What sounds like fun to me?" These questions will get you in touch with your unique preferences, which are an important aspect of yourself. Another way to do this is to identify a choice you have between two options and ask yourself which would be more enjoyable. Then choose the more enjoyable one, if at all possible. This will give you practice noticing what you prefer and, ideally, also some practice acting on your preference.
- Some people find it easiest to check in with themselves and get grounded first thing in the morning, before tackling the day. The following are some writing prompts that are designed to help you get grounded in your unique self before the day gets complicated. Experiment with some of them and see if you like them.
  - I am grateful for_____.
  - I am looking forward to _____.
  - The kind of person I want to be today is _____.
  - Thoughts I want to think today are _____.
  - Five enjoyable, beautiful, or pleasant things around me right now are _____.
  - The sensations I'm experiencing in my body right now are _____.
  - The emotions or feelings I'm experiencing right now are _____.
  - I would like to feel_____, and some thoughts that bring that feeling up are _____.

NEEDS VERSUS DESIRES

We often use the word *need* to communicate that something is important to us. Unfortunately, the word *need* can feel a little bit like an ultimatum to the listener. It can invite defensiveness or a guarded response, which is the last thing you want when something is really important to you.

Hard conversations with your partner will go better if you figure out how to discuss desires and preferences rather than needs, even when it comes to things that feel important to you. This exercise is intended to help you practice reframing statements in terms of desires and preferences rather than needs.

1. Write down a list of the things you strongly desire. Anything you have told someone you "need" should go on this list.
2. Rewrite each item on your list in a sentence that expresses something about desire, preference, and hopes. For example, you might write, "I would really love to experience (fill in the blank)."
3. Add a phrase that addresses the importance of the issue or how strong your feelings are about the topic and why it feels important to you. Using the aforementioned example, you might continue, "I feel strongly about this because (describe why it feels important to you)."
4. Any time you notice yourself thinking or saying "I need," challenge yourself to figure out a way to express your desire and preference. Make sure you also express the importance of the issue to you. The point isn't to minimize the importance or remove a sense of urgency, but rather to express your preferences and add emphasis in ways that aren't as likely to result in defensiveness.

HOLDING STEADY SELF-COACHING WORKSHEET

Thoughts lead to feelings, which is why self-talk, or, in other words, careful management of thoughts, is such a powerful tool for staying steady in a difficult situation or conversation. Imagine you have an internal coach who can give you just the right pep talk for any given situation. That internal coach might have to interrupt your internal heckler to get a word in edgewise, but the effort will pay off because good coaching really makes a difference in how well we perform.

Imagine being at the gym, lifting weights. Your internal heckler starts up: "You're so weak, you can't lift anything. I don't even know why you try. You'll never amount to anything. You don't look as good as all these other people at the gym either. You shouldn't have even bothered coming." Obviously, with coaching like that, you will have to work 10 times as hard to make any progress at all.

Okay, now imagine replacing your heckler with a good coach, someone who inspires you to keep going, compliments your effort, and supports your growth: "Look at you go! You're amazing! You've definitely got this. Everyone feels tired sometimes; just focus and see if you can do one more rep. You're making a strong, healthy, beautiful body with perfect muscles!"

Now imagine you're in a different type of challenging situation. You're having a hard conversation with your partner. The two of you disagree, and you're trying to manage your emotional responses and really understand what your partner is telling you without getting angry and defensive or shutting down. What kind of coaching do you want to provide for yourself in this situation?

Write down a list of things your internal coach might say that would help you stay with the conversation a little longer and a little stronger.

Here are a few examples for you to consider. Feel free to rewrite them to fit your circumstances and eliminate any that don't fit for you. Add your own if you can. The only requirement is that your internal coaching should help you stay steady, inspired, and focused on being your best self, even when it is hard.

- "I will make up my own mind in the end, but until then I'm going to explore everything I can."
- "I can do this. I am strong enough to hear the truth from my partner. I am strong enough to stay with the conversation and show up with my true self, and my true opinions."
- "No one is forcing me to do anything I don't want to. Thinking, talking, and imagining are not the same as acting."

- "I can run an experiment and see how it goes, and then I can revise the plan until we come up with something that works for all of us."
- "My vote is the deciding vote in my own life and decisions."
- "If the relationship doesn't work out, I want to know I explored all possibilities and really deeply came to understand my partner's perspective."

See if you can distill your self-coaching to two or three really powerful statements. Put them somewhere prominent; write them on your hand for the day or week, or put them in your notes on your phone or on an index card in your wallet. Look at these powerful coaching statements any time you feel wobbly. Don't let the heckler get too far out front; get the compassionate coach in there to help you!

TIME-OUT EXERCISE

Reptile Brain Review

Having a time-out strategy in place is crucial for managing escalation in difficult situations and hard conversations. We all have a limbic system and a lizard brain, the parts of the brain Dan Siegel describes as the "downstairs brain," or "thumb," and brainstem, or "palm," in his hand model of the brain. (You can learn more about this directly from Dr. Siegel on YouTube. Look for Dan Siegel, "Hand Model of the Brain.")

These are the parts of the brain that store emotional memory; scan for danger; and cause us to immediately fight, freeze, or flee when something potentially life-threatening happens. These parts of our brain are responsible for the survival of our species; they motivate us to save ourselves at the expense of others, if necessary. Without this lifesaving capacity, our ancestors would have been eaten by predators long ago and we wouldn't be here today. When our self-protective brain perceives threat, it dumps a cascade of stress-related chemicals into the bloodstream so you can outrun a tiger or lift a boulder off your foot. This part of the brain is not smart, just reactive. It has no logic and no empathy. It's not interested in being polite.

In the 21st century, we don't have nearly as many saber-toothed tigers, but our self-protective brains are still fine-tuned for life-threatening danger. Remember, your reptile and limbic brain's jobs are *not* discernment. They will respond in less than a millisecond to anything that might match a memory of trauma, embarrassment, disappointment, or pain. So, when your spouse snaps at you, you get a dump of stress hormones that makes you respond as if they were a guy with a machine gun coming at you fast. Your self-protective mechanism doesn't discern between an embarrassing moment and a life-threatening one. It helps you avoid all perceived threats.

What Happens When You're Triggered

When triggered, you can no longer access the parts of your brain that use logic or, possibly more importantly, empathy. The thinking, connecting, and processing parts of your brain are disconnected in this stressed-out state. It takes quite a bit of time to metabolize all those stress hormones and become able to access logical thought, curiosity, and empathy again. In a relationship context, the pivotal moment is the one when a discussion turns into a fight. Voices are raised, fingers pointed, and doors slammed, and you see your partner as "them" rather than "us" and go to war. You or your partner are likely to say hurtful things that you will later regret.

Later, if you try to remember exactly what happened during the fight, you're going to remember every bad feeling and every hurtful thing that was said. So will your partner, but the two of you probably won't be able to agree on the sequence of events that led to this situation or exactly what happened. Once that discussion became a fight, your self-protective brain took charge of focusing on every negative feeling or perceived slight, and the logical and connecting parts of your brain couldn't establish a coherent sequence of events and store it in an orderly fashion. This is why it is not productive to go back over an old fight blow by blow.

Time-Out!

If you get triggered during an argument with your partner, anything you say or do is likely to damage your relationship. When you're triggered, your options quickly become limited to fight, flee, fawn, faint, or freeze. If you fight, you will say hurtful things you can't take back. If you shut down or leave the scene, your partner will perceive it as abandonment, which may be less dramatic but is just as damaging.

Because you love your partner and don't want to say or do hurtful things, or create a messy tangle that is hard to unravel later, you both need to agree on a strategy that reminds you to stop talking, interacting, and causing damage, and start self-soothing, dialing back the stress, and getting some calm under your feet.

Here's the strategy: When an interaction starts to heat up, you take a "time-out." No last words, no final attempts to "win"—just time out. You can return to the issue later, when you can once again access empathy, logic, and curiosity.

When you call a time-out, it's important to do it in an intentional way. You might want to say it in a nasty voice and storm out, tossing a rude gesture or insult over your shoulder as you slam the door, but that's probably not the most effective way to leave the discussion. Later on, your partner is going to remember that attempt to end the conflict as cruelty not kindness.

Of course, it would be better if you could say something like, "I love you, and because I don't want to hurt you by saying something I'll regret later, I'm going to take a time-out and go to the gym. Don't forget I love you, and I'll be back soon." That would be ideal, but most of us can't manage that level of kindness and warmth when we're triggered. The time-out method is designed to help you call a time-out quickly, efficiently, and without causing damage.

The following is a step-by-step walk-through of how to use the time-out method in your next fight.

Step 1: Plan Ahead

Maybe it sounds silly to plan ahead for a fight, but it's essential that you and your partner talk about your time-out strategy *before* you're in the middle of a conflict.

1. *Reflect with your partner on your conflict styles.* Think: What do you do when you get triggered? Do you try to escape, convince, stonewall, or attack? Do you get defensive, roll your eyes and cross your arms, get sarcastic, become whiny and overly conciliatory, or just shut down? What kind of damage does that do? Note how your self-protective brain is affecting you and recognize that those are defensive postures designed to save you, not help your partnership. Think about how your partner responds to being triggered, too. When you can identify your partner's go-to conflict style, it can also help you not take it so personally when they go on the attack or shut down. They're just triggered. It's not personal. It's their "downstairs" brain. If you want them to forgive you when you're triggered, it's only fair that you also forgive them. Better yet, call a time-out and have less to apologize for.

2. *Agree on the importance of having a time-out* so you don't continue to hurt one another and set your intention now to use it next time a discussion becomes a fight.

3. *Come up with an easy-to-use signal*—something that you can both agree means "I love you, and I'm calling a time-out so we don't hurt one another," but that you can realistically do when you're upset. This could be a hand gesture (preferably not a rude one), a word, a phrase, waving a little white flag you keep on your fridge, or anything else you decide will work.

4. *Pay attention to your reactions.* Prepare yourself to use a time-out effectively by learning more about what happens to you when you get triggered and how you can control your response. Getting triggered is a physiological reaction. Even before your conscious brain quite knows what's happening, your body will react. Next time a minor annoyance interrupts your

daily routine, notice if your heart starts to pound or your breathing starts to feel rushed. Learn how your body signals its stress. Recognizing your reaction will give you a chance to control how you proceed, like an early-alert system that tips you off before the fight starts—and therefore gives you a chance to stop, or at least minimize, the damage.

5. *Practice slowing down your response.* It's the nature of a stress reaction to escalate. Your job is to keep that from happening—to get ahead of your own reaction and slow it way down. Otherwise, you won't be able to access the rational voice that tells you to take a time-out. Understanding how your body responds to being triggered will help you master the skill of slowing down and controlling your response. The good news is that everyday life will probably afford you lots of opportunities to practice. Next time you start to feel your stress reaction, pause and take a deep breath. It's not as minor as it sounds: Long, slow exhales can actually lower your blood pressure and cortisol levels, shifting you from the threat-response sympathetic nervous system to the calming parasympathetic nervous system. This gives you the chance to slow down and remember your time-out strategy. The more you practice this calming response, the more likely it is that you'll be able to access it when you and your partner fight.

Step 2: Call a Time-Out

Now that you've established your signal, keep it in mind until you and your partner come into conflict or, better yet, when you first start to feel your body reacting in a stressful way. To make this work, you have to be able to identify when you or your partner are starting to get triggered. Watch for these warning signs:

Your voice is rising.

You're convinced there is only one point of view and that your partner is 100% wrong.

Your heart is racing.

You feel nauseous.

Your face is flushed.

You're pointing your finger at your partner and saying "*You . . .* "

You're thinking in overgeneralized terms like, "He *never* supports me" or "She *always* dismisses my ideas."

Pay attention to your reactions so you can notice as soon as your self-protective brain starts to kick in. As soon as you notice that a conversation is starting to turn into a fight, use your time-out signal.

Step 3: Separate and Soothe

Once you've called a time-out, the conversation is put on pause. You can (and should) return to it later, but you need this time to quiet your brain, metabolize the associated stress hormones, and return to the point from which you can hear your partner's point of view without getting defensive. Depending on how upset you were, this might take a few seconds, or a few hours, or a full night's sleep. Here's how to handle your time-out:

1. *Go to separate spaces.* You and your partner need some time apart to return to equilibrium. If you call a time-out but don't take time off, you'll jump right back into the conflict without improving anything. Trust me. Take some time to yourself to calm down.
2. *Figure out your self-care plan.* This will be different for everyone. The important point is that whatever you choose to do during this time should soothe you, not work you up further. For some people, a treadmill or a run is a really good way to get calm. But for other people, exercise will whip them into a frenzy. You could go to a quiet room and write in your journal, but if you spend that time griping about your partner, you're going to keep renewing and fueling the upset. Thoughts create feelings; if you have difficulty controlling your thoughts, you might need to take a break from thinking or talking and do something that is purely physical, and purely pleasant. Check out the list at the end of this handout as you consider what will be an effective plan for you. Be mindful of what is likely to work for you and what is likely to be counterproductive, and be prepared to try something and adjust if it doesn't work.
3. *Take at least 45 minutes.* It takes a while for your body to process those stress chemicals. If you took a time-out early, before you got totally triggered, you might be able to get by with just a few deep breaths or a walk around the block, but if you're fully triggered, you might not really be calm and logical until the next morning or even longer. Don't engage in the conversation again until you and your partner are both completely calm, even if that means you have to wait a few days. You will know you are ready to

talk again when you can honestly get curious about what your partner was experiencing, why they were upset, or what they were trying to tell you.

Step 4: Reapproach

After you've taken the time to calm down, you can decide when to return to the topic. You shouldn't try to discuss the topic again until you are really ready, but you will need to reapproach and say something connecting or reassuring pretty soon. The person who called the time-out will be in charge of approaching the other. That's because a time-out can feel like abandonment to the other partner; initiating reconnection will help repair any lingering sense of abandonment. Also, particularly if you have a habit of not returning to conversations about tough topics, it is crucial to establish that a time-out is not an avoidance tactic. If you have a lot of difficulty talking about tough topics, engage a therapist or coach to help you, but don't just sweep it under the rug.

1. *Initiate conversation* with something like, "Okay, that was rough. I want to make sure that we don't just leave this hanging. So let's schedule a time that works for both of us to talk about this again." This will reassure the other partner that, even though you called a time-out, you're not simply dropping the topic.
2. *Schedule a time to discuss again.* Often, "right now" is not the best time. Make sure you both have had enough time to calm down completely and try to choose a moment at which you won't have other stressors or distractions to deal with.

Step 5: Revisit the Conversation

How exactly you approach the conversation will depend on your particular circumstances. Take some time to figure out how and when to proceed.

1. *Assess your own state of mind.* Consider: Are you ready to listen with an open mind to what your partner thinks, feels, and prefers? Are you able to express your thoughts and feelings without blame or finger-pointing? Can you get through a conversation without trying to convince your partner to agree with you? Also take into account how difficult the material you're trying to discuss is. How triggered did you each get last time?

- If you both feel ready, by all means sit down and talk.
- If you're not quite there yet but know you can get there, give it some time. Wait until you're truly calm and feel open, warm, kind, and generous.
- Start warm. Spend a few minutes connecting, either by quietly holding hands or exchanging positive feedback or things you love and appreciate about one another. This can help you both get completely relaxed, which is a good place to start a conversation from. You can take short, frequent breaks and help one another calm down in this manner whenever you wish. Starting and ending with positivity and sprinkling lots of positive moments into the conversation will help both of you feel less anxious and guarded about talking together.
- If you are feeling shaky, not sure you can get to a really good place, then go slow, carefully monitor your responses, and be ready to call a time-out again.

2. *Control the conversation.* Here's a great strategy if you're dealing with a particularly triggering topic: Set a timer for 20 minutes, or even less, and stop when the timer goes off. The time limit minimizes the chances that one or both of you will get emotionally exhausted or retriggered. There are a few different ways to handle this technique:
   - Some couples like to take turns, splitting that time in half.
   - Some prefer to have one partner use all the time and schedule another time for the second partner to have their say.

Feel free to figure out what works best for you. Remember: You can always come back to the conversation and discuss another aspect later. In fact, with a big topic, you may have to come back to it many times, and you can use this technique whenever you do.

Step 6: Time-Out Again?

During your conversation, if you start to feel things spiraling out of control, do the following:

1. *Focus on getting grounded.* If you start to feel upset, take a few breaths and slow down.
2. *Pause the conversation* and have a feel-good moment together. Hold hands, talk about positive things you appreciate about one another, or go

for a little walk together. Remind one another that your love and connection is the entire point of talking things through.

3. *Take a mini time-out.* If you catch it early, you might be able to just take a quick walk around the block, go to the bathroom and splash water on your face, or give yourself some other brief moment of calm.

4. *Take another time-out* if that doesn't help.

5. *Take as many breaks as you need* to make sure you are only having hard conversations when you have your entire brain onboard. After all, it is the hard conversations you really *need* your brain for.

Remember, you're not going to get to any kind of resolution if either of you is too triggered.

Time-Out FAQs

Is It Like This Forever?

No. With practice, you will get better at noticing that you are getting upset before you're fully triggered. That will make it easier for you to control your responses to conflict. You might be able to just take a couple minutes and walk around the block, and come right back to it. Or the two of you might be able to go for a walk and continue the conversation calmly because you're moving your bodies or holding hands. Some couples can take a mini time-out by being silent together but connecting by walking the dog or holding hands. Believe it or not, tossing a ball back and forth between you might make it possible for you to continue to talk.

Eventually, you will be able to take a deep breath and remember your point of view is just that—a point of view—and your partner is someone you deeply love and admire, not a wild animal you have to skewer or run from. Wouldn't it be amazing if you could *truly* know and understand your partner's point of view, even if you don't agree with it? When you can get curious and calm, and listen without convincing or blaming, you are ready to talk.

What If We Can't Do It?

If this technique just isn't working, for any reason, it might be time to bring a couples therapist into the conversation. The time-out strategy is *hard*. It involves working against the natural instincts of a part of your brain that has protected you effectively for years and will continue to protect you, thank goodness. The project is learning to discern *realistic* levels of danger and override the downstairs brain response when things aren't *actually* life-threatening. This is not at all easy; however, getting good at this will be necessary for the success of your relationship. Get whatever help you need to have a hard conversation well. You and your relationship are worth it.

Ideas for Self-Soothing

This is a big list of ways to self-soothe. Some of these may work for you, and others may not. Some will get you out of the house, and some you can just do in the next room while the two of you cool down. Take some time to scan the list and really consider which of these activities seem comforting to you. You could even circle some of the most likely options, and refer back to your notes next time you have a fight. Keep in mind that thoughts create feelings; look for strategies that either stop you from thinking entirely, engage your body in pleasant sensations, or shift your thinking to something positive.

- Take a walk outside.
- Read a beloved novel.
- Soak in a warm bath.
- Write in your journal. (Do not rehash the fight. You're trying to break the thought/feeling spiral, not strengthen it.)
- Draw or paint.
- Meditate.
- Go for a jog.
- Call a friend and ask them to distract you with something positive or fun. (Do not rehash the fight. You're trying to break the thought/feeling spiral, not strengthen it.)
- Do a yoga routine.
- Go swimming.
- Listen to soothing music.
- Put on an upbeat song and dance.
- Watch cute animal videos online.
- Write a letter or an e-mail to a beloved friend (but don't use this as an opportunity to rehash the fight or complain about your partner).

- Garden.
- Cuddle or play with your pet.
- Watch a movie.
- Go for a bike ride.
- Find a nice nature spot and sit on the grass, watching for wildlife.
- Try out a new recipe.
- Go to the library or your local bookstore and browse the shelves.
- Look through the pictures in a beloved picture book or art book.
- Knit, crochet, or sew.
- Do a jigsaw puzzle, word puzzle, or something else engaging and absorbing but not stressful.
- Color in a coloring book.
- Listen to a podcast.

CHALLENGING THE THOUGHT/FEELING/MEANING SPIRAL

You are having feelings. That's okay, it happens to everyone from time to time. Thoughts and feelings are intimately intertwined. Thoughts lead to feelings, and when feelings are uncomfortable, we create an entire story about why we are experiencing something uncomfortable. You can think thoughts that make your feelings stronger, bring different feelings, or reduce the intensity of your feelings. This is crucial when you are experiencing painful feelings. Getting some control of your thoughts, so you can experience less suffering, is extremely important to happiness. Making any decisions about actions to take in your relationship is another subject and should be kept separate from managing thoughts and feelings.

Let's consider the topic of jealousy in a polyamorous relationship. Imagine Mary's partner goes on a date with Rosie and Mary experiences jealousy, along with anger, resentment, fear, or any other uncomfortable emotion. Mary might have such thoughts as, "My partner is probably going to leave me for Rosie," or "Rosie is more attractive than I am," or "Rosie wants to break up my relationship with my partner," or "My partner doesn't care about my feelings." Any of these thoughts reinforce the uncomfortable feelings Mary is experiencing.

Use these steps to identify your feelings, expand your thinking, and calm yourself. Remember, this is not a decision-making process, it is a process of managing the thought/feeling/meaning spiral. Any decision you need to make will be better made at a time when you can think more clearly.

1. What emotions are you experiencing? (Examples include jealousy, fear, anger, resentment, envy, and many more, but it is important to know this worksheet is relevant to any thought/feeling/meaning spiral, not just those having to do with jealousy.)
2. What thoughts are you thinking that lead to those feelings? Write down the thoughts that strengthen the feelings you are experiencing. (See the aforementioned examples if you are having trouble identifying your thoughts.)
3. Now flip these thoughts or stories upside-down. You might ask yourself, for one thought at a time, "Am I 100% sure this is true?" Whatever your answer is to that question, next write down a few statements that are opposite your initial thought/story. For instance, if your first thought was, "My partner likes their new lover better than they like me," some opposite statements would include, "My partner likes me better than their new lover" and "My partner doesn't like their new lover better than they like me."

4. Now that you have a list of opposite statements, make a list of the other possible stories you can think of that might explain the current circumstances. For instance, if your partner is late coming home, "They are in a ditch dying" isn't going to help you function well, feel good, or help in an emergency. It would be helpful to think, "I'm sure they just lost track of time," or "Maybe they stopped at the store," or "Their phone might have run out of battery, and that's why they haven't called yet." The truth of the matter is not important right now; what is important is letting your self-protective brain know there are options other than the catastrophic thoughts you have been thinking. For any given situation, think up as many alternative stories as you can. These alternative stories are what I refer to as "meanings," as in "this is the meaning I make of that."

Next, take a break from thinking about this. Do your best to take gentle care of yourself. What would feel pleasant right now? What would be a good distraction for you? A hot bath? Making a nice soup? Putting on some peppy music? Doing an art project? Going to the gym? Whatever you choose, make sure it is enjoyable. This might be easier if you give yourself a time-related plan for your mini-vacation, for instance, "I'm not going to worry until 7 a.m." or "I'm not going to make a decision about my relationship's future for at least a week."

When you are ready, sleep on it. If you have trouble winding down, use a guided meditation to help you relax, listen to a story, or read a pleasant but boring book so you can think about something else.

In the morning, revisit this exercise and decide if there are any questions you have for your partner, assumptions you want to check out, or aspects of your experience you want to share with anyone.

Give yourself some positive strokes for your hard work. You might also ask your partner or a support person for positive strokes. It is a big deal to challenge your own negative thinking, and you are a rock star for doing it.

Preparation for Communication Worksheets

These worksheets are designed to help with the steps that come before actually starting a conversation about something that is important to you. If it is hard for you to get clear on what you want to say, say it clearly, stay with it, stay calm, or stay on track and warm when someone else reacts emotionally to something you say, these worksheets will help. Included are the following:

- Preparing to Communicate
  - Helps you get clear on what you want to express and start the conversation with a step-by-step guide, complete with examples.
- Rehearsing Tough Conversations
  - Addresses the anxiety you may feel related to an upcoming hard conversation and prepares you to respond well to any reaction, response, or rebuttal.

PREPARING TO COMMUNICATE

Are you considering communicating with someone about your thoughts and feelings? If so, that's great. If you sometimes find it difficult to gather your thoughts, stay steady if your partner starts to feel distressed, or fully express what you want to say it will help to prepare for the conversation ahead of time. The following are some questions to help you sort out your thoughts, followed by some suggestions for how to express yourself in ways that make it more likely you will feel heard and understood. Read through all the steps before you start the conversation with your partner, because there are a lot of ways you can prepare, particularly if it is a conversation you are worried about. Even if you don't do all the steps, it will be helpful to read them.

Step 1: Get Clear

It is helpful if you can be clear about your topic, as well as your thoughts and feelings about it, before you begin talking with your partner. I recommend working through this on your own in writing, to get clear about what your topic is and what you think, feel, believe, perceive, desire, etc., about that topic. Ask yourself these questions, and write down the answers:

- What is the most pressing topic? (If there are several, write them down and pick just one for now. You have a lifetime to communicate, so bite off just one topic at a time.)
- What do I *think* about this topic?
- What *feelings* come up for me about this?
- On a scale of 1–10, with 1 being hardly any and 10 being a lot, how important is the topic for me?
- What beliefs are coming into this issue for me?
- What assumptions am I making about my partner or my partner's perceptions, thoughts, feelings, or beliefs?
- What is my goal in having this conversation (e.g., my partner hears me, my partner understands me, my partner and I can come to a decision that works for both of us, etc.)?
- What are my desires about this topic? What do I want to have happen, and why do I want that?

- What stories or meanings am I making up about this topic? In other words, what does it mean to me that we are talking about this? What would it mean if we agreed? What would it mean if we didn't agree?
- Do I have perceptions about this that my partner might not share? What does my partner need to know about my perceptions of events to understand what's going on for me?

Step 2: Share Your Goal

Start by telling your partner your goal in having the conversation. Do you want them to just listen? Do you want them to show you that they understand what you're saying? Do you want help thinking something through? Are you hoping to make a decision for yourself? Are you hoping the two of you can make a decision together about something that affects both of you? Telling your partner up front what you are hoping to get out of having this discussion will help them understand where you're coming from and make it more likely that the conversation will be productive.

If you have just started talking about an issue, I recommend that you do not attempt to come to a resolution or make a decision yet. An early step would be to express your perspective as clearly as you can, asking your partner to hear you, help you clarify your thoughts, and hopefully understand you better. Then ask your partner to do the same: Help them get clear and express themselves more fully, and show that you understand them. Decision-making is a much later step, so don't confuse things by asking for a decision in the early stages.

Step 3: Stick to Your Topic

When you communicate, it is often helpful to separate what you are expressing about your perceptions from your feelings and the meanings you are making. It is also helpful to stick with just one thought at a time. Remember, in the course of a long-term relationship, you have ample time to explore and reexplore topics; you can say more or go off on a tangent later. For now, figure out what you want to express to your partner about one concise topic. Regarding that topic, what do you want your partner to understand about your perceptions, feelings, and the meanings you are making? Writing this down now will help you be concise later, during the actual conversation.

Here's an example: "Yesterday morning, when I came into the bathroom and there were towels on the floor, I assumed you had left them there, and I felt angry and frustrated. The meaning I made was that you take me for granted and think it is my job to pick up after you." Here's another example: "The other day, I had a conversation with George about his open relationship. I felt excited about what he was saying because he seems really happy, and it sounds like he and his wife are doing really well and having a lot of fun. I think I would like to explore whether we could have an open relationship, but I'm concerned that you might not like that idea."

Step 4: Acknowledge Your Perspective

Make sure you have taken responsibility for your own thoughts, feelings, beliefs, perceptions, and preferences, and acknowledged that your partner might be in a different place, without making them feel bad about it. You will have a much easier time talking about deep topics with high levels of grace and low levels of drama if you frame beliefs, perceptions, and opinions as such, rather than assuming that everyone agrees with you (or should agree with you) about universal truths. In fact, for the purposes of having tough conversations about charged topics with people you care about, I recommend striking the word *truth* from the vocabulary and instead talk about theories, beliefs, thoughts, feelings, preferences or desires, and perceptions.

The following are some examples of how this shift might look in real life:

- Version 1: We have to go to church.
- Version 2: I believe in God, and I hold the opinion that it is important that we go to church. I have a strong preference that I, at least, attend church, even if you don't. My perception is that many positive things come from going to church. My hope is that if we go together, we will grow together in some important ways as a result of having shared experiences. I imagine us discussing things that happen at church during dinner, and in my imagination, sometimes we disagree; however, when I think about those discussions, even if we disagree in them, I imagine feeling cozy, connected, and curious.

- Version 1: Polyamory is a sin, causes harm, and destroys relationships.
- Version 2: I believe polyamory is a sin, and I have an opinion that polyamory can cause harm, but that might be more of a fear than an opinion. Also, it is my perception that Bob and Sally's open relationship has been bad for

both of them. My theory is that if they hadn't opened their relationship, they would still be together now. When I think about opening our relationship, a lot of feelings come up, including fear of losing the connection we have. I am afraid that the fact that you are interested in exploring polyamory means that you don't find me attractive anymore or are tired of our relationship.

- Version 1: We need to talk about opening our relationship.
- Version 2: I believe I am a person who experiences frequent attractions; historically, it has been true. I predict that at some point in the future I will develop a crush on someone other than you, and because I might want to act on it, I'd like to discuss that possibility with you now, so I understand your thoughts about it and how you would like me, and us, to handle it if and when that happens. To me, discussing polyamory doesn't mean we have to act on it. First, I would like to think about it, ideally with you, so we are on the same page, and I'm not having a lot of private fantasy-type thoughts about it that you aren't aware of.

- Version 1: What did I do to make you angry yesterday morning?
- Version 2: My perception is that yesterday morning you were angry with me. As I remember it, you threw the dish towel on the floor and slammed the door as you were leaving, which to me suggests you were angry with me. My point in bringing this up is to find out what was actually happening for you. Were you angry with me, and, if so, why?

- Version 1: I need to stay home tonight.
- Version 2: My preference would be to stay in tonight and have a quiet evening at home. My perception is that I haven't done that for a long time, and I miss it. It feels important to me because I've been stressed and anxious all week. I would love to relax and not have to think about anything tonight.

Now it's your turn. Write down some things you might want to express to someone else, and review each statement carefully. Make sure you are acknowledging that your perceptions are yours alone, rather than the truth. Identify your preferences, rather than calling them needs. If something feels important, see if you can figure out what emotion or feeling goes with it, and figure out a way to express that without upping the emotional ante by raising your voice, issuing an ultimatum, or describing something as a need.

REHEARSING TOUGH CONVERSATIONS

Do you anticipate a difficult conversation? If so, you can work through a lot of it on your own, using a method involving two chairs. Here's how it works.

Set up two chairs facing one another. Sit in one chair, facing the other, and pretend you're looking at your partner (or the person you want to have the conversation with) in the other chair. Express what's on your mind to the best of your ability. Don't worry about perfection, just spit it out as best you can, but do make an effort to say it as if you were actually talking to the other person and bringing your best self to the project. Now switch chairs. Be your partner, and respond in the way you think they will respond. Switch back to your own chair and respond back to your partner from a grounded, warm, empathic place. Switch chairs again, and be your partner again, responding to what you just said to them.

As this exercise continues, make sure you respond from your partner's chair in the ways you are most worried they might respond, so you can have the experience of figuring out how to handle your own worst-case scenarios. Continue with this exercise until you have prepared a balanced and values-informed response to the things you are afraid they will say. If you get stuck and can't think of a way to respond that will be helpful, get some ideas from a wise friend, coach, or therapist. This exercise should result in you feeling prepared for any response and much less anxious about how the conversation will go.

Relationship Enrichment Handouts

This handout set is a necessary toolkit for strengthening relational skills. The "Time-Out Exercise" also fits here, so don't miss it in appendix B, "Emotional Balance Worksheets." This set includes the following:

- How to Get the Most out of Relationship Therapy or Coaching
  - Contains two exercises I ask all relational therapy clients to do before our first meeting. This handout is an excellent starting place and worth revisiting every now and then.
- Initiator: Revealing One's Self
  - Provides a concise description of the skills involved in the initiator role of the initiator/inquirer process. This handout was generously provided by the Couple's Institute.
- Inquirer: The Effective Listener
  - Describes the skills involved in the inquirer role of the initiator/inquirer process. This handout was generously provided by the Couple's Institute.
- 30 Ideas No Matter How Silly: Brainstorming Process
  - For use by couples or individuals, guides a process of expanding options in a playful and effective way. Excellent for any situation where there seems to be a failure of imagination about potential options or actions.
- Co-Creating a Trusting Relationship
  - A guide that fosters an understanding of the relational dynamics that support truth-telling. Building trust is not an individual project; it requires strengthening multiple aspects of the relationship system. If trust has been a problem in your relationship, this handout will help identify where to focus your energy.

- Making a Good Repair
  - A step-by-step guide that explains how to make an effective repair, which is a skill every partner should cultivate. Doing it well saves a lot of time and energy, and is a necessary step in strengthening trust after any large disappointment or broken agreement.

HOW TO GET THE MOST OUT OF
RELATIONSHIP THERAPY OR COACHING

I value your commitment to your relationship and respect your investment of time, energy, and financial resources. I appreciate your faith in me as a helper and facilitator for the growth you want in yourself and your relationship. I want our work together to be extremely successful. To this end, I have created this handout. I want you to start thinking about yourself, your relationships, and the changes you desire in ways that will create positive change, even before our first meeting. In fact, I have some homework for you to do before we meet.

Envisioning Your Future Relationship (Exercise 1)

Take some time to reflect, and then answer these questions:

- What kind of relationship do you want to create? Think about what your relationship might feel like when you are deeply happy in it. Imagine you are coming home at the end of a long day and feeling pure joy and anticipation when you park and enter the house. You are looking forward to your time with your partner. Now here's the question: What are the features of the relationship that you are excited to come home to? What does that relationship look and feel like, from your perspective?
- When you imagine yourself in that amazing, fulfilling relationship, how are you showing up? What kind of a partner are you being, in your fantasy of a deeply happy relationship?
- How far are you from that ideal right now? Be honest: How are you currently showing up that isn't your best self? How would you like to be showing up, in accordance with your values and congruent with the relationship that you want to create?

Putting Relational Therapy and the Change Process in Perspective

In my experience, the difference between effective and ineffective relationship therapy is whether each partner is able to identify meaningful goals for themselves (not for their partner). What is a meaningful goal? Goals that move therapy forward effectively have several key qualities:

1. These goals represent how you want to be as a person. They are in alignment with your values and feel important to you because they represent steps toward your own personal growth objectives.
2. Achieving these goals will benefit not only you, but also your partner and your relationship. The best goals have a clear payoff directly to you, the person who holds the goal. These goals will also benefit the relationship and make a difference to your partner.
3. These goals are quite specific and actionable. If you can't picture a person in a movie performing the goal activity, it isn't specific enough.

Here is an example of a goal that meets the criteria: "I want to listen to my partner without interrupting. This is in alignment with my values because I believe being a good listener is an important quality in a partner, and I aspire to be a good partner. It will also benefit me to listen without interrupting, because then I will get to know my partner, which I would love; after all, I often wonder what they think and feel. I would feel good about myself, and them, if they told me what they think and feel, even if I didn't agree with everything they say. I also think it will benefit my relationship when I reach this goal, because sometimes my partner tells me they don't feel heard. When I become good at listening, my partner will feel more emotionally safe, and that will definitely benefit our relationship."

Here's another example: "I want to stop being defensive when my partner is telling me something. I don't feel good about myself when I'm defensive, so it is in accordance with my values to stop that behavior. It will benefit me directly to stop being defensive, because then my partner will be able to speak freely without getting distracted by my perspective; I will get to know them better. Our relationship will benefit, because defensiveness often leads to a fight. When I stop being defensive, we will certainly fight less."

Notice that these goals *do not require that you know how to achieve them.* That is where therapy and coaching come in. Your job is to get clear on what you want to change about yourself, and my job is to help you get there.

Setting Meaningful Goals for Personal Change (Exercise 2)

Now it's your turn. Think about what you would like to change about how you show up in your relationship. What might you want to change about yourself that will make a difference to you and in your relationship, and be in alignment with your values?

Make a list of things you would like to change about yourself. It could be one or two things, or 10. Put a star by the two that you think will make the biggest difference in the quality of your relationship. For extra credit, write down how you will feel after you have achieved those changes. What emotions will you experience when you are showing up in the new way you aspire to?

This handout is modified from the work of my mentors, Ellyn Bader and Peter Pearson, who created the Developmental Model of Couples Therapy.

INITIATOR: REVEALING ONE'S SELF

Focus on One Issue Only

Before you begin, get clear on your main concern. Check your partner's
readiness.
Stay on track with this one issue. Describe what you want.

Express Your Feelings and Thoughts

Feelings are often complex and can even be contradictory. Are you sad,
scared, angry, or happy?
Go beyond simply expressing one feeling.
Look for the vulnerability that may be underneath your initial feeling, e.g.,
sadness, fear, jealousy, hurt, guilt, etc.

Remind Yourself

This is my problem. It's an expression of who I am. It's about me revealing
myself and being willing to express my own thoughts and feelings.

Avoid Blaming, Accusing, or Name-Calling

Blaming stops you from knowing yourself. You have a role to play in being heard.
You may wish to acknowledge some positive aspects of the situation.

Be Open to Self-Discovery

Explore your personal, inner experience. Keep going deeper into how you feel.
What does this tell you about yourself? How do you respond?
How do you think and feel?

Remind Yourself

This process is about my willingness to take a risk to speak or discover my
truth and increasing my ability to tolerate the expression of our differences.

INQUIRER: THE EFFECTIVE LISTENER

Listen Calmly

Don't defend yourself, argue, or cross-complain.

Remind yourself that you don't have to take what's said so personally. Hold on to the "big picture."

Ask Questions

Develop an interested and curious state of mind.

The questions you ask are designed to understand your partner's experience.

Can you come up with any examples on your own that will let your partner know you really understand?

Remind Yourself

Am I in a place to listen with openness? I do not own this problem.

I do not need to get upset.

It's up to me to manage my reactions.

Recap

Repeat back to your partner, as accurately and completely as you are able, what you've understood.

Check it out with your partner to see if it's complete and accurate.

Empathize

Do your best to put yourself in your partner's shoes. Respond with empathy.

Keep making empathetic statements until a soothing moment occurs.

You can hold onto yourself and still imagine what it's like for the other person.

Remind Yourself

My partner is a separate person with their own feelings, thoughts, personality, and family history. I only need to listen, not look for solutions.

30 IDEAS, NO MATTER HOW SILLY: BRAINSTORMING PROCESS

This process can be used for many situations. Maybe you're trying to come to a decision on a course of action, sort out a household system, find more ways to connect with one another, or think of things you'd enjoy doing on your own while your partner is away. Most things in life would benefit from a brainstorming list. We often allow ourselves to be limited by what we can imagine, because we imagine only what we already assume is possible. This is your opportunity to imagine what is possible from an unlimited, creative, even silly place.

Step 1: Access a sense of vast possibility. The sky's the limit. Encourage yourself to feel playful and creative. You might even get stilly, and that's good. This is a creative process; it should feel like fun instead of hard work.

Step 2: Get a piece of paper and get ready to generate a lot of ideas. You might number your page 1–30, because you will be brainstorming your way to at least 30 ideas, if not more.

Step 3: Identify the problem you want to solve and write it in the blank in this heading at the top of the page: "Thirty Ideas, No Matter How Silly, for

_____."

Step 4: Turn off your inner censor and generate ideas as fast as you can. Write down each idea as it comes to mind, even if it seems ridiculous or illogical. Don't stop to consider whether it's practical, affordable, or in compliance with how you think the world works. If you are on a team of idea-generators, so much the better, but you can also do this alone. If you have partners, take turns generating ideas. No cross-talk; don't shoot down one another's ideas or even your own. Instead, use every idea as a jumping-off place for even better—or even more silly—ideas. No idea is too ridiculous. This is a creative expansion exercise, not a list for narrowing your focus or settling on a decision. Your goal is to get past what you thought was or wasn't possible with your previous limited thinking.

Step 5: Go through your list and do some refining. Everything on the list was important for idea-generating, but some items may not need to stay on the list. For each idea you cross off, make sure there are several ideas still on the list that address the kernel of what was attractive about the thing.

- Remove any items that are not in accordance with your values. For instance, if you put "go to bed and never get up again," consider what it points to that is missing in your current life. For this example, you might add, "Take more naps, learn stress-reduction strategies, take a meditation class, take a day off in the next week."

- Remove anything that is totally unrealistic, but again, make sure you address what it points to that you might benefit from adding to your life. For instance, if you put "join a circus" and given your age or circumstance you know for sure you won't be doing that, think about the feeling it generates and add to your list. Ideas might include taking a dance class, wearing playful clothing, learning to juggle, or seeking out opportunities to perform. Have respect for your desires.

Step 6: Now that you have a list, you can post it somewhere prominent. Is it a list of fun things you could do together? Put it on the fridge. Is it a list of fun things you could do alone? Post it by your bedside or on your mirror. Is it a list of ways you might handle a household dilemma? Put it in your Household Matters Monthly Meeting Notes book.

Step 7: If you made your brainstorming list as a step toward decision-making, the next step is to use it to come up with experiment 1. Remember not to get too serious about it, just pick something that feels like a good starting place for everyone involved and give it a try for a limited amount of time. Schedule a date to revisit and evaluate the experiment.

CO-CREATING A TRUSTING RELATIONSHIP

Honesty is at the root of trust. I don't think it is possible to create a trusting connection without a substantial foundation of honesty; however, honesty is a more
complicated topic than you might think. For one thing, no one is honest all the
time, even in thriving relationships. For another, while being an honest person
may be part of a personal values system, honesty is also a team sport.

There are multiple kinds of lies, and they are not all created equal. In this
document, I describe a variety of common types of lies and when they tend to
crop up; for each type, I share some action steps you can use to strengthen your
truth-telling skills. The taxonomy of lies I share was developed by Ellyn Bader
and Peter Pearson of the Couple's Institute, and you can learn more about it in
their book *Tell Me No Lies.*

Some lies are kindhearted attempts to soothe or lift someone's spirits, for
instance, "You look great in those pants." These *loving lies* are very common in
relationships and not malicious, and they rarely do any real damage.

Action steps:

- Any time you are thinking of telling a loving lie, consider whether that well-
  intentioned untruth will strengthen your intimate connection or damage it.
  Ask yourself if your partner would agree with you.
- Initiate a conversation with your partner about this. One person's loving lie
  will be another person's trust-breaker, so get clear with one another about
  the topics and situations for which you each prefer total honesty.

Another type of lie is a *conflict-avoidant lie.* Every small child learns how to
craft or spin a story to avoid getting in trouble and then hones that skill throughout the span of many years. No one is immune, so you can let go of the idea that
lying makes you, or your partner, a bad person; however, lies that are intended
to avoid a negative consequence can easily undermine trust.

Action steps:

- Take a good look at how you handle conflict. When you and your partner
  disagree, do you feel comfortable speaking up? If not, why not? What are
  you afraid will happen? Be honest with yourself, and identify if you have a

tendency to avoid conflict by telling lies, hiding the truth, or avoiding tough conversations.

- Initiate a conversation with your partner about managing disagreements between the two of you. Do you both agree it would be good to be able to disagree without creating a lot of drama or tension? Do you need some help with this? If so, agree to find a coach or therapist to help you.
- Start growing your muscle for truth-telling. Some people think that if they are going to be honest, they will have to give up a lot of things they don't want to give up. In truth, all you have to give up is lying. Instead of lying, tell your partner what you think, feel, believe, or prefer. Let the disagreement happen, and prove to yourself and one another that having a difference of opinion won't kill you.
- For some, disagreeing and staying connected is hard. If you and your partner are unable to do it despite your best efforts, get some help from a therapist or coach. This is a learnable skill. It will make you happier and your relationship stronger.

Learning to *invite truth-telling* is just as important as learning to tell the truth. Just as many of us have learned to lie from childhood onward, many of us have learned to discourage truth-telling in our interactions. When we respond badly to something we're not comfortable hearing, we make it harder for people to come to us with uncomfortable truths in the future.

Action steps:

- Take a good look at how you respond when someone tells you something you don't want to hear. Do you cry, yell, run away, shut down, or leave the house in a huff? Have you ever heard yourself say, "Don't ever talk to me about that again!"? If any of this describes you on a bad day, you could get better at inviting your partner to be honest with you.
- Trust yourself. You can handle some hard stuff. You'll be okay. Learn to trust that you will live through getting bad news, learning something uncomfortable about your partner, and considering new ideas. Develop some grit.
- Identify your goals. How will it benefit you to hear more honest truth from your partner? Certainly you will then know them better and be better able to figure out if you like them. Are there other benefits? You are learning to get some control of your emotional reactions so your partner can more

easily talk honestly to you; it will help if you keep your reasons for doing so at the front of your mind, because it won't always feel comfortable. Know why you're doing it.

Learning to co-create a comfortable environment for discussing, potentially disagreeing about, and certainly disclosing uncomfortable truths is the best thing you can do to strengthen trust in your relationship. Partners must work together to do this.

The following are some discussion points to get you started in creating a relationship based on trust. As you discuss these items, ask one another questions until you can accurately say back what your partner is expressing but using your own words.

- How important is honesty to you and why?
- How comfortable are you telling untruths? What types of things have you lied about (for instance, in previous relationships or your childhood)? What types of things have motivated you to lie?
- Give your partner examples of the kinds of things that feel important to you to know and the kinds of things that don't feel important to you to know. Maybe there are even some things you don't want to know. Discuss this with enough examples that you both feel confident that you understand one another's preferences, which might be very different from one another. Do not assume your partner wants to know (and not know) the same types of things you do. Ask. Tell. Be specific.
- What do you do to actively create an environment of trust and honesty in your relationship? What does your partner do?
- What do you do to create a soft landing-place for your partner to make difficult, honest, and vulnerable disclosures? Check with them to see if your efforts are helpful to them or find out what strategies might work better for them.
- When you have a choice to make that you know will affect your partner, and you suspect you and your partner will disagree about what you should choose, what feelings do you experience, and what is your thought process? Discuss how you want to show compassion for one another in situations like this.

- When you make a mistake that affects your partner, or when your partner feels hurt by something you have done, what emotions do you experience? How do you handle those emotions? How would you like to handle them? Discuss how you each would like to show compassion for one another in situations like this.

MAKING A GOOD REPAIR

There are many situations when a repair is needed. Maybe you said something you regret, told a lie, or caused harm in some way. Maybe you made a choice your partner didn't agree with or did something your partner feels is a betrayal. Perhaps there is something in your shared past that keeps coming up again and again. Learning to make an effective repair can help in any of these situations, but a good repair goes far beyond "I'm sorry." This document will guide you through the process of making a good repair. I direct this handout to the person who is initiating a repair for something they did that was hurtful to their partner, but the steps for getting ready are just as applicable to the other partner. A repair takes grit, grace, and stamina for everyone concerned. Don't rush it, and take breaks if you need to.

Action steps for getting ready to repair:

- Get grounded. How will you benefit from a good repair? It will take some time and energy, so get clear on why you think it is important and what you will get out of it.
- Trust yourself. You're strong enough to admit your mistakes and live through it.
- Forgive yourself, but don't let yourself off the hook. Everyone makes mistakes. And all actions have consequences. You are a fabulous human being— and even more so when you take responsibility for your actions, make a good repair, and build a safe and trusting connection that gets stronger throughout time.
- Prepare for some discomfort. It is not reasonable to expect trust to grow if you don't have the grit to really hear your partner's point of view. For many people, that is very difficult, particularly if you caused discomfort or harm. Some people prepare for discomfort by bracing themselves, but I think it is more effective to get in touch with your highest and best intention, your very best self, and do whatever it takes to stay in touch with that part of you.
- While you are in touch with your best self, it should be easy to find generosity in your heart. You will need it for this process to work. If you are not feeling loving and generous, get a therapist, coach, or friend to help you get there first. Making a pseudo-repair from a resentful or cranky place will not build trust or any meaningful connection.

- Get comfortable. The best repair takes some time and focus, and that focus should initially be on the injured party or the most distressed person. Prepare to focus on your partner without explaining your perspective for quite some time.

Action steps for making the repair:

- Get curious about what your partner's experience was. What hurt? What was hard? How did your partner perceive events? What interpretation did they put on those events? Make sure you stay with this process until you are very clear and able to say back what went wrong from your partner's perspective. How would they prefer for you to have handled the situation and why? You need to know it all, and ending this process too soon won't benefit you, difficult as it may be. Stay with it and show genuine curiosity until you have a feeling of, "Oh! I get it!" Then make sure you can say it back and your partner agrees that you got it.
- Express empathy. Once you understand what happened from your partner's point of view, you can express empathy. That means indicating that you understand how they felt and it makes sense to you. When it goes well, this is what it sounds like: "I now understand that when I did (x), this is what happened for you (description of your partner's internal experience). I see how you felt (x), and it makes total sense to me that you would feel that way, given the combination of what I did and what it meant to you."
- Apologize. Explain to your partner why you are sorry. Continue to focus on your partner, and resist the impulse to explain your perspective. It will be much better if you save your point of view for later.
- Explain what you plan to do differently in the future (if anything). This should go beyond, "It was a mistake, and it won't happen again." Your new understanding of the situation will inform your future choices; however, think this through carefully because you *must not* agree to something you can't or don't want to follow through on. The following are some ideas:
  - What exactly would you do differently if you had it to do over again? Think about the choices you made and the choice points as the situation evolved.
  - Would you want to think about things differently, take responsibility, check in more, and/or communicate more fully?

- ○ Maybe there is a way you would like to *prevent* this situation from occurring again. This should go beyond, "This situation is not likely to recur so let's move on." If a similar situation did happen, how would you want it to go?
- ○ Are there emotions you would like to deal with differently, to prevent a similar situation from coming up again? Sometimes such emotions as boredom, anxiety, anger, dissatisfaction, or depression can be involved in choices we later regret.

- Acknowledge that your partner might have some doubts about your ability to follow through effectively with your plan. This is particularly important if there have been major or recurring breaches of trust in the past. For instance, this might be an acknowledgment that years have gone by with many lies and that it would be a lot to expect a partner to suddenly trust in change just because of one heartfelt conversation. While certainly difficult, this level of repair is respectful of the reality of particularly difficult situations. It is extremely challenging to stick with someone while they do battle with their inner conflict-avoidant demons or tendency toward abundant untruths. Acknowledging that you are asking something big from your partner in the way of newfound trust is a very respectful thing to do. (Thank you to Pete Pearson from the Couples Institute for this concept.)

Creating Change Worksheet Set

This set of worksheets is a deep dive into the change process. From identifying useful goals, to working with the neural network of habit and the change process, to getting through blocks, this is a powerful toolkit for changing any aspect of your life, large or small. It includes the following:

- Getting Clear on Your Goals
  - Covers the difference between a goal you can meet and a goal that is impossible and will just lead to frustration. This worksheet creates an internal shift that enables the change process to begin.
- Creating Personal Change
  - Identifies where you want to go and what it will look like when you get there. This worksheet is about finding the parts of a neural network that holds up a mindset and choosing the mindset you want.
- Accessing Motivation
  - Identifies why you are not reaching your goals. Motivation is an important key to success, and accessing personal motivation is an art form.
- Creating Change Action Plan
  - Guides a step-by-step process of moving forward in a way that will help you be effective in the ways that are most important to you.
- Resolving a Dilemma Using Two Chairs
  - Guides a classic therapy technique from Gestalt therapy. This handout provides magical tools for identifying and working through the inevitable blocks that present themselves when we try to change something.

GETTING CLEAR ON YOUR GOALS

Getting clear on your goals and framing your desires and aspirations for yourself and your relationship in a form you can actually make headway with is crucial. Then begins the process of change. There are several steps you can take that will help you achieve the necessary clarity so you can actually make change happen and start to notice some results.

1. Make a list of goals you have for yourself. These might start with, "I want to . . ." or something similar. Really consider how you want to show up in your life and your relationship, and what you want to create for yourself. Examples include, "I want to be more creative," "I want to feel more emotionally balanced," "I want to feel grounded and patient in discussions with my partner," "I want to be more vulnerable and less guarded in tough discussions," etc.
2. Make a list of desires you have for your partner. These might start with, "I would like it if my partner would. . ." or something similar. It is important to distinguish between things you want to change in yourself (question 1) and things you would like your partner to change (question 2). Examples of desires you have for change in your partner might include the following: "I want my partner to listen to me when I'm upset," "I want my partner to admit how they hurt me and apologize," "I want my partner to feel more empowered and happy," etc.

Now let's revisit your first list. For each item on your list of things you would like to create in your life, write down any ideas you have about what might be blocking you. For instance, if you wrote, "I want to be more creative," you might write down such things as the following:

- One block to being more creative is poor time management.
- I also tend to minimize the importance of creative pursuits and don't prioritize them.

Still considering the first list, generate some action steps for each item, based on what you learned from the list of blocks. Using the example of being more creative, what you write down might be as follows:

- I could be more creative in how I go about some mundane tasks.
- I could spend 15 minutes less on social media and use that time to do something that feels creative.

Now let's revisit your list of desires for your partner. Since you can't actually make your partner do these things (or any things), you will have to think about this list differently from the list of goals for yourself.

First, consider each item on the list and decide if there is something about it you want to tell your partner. This might be telling them that something is important to you. Or it might be telling them that you are hoping they will do a particular thing. Put a mark by any of the things on this list that you would like to communicate with your partner about. Communicating about these things is an important step and ideally should be done without blaming or making them feel badly; you just want to let them know what is important to you and why, and what you are hoping they will do in your future together.

Next, you will have to figure out what you might be doing, or not doing, that is making it difficult for your partner to give you want you want with regard to the things on this list. We all have the ability to make it difficult for other people to give us what we want, and, similarly, we also have the ability to make it easier. For each item on your list of things you would like your partner to do, write down a sublist of things you do, have done, or don't do that make it harder for your partner to accommodate your wishes with regard to those things. For instance, if you put something like, "I would like my partner to own how he has hurt me," you would ask yourself, "What have I done or said that makes it hard for him to own how he has hurt me?" Some possible examples might be as follows:

- I lose my temper or break down crying when we talk about hard things, which makes it hard for my partner to hold up well in those conversations.
- I feel resentful but haven't communicated that to him in a direct and calm way that describes my feelings without shaming or blaming him.
- I haven't really taken the time to think about what would facilitate a repair, so I haven't really made a concrete request that he could respond to.

Now consider some positive steps you could take that might make it easier for your partner to do what you would like them to do. Look at my examples from earlier and notice how they point to some slight pivots that would probably make a difference in the outcome. In the first example, I might decide to manage my emotions so I don't break down crying. In the second, I might give some thought to how to describe my own emotions without shaming or blaming my partner for them. In the third example, I might think about what a good repair would feel like and have a specific discussion about why that would feel important to me, and ask how my partner would feel about doing those things.

If you have no ideas about what you could do that might make a difference to your partner in some of these areas, your action step would be to ask them. For instance, "I really wish you would clean up the kitchen after you cook. I wonder if there is anything I could do that would help you feel willing or able to do that?" Of course, your partner might not have any interest in doing it, but if they do have at least a little interest in the project, and can give you some feedback, it will be very helpful for making progress in that area.

Now that you have worked your way through these exercises, you may have identified a lot of possible goals for yourself. It won't help if you get flooded, and it won't help to divide your attention in too many ways, because then you won't have the amount of focus you need to actually create change.

Making the Rubber Meet the Road

Look at your lists and see if you notice any themes. For instance, you might see a theme that has to do with managing your emotions in a variety of circumstances. Or you might see a theme that has to do with sharing things about your thoughts, feelings, or desires with your partner more openly or without blame. Or you might notice that you haven't communicated many of your desires to your partner, in which case just doing that may be a sufficient first step. If there are any themes, write them down.

Select one thing or theme that you plan to focus on first. This should be something that, when it shifts, will make a big difference in your life and, ideally, also your relationship. Write down the one thing you will focus on first, and commit to it. Write at least one positive statement, a mission statement, that includes the goal, the reason the goal is important to you, and the benefit you will experience when the shift is complete: "I commit to focusing on . . ." or "This is important to me because . . . and when I have achieved this change, it will have been so worth the effort because . . ."

My mission statement is:

Keep that statement of commitment front and center while you are working on it so you don't forget. To keep it on your radar, you could put Post-its throughout your house, tell an accountability partner or other friend, make it into a mantra, or write it on your arm.

CREATING PERSONAL CHANGE

Thoughts, actions, and emotions are closely linked. Thoughts create emotions. Emotions lead to meaning-making, or thinking about the meaning of the emotions. Actions can spring from thoughts and feelings but also result in thoughts and feelings. Shifting one of these factors will shift the rest. If you want to create change in your life, putting a thought together with an action, and then feeling a feeling, is the way to go. Or you could feel the feeling you aspire to experience, and then it will be easier to choose an action and think thoughts that go with the positive emotion. Whichever way you go, all three parts are important and intertwined with one another.

This worksheet is designed to increase awareness of which thoughts, emotions, and actions are linked for you and what outcome they support. Getting clear on an outcome you want (a goal) and then stretching to identify the thoughts, actions, and emotions that support that outcome is a very powerful step. I use this format frequently on a whiteboard in my therapy room and learned it from Vann Joines, Ph.D. It also makes a powerful self-help project.

CREATING PERSONAL CHANGE

One change I would like to make in myself, that will make a big difference in my life is:

Currently, regarding this issue, the feelings I experience are:	When the change is complete, the feelings I will experience are:
Currently, the thoughts I think that bring these feelings are:	Things I would rather think include:

Include thoughts about yourself, others, and your destiny

Things I do when I think these thoughts and feel these feelings are:	Actions that go with the new thoughts and feelings are:
I will have to give up:	I will gain:

If I really wanted to sabotage the project, I would:

Developed by Bill Holoway, M.D. and revised by Vann Joines, Ph.D.

ACCESSING MOTIVATION

Finding motivation involves being able to see how the change you are considering making would benefit you. Let's imagine you would like to become able to manage automatic emotional responses so you can respond to your partner calmly and without defensiveness or anger. How will your life be better when you have figured out how to do this? Imagine yourself in a tough conversation, and you are being an empathetic, openhearted, calm, curious listener and participant in the conversation. How does this benefit you? If this sounds like a selfish perspective, it is, but in the best possible way. This is about *your* stake in the situation. Yes, it would probably also benefit your partner and your relationship, but finding your own motivation, *separate from any benefit to anyone else*, is crucial to success with any change you might want to make. The more difficult the change, the more in touch with your own motivation you will need to be.

First, envision the rewards you might reap if you were able to do the thing you are considering. Using the example of managing your automatic emotional responses, make a list of every benefit you can think of, small and large. How would it benefit *you* to stay calm enough to fully understand your partner's perspective on something you disagree about?

Now, consider your list. Refine it. If there are things on the list that are benefits to your partner, see if you can figure out a way that those things also benefit you directly. It is fine for there to be benefits to others, but when the rubber meets the road, you're the one who's going to be facing the challenge, so make sure you are clear in your mind about why it is important to you.

Look over your list of motivations for change. Can you distill or refine the list into an image or a single word or short phrase that symbolizes why this is important to you? Maybe the things on your list conjure up a fictional figure or a word that describes how you feel when you embody the traits you are cultivating. You will need to be able to call up your motivation when you need it or your automatic responses will take over in a split second. In that split second, it will help if you have a mantra, an image, or an emblem that can remind you to take a deep breath and respond in the way you planned.

- My word, phrase, or image is _____.
- My plan for keeping my word, phrase, or image at the top of my awareness at all times is _____.

CREATING A CHANGE ACTION PLAN

To make a change in your life, you will need concrete goals that are about you (see the "Getting Clear on Your Goals" worksheet in this appendix), as well as clarity regarding the thoughts, feelings, and actions that you are now engaging in, and those that better match the goal you aspire to (see the "Creating Personal Change" worksheet, also in this appendix). Once you have done that foundational work, you are ready to make the rubber meet the road with a concrete action plan comprised of what I would describe as a series of experiments.

Your first action-based experiment might be to change a habitual thought that isn't serving you into one that serves you better. Or it might be engaging in a regular mindfulness practice of intentionally shifting toward such emotions as appreciation, love, and gratitude. It might be doing a particular action over and over again to build a new habit while also creating a shift in thoughts and feelings. My point is, your experiment requires you to do something different, but it might be a thought experiment, a feeling experiment, or a purely action-based experiment. It might also be an experiment that has an action, accompanied by an intentional shift of emotion or thought. For instance, imagine you have decided to run an experiment that involves listening when your partner is talking, and instead of interrupting or responding defensively, you plan to get curious and ask some good questions. It will be easier to do that if you are aware of the thoughts you think when your partner starts talking that often result in you interrupting and defending yourself. With that self-awareness, you can coach yourself to think different thoughts when your partner is talking, which will set you up to have more success managing the automatic response of interrupting.

Once you have identified your experiment, write it down in detail. If your experiment is to not interrupt, make sure to write down what you will do instead so you have positive action steps. That might be, "Instead of interrupting, I will take three deep breaths and remember that I want to know what my partner thinks. I will ask at least one follow-up question to what my partner is saying." Don't overcomplicate this; keep it to just one concise experiment so you can really focus on it and succeed.

Now, write down why this is important to you and how your life will be improved when you have mastered this skill (refer to your mission statement in the "Getting Clear on Your Goals" worksheet or, for a deeper dive, use the "Accessing Motivation" worksheet). This might be something like, "It is important to me to listen well and get curious because I want to know what my partner thinks on deeper levels than we usually discuss, so I can understand my partner more fully. I think knowing my partner better will lead to me loving and respecting them more fully, which would be wonderful and will lead to me feeling more energetic and positive about myself, my life, and my relationship."

My first experiment is to _____

_____.

This is important to me because _____

_____.

My life will be better in the following ways when I'm good at this: _____

_____.

The next challenge is to keep your attention on this project so you can succeed. Remember, repetition and consistency are key. This action plan must become a daily practice that involves honoring your desire and motivation to change. With your attention on the project, you can give yourself good support and self-coaching for the effort.

Some experiments require total focus for weeks. Others evolve more quickly and can be tweaked every day depending on circumstance. The most important thing is to keep your goal on your radar, and stay focused on one primary goal at a time so you don't become confused or overwhelmed.

Every morning when you start your day, ask yourself (either on paper or in your mind), "What am I going to do today that will move that goal forward and why?" This might look exactly like it did on the first day you did it, or it might evolve a little throughout time.

Each day's action step should feel completely manageable. Be realistic: If it's the busiest day of the year, don't put down something that will take an hour; instead, put down something that will take less than a minute. You must create manageable action steps if you want to succeed at change. Every day is different, so assess your day. What feels manageable today? Might it even feel fun?

Now, be a good coach for yourself and imagine the entire sequence, including your success and positive emotions. Get the goal clear in your mind, and picture yourself doing the action step that day. Imagine feeling empowered, happy, effective, or any other positive emotion during and after the action. Get clear about what amazing benefits will come of your effort, and feel the gratitude and appreciation for those amazing benefits. This is you, being a positive, motivating coach for yourself. If you can make the entire process fun, that's even better.

Review each night, perhaps right before you fall asleep or in a notebook where you track your intentions, follow-through, and gratitude each day. Did you meet your goal? What went well? Give yourself positive feedback for doing what you intended to do: "I am a total rock star! I decided to send a loving text at lunchtime, and I did it! This is me taking charge of change in my life, and I'm proud of myself for it!" If you fell short of what you had hoped to do, compliment yourself for what you *were* able to do and acknowledge a desire to improve the next day. Be specific about what you plan to do differently and why it is important to you. Remember to be a cheerful, uplifting, inspiring coach, not a punitive, punishing one.

If it is proving to be challenging to follow through on your action plans, you might tweak them to feel more manageable. Or you might work on increasing how fun it is, add more positive feedback from your inner coach, or add a reward of some sort. I often write myself a pep-talk note for the following morning in a journal beside my bed. Then I read it when I wake up. This might be something like, "You've totally *got this* for today! Here's why this is fun and important, and I know you can do it. Also, right after you *do* it, you get to go buy yourself your favorite coffee drink, or go for a walk in your favorite place, or *both!*" The important part is to lift your mood and start off with a strong vote of confidence, a positive attitude, and an expectation of success combined with fun. Another helpful support if you are encountering blocks to success is the exercise "Resolving a Dilemma Using Two Chairs," in this appendix, which will help you sort out what is going on that might be blocking your progress.

RESOLVING A DILEMMA USING TWO CHAIRS

A dilemma is a situation in which you have choices but don't yet know which direction to go. One part of you wants to do (fill in the blank), and another part of you isn't so sure that's a good idea. Everyone has a dilemma from time to time, and, in fact, when you're stewing about a problem, and feeling stuck, you might try asking yourself what your dilemma is. This can help you get to something less tangled. Are there internal parts of you that want different things? Are you having an internal dialogue or battle between those viewpoints? If so, you can get a deeper understanding of what is going on for you by using this exercise, which is an extremely useful and effective way to work with any two-part dilemma. You can do it with the help of a therapist or coach, or you can do it as a self-help exercise. This exercise has its roots in Gestalt therapy.

The following are some examples of dilemmas you might use the two-chairs technique to resolve:

- One part of me wants to stay in this relationship, and another part wants to leave.
- One part of me wants to agree to what my partner wants, and another part of me doesn't.
- One part of me wants to open the relationship, and another part is not so sure.
- A part of me wants to follow through on my agreement with my partner, but another part of me wants to do my own thing.
- One part of me thinks it would be a good idea to come out to my mother, and another part of me thinks that is not such a good idea.
- One part of me wants to buy a house, and another part is not quite ready.
- One part of me wants to have another baby, and another part is not so sure.

You get the idea. The point of the exercise is to allow yourself to give voice to both sides of your internal dilemma, listening fully to what each part of you has to say. Usually, this is done by setting up two chairs. One chair represents the part of you that holds position A, and the other represents the part of you that holds position B. Any two chairs will do. Set them up facing one another. State your dilemma in terms of, "One part of me (this) and another part of me (that)." Choose which you want to start with, and sit in one of the chairs. Take a deep breath, and allow yourself to get fully in touch with the emotions and thoughts of this viewpoint. When you're in touch with that part, fully express that part of yourself, and *only that part* of yourself. When you feel the other part wanting to interrupt, just tell it to wait a minute and it will get its turn. Why do you, from this part of you, want what you want? Why does it feel important? What is at stake? What does it mean to you? When you feel like you've expressed that part fully, switch chairs.

Now take a breath, and get in touch with the alternate opinion within yourself. This is the part that wanted to butt in a few minutes ago. In this chair, you might start by saying, "I disagree. From my perspective, you missed a few important points . . ." Let the other part know what *this* part of you thinks, feels, and wants. Why does this issue feel so important to this part of you? What is at stake?

When this part has said its piece, switch chairs again. Before you start talking, make sure you are in touch with the thoughts and feelings of the first part again. Look right at the other chair, and talk to it. What did that other part miss? Help the other part see this through your eyes, when you are sitting in this part of yourself.

Continue moving back and forth, staying in each perspective for long enough to carry the conversation a little deeper than before. Don't just switch at the first impulse to do so, or you'll end up with a somewhat superficial argument between two dueling parts, and you won't make much progress.

When things start to wind down, take a minute to take stock. It might help to respond to these points:

- Restate the dilemma. Sometimes moving between chairs reveals that the dilemma is exactly what you thought it was, and other times it turns out that it is a little different than you originally thought. "A part of me thinks _____, and another part of me thinks_____."
- Sometimes things become confusing because a third viewpoint arises. Give it its own chair, and see what emerges.
  - Sometimes a third (or fourth!) part is a subset of one of the other parts. In that case, as you continue moving between chairs exploring your dilemma, they might reintegrate.
  - Sometimes they actually belong to a tangential dilemma. In that case, let them know you are focusing on just one dilemma at a time. They will get their turn next time.
  - Other times, a third part is entirely different. For instance, sometimes a really critical, semi-self-abusive part may emerge. If a scolding, shaming,

or punitive side appears, you will need to figure out a way to deal with the critical part, so you can take a deep breath and start to feel some freedom of choice again. That might be a project you can undertake on your own, if you are good at assessing and making changes in your life in the direction of self-love and self-care. Otherwise, a therapist can certainly help you with this project.

- Can you identify a part that aspires to grow, change, or stretch in a positive way, and another part that is frightened, cautious, or reluctant to make that change, or rebellious, pissed off, and resentful about considering making a change?
  - If so, the next step is to facilitate a conversation between those two parts. From your aspirational part, ask the worried, rebellious, or resentful part about its feelings and concerns, until you are quite clear what that part is protecting you from. What kind of negative outcome is it trying to prevent by getting in the aspirational part's way?
  - From the aspirational part, thank the protective part for doing its job of protection. The protective part came about some time ago, possibly when you were very young, for the purpose of preventing something bad from happening. Thank goodness it has been on board, helping you out all this time. Don't make the mistake of suggesting that this part has to go. You would never have made it this far without all the protective parts you have. Thank them and honor them. Then make some decisions about how they are needed today, on a case-by-case basis, with the understanding that now you have adult resources and capabilities.
  - Assess whether there is still a clear and present danger, or if the perception of danger is being blown out of proportion. Most protective parts (but not all) are acting on old information, based on past experiences in which we were much less powerful or much more dependent than we usually are as adults.
  - If your adult self is not in real danger, see if you can come up with a short-term experiment the aspirational part could run to explore the territory. This experiment would allow you to investigate whether you, as a whole adult person, might have some effective strategies for keeping yourself safe, so that the protective part can take a step back and relax for a minute.
- When you start to see a possible action-based experiment emerging, frame it as such, and use your two chairs to explore how both parts could agree to

collaborate to run that experiment. To succeed, you will have to honor both parts, meet their needs, address their concerns, and follow through on any agreement you make to reassess after a period of time. For example, let's say you're working with a dilemma about whether to stay in a relationship or leave. One experiment might be to speak up in your relationship about things that are important to you that you didn't used to speak up about, for a month just to try it. You would have to figure out how to handle your discomfort and any fears you have about consequences so your protective part can relax enough to allow the experiment, but if your other option is to leave, it makes sense to try this or another meaningful experiment first.

Any time you feel confused or uncertain about a course of action or it turns out that you didn't follow through on something in the way you hoped or thought you would, or you are ambivalent about making an agreement with a partner, it is worth delving into what internal dilemma might be right under the surface. This exercise is often used by therapists but can just as easily be done at home. If you think you might get into some challenging material and want a therapist for support, do it for the first few times in a therapy room. But if you feel pretty confident you will be able to manage whatever comes up, go ahead and try it on your own.
Variations:

- You can do this exercise without moving between chairs by referring to something like, "On one hand . . . and on the other hand."
- You can do this quietly, and without chairs, using a journal. Write the different viewpoints on separate pages or with different colored ink, but don't skimp on getting in touch with the feelings of the parts of the dilemma.
- Play with it, and see if other variations emerge and feel useful to you.

Crafting Your Unique
Open Relationship Handout Set

These handouts relate specifically to creating an open relationship and cover discussion points, as well as handling common stumbling blocks. Included are the following:

- Imagining Many Forms of Open
  - Helps identify, as an expansion exercise, what is important to you and helps you figure out how to craft a relationship that will help you get it.
- Discussion Topics for Intimate Relationships
  - Provides a robust list of topics people might consider discussing when opening their relationship, organized by category. Most are also relevant to monogamous relationships.
- Consolidating Information, Working Toward Action
  - Guides the transition from exploration of topics, thoughts, feelings, and preferences to decision-making, by offering processes that support effective action plans.
- How I Plan to Handle New Relationship Energy
  - Helps create an individual and effective plan for predictable challenges that enables careful thought and values-led guidance that would be difficult to achieve in the throes of emotion.

IMAGINING MANY FORMS OF OPEN

There are infinite ways to arrange an open relationship. Good news: That means the sky's the limit. But it also means it is worth taking the time to consider what you think might actually work for you and what you would prefer not to try quite yet. Open relationships tend to evolve throughout time. Partners may run a cautious experiment and see how it goes; if it goes well, their confidence and feeling of safety grows, and they may eventually end up with a form of open relationship they would not have originally thought possible. There's plenty of room to explore and discover what works for you, and there's no reason to go for the hardest thing you can imagine right from the start.

Use these questions to guide your thinking and discussion about your preferences. Ask yourself what feels fairly easy to you and what feels challenging. Make sure you identify *what* would be challenging about it or *what* could potentially make it work; those details are the keys to figuring out a good plan with a high chance of success.

These questions are designed to help you consider a full range of options. Don't let yourself be limited by my questions or what you think a relationship must look like; feel free to think up your own questions and your own unique relationship configurations. If you have a fear or an idea that doesn't appear on my list, put it on the list and discuss it. Also, while I've listed these in brief form, each question could certainly prompt a detailed and in-depth conversation. Make sure to discuss any that bring up strong feelings for you; it's better to have a charged discussion of a hypothetical issue than discover those strong feelings by accident at an inconvenient moment.

At the end of the exercise, there is a place to take notes. You can use it to keep track of those topics you need more information about so you can do further research on your options.

- The kinds of relationships that interest me most are those that have the following qualities:
- I'm mostly interested in relationships that allow me to have the following kinds of experiences:
- I'm mostly interested in relationships with the following amounts of depth and emotional closeness:
- I'm mostly interested in relationships with the following amounts of physical and/or sexual closeness/activity:

- I currently imagine myself being with the following types of partner(s):
- The type of relationship I imagine having with my metamours (my partners' partners) is . . .
- The type of relationship I imagine my partner(s) having with my other partners is . . .
- When I imagine someone I'm involved with falling in love with someone else, I feel . . .
- When I imagine myself falling in love with someone, while also having another partner, I feel . . .
- One thing I think would really work well for me would be . . .
- When I imagine my ideal relationship situation, I picture . . .
- My thoughts about hierarchy in a nonmonogamous relationship are . . .

As you consider your thoughts about these questions, you might want to review chapter 1, "Consensual Nonmonogamies," for definitions and broad strokes describing various existing relationship types, so you can consider nuanced combinations of monogamy, mongamish, swinging, polyamory, polyfidelity, etc. Remember, if you can imagine it, you can try it.

DISCUSSION TOPICS FOR INTIMATE RELATIONSHIPS

The first two topics on this list, fidelity and connection, will help any partners clarify their feelings about important material. Lack of discussion of these topics has led to all sorts of relationship misunderstandings, so please roll up your sleeves and have some talks. You don't have to be planning to open your relationship to have these discussions.

Safety; primacy; visibility; time, money, and other resources; disclosures; and negotiation are all topics that are relevant to any form of open relationship. Discussing these topics can help you figure out what type of open relationship might serve you, if any. These conversations will surface some issues that can blindside you if not discussed, and it is better to see them coming.

If you would benefit from having some structure for your discussions, use the initiator/inquirer process.

If you need to generate some extra ideas or get help thinking outside the box in any of these areas, refer to the "30 Ideas No Matter How Silly: Brainstorming Process" handout in appendix D.

Fidelity:

- What does fidelity mean to you?
- When do you feel secure emotionally?
- What do you do to make yourself feel emotionally secure?
- What does your partner do that results in you feeling emotionally secure?
- There are many aspects of sexuality, and your feelings about all of them may not be the same. Your feelings might also be situational or specific to a particular person or gender. Here are some topics that commonly come up when discussing fidelity, or perceiving infidelity:
  - Fantasy about other people
  - Fantasy about particular activities we don't do together
  - Watching pornography
  - Reading erotic stories
  - Self-pleasure when alone
  - Self-pleasure with your partner present
  - Sexting
  - Flirting
  - Connecting emotionally

- ○ Connecting emotionally or socially on social media, or sexually with an ex, or with another specific person
- ○ Discussing your relationship with someone else/another friend or partner
- ○ Erotic connection using technology

Connection:

- What does your partner do that really lights you up?
- What do you do that lights your partner up?
- What do you do that lights *you* up?
- Who else is in your life that contributes to you feeling whole and amazing?
- Who do you have special connections with that you don't want to lose? What is special about those connections? What do they bring to you and your relationships with others?
- Do you have any special connections with others that make you nervous in any way?
- Does your partner have any special connections that make you nervous?
- Regarding connections that make you nervous, what are you nervous or fearful about?
- What type of connections would you like to have more of in your life?
- What people or activities do you think would add to your experience of connection?
- What types of outside connections do you think strengthen your relationship(s) with others?
- What types of outside connections do you think weaken your relationship(s)?

Safety:

- What are your thoughts and feelings about physical safety when dating others?
- What are your thoughts and feelings about sexual safety when dating others?
- Do you know what you need to know about sexually transmitted infections to make good decisions and strong agreements?
- If not, what do you need to know? The American Sexual Health Association is a great resource, as is Planned Parenthood.

- What are your thoughts and feelings about the safety of your children, housemates, or other family members when dating others?
- Do you have fears about any of your shared resources or any other safety concern to discuss?

Primacy:

- Do you imagine having a primary/secondary relationship structure if you decided to try polyamory? If not, what do you imagine instead?
- What is it about primary/secondary that you like and are drawn to?
- What is it about primary/secondary that worries you or that you think could be problematic?
- Are there things you do with your partner that you would like to reserve for doing just with them? (This could be anything from kissing to going on international trips.)
- What is it about those things that feels special?
- What are some ways you could keep those things special?
- How do you imagine handling a difference of opinion with a partner about doing certain activities with others?
- Are there some things that are particularly difficult for you to think about your partner doing with other people or another person?
- What is it about those things that feel special, important, or unique?
- What are some ways you could keep your relationship feeling special and unique? (Think of some ways that don't limit activities and some that do.)
- How do you feel when you imagine having your activities with another person curtailed by your partner's preferences? Are there some activities you have stronger feelings about than others?
- How do you feel when you imagine requesting that your partner curtail their activities to match your comfort level or preference? Again, are there certain activities you have stronger feelings about than others?

Visibility:

- What are your feelings about other people, family, friends, or coworkers knowing about your (some form of open) relationship?
- How do you feel when you think about telling other people? (Your feelings might vary from person to person; discuss any that feel relevant.)

- How do you feel when you think about *not* telling others and keeping it private?
- What are the pros and cons of telling/not telling important people?
- What are your thoughts about telling your children about your open relationship?
- How do you feel about public displays of affection with another partner?
- Do you care if your partner has PDAs with others?
- What constitutes a PDA?
- How do you want to handle questions or judgments someone might have about, for instance, a perception of some infidelity as a result of not knowing about your relationship agreements?
- Is there at least one person you can agree would be a safe person to discuss opening your relationship with? If there is more than one person, make a list. It can backfire if you don't have sufficient support, so see if you can find at least one person to agree on, or else find a therapist or coach to meet that need.

Time:

- When you imagine opening your relationship, what challenges do you imagine arising regarding allocation of time?
- How much time do you imagine spending with other partners?
- How much time do you imagine your partner(s) spending with other partners?
- Do you feel relaxed and secure about the amount of time you spend with your current partner(s)? If not, why not?
- Does time feel like a limited commodity?
- Do you know where your time goes? If not, write it down for a week and see where you might be able to reallocate some time from less important things to more important things
- Do you feel connected when you are with your partner? If not, what could increase the feeling of connection you get with the time you have together?
- Do you feel relaxed and connected to yourself? If you aren't getting high-quality time alone and you need it, the lack will undermine multiple aspects of your life.

- What do you most love to do alone? Make a list of things you love to do alone. Keep it handy. This can help you find something enjoyable to do if you ever find yourself alone with nothing to do.
- What do you love to do with your partner? Make a list and keep it handy, too. This will help you choose high-reward activities when you have the opportunity to make a conscious choice.
- Are there times you and your partner particularly love being together and times you don't so much? What activities do you enjoy together, and what things don't you like to do together? If so, that information might help you plan how and when to spend time with others. For instance, maybe that other date is your yardwork buddy, or is amazing at helping with the kids, or really enjoys batch-cooking meals for the week.

Money and Other Resources:

- Does money feel like a limited commodity to you? To your partner?
- Do you have concerns about financial resources in your current relationship situation? What are your concerns?
- Do you have concerns about financial resources related to opening your relationship? What are your concerns?
- Are there resources other than time and money that you have concerns about related to opening your relationship? What are your concerns?
- How comfortable are you talking about money?
- What are some ways you can imagine handling money matters regarding opening up your relationship that would feel comfortable to you?

Disclosures:

- When do you want to know that your partner(s) is interested in someone new?
- When do you want to tell your partner(s) that you are interested in someone new?
- How much do you want to know about what your partner does with other people?
- How much do you want to share about your activities with other people?
- How comfortable are you with either of you discussing your relationship, challenges, struggles, or issues with another partner? Are there circumstances or topics where your feelings about this vary?

- How much do you want to hear about struggles your partner(s) might be having with another partner?
- How much would you like to tell your partner(s) about struggles you might be having with another partner?
- If you are considering don't ask/don't tell, how would you like to handle emergencies that might require sharing information?

Negotiation:

- How much advance notice do you like to have for changes in plans? Does it matter whose plans?
- Are there exceptions? How would you like to handle emergencies that result in changes in plans or exceptions to agreements you have in place?
- When do you want to hear about your partner's desire to renegotiate some aspect of your relationship agreements? (Tip: Don't wait until it's time sensitive.)
- How do you plan to make it easy for your partner to share something uncomfortable with you?
- How willing are you to bring up something that your partner might have trouble hearing?
- How confident are you that you and your partner(s) can be honest with one another and discuss the hidden assumptions and particulars of any given agreement? This is important, because if you are not confident about that or you have a partner who is not confident about it, that would be a reason to get to know a therapist or coach who can help you every now and then.
- How comfortable are you discussing the particulars of your relationship agreements? How comfortable is your partner?
- Do you tend toward oversharing or undersharing? Do you tend to avoid conflict or thrive on a spirited exchange of views? How about your partner(s)? Discuss your different unique styles of conversation and what might be challenging topics, so you know how to help one another and make sure you cover the ground with important discussions. For instance, if vacations are a hot-button issue for one of you, the other(s) should not wait until the last minute if they want to discuss something about vacation or renegotiate an agreement. A difficult topic will benefit from especially careful communication and lots of positive feedback for the struggling partner(s).

CONSOLIDATING INFORMATION, WORKING TOWARD ACTION

You should now be aware of some areas of agreement and disagreement, and know which areas bring up emotions and blocks, and which areas are relatively easy and straightforward. Use this worksheet or a spreadsheet modeled on it to consolidate information from your conversations and reflections, and assess whether you are ready to make some decisions. This worksheet can be used by you individually if you are trying to figure out how you want to set things up for yourself, or it can be used by a couple, throuple, or more. Just adjust the questions to fit your situation.

1. List the things you have identified that you are at least 80% clear on with yourself. If you are making decisions with a partner or partners, list the things that all of you are in at least 80% easy agreement on.
2. List the things you have identified for which there is a lot of emotional load *and* a lack of clarity about how to resolve the issue.
3. List the things you have identified for which there is a lot of emotional load but you are at least 75% clear on a course of action that might be a good starting point.
4. List the things you need more information about and make a note about where you think you might be able to get that information.

Go back to item 1. These are the aspects of your relationship you are most clear about or have the most agreement on. This would be a logical place to start because there is less emotional load here and near-perfect agreement. Make a list of manageable experiments you could run regarding these issues. Be prepared for things to evolve; just because you have near-perfect agreement doesn't necessarily mean things will go according to plan. Even with a strong start, for example, 80% agreement across the board, plan to try an experiment or set of experiments and revisit after a reasonable interval.

Go back to item 2. This is a list of topics to focus on, in either therapy or structured, careful initiator/inquirer-type discussions on your own.

Go back to item 3. This list is a place where you might run some experiments but with careful consideration for those who are experiencing a lot of emotion or challenge. What supports or structures might you put in place to help those who are stretching? Stretching yourself to experience something you think may be uncomfortable is an honorable project. If you or a partner are in that situation, it is important that they not feel alone or unsupported. Consider starting with one small experiment in one of these areas, and practice giving a lot of positive feedback for courage, bravery, holding steady, building new skills, trying new things, and generally being a superhero of personal and relational growth. Revisit the experiment after a relatively short interval.

Go back to item 4. Open relationships involve pretty big learning curves for most people. It's useful to figure out what you need to know more about to make good decisions, support yourself and your partners, or move forward in any manner. What have you discovered that you would like to know more about? I've listed some typical items that come up fairly frequently and included some potential resources for each entry, but you may have others. Do some internet research about anything you need help with, or reach out to your local CNM (consensual nonmonogamy) community.

- Practice safer sex to avoid contracting or spreading sexually transmitted infections.
  - Planned Parenthood website.
  - American Sexual Health Association website.
- Access your local polyamory groups and supports.
  - Look for meetup groups, poly cocktails, or sex geeks meetings, or do an internet search for polyamory in your area.
- Learn more about various configurations of possible relationships and decision-making structures, and how people have made polyamory work.
  - The following books come to mind. Feel free to do your own research and look for others.
    - *Designer Relationships* by Mark A. Michaels and Patricia Johnson
    - *Stories from the Polycule: Real Life in Polyamorous Families* by Elisabeth Sheff.
- Explore swinging.
  - Do an internet search for swinger lifestyle (your state).
- Explore kink.
  - Do an internet search for BDSM (your state) and kink (your state).
  - Join Fetlife, a social media group for kinky people, with a lot of overlap with consensual nonmonogamy.
- Find support for LGBTQIA+ identity.
  - Do an internet search for LGBTQ (your state).

- Look up PFLAG (Parents, Families, and Friends of Lesbians and Gays). It's the oldest and largest support group for LGBTQIA+ people and their families and allies. They are also inclusive of trans and other queer identities.
- Handle difficult emotions, for instance, jealousy.
  - Refer to chapter 13, "Understanding and Addressing Jealousy."
  - Get a copy of *Jealousy Survival Guide: How to Feel Safe, Happy, and Secure in an Open Relationship* by Kitty Chambliss.
  - Get a copy of *The Jealousy Workbook: Exercises and Insights for Managing Open Relationships* by Kathy Labiola.
  - Check out any book about emotional self-regulation; I recommend the works of Daniel G. Amen and Dan Siegel.

Whatever topics you would like to know more about, put your research plan on your action list.

Things I still need to learn more about to make good decisions moving forward:

Where/how I will seek that information:

Notes:

HOW I PLAN TO HANDLE NEW RELATIONSHIP ENERGY

Fill out this worksheet and put it somewhere you will be able to find it when you or your partner are falling in love with someone new. When the time comes and either you or a partner are experiencing new relationship energy, find this worksheet. Carry it with you or post it prominently, and read it often. Don't lose sight of this material; keep it front and center, and follow your own advice about how to manage your relationships. The success of your polyamorous relationship, and all the important relationships in your life, depends on how you handle yourself when you, or your partner, fall in love with someone new.

- The kind of person I aspire to be is . . . (List at least three qualities you display when you are at your best. A good prompt is to ask yourself, "How would I want the people I love to describe me at my funeral?")
- In my most important relationships, I show those qualities by . . . (It can help to imagine you're watching your life as if it's a movie. How would the movie show, through your character's actions, that you have the qualities you listed? List the actions.)
- The people I want to make sure I stay connected to are . . . (List your most important people: partner(s), children, best friends, closest family members, etc.)
- My favorite qualities of this person are . . . (For each person on the list, give five to 10 of their best qualities. As you consider each person, really allow yourself to feel the love, respect, and admiration that their qualities invoke in you.)
- Fun things I love to do with those people are . . . (List several things for each person. Challenge yourself to find a lot of fun things you can do with the people you love.)
- I feel connected with each of those people when . . . (List moments or activities that make you feel close. Maybe these are already on the fun list, or maybe not. Make sure you identify at least one or two activities that feel deeply connecting or rewarding with each person on your list.)
- Fun things I love to do alone are . . . (See if you can list 30 or more things that you have fun doing alone.)
- Describe how you want your partner to feel about you.
- Describe how you want your partner to feel about your polyamorous relationship.

- List some things you can do to elicit those feelings in them, both in the throes of new love and in regular day-to-day life. If you can't think of anything, ask them. It is crucial that you know how to delight your partner and understand what makes them feel good about polyamory.

Start each day by looking at these lists and figuring out at least one small action you can do to show the most important people that you love, enjoy, and appreciate them. Commit to making all your relationships fun, not just the new ones.

To take it one step further, you might choose to write two letters to your future self. In the first letter, describe how you want to handle your intense feelings when you are experiencing NRE with someone new. How do you want to show up for your partner(s) and why? How do you benefit, and what is the payoff? In the second, describe how you want to handle your relationship when your partner experiences NRE. How do you want to show up? Why? What is the benefit to you of showing up in that way?

Bibliography

*Arranged by topic

ATTACHMENT, DIFFERENTIATION, AND NEUROSCIENCE

Atkinson, B. J. (2005). *Emotional intelligence in couples therapy: Advances from neurobiology and the science of intimate relationships.* New York: W. W. Norton.

Birnbaum, G. E., Reis, H. T., Mikulincer, M., Gillath, O., & Orpaz, A. (2006). When sex is more than just sex: Attachment orientations, sexual experience, and relationship quality. *Journal of Personality and Social Psychology, 91*(5): 929–43.

Brassard, A., Peloquin, K., Dupuy, E., et al. (2011). Romantic attachment insecurity predicts sexual dissatisfaction in couples seeking marital therapy. *Journal of Sex and Marital Therapy, 38*(3), 245–62.

Cozolino, L. J. (2006). *The neuroscience of relationships: Attachment and the developing social brain.* New York: W. W. Norton.

Dana, D., & Porges, S. W. (2018). *The polyvagal theory in therapy: Engaging the rhythm of regulation.* New York: W. W. Norton.

Fern, J. (2020). *Polysecure: Attachment, trauma, and consensual nonmonogamy.* Portland, OR: Thorntree.

Ferreira, L. C., Narciso, I., Novo, R. F., & Pereira, C. R. (2014). Predicting couple satisfaction: The role of differentiation of self, sexual desire, and intimacy in heterosexual individuals. *Sexual and Relationship Therapy, 29*(4), 390–404.

Fishbane, M. D. (2011). Facilitating relational empowerment in couple therapy. *Family Process, 50,* 337–52.

Fishbane, M. D. (2007). Wired to connect: Neuroscience, relationships, and therapy. *Family Process, 46*(3), 395–412.

Goldstein, S., & Thau, S. (2006). Integrating attachment therapy and neuroscience in couple therapy. *International Journal for Applied Psychoanalytic Studies, 1*(3), 214–23.

Hardy, N. R., & Fisher, A. R. (2018). Attachment versus differentiation: The contemporary couple therapy debate. *Family Process, 57*(2), 557–71.

Jenks, R. J. (1985). Swinging: A test of two theories and a proposed new model. *Archives of Sexual Behavior, 14*(6), 517–27.

La Guardia, J. G., Ryan, R. M., Couchman, C. E., & Deci, E. L. (2000). Within-person variation in security of attachment: A self-determination theory perspective on attachment, need fulfillment, and well-being. *Journal of Personality and Social Psychology, 79*(3), 367–84.

Page, E. H. (2004). Mental health services experiences of bisexual women and bisexual men: An empirical study. *Journal of Bisexuality, 3*, 137–60.

Porges, S. W. (2011). *The polyvagal theory: Neurophysiological foundations of emotions, attachment, communication, and self-regulation.* New York: W. W. Norton.

Ramirez, O. M., & Brown, J. (2010). Attachment style, rules regarding sex, and couple satisfaction: A study of gay male couples. *Australian and New Zealand Journal of Family Therapy, 31*(2), 202–13. doi.org/10.1375/anft .31.2.202

Richards, C. (2010). Trans and nonmonogamies. In M. Barker and D. Langdridge (Eds.), Understanding nonmonogamies (pp. 121–33). New York: Routledge.

Roberts, A., & Pistole, M. C. (2009). Long-distance and proximal romantic relationship satisfaction: Attachment and closeness predictors. *Journal of College Counseling, 12*, 5–17.

Siegel, D. (2017). Dr. Dan Siegel's Hand Model of the Brain. *YouTube.* Retrieved March 11, 2020, from https://www.youtube.com/watch?v=f-m2Y cdMdFw.

Siegel, D. (2010). *The mindful therapist: A clinician's guide to mindsight and neural integration.* New York: W. W. Norton.

Siegel, D. (2007). *The mindful brain: Reflection and attunement in the cultivation of well-being.* New York: W. W. Norton.

Siegel, D. (2006). An interpersonal neurobiology approach to psychotherapy. *Psychiatric Annals, 36*(4), 248–58.

Siegel, D. (1999). *The developing mind: How relationships and the brain interact to shape who we are.* New York: Guilford.

Tatkin, S. (2013). *Your brain on love: The neurobiology of healthy relationships*. Audible Original Audiobook.

Tatkin, S. (2011). *Wired for love: How understanding your partner's brain and attachment style can help you defuse conflict and build a secure relationship*. Oakland, CA: New Harbinger.

Timm, T. M., & Keiley, M. K. (2011). The effects of differentiation of self, adult attachment, and sexual communication on sexual and marital satisfaction: A path analysis. *Journal of Sex & Marital Therapy, 37*(3), 206–23.

Zhang, F., & Labouvie-Vief, G. (2004). Stability and fluctuation in adult attachment style over a six-year period. *Attachment & Human Development, 6*(4), 419–37.

DEVELOPMENTAL MODEL OF COUPLES THERAPY AND RELATED THERAPIES

Bader, E., & Pearson, P. (2001). *Tell me no lies: How to stop lying to your partner—and yourself—in the four stages of marriage*. New York: St. Martin's.

Bader, E., & Pearson, P. (1988). *In quest of the mythical mate: A developmental approach to diagnosis and treatment in couples therapy*. Florence, KY: Brunner/Mazel.

Goulding, M. M., & Goulding, R. L. (1979). *Changing lives through redecision therapy*. New York: Brunner/Mazel; revised edition Grove Press, 1997.

Kellogg, S. (2015). *Transformational chairwork: Using psychotherapeutic dialogues in clinical practice*. Lanham, MD: Rowman & Littlefield.

Stewart, I., & Joines, V. (2012). *TA today: A new introduction to transactional analysis*, 2nd ed. Chapel Hill, NC: Lifespace Books.

INFIDELITY

Anderson, E. (2012). *The monogamy gap: Men, love, and the reality of cheating*. New York: Oxford University Press.

Anderson, E. (2010). At least with cheating there is an attempt at monogamy: Cheating and monogamism among undergraduate heterosexual men. *Journal of Social and Personal Relationships, 27*(7), 851–72.

Duncombe, J., Harrison, K., Allan, G., & Marsden, D. (2004). *The state of affairs: Explorations in infidelity and commitment*. Mahwah, NJ: Lawrence Erlbaum.

Fincham, F. D., & May, R. W. (2017). Infidelity in romantic relationships. *Current Opinion in Psychology, 13*, 70–74.

Fisher, H. (2017). *Anatomy of love: A natural history of mating, marriage, and why we stray.* New York: W. W. Norton.

Martin, W. (2018). *Untrue: Why nearly everything we believe about women, lust, and infidelity is wrong and how the new science can set us free.* New York: Little, Brown Spark.

Nelson, T. (2012). *The new monogamy: Redefining your relationship after infidelity.* Oakland, CA: New Harbinger Publications.

Oppenheimer, M. (2011, July 3). Married, with infidelities. *New York Times Magazine.* Retrieved March 11, 2020, from https://www.nytimes .com/2011/07/03/magazine/infidelity-will-keep-us-together.html.

Oswalt, S. B., & Wyatt, T. J. (2011). Of course we're exclusive: Hispanic college students' ideas about monogamy. *Journal of Hispanic Higher Education, 10*(4). DOI: 10.1177/1538192711410700

Schmitt, D. P. (2005). Sociosexuality from Argentina to Zimbabwe: A 48-nation study of sex, culture, and strategies of human mating. *Behavioral and Brain Sciences, 28*, 247–311.

Treas, J., & Giesen, D. (2000). Sexual infidelity among married and cohabitating Americans. *Journal of Marriage and the Family, 62*(1), 48–60.

KINK/BDSM

Bauer, R. (2010). Nonmonogamy in queer BDSM communities: Putting the sex back into alternative relationship practices and discourse. In M. Barker and D. Langdridge (Eds.), *Understanding nonmonogamies* (pp. 142–53). New York: Routledge. DOI: 10.4324/9780203869802–22

Bezreh, T., Weinberg, T., & Edgar, T. (2012). BDSM disclosure and stigma management: Identifying opportunities for sex education. *American Journal of Sexuality Education, 7*(1), 37–61. DOI: 10.1080/15546128.2012.650984

Brame, G. G. (2000). *Come hither: A commonsense guide to kinky sex.* New York: Fireside.

Brame, G. G., & Brame, W. (1996). *Different loving: The world of sexual dominance and submission.* New York: Villard.

Carlström, C., & Andersson, C. (2019). The queer spaces of BDSM and non-monogamy. *Journal of Positive Sexuality, 5*(1), 14–19.

Connolly, P. (2006). Psychological functioning of bondage/domination/ sadomasochism (BDSM) practitioners. *Journal of Psychology and Human Sexuality, 18*(1), 79–120.

Dunkley, C. R., & Brotto, L. A. (2018). Clinical considerations in treating BDSM practitioners: A review. *Journal of Sex & Marital Therapy, 44*(7), 701–12. DOI: 10.1080/0092623X.2018.1451792

Easton, D., & Liszt, C. A. (2000). *When someone you love is kinky.* Emeryville, CA. Greenery.

Fennell, J. (2015). Does this look sexual to you? Why do people do BDSM? *Presentation to the DC Sociological Society*, Washington, DC.

Harrington, L. (2012). *Playing well with others: Your field guide to discovering, exploring, and navigating the kink, leather, and BDSM communities.* San Francisco, CA: Greenery.

Hoff, G., & Sprott, R. A. (2009). Therapy experiences of clients with BDSM sexualities: Listening to a stigmatized sexuality. *Electronic Journal of Human Sexuality, 12*. Retrieved March 11, 2020, from http://www.ejhs.org /Volume12/bdsm.htm.

Kink Clinical Practice Guidelines Project. (2019). Clinical practice guidelines for working with people with kink interests. *Kinkguidelines.com.* Retrieved March 11, 2020, from https://www.kinkguidelines.com.

Kleinplatz, P. J., & Moser, C. (2006). *Sadomasochism: Power pleasures.* Binghamton, NY: Harrington Park Press.

Langdridge, D., & Barker, M. (2007). *Safe, sane, and consensual: Contemporary perspectives on sadomasochism.* New York: Palgrave Macmillan.

Ortmann, D., & Sprott, R. A. (2013). *Sexual outsiders: Understanding BDSM sexualities and communities.* New York: Rowman & Littlefield.

Richters, J., De Visser, R., Rissel, C., Grulich, A., & Smith, A. (2008). Demographic and psychosocial features of participants in bondage and discipline, sadomasochism, or dominance and submission (BDSM): Data from a national survey. *Journal of Sexual Medicine, 5*(7), 1,660–68. DOI: 10.1111/j.1743–6109.2008.00795.x

Rodemaker, D. (2008). *Altsex: The clinician's guide to BDSM.* Doctoral dissertation, Chicago School of Professional Psychology, Chicago. Proquest Dissertations and Theses. UMI 3436690.

Sagarin, Brad. The science of BDSM. www.scienceofbdsm.com

Sandnabba, N. K., Santilla, P., Alison, L., & Nordling, N. (2002). Demographics, sexual behavior, family background, and abuse experiences of practitioners of sadomasochistic sex: A review of recent research. *Sexual and Relationship Therapy, 17*(1), 39–55.

Shahbaz, C., & Chirinos, P. (2017). *Becoming a kink-aware therapist.* New York: Routledge.

Sprott, R. A., & Benoit Hadcock, B. (2017). Bisexuality, pansexuality, queer identity, and kink identity. *Sexual and Relationship Therapy, 33*(1–2), 214–32. DOI: 10.1080/14681994.2017.1347616

Taormino, T., & Carrellas, B. (2012). *The ultimate guide to kink: BDSM, role play, and the erotic edge.* Berkeley, CA: Cleiss.

van Anders, S. (2015). Beyond sexual orientation: Integrating genders/sex and diverse sexualities via sexual configurations theory. *Archives of Sexual Behavior, 44*, 1,177–213. DOI: 10.1007/s1050801504908

Wiseman, J. (1996). *SM 101: A realistic introduction.* San Francisco, CA: Greenery.

Wismeijer, A., & van Assen, M. (2013). Psychological characteristics of BDSM practitioners. *Journal of Sexual Medicine, 10*(8), 1,943–52. DOI: 10.1111/jsm.12192

Wright, S., Stambaugh, R., & Cox, D. (2015). *Consent violations survey tech report.* Retrieved March 11, 2020, from https://ncsfreedom.org/images /stories/2015_Survey_PDFs_ETC/Consent%20Violations%20 Survey%20 Analysis%20final.pdf.

Yost, M. R., & Hunter, L. E. (2012). BDSM practitioners' understandings of their initial attraction to BDSM sexuality: Essentialist and constructionist narratives. *Psychology & Sexuality, 3*(3), 244–59. DOI: 10.1080 /19419899.2012.700028

POLYAMORY AND OTHER CONSENSUAL NONMONOGAMIES

Anapol, D. (2010). *Polyamory in the 21st century: Love and intimacy with multiple partners.* Lanham, MD: Rowman & Littlefield.

Aviram, H. (2010). Geeks, goddesses, and green eggs: Political mobilization and the cultural locus of the polyamorous community in the San Francisco Bay Area. In M. Barker and D. Langdridge (Eds.), *Understanding nonmonogamies* (pp. 99–105). London: Routledge.

Bairstow, A. (2017). Couples exploring nonmonogamy: Guidelines for therapists. *Journal of Sex and Marital Therapy, 43*(4). doi.org/10.1080/00926 23X.2016.1164782

Balzarini, R. N., Campbell, L., Kohut, T., Holmes, B. M., Lehmiller, J. L., Harman, J. J., & Atkins, N. (2017). Perceptions of primary and secondary relationships in polyamory. *PLoS One, 12*(5), 1,020. DOI: https://journals .plos.org/plosone/article?id=10.1371/journal.pone.0177841

Balzarini, R. N., Dharma, C., Kohut, T., et al. (2018). Demographic comparison of American individuals in polyamorous and monogamous relationships. *Journal of Sex Research,* *56*(6), 681–94. DOI: 10.1080 /00224499.2018.1474333

Balzarini, R. N., Dharma, C., Muise, A., & Kohut, T. (2019). Eroticism versus nurturance: How eroticism and nurturance differs in polyamorous and monogamous relationships. *Social Psychology, 50,* 185–200.

Barash, D. P., & Lipton, J. E. (2002). The myth of monogamy: Fidelity and infidelity in animals and people. New York: Henry Holt.

Barker, M. (2011). Monogamies and nonmonogamies: A response to "The challenge of monogamy: bringing it out of the closet and into the treatment room" by Marianne Brandon, *Sexual and Relationship Therapy, 26*(3), 251–87. doi.org/10.1080/14681994.2011.595401

Barker, M. (2005). On tops, bottoms, and ethical sluts: The place of BDSM and polyamory in lesbian and gay psychology. *Lesbian and Gay Psychology Review, 6*(2), 124–29.

Barker, M. (2005). This is my partner, and this is my . . . partner's partner: Constructing a polyamory identity in a monogamous world. *Journal of Constructive Psychology, 18*(1), 75–88.

Barker, M., & Langdridge, D. (Eds.). (2010). *Understanding nonmonogamies.* New York: Routledge.

Baumgartner, B. (2009). A multiplicity of desire: Polyamory and relationship counselling. *International Journal of Narrative Therapy and Community Work, 2,* 59–63.

Brandon, M. (2016). Monogamy and nonmonogamy: Evolutionary considerations and treatment challenges. *Sexual Medicine Reviews, 4*(4), 343–52.

Berry, M. D., & Barker, M. (2014). Extraordinary interventions for extraordinary clients: Existential sex therapy and open nonmonogamy. *Sexual and Relationship Therapy, 29*(1), 21–30.

Bergstrand, C. R., & Sinski, J. B. (2010). *Swinging in America: Love, sex, and marriage in the 21st century.* Santa Barbara, CA: ABC-CLIO.

Bergstrand, C. R., & Williams, J. B. (2000). Today's alternative marriage styles: The case of swingers. *Electronic Journal of Human Sexuality, 3.* Retrieved March 11, 2020, from http://www.ejhs.org/volume3/swing/body .htm 1/9.

Bettinger, M. (2005). Polyamory and gay men: A family systems approach. *Journal of GLBT Family Studies, 1*(1), 97–117.

Brandon, M. (2011). The challenge of monogamy: Bringing it out of the closet and into the treatment room. *Sexual and Relationship Therapy, 26*(3), 271–77. DOI: 10.1080/14681994.2011.574114

Bricker, M. E., & Horne, S. G. (2007). Gay men in long-term relationships: The impact of monogamy and nonmonogamy on relational health. *Journal of Couple and Relationship Therapy, 6*(4), 27–47.

Brunning, L. (2016). The distinctiveness of polyamory. *Journal of Applied Philosophy, 35*(3), 513–31. doi.org/10.1111/japp.12240

Cascais, F., & Cardoso, D. (2012). "Loving many": Polyamorous love, gender, and identity. In N. de H. García & M.-A. Tseliou (Eds.), *Gender and love: Interdisciplinary perspectives* (pp. 21–29). Oxford, UK: Inter-Disciplinary Press.

Chambliss, K. (2017). *Jealousy survival guide: How to feel safe, happy, and secure in an open marriage*. CreateSpace Independent Publishing Platform.

Chapman, M. (2010). *What does polyamory look like? Polydiverse patterns of loving and living in modern polyamorous relationships*. Santa Fe, NM: iUniverse.

Cohen, M. T. (2016). The perceived satisfaction derived from various relationship configurations. *Journal of Relationships Research, 7*(10), 1–7. DOI: 10.1017/jrr.2016.12

Conley, T. D., Matsick, J. L., Moors, A. C., & Ziegler, A. (2017). Investigation of consensually nonmonogamous relationships: Theories, methods, and new directions. *Perspectives on Psychological Science, 12*(2), 205–32.

Conley, T. D., & Moors, A. C. (2014). More oxygen please! How polyamorous relationship strategies might oxygenate marriage. *Psychological Inquiry, 25*, 56–63.

Conley, T. D., Moors, A. C., Jatsick, J. L., & Ziegler, A. (2013). The fewer the merrier? Assessing stigma surrounding consensually nonmonogamous romantic relationships. *Analyses of Social Issues and Public Policy, 13*(1), 1–30.

Conley, T. D., Moors, A. C., Ziegler, A., & Karathanasis, C. (2012). Unfaithful individuals are less likely to practice safer sex than openly nonmonogamous individuals. *Journal of Sexual Medicine, 9*(6), 1,559–65.

Conley, T. D., Ziegler, A., Moors, A. C., Matsick, J. L., & Valentine, B. (2012). A critical examination of popular assumptions about the benefits and outcomes of monogamous relationships. *Personality and Social Psychology Review, 17*(2), 124–41.

Copulsky, D. (2016). Asexual polyamory: Potential challenges and benefits. *Journal of Positive Sexuality 2*, 11–15.

Cox, D. W. (2016). *Exploring the health of consensually nonmonogamous individuals: A mixed methods approach*. Doctoral dissertation, University of Oklahoma, Norman, OK.

Davidson, J. (2002). Working with polyamorous clients in the clinical setting. *Electronic Journal of Human Sexuality, 5*. Retrieved March 11, 2020, from http://www.ejhs.org/volume5/polyoutline.html.

de Visser, R., & McDonald, D. (2007). Swings and roundabouts: Management of jealousy in heterosexual swinging couples. *British Journal of Social Psychology, 46,* 459–76. DOI: 10.1348=014466606X143153

Deri, J. (2015). *Love's refraction: Jealousy and compersion in queer women's polyamorous relationships.* Toronto: Buffalo London.

Driskell, S. (2018, June 5). New research on the prevalence of consensual non-monogamy. *Indiana University Bloomington.* Retrieved March 11, 2020, from https://blogs.iu.edu/sciu/2018/06/05/consensual-non-monogamy/.

Emens, E. (2004). Monogamy's law: Compulsory monogamy and polyamorous existence. University of Chicago's Public Law and Legal Theory Working Paper, no. 58, University of Chicago Law School, Chicago, IL. Retrieved March 11, 2020, from https://chicagounbound.uchicago.edu/cgi/viewcontent.cgi?referer=&httpsredir=1&article=1193&context=public_law_and_legal_theory.

Fairbrother, N., Hart, T. A., & Fairbrother, M. (2019). Open relationship prevalence, characteristics, and correlates in a nationally representative sample of Canadian adults. *Journal of Sex Research.* doi.org/10.1080/00224499.2019.1580667

Ferrer, J. N. (2017). Beyond the non/monogamy system: Fluidity, hybridity, and transcendence in intimate relationships. *Psychology and Sexuality, 9*(1), 3–20.

Ferrer, J. N. (2007). Spirituality and intimate relationships: Monogamy, polyamory, and beyond. *Spiritual Activism, 1,* 37–62.

Fincham, F. D., & May, R. W. (2017). Infidelity in romantic relationships. *Current Opinion in Psychology, 12,* 70–74.

Finn, M. D. (2014). Questioning the rule-making imperative in therapeutic stabilizations of nonmonogamous (open) relationships. *Forum: Qualitative Social Research, 15*(3). Retrieved March 11, 2020, from http://www.qualitative-research.net/index.php/fqs/article/view/2042/3700

Finn, M. D., & Malson, H. (2008). Speaking of home truth: (Re)productions of dyadic-containment in nonmonogamous relationships. *British Journal of Social Psychology, 47*(3): 519–33.

Fleckenstein, J., & Cox, D. (2015). The association of an open relationship orientation with health and happiness in a sample of older U.S. adults. *Sexual and Relationship Therapy, 30*(1), 94–116. DOI: 10.1080/14681994.2014.976997

Ford, M. P. (2003). Therapists' sexual values for self and clients: Implications for practice and training. *Professional Psychology, Research, and Practice, 34*(1), 80–87.

Friederichsen, R. M. (2017). *Culturally competent counselling with consensually nonmonogamous clients: A narrative inquiry.* Doctoral dissertation, University of British Columbia, Vancouver.

Garner, C., Person, M., Goddard, C., Patridge, A., & Bixby, T. (2019). Satisfaction in consensual nonmonogamy. *Family Journal, 27*(2), 115–21. DOI: 10.1177/1066480719833411

Girard, A., & Brownlee, A. (2015). Assessment guidelines and clinical implications for therapists working with couples in sexually open marriages. *Sex and Relationship Therapy, 30*(4), 462–74. DOI: 10.1080 /14681994.2015.1028352

Goss, R. E. (2004). Proleptic sexual love: God's promiscuity reflected in Christian polyamory. *Journal of Theology & Sexuality, 11*(1), 52–63. DOI: 10.1177/135583580401100105

Graham, N. (2014). Polyamory: A call for increased mental health professional awareness. *Archives of Sexual Behavior, 43*, 1,031–34.

Griebling, B. (2012). The casualization of intimacy: Consensual nonmonogamy and the new sexual ethos. Doctoral dissertation, University of Pennsylvania, Philadelphia, PA. Retrieved March 11, 2020, from http://repository. upenn.edu/edissertations/638.

Grunt-Mejer, K., & Campbell, C. (2016). Around consensual nonmonogamies: Assessing attitudes toward nonexclusive relationships. *Journal of Sex Research, 53*(1), 45–53.

Hardy, J. W., & Easton, D. (2017). *The ethical slut: A practical guide to polyamory, open relationships, and other freedoms in sex and love*, 3rd ed. New York: Crown.

Haupert, M. L., Gesselman, A. N., Moors, A. C., Fisher, H. E., & Garcia, J. R. (2017). Prevalence of experiences with consensual nonmonogamous relationships: Findings from two national samples of single Americans. *Journal of Sex & Marital Therapy, 43*(5), 424–40.

Heaphy, B., Donovan, C., & Weeks, J. (2004). A different affair? Openness and nonmonogamy in same-sex relationships. In J. Duncome, K. Harrison, & D. Marsden (Eds.), *The state of affairs: Explorations in infidelity and commitment* (pp. 167–86). Mahwah, NJ: Lawrence Erlbaum.

Henrich, R., & Trawinski, C. (2016). Social and therapeutic challenges facing polyamorous clients. *Sexual and Relationship Therapy*. DOI: 10 .1080/14681994.2016.1174331

Herbert, M., & Zika, E. (2014). Why (not) simply loving? Polyamorous reflections. *International Journal of Narrative Therapy and Community Work, 3,* 17–20.

Hutzler, K. T., Giuliano, T. A., Herselman, J. R., & Johnson, S. M. (2016). Three's a crowd: Public awareness and (mis)perceptions of polyamory. *Psychology and Sexuality, 7*(2), 69–87.

Johnson, S. M., Giuliano, T. A., Herselman, J. R., & Hutzler, K. T. (2015). Development of a brief measure of attitudes towards polyamory. *Psychology and Sexuality, 6*(4), 325–39.

Jordan, L. S. (2018). "My mind kept creeping back . . . this relationship can't last": Developing self-awareness of monogamous bias. *Journal of Feminist Family Therapy, 30*(2), 109–27. DOI: 10.1080/08952833.2018.1430459

Jordan, L. S., Grogan, C., Muruthi, B., & Bermudez, J. M. (2016). Polyamory: Experiences of power from without, from within, and in between. *Journal of Couple and Relationship Therapy, 16*(1), 1–19. DOI: 10.1080 /15332691.2016.1141135

Kauppi, M., & Wittwer, N. (2012). *Longevity and intimacy in polyamorous relationships.* Master's thesis, Edgewood College, Madison, WI.

Kimberly, C., & Hans, J. D. (2017). From fantasy to reality: A grounded theory of experiences in the swinging lifestyle. *Archives of Sexual Behavior, 46*(3), 789–99.

Klesse, C. (2006). Polyamory and its "others": Contesting the terms of nonmonogamy. *Sexualities, 9*(5), 565–83. DOI: 10.1177/1363460706069986

Kolesar, A. E. A. (2010). *Spiritual identities of multiply partnered people.* Doctoral dissertation, Institute of Transpersonal Psychology, Palo Alto, CA.

Labriola, K. (2013). *The Jealousy Workbook: Exercises and Insights for Managing Open Relationships.* Eugene, OR: Greenery.

Labriola, K. (2010). *Love in abundance: A counselor's advice on open relationships.* Eugene, OR: Greenery Press.

Lehmiller, J. J. (2015). A comparison of sexual health history and practices among monogamous and consensually nonmonogamous sexual partners. *Journal of Sexual Medicine, 12*(10), 2,022–28.

Levine E. C., Herbenick, D., Martinez, O., Fu, T. C., & Dodge, B. (2018). Open relationships, nonconsensual nonmonogamy, and monogamy among U.S. adults: Findings from the 2012 national survey of sexual health and behaviors. *Archives of Sexual Behavior, 47*(5), 1,439–50.

Levitt, E. E. (1988). Alternative lifestyle and marital satisfaction: A brief report. *Annals of Sex Research, 1*(3), 455–61.

Manley, M. H., Diamond, L. M., & van Anders, S. M. (2015). Polyamory, monoamory, and sexual fluidity: A longitudinal study of identity and sexual trajectories. *Psychology of Sexual Orientation and Gender Diversity, 2*(2), 168–80.

Martin, S. A. (2017). *Relationship agreements and communication in monogamous and consensually nonmonogamous relationships.* Master's thesis, University of Guelph, Guelph, Ontario, Canada. Retrieved March 11, 2020, from https://atrium.lib.uoguelph.ca/xmlui/bitstream/handle/10214/12114/Martin_Sophie_201712_MSc.pdf?sequence=7&isAllowed=y.

Matsick, J. L., Conley, T. D., Ziegler, A., Moors, A. C., & Rubin, J. D. (2014). Love and sex: polyamorous relationships are perceived more favorably than swinging and open relationships. *Psychology & Sexuality, 5*(4), 339–48.

McCarthy, B., & Ross, L. W. (2018). Therapist values: Assessing and treating traditional and nontraditional relationships. *Family Journal, 27*(1), 11–16. doi.org/10.1177/1066480718811327

McCoy, M. A., Stinson, M. A., Ross, D. B., & Hjelmstad, L. R. (2013). Who's in our clients' bed? A case illustration of sex therapy with a polyamorous couple. *Journal of Sex and Marital Therapy, 41*(2), 134–44. DOI: 10.1080/0092623x.2013.864366

McCullogh, D., & Hall, D. S. (2003). Polyamory: What it is and what it isn't. *Electronic Journal of Human Sexuality, 6.* Retrieved March 11, 2020, from http://www.ejhs.org/volume6/polyamory.htm.

McLean, K. (2008). Negotiating (non)monogamy. *Bisexuality and Intimate Relationships, 4*(1–2), 83–97.

Michaels, M., & Johnson, P. (2015). *Designer Relationships.* Jersey City, NJ: Cleis.

Mitchell, A., & Barger, M. (2013). *Polyamory: What therapists need to know.* Master's thesis, Edgewood College, Madison, WI.

Mitchell, M. E., Bartholomew, K., & Cobb, R. J. Need fulfillment in polyamorous relationships. *Journal of Sex Research, 51*(3), 329–39.

Mogiliski, J. K., Memering, S. L., Welling, L. M., & Shackelford, T. K. (2017). Monogamy versus consensual nonmonogamy: Alternative approaches to pursuing a strategically pluralistic mating strategy. *Archives of Sexual Behaviors, 46*, 407–17.

Mogiliski, J. K., Reeve, S. D., Nicolas, S. C., et al. (2017). Jealousy, consent, and compersion within monogamous and consensually nonmonogamous romantic relationships. *Archives of Sexual Behavior, 48*(2). DOI: 10.1007/s10508-018-1286-4

Moors, A. C., Conley, T. D., Edelstein, R. S., & Chopik, W. J. (2015). Attached to monogamy? Avoidance predicts willingness to engage (but not actual engagement) in consensual nonmonogamy. *Journal of Social and Personal Relationships, 32*(2), 222–40.

Moors, A. C., Matsick, J. L., & Schechinger, H. A. (2017). Unique and shared relationship benefits of consensually nonmonogamous and monogamous relationships. *European Psychologist, 22*(1), 55–71.

Moors, A. C., Rubin, J. D., Matsick, J. L., Ziegler, A., & Conley, T. D. (2014). It's not just a gay male thing: Sexual minority women and men are equally attracted to consensual nonmonogamy. *Journal fur Psycologie, 22*(1), 38–51.

Moors, A. C., Selterman, D. F., & Conley, T. D. (2017). Personality correlates of desire to engage in consensual nonmonogamy among lesbian, gay, and bisexual individuals. *Journal of Bisexuality, 17*(4), 418–34. DOI: 10.1080/15299716.2017.1367982

Morrison, T. G., Beaulieu, D., Brockman, M., & Beaglaoich, C. (2013). A comparison of polyamorous and monoamorous persons: Are there differences in indices of relationship well-being and sociosexuality? *Psychology & Sexuality, 4*(1), 75–91. doi.org/10.1080/19419899.2011.631571

Orion, R. (2018). *A therapist's guide to consensual nonmonogamy: Polyamory, swinging, and open marriage.* New York: Routledge.

Orleans, E. (1999). Poly wants a lover. *Journal of Lesbian Studies, 3*(1–2), 63–65.

Pincus, T., & Hiles, R. (2017). *It's called polyamory: Coming out about your nonmonogamous relationships.* Portland, OR. Thorntree.

Philpot, S. P., Duncan, D., Ellard, J., et al. (2017). Negotiating gay men's relationships: How are monogamy and nonmonogamy experienced and practiced over time? *Culture, Health, and Sexuality, 20*(8), 915–28.

Powell, L. (2018). *Building open relationships: Your hands-on guide to swinging, polyamory, and beyond!* Portland, OR: Liz Powell International.

Ritchie, A., & Barker, M. (2006). "There aren't words for what we do or how we feel so we have to make them up": Constructing polyamorous languages in a culture of compulsory monogamy. *Sexualities, 9*(5), 584–601.

Robinson, M. (2013). Polyamory and monogamy as strategic identities. *Journal of Bisexuality, 13*(21), 21–38.

Rossman, K., Sinnard, M., & Budge, S. (2019). A qualitative examination of consideration and practice of consensual nonmonogamy among sexual and gender minority couples. *Psychology of Sexual Orientation and Gender Diversity, 6*(1), 11–21.

Rubel, A. N., & Bogaert, A. F. (2015). Consensual nonmonogamy: Psychological well-being and relationship quality correlates. *Journal of Sex Research, 52*(9), 961–82. doi.org/10.1080/00224499.2014.942722

Rubel, A. N., & Burleigh, T. J. (2018). Counting polyamorists who count: Prevalence and definitions of an under-researched form of CNM. *Sexualities, 23*(1–2), 3–27. doi.org/10.1177/1363460718779781

Rubin, A. M., & Adams, J. R. (1986). Outcomes of sexually open marriages. *Journal of Sex Research, 22*, 311–19. DOI: 10.1080=00224498609551311

Rubin, J. D., Moors, A. C., Matsick, J. L., Ziegler, A., & Conley, T. D. (2014). On the margins: Considering diversity among consensually nonmonogamous relationships. *Journal für Psychologie, 22*(1), 19–37.

Ryan, C., & Jetha, C. (2011). *Sex at dawn: How we mate, why we stray, and what it means for modern relationships*. New York: HarperCollins.

Sartorious, A. (2004). Three and more in love. *Journal of Bisexuality, 4*(3), 79–98.

Schechinger, H. A., Sakaluk, J. K., & Moors, A. C. (2018). Harmful and helpful therapy practices with consensually nonmonogamous clients: Toward an inclusive framework. *Journal of Consulting and Clinical Psychology, 86*(11), 879–91. DOI: 10.1037/ccp0000349

Scherrer, K. (2010). Asexual relationships: What does asexuality have to do with polyamory? In M. Barker & D. Langdridge (Eds.), *Understanding Nonmonogamies* (pp. 154–59). New York: Routledge.

Sheff, E. A. (2019, May 27). Updated estimate of number of nonmonogamous people in U.S. *Psychology Today*. Retrieved March 11, 2020, from https://www.psychologytoday.com/us/blog/the-polyamorists-next-door/201905/updated-estimate-number-non-monogamous-people-in-us.

Sheff, E. (2015). *Stories from the polycule: Real life in polyamorous families*. Portland, OR: Thorntree.

Sheff, E. A. (2013). *The polyamorists next door: Inside multiple-partner relationships and families*. Lanham, MD: Rowman & Littlefield.

Sheff, E. A. (2013, January 10). Not necessarily broken: Redefining success when polyamorous relationships end [blog post]. *Woodhullfoundation.org*. Retrieved March 11, 2020, from https://www.woodhullfoundation.org/2013/01/10/not-necessarily-broken-redefining-success-when-polyamorous-relationships-end/.

Sheff, E. A. (2012, October 23). Polyamory and divorce [blog post]. *Elisabethsheff.com*. Retrieved March 11, 2020, from https://elisabethsheff.com/2012/10/23/polyamory-and-divorce-3/

Sheff, E. A. (2006). Poly-hegemonic masculinities. *Sexualities, 9*(5), 621–42.

Sheff, E. A. (2005). Polyamorous women, sexual subjectivity, and power. *Journal of Contemporary Ethnography, 20*(10), 1–34. DOI: 10.1177/0891241604274263

Sheff, E. A., & Hammers, C. (2011). The privilege of perversities: Race, class, and education among polyamorists and kinksters. *Psychology & Sexuality, 2*(3), 198–223.

Scherrer, K. S. (2010). Asexual relationships: What does asexuality have to do with polyamory? *Understanding non-monogamies* (pp. 154–59). London: Routledge.

Sizemore, K. M. (2016). *Examining consensual nonmonogamy among emerging adult samples: A collection of studies.* Doctoral dissertation, University of Tennessee, Knoxville, Knoxville, TN. Retrieved March 11, 2020, from https://trace.tennessee.edu/utk_graddiss/3965/.

Smiler, B. (2011). There's no such thing as polyamory. *Electronic Journal of Human Sexuality, 14.* Retrieved March 11, 2020, from http://www.ejhs.org/volume14/NoSuch.htm.

Smith, C. N. (2017). Open to love: Polyamory and the black American. *Journal of Black Sexuality and Relationships, 3*(2), 99–129.

Song, S. (2012). Polyamory and queer anarchism: Infinite possibilities for resistance. In C. B. Daring, J. Rogue, D. Shannon, & A. Volcano (Eds.), *Queering anarchism: Essays on gender, power, and desire* (pp. 165–72). Oakland, CA: AK Press.

Spears, B., & Lowen, L. (2010). *Beyond monogamy: Lessons from long-term male couples in nonmonogamous relationships.* CreateSpace Independent Publishing Platform.

Taormino, T. (2008). *Opening up: A guide to creating and sustaining open relationships.* San Francisco, CA: Cleis.

Thompson, A. E., Bagley, A. J., & Moore, E. A. (2018). Young men and women's implicit attitudes towards consensually nonmonogamous relationships. *Psychology and Sexuality, 9*(2), 117–31.

Veaux, F., & Rickert, E. (2014). *More than two: A practical guide to ethical polyamory.* Portland, OR: Thorntree.

Visser, R., & McDonald, D. (2007). Swings and roundabouts: Management of jealousy in heterosexual "swinging" couples. *British Journal of Social Psychology, 46*, 459–76.

Weitzman, G., Davidson, J., Phillips, R. A., et al. (2014). What psychology professionals should know about polyamory. Baltimore, MD: National Coalition for Sexual Freedom. Retrieved March 11, 2020, from https://secureservercdn.net/198.71.233.68/9xj.1d5.myftpupload.com/wp-content/uploads/2019/12/Poly_Booklet_2014_09_27_2014–10–09.pdf.

Wilkins, A. (2004). "So full of myself as a chick": Goth women, sexual independence, and gender egalitarianism. *Gender and Society, 18*(3), 328–49. DOI: 10.1177/0891243204264421

Willey, A. (2006). "Christian nations," "polygamic races," and women's rights: Toward a genealogy of non/monogamy and whiteness. *Sexualities, 9*(5), 530–46. DOI: 10.1177/1363460706069964

Williams, D. J., & Prior, E. E. (2015). Contemporary polyamory: A call for awareness and sensitivity in social work. *National Association of Social Workers, 60*(3), 268–70. DOI: 10.1093/sw/swv012

Winston, D. (2017). *The smart girl's guide to polyamory.* New York: Skyhorse.

Wolfe, L. P. (2003). *Jealousy and transformation in polyamorous relationships.* Doctoral dissertation, Institute for Advanced Study of Human Sexuality, San Francisco, CA.

Wosick-Correa, K. (2010). Agreements, rules, and agentic fidelity in polyamorous relationships. *Psychology & Sexuality, 1*(1), 44–61.

Ziegler, A., Matsick, J. L., Moors, A. C., Rubin, J. D., & Conley, T. D. (2014). Does monogamy harm women? Deconstructing monogamy with a feminist lens. *Journal fur Psychologie, 22*, 1–18.

Zimmerman, K. J. (2012). Clients in sexually open relationships: Considerations for therapists. *Journal of Feminist Family Therapy, 24*(3), 272–89.

Index

About the Author

Martha Kauppi is a marriage and family therapist, educator, AASECT-certified sex therapist, and supervisor. She has a private practice in Madison, Wisconsin, where she specializes in complex relational therapy, a broad variety of sex issues, and consensual non-monogamies. Her unique approach to sex therapy is informed by her medical background as a midwife and has been honed through years of training physicians, nurses, counselors, coaches, and therapists to work more effectively with every conceivable issue related to sexuality. Kauppi is known for her warmth, humor, creativity, and ability to inspire, and she has a proven track record of providing effective, accessible skills and techniques therapists can use in their practices right away. Her mission is to create a cultural shift: What if every therapist felt comfortable, competent, and confident including discussion about sex in the normal course of therapy? What if every client could expect their therapist to be able to hold steady and help skillfully with *any* topic—even sex?